Principles
of
World
Politics

George Modelski

PRINCIPLES
OF
WORLD
POLITICS

The Free Press NEW YORK
Collier-Macmillan Limited LONDON

THE FREE PRESS
A Division of The Macmillan Company
866 Third Avenue, New York, New York 10022

COLLIER-MACMILLAN CANADA LTD., Toronto, Ontario

Library of Congress Catalog Card Number: 70–163237

Printing Number
1 2 3 4 5 6 7 8 9 10

Contents

List of Tables

List of Illustrations

Preface

THIS BOOK has many sources of inspiration; few if any can be adequately acknowledged. It can best be described as a synthesis of ideas evolved by the author from his own experience and from the numerous influences that have challenged him in the past two decades. It is also a response to the profusion of specialized International Relations research and technology that has been part of the spectacular expansion of the social sciences since 1945.

Although thought about for a long time, the book became an actual writing project only when Klaus Knorr prompted commitment to it at the Center of International Studies of Princeton University in 1964–1965. The substance of the book developed in the years that followed in lectures and courses given at the Australian National University, Monash University, Stanford University, and finally at the University of Washington. At each of these institutions the discussion helped to shape the unfolding argument. Particularly valuable, in the past few years, have been discussions in the World Society Seminars at the University of Washington.

A student of World Politics necessarily paints in broad strokes on a large canvas. For best results, he needs a global perspective: an understanding of the evolution of mankind, a map of present-day world structures and processes, and also a vision of the future. The present work offers some of each of these materials.

That the nation-state system, the contemporary constitution of the world, is capable of steady change, improvement, and adjustment is a thought that needs to be taken beyond the stage of rhetoric. This book elaborates this thought and gives it substance. Its impact is intended to be architectonic, in a special sense: presenting blueprints not for an ideal structure but for a world habitat capable of infinite additions, accretions, and modifications, subject only to the overriding determination to reconcile order with justice. These are not blueprints to be carried out by one world authority, but rather guides to universal conduct—principles in terms of which day-to-day decisions may be ranked by all members of world society. For, in the ultimate analysis, world order rests not on the actions of any one organization or agency, but on the responsibilities that are willingly assumed by all.

GEORGE MODELSKI

Seattle, Washington

I

Introduction

 T HE INTELLECTUAL SOURCE OF THE present work is International Relations, a field of academic enterprise that was born in the twentieth century. Its very name suggests its intimate connection with the concerns and the predicaments of contemporary international politics.

The Study of International Relations

In academic and everyday language, "international relations" means "relations among nations." However, inasmuch as the terms "nation" and "state" are in this context interchangeable, and inasmuch as states are represented by governments, the subject necessarily reduces itself almost entirely to "intergovernmental relations," "relations among independent governments" or "relations among nation-states." [1] The substance of the field thus concerns states and their behavior toward each other in war and peace, in diplomacy, and in international organization. All of this is, of course, politics, but in practice the study of International Relations has had little connection with Political Science. [2]

For Political Science, the focus of interest also is the state and (more recently) the political system, viewed as the national community organized by the state. In the tradition of Aristotle (whose conception of the ideal *polis* is that of the single city-state), political scientists usually discuss states as though they were isolated, self-contained and self-sufficient entities. They see political change as self-generated—that is, endogenous to the national community—while influences from "outside" the community are alien, illegitimate, if not positively subversive. Confined as it has been to within the restrictive boundaries of the state, and thus developing, in effect, in conditions of intellectual incest, Political Science has been barren of ideas constructive of world order. The typical Political Science prescription for world order has been based on the copying of "models" of national political systems, their transplanting to conditions that have usually been inhospitable to them.

In the preeminent role they assign to the state, the premises of International Relations and of Political Science thus complement each other. The postulated nature of the state, moreover, is also the *differentia* that determines the boundary between the two fields of study.[3] Thus Political Science studies states as political systems that are characterized by community, consensus, and a monopoly of the legitimate means of violence. As a result of these conditions, states are believed to be characteristically in a condition of peace;[4] and domestic tranquillity serves as the distinguishing feature of the national political order. International Relations, on the other hand, studies relations among states, these relations being understood as lacking in community, consensus and monopoly of the legitimate means of violence. The distinguishing characteristic of international relations is therefore the state of war—if not actual war, then at least potential war. Just as authority and order characterize national or domestic politics, so the push and pull of influence, disorder, anarchy or at best controlled chaos are the distinguishing marks of international politics.[5] It is on such an optimistic opinion of the quality of national life, and such a partial view of the realities of world order, that has come to rest the paradoxical distinction between traditional Political Science and International Relations.

The tendency to focus political thought on the nation-state may perhaps be described as ethnocentric. In general this term depicts a propensity for regarding one's own ethnic group as the center of culture —a propensity that tends to degenerate into an inability to view other cultures dispassionately. Inasmuch as the state is itself an ethnocentric institution, a political science that focuses on it might labor under similar disabilities.

The study of politics is not either inherently or necessarily ethnocentric. In the classical Mediterranean world, the Greeks' small and self-contained *polis* found its counterpart in Rome's huge and overpowering *cosmopolis*—the "city of the world," of which all men were citizens. The Roman Empire was the political embodiment of the cosmopolis; its doctrines were carried through into the Middle Ages by the Roman Church, which also inherited some of its physical and organizational capital. The "natural-law" tradition, which was strong in certain phases of the development of international law, drew on just such roots.

The attack on the authority of the Church in the Reformation, along with the emergence of autonomous princes and principalities in Europe at the close of the medieval period, brought about a gradual return to the ideas of the Greeks and the ideals of independence. Of modern political thinkers, Thomas Hobbes is probably the clearest and most persuasive exponent of the authority of the state and of the need for it as the guarantor of domestic peace. His plea on behalf of the "Leviathan" remains to this day the best recipe for a strong centralized state, as well as a powerful statement of organization theory. The trend of thought he espoused found other eloquent spokesmen: the writers of the *raison d'état* school of the seventeenth and eighteenth centuries,[6] nineteenth-century diplomatic and national historians of the class of Leopold von Ranke, international lawyers of the Positivist school—all these fall within the same pattern. Thus, the preponderance of scholarly thought, prior to the twentieth century, lay in largely state-oriented approaches; and this despite the universalist traditions of international law (known before the nineteenth century as *ius gentis*) and the earlier tradition, still strong in history and in political writing, for depicting all of Europe as one "federal" community.

The growth of learning and the expansion of universities in the nineteenth century added greater resources to the study of politics, and attention now came to focus squarely on the state. International Relations followed early in the twentieth century, in a complementary fashion: its formal inauguration may be dated at 1910, when the newly established Carnegie Endowment for International Peace brought out the first scholarly periodical devoted especially to world affairs: *International Conciliation*. As these events suggest, the direct concern of the newly mobilized scholarly concern was the cause of international peace. Added impetus was soon provided by the foundation of the League of Nations after World War I, and by the widely felt concern for doing something about what had formerly been called "foreign" affairs. Equally important has been the general expansion of the social sciences, within which both Political Science and International Relations have found a home.

The earliest professional students of International Relations had no readily identifiable theoretical orientation. Indeed, the study itself remained in a pre-theoretical (even if by now undoubtedly scholarly) stage of development. The prevailing approach could best be described as "eclectic"[7]; its practitioners came from a variety of academic and professional backgrounds, international law, history, government and international service being particularly well represented. Among the prominent names during this early phase was those of Alfred Zimmern, who was teaching at Oxford and writing in particular on the role of international organization in the nation-state system, and Quincy Wright, whose project at the University of Chicago on the "Causes of War" was an early model of social science research. Wright's *Study of War*, a fine example of an eclectic approach, was a major work of scholarship; it still holds its ground as a source of knowledge on this crucial subject.

World War II, as well as the turbulent and traumatic years that preceded and followed it, had a profound effect on thinking about International Relations. In their wake came a group of writers, self-described as the Realists, whose views and conceptions of the subject set the terms of debate for an entire generation of scholars and students. Among the most influential Realists were Edward Hewlett Carr, whose *Twenty Years Crisis*, published in London in 1939, was a withering critique of the "utopian" political attitudes of the years between the wars, and established realism as a term of political analysis; Nicholas Spykman, founder of the Yale Institute of International Studies, whose *America's Strategy in World Politics* (1942) was strongly influenced by geographical and geopolitical conceptions; and Hans Morgenthau, whose *Politics among Nations* (1948) proved a popular text and exercised a significant influence on large numbers of students in their approach to the subject. Raymond Aron's *Peace and War* is a more recent major work, essentially in the same tradition.

The Realists provided International Relations with coherence, thereby transforming it into an organized body of thought; but they gained this coherence at the expense of flexibility and adaptability. While their message came through loud and clear, it had a shrill and dogmatic tone. In their emphasis upon the role of the state, and in particular of those states that hold great power, they were the direct descendants of Hobbes and Ranke. They delighted in "showing up" those naive observers of the world scene who were neglecting to take into account the factor of power. Depressed and disappointed by the evident weakness of world order and the revealed fragility of the international community, they proceeded to argue the impossibility of achieving such order unless it was founded upon national power. The core of this thinking was the unreality of all community except the national one. In their teaching, they cultivated connoisseurship: the faculty of appreciating a fine game of international affairs while it was in progress, but without questioning the rules, or the status of the players. In a broad sense, they supplied an ideology for an era that finally consolidated the nation-state as the dominant political institution of the world system; in that sense, they enshrined ethnocentrism at the heart of International Relaions.

While the Realist position was significant as a stage in the development of the subject, it did not shed very much light on what the world was "really" like. Its ideological resources carried little of the explanatory power that one has the right to expect from social science models. The idea that states seek power does alert the student to certain "facts of life" about international affairs, and in that regard it may have been a useful corrective to earlier tendencies of popular thought. The declaration that all of politics has to do with problems of power is even less illuminating; utilized too often, it tends to result in the worst forms of reductionism. The rediscovery that the supreme guide to conduct in world affairs should be the national interest by itself represented a high-water mark of ethnocentrism.

The everyday work of students of International Relations during the Realist phase was of a topical, chronological and dryly descriptive character. Typical subjects of interest were questions such as United States policy toward Asia, or the progress of the Sino-Soviet dispute—with little attempt at either theoretical inquiry or explanation. Such theoretical work as was undertaken was along the lines of "foreign policy" analysis: the study of governmental organizations and procedures; the explication of foreign policy (or what Aron called "strategic-diplomatic action"); the examination of foreign policy and strategic decision-making. Generally, there was a good deal of interest in foreign countries and foreign areas, as objects of foreign policy. Particularly in the United States (where, during the immediate postwar years, the field experienced rapid growth) writers assumed a foreign policy orientation, and became advisors to the government on questions such as: "What should we do about NATO?" or "How can we develop Asia?" Consequently, the rest of the world tended to be viewed in an instrumental perspective, derived from nation-centered foreign policy objectives. Inevitably, too, one of the favorite phrases of the period became "instrument of foreign policy": the United Nations as an instrument of foreign policy; foreign aid as an instrument of foreign policy; even food as an instrument of foreign policy.

There is no need at this point to develop a critique of Realism; that has been done many times before. Beyond noting its influence and its undoubted contribution, it is necessary only to underscore its presocial scientific character and its ethnocentric perspective, two features that were mutually interacting. What was lacking was a strong explanatory theory, linked with a comprehensive picture of the world. But such a theory was unattainable within the time-bound perspectives of the Realists: their frame of reference was the European world of the nineteenth century, and of the twentieth century, which "turned out to be different." They were neither aware of the real past nor attuned to the real future. Some of them wrote as though their prescriptions for politics had the qualities of eternal truth. Yet, upon close inspection, these verities turned out to contain little more than the conventional diplomatic wisdom of the last century; they were little more than commentaries on the aphorisms and bon-mots of a Talleyrand, or on the political slogans of a Bismarck.

By about 1960, the study of international relations had entered a new phase: it became theoretically self-conscious, and a subfield, the theory of International Relations, was born. An early sign of this trend was the foundation of two new journals: *World Politics* (1949), which opened up its pages to a variety of contributors from the social sciences, and the *Journal of Conflict Resolution* (1958), which was decidedly and overtly behavioral. Stanley Hoffmann's critical essay "The Long Road to Theory in International Relations" (1959)[8] signaled a change of mood and a change of approach.

One prominent aspect of the decade that followed was the ascendancy of the systems approach. Spurred by wide interest in social-system theory, as expounded by Talcott Parsons, and by parallel developments in Political Science (David Easton's *The Political System* (1953)), students of International Relations revived an old and long-standing interest of commentators in world affairs. Attention-getting viewpoints have been those expressed in Morton Kaplan's *System and Process in International Politics* (1957), and in such collections as Rosenau's *International Politics and Foreign Policy* (1961) and Knorr and Verba's *The International System: Theoretical Essays* (1961). Karl Deutsch has been influential in raising the standards of theory and research.

The degree of innovation that was associated with the rediscovery of the concept of "international system" was not really outstanding. The term had good currency in eighteenth- and nineteenth-century writings on European diplomacy; it was an important part of traditional Balance of Power theories.[9] But the change of orientation that was associated with the revival of this concept nevertheless did have certain important consequences.

One important result was to shift the center of gravity of the entire field: the range of interests of International Relations scholars became extended, away from foreign policy—most often, in fact, American and Soviet foreign policy—and to the international system as a whole. At a time of wide-ranging social change, explicit concern with the state of the entire global system facilitated the description of large-scale processes. In the same way, express involvement with the total field of international politics corrected the ever-present tendencies toward "local determination": the inclination to explain events by local factors and to ignore chains of systemic interdependence.

The principal merit of the systems approach was to establish a viable characterization for phenomena of global interdependence, and to signal the need for a greater understanding of particular interdependencies. For to say that the world now forms an international system is at the same time to assert that various parts of that system not only interact but also cohere, that changes in one part of the system inevitably set in motion changes in other parts. This serves as a corrective to the unsubstantiated images of chaos, if not anarchy, that were frequently associated with perceptions of international politics; it thereby helps to organize thought about the world around the premises of coherence, regularity and persistence that underlie the concept of a system.

Another merit of the systems approach has been the tendency to favor generalization and abstraction—that is to say, those conditions that are indispensable to the creation of theory. It coincided with the trend—known in all of Political Science as behaviorism—toward stricter methodologies and closer attention to empirical data, methods of data collection and analysis. It meant bringing systematic methods to a subject that was only just emerging from a traditional concern with national and historical idiosyncrasies, which expressed itself in impressionistic and intuitive analyses, frequently shading over into high-class journalism, if not armchair strategy. Depicting contemporary international politics as one kind of system naturally and inevitably raised some questions about both past and future systems, and thus invited inquiry into processes of growth and transformation, as well as directing attention to similar or analogical processes in other social sciences and in other political systems. Unfortunately, efforts to answer such questions and to engage in inquiries of that sort have not been carried far enough.

The fact was that methodological innovations, such as the systems approach in general, were still handicapped by an underlying theory that remained essentially nation-state-oriented and Realist in tone. The basic paradigm continued to be ethnocentric: the nation-state as the basic unit of analysis; emphasis on differences between internal and external policies; stress on nation-state characteristics as explanations of world phenomena. Elaborate technique and sophisticated "hardware" became substitutes for asking sound questions and proceeding from sound theory. The technical advances of these years did little more than give some quantitative dimensions to familiar Realist theories.[10]

After an initially favorable impact, the systems approach failed to develop much subsequent momentum. One problem was the generality of the concept, and consequently the wide variety of ideas that are all able to travel under that label. Thus, what is true of all systems, even though it may be relevant to the international system, is most often not sufficiently specific to add greatly to our appreciation of a much more narrowly defined, yet promising field. The systems approach has furthermore lent itself to a great deal of needless mystification at the level of language, giving the impression that the frequent utterance of the magic word "system" not only granted admission to the sanctum of the initiated, but like "Sesame" opened a great treasure of political wisdom. The usefulness of a specifically systems approach to international relations may now be approaching its end, despite the fact that the influence exerted by it will undoubtedly prove to have been a lasting one.

The Poverty of Contemporary Theory

Throughout most of this century (that is, over the time span of the academic study of International Relations), the dominant paradigm has been that of the nation-state system and the style of approach basically ethnocentric. As has already been pointed out, to some extent this echoed the state of international affairs under the impact of the great wars, as well as reflecting the process of nation-building that was then under way in most parts of the world. Whatever the reasons, the influence of this concept has been generally restrictive: it has narrowed the range of theoretical inquiry, and limited the opportunities for shaping the course of political change in the world. It has, in fact, made it possible for the conviction to gain ground that the basic political framework of the world is, for all practical purposes, unchangeable—to be taken as given.

The dominance of this theoretical paradigm has been a persistent cause of the weakness of International Relations as a field of scholarly inquiry, and its concomitants, incomplete professionalization and the correspondingly important role played by "amateur" commentators. Professionalization means the development of universally acknowledged criteria of knowledge and judgment; it provides immunity against parochial pressures and swings of fashion. As a rule, professionalization emerges as a function of the size of the general scholarly (and in this case, social-scientific) community, as well as of the number and quality of specialists in a given field. The rate of growth of International Relations since the beginning of this century has been quite rapid, probably faster than the growth rate of science during the same period.[11] But the start was late and the absolute numbers correspondingly low. In the years between the two world wars, the total number of International Relations scholars in the world would have been in the hundreds—in fact, it may have been only in the region of about one hundred. In the mid-nineteen-sixties their numbers could be counted in the thousands, yet it is doubtful whether the total of Ph.D.-level specialists, on a worldwide scale, greatly exceeded one or two thousand, about one-half of whom were to be found in the United States. Thus it is only recently that the field assumed a shape that permitted autonomous theoretical and professional growth.

As the result of its persistent tendencies toward ethnocentrism and of the historically low degree of professionalization, mainstream International Relations may be said to have functioned as an "ideology" of the nation-state system, rather than as a "social-science-type" explanatory theory. In other words, International Relations described, explained and justified the political system that, in common with Political Science, it assumed to exist in the contemporary world. Rarely if ever were more fundamental questions asked, so that the result was a field of insufficient intellectual excitement and curiosity, despite the great possibilities so obviously inherent in it. One indication of the resulting malaise was the growth of enterprises—for example those in peace research—that were basically concerned with identical problems, yet were capable of mobilizing the interests of a variety of specialists, not only in the social but also in the natural sciences. In recent years, peace research has been the source of some of the most interesting work in International Relations. A different indication of spiritual malaise was the sterile nature of the intellectual debates—such as the unproductive arguments over the respective virtues of classicism and scientism.

Some students of the subject have recognized this dilemma. Martin Wight has argued persuasively that "international theory is marked, not only by paucity but also by intellectual and moral poverty"; he rightly attributed this principally to the "intellectual prejudice imposed by the sovereign state." Yet he himself, in effect, refused to abandon such prejudice, arguing at some length that not only was there no international theory worthy of the name, but that there could not be any.[12]

Such pessimism is unacceptable. The professionalization of the field, combined with the growth of the entire study of politics, has now provided the intellectual base for a scholarly enterprise that can outgrow its own state-bound origins. The growing self-awareness and interdependence of mankind provide the social and public conditions for the growth of a theory that is strong enough to survive the swings of public fashion, as well as periods of high political tension. What is needed is a challenge to the ruling model of the nation-state system as the only one among several possible ways (and not necessarily the best) of organizing world society.

The Politics of World Society

The time might now be ripe for enlarging the small area that has housed International Relations, and for reconstructing it so as to accommodate within it larger and more spacious conceptions. The first step in such an undertaking would be to give it a new name; this could only be "World

Politics." Within the study of world politics, International Relations is a subfield, concerned with world systems that are still characterized by the dominance of interstate relations.

The general field of World Politics may be defined as the study of the politics of world society; that is the basic conception underlying the present work. The primary referents of this analysis are the planet Earth and nature, along with man and his works upon that planet. In an era that has launched upon space exploration, what had already been known by astronomers for some centuries has become a property of public consciousness—namely, that the Earth is a small and fragile island of life in a vast and inhospitable expanse of space.

On that Earth man has, in recent centuries, woven an intricate pattern of global interactions; it is to the totality of those interactions that the title of world society belongs. For students of world politics, the basic problem then becomes: how does this world society govern itself? what are the influences shaping its politics? what effect does its political organization have upon its other aspects and upon the rest of life on Earth? Description, explanation and appraisal of the politics of world society is thus the chief purpose of this study.

Its first and fundamental concern will be the political life of contemporary world society. This is the world whose political arrangements need to be explained, insofar as its future will arise out of these present-day arrangements. They are the only political structures and processes that are still accessible to human intervention.

The contemporary world and its relatively self-sufficient, necessarily self-governing, social system thus become the anchor point of political analysis.[13] World societies are concrete social structures, whose age and character can be afforded precise determination, in each case. Initiation of the present-day global society may be dated to the Age of Discoveries of the fifteenth and sixteenth centuries; its age thus does not exceed a score of generations. Its uniqueness consists in its globality: this is the first society that, through a process of globalization lasting a few centuries, has come to satisfy such criteria as global awareness, global interaction, and some degree of worldwide value commonality.

In its worldwide extension and operation, and, most importantly, also in its size, present-day society is one of a kind; but if it is assigned to the class of large-scale, complex and relatively self-sufficient social systems, it might have to be recognized as one member of a larger group. There have been in history, prior to the onset of globalization, societies that have satisfied these criteria so that, for present purposes, they too can be described as world societies. Classical China, through much of its history, or the dominion of the Incas, may be adduced as examples of earlier world (although not global) societies. Their record and their achievements are worthy of close attention by students of world politics, if only because their weaknesses make it possible to understand certain important problems of contemporary world society, and therefore of all world societies.

The study of the politics of world society thus rests on the historical time dimension of our own global society, as well as an understanding of other historical world orders. In addition, the study extends into the future, so that it includes projections and programmes for the future of world society. The imaginative construction of complexity on a global scale is a daring and obviously "utopian" enterprise; but without it mankind would be able to do no better than drift along paths of accidental fortune and unanticipatable disaster. The study of the politics of world societies thus has a future dimension as well, in relation to which the application of principles of world politics assumes especial importance.

World society in this context means, to begin with, man on earth and the patterns of his interrelations. But man is no more than the most salient feature of life on earth, and he cannot exist and flourish apart from and without the rest of nature. In a broad sense, world society is therefore life on this planet. Its politics is fundamentally concerned with the survival and enhancement of all life on earth.[14]

Politics, Order and Justice

For any given society, politics is that set of activities that is concerned with the achievement (or "production") of order and justice. World politics is the set of activities that is concerned with the achievement of order and justice for world society.

Such an approach is, to begin with, broadly functional to the extent that it relates politics to a larger framework. Politics is not a self-contained or self-generated activity, but rather a complex of behavior that acquires meaning through its relationship to a greater whole. For world society, politics performs certain specialized functions (or produces certain specialized goods) and not others; it may perform these functions either well or inadequately. The study of world politics thus entails the cultivation of judgment about the quality of politics in the whole of world society.

The functional approach implies that politics is a "useful" activity, on a par with other socially useful activities, such as industry or art. Experience moreover suggests that some degree of political activity is found in all societies, so that politics is, in effect, an unavoidable social function. But the attribution to it of usefulness—or better, perhaps, of meaning—does not confer upon politics a status that is distinct from that of any other social activity. Politics cannot be regarded *a priori*, as either elevated or superior, or else as tainted and inferior. Different societies assign different priorities to politics; depending on the problems they confront, societies may give more or less attention to it.

The "products" of politics are order and justice—no matter whether the politics in question be local, national or global. The precise determination of the nature and quality of such products, or goods, however, is neither easy nor simple. Both "order" and "justice" are general concepts, capable of standing for a wide range of conditions and involving many concrete predicaments. Yet, however hard it may be to depict order and justice in positive terms, a breakdown of order or the negation of justice is always quickly sensed and easy to describe. Politics arises because social orders tend to run down and perfect justice is unattainable.

The common denominator of order and justice is force. At the center of politics stands force and the terrible abuses to which it is sometimes put; politics is the use, abuse and control of force. One reason why politics is important is that force easily loses its instrumental quality, slides into violence, and then takes to spreading destruction, as fire does. Because of its morbid interest in force, politics needs to be watched constantly, as well as kept responsible. Another common denominator of order and justice is consensus.

A conception that thus points to the close and fateful link between politics and force should not however, be identified with Max Weber's much quoted definition of politics as the activity of leading the state, the state being "a human community that claims the monopoly of the legitimate use of violence within a given territory." [15] Weber's definition is part of the nation-state system paradigm, which identifies states with order and world politics with the lack of power monopoly and hence with disorder. But it also insinuates the thought that an orderly (hence desirable) state of affairs for a society is the condition in which power or the legitimate use of force is indeed monopolized.

This is far from being a proven doctrine of Political Science and it should be examined with the utmost care.[16] Politics is, as previously maintained, directly concerned with the organization of force; but the condition of monopoly of power is only one of a variety of possible arrangements; it is by no means obviously the most productive of order or justice. Hence, politics needs to pay attention to an entire spectrum of "production alternatives," or models for the employment of force, ranging all the way from monopoly to perfect competition. And the conception of the nation-state as founded upon the monopoly of the legitimate use of force also needs drastic revision.

David Easton's conception of politics is of a "set of interactions through which binding (that is authoritative) decisions over the distribution of values are made for society." [17] The first point to consider is the nature of the society for which decisions are made: is it the world society? The second point to give thought to is the notion that the subject matter of politics is the distribution of values for society. While politics is indeed one of the avenues through which changes are made in the distribution of values, it is by no means the only one. Generational change or shifts in public tastes and priorities all bring about a continual redistribution of values. The condition in which political organizations arrogate to themselves alone the exclusive right, or even only a standing right, to redistribute values brings instability and disorder; it is also unjust in that a conception of politics that restricted politics to this particular function would have to be completely dysfunctional. The only condition in which politics uniquely determines the allocation of values is a monopoly of force. Hence Easton's conception is, in fact, dependent upon Weber's, and the two of them are equally open to criticism.

Since order and justice are interdependent, good politics must reconcile their requirements; but it may not be able to maximize both at the same time. Both order and justice restrict autonomy and individual freedom and any society can tolerate only so much infringement upon both. In turn, the greater the individual freedom or the organizational autonomy, the more direct is the possibility of chaos and disruption. Societies can be distinguished by the relative weight they assign to order and justice, and hence to autonomy and freedom.

Order and justice may be called public (as distinct from private) goods, inasmuch as they are consumed by a public, and their benefits accrue jointly to many people.[18] Provision for them affects the welfare of entire societies, and their existence is therefore of some importance. But one consequence of viewing politics as the supply of public goods is that it leaves open the question of how they are to be produced. Simple-minded concepts, which identify the production of public goods solely with the state, are obviously unsatisfactory: even though states are among the organizations that do produce order and justice, they are not the only such "producers"; moreover, the production of public goods on a world-wide basis demands more complex and more varied arrangements.

In the most general terms, order and justice could be seen as the product of two types of arrangements: organizations, and networks. Organizations would include such familiar arrangements as the nation-state, City Hall, and the United Nations; but large-scale organizations of every type, including corporations and universities, also produce (or fail to produce) some order and some justice. Finally, individuals may be assimilated analytically to organizations (to which they are similar because they have an identity, continuity, etc.), and thus regarded as contributors to the output of public goods. Networks, too, produce public goods even though their "product" is much harder to identify. One example of a network is markets: all markets involve problems of order and justice (for instance, through the policing of fair-trading practices); elite networks are informal patterns of influence, but usually also have significant capacity for order. In large-scale societies, the production of order and justice will be found to a large degree in the keeping of specialized organizations and networks; but it would be misleading to assert that political activity is exhausted by the actions of such specialists.

Viewing politics as the production of order and justice does not resolve all the conceptual ambiguities of Political Science. The identification of such goods remains, in particular circumstances, an open question, and their measurement a matter of some difficulty. Given the variety of agents who are capable of producing such intangibles, some effort must be made to focus attention, in the first place, on those organizations and networks that specialize to a high degree in the supply of these goods. Indeed, the precise manner in which order and justice can be conceived as organizational or network outputs, even of these specialized political bodies, is still an open question. But there is considerable advantage to delimiting the field of politics otherwise than by merely confining it solely to the state, and there are advantages of flexibility and adaptability in well-understood concepts that focus attention on the basic purposes of all politics.

Politics, viewed in functional terms, takes for granted the framework of society and derives its purposes from it. Such a conception cannot always be adequate, because there are times when political activity either establishes or reconstructs a framework. This can occur in all phases and levels of politics; even world society itself can be seen as the product of political activity, and will be so depicted on a number of occasions to follow. The student of politics cannot ignore such processes, nor can he afford to shrug them off. We can, however, label them as exceptions or aberrations—as occasions on which the political element assumed dominance and overrode the necessary balances and harmonies of society. For purposes of "normal" political analysis, the meaning of world politics should be derived from the sense and welfare of the entire human community. World society is, of course, the only large society that is capable of providing the basic framework of such politics, as well as its basic point of reference.

Fundamentals of Geocentric Politics

The bases have now hopefully been laid for a reversal of conventional thinking and for the abandonment of conventional conceptions. These bases are: first, the recognition of world society as the field whose politics constitutes world politics; second, a view of politics that abandons notions of special authority, monopoly of force and dependence on the state, and opens the way for a revival of interest in basic purposes. Both these views are necessary ingredients of basic change. It is not enough merely to project the old Political Science to the level of global politics; politics itself will undergo a radical conversion in the process of being projected on a global scale. World politics becomes the study of the politics of large world societies, and hence a study of some degree of generality and abstractness. At the same time, the notion of world society is historically and factually circumscribed: in practice, its field is rather narrow, for it is fundamentally earth- and time-bound.

A label is needed to describe the nature of the reversal, the retreat from traditionally ethnocentric conceptions: at issue is not only a renewal of traditional conceptions of International Relations, but also a re-ordering of Political Science. Eventually, what will remain will be a new, generalized conception of the study of Politics; but in the meantime resort might be had to some term that represents the global orientation needed in the new politics. To take advantage of a contrasting expression, the new approach might be described as earth politics, or as "geocentric politics"; for an even shorter term, "geopolitics" [19] might serve.

The dictionary defines "geocentric" as "taking . . . the earth as the center of perspective and valuation"—which is a good description of the tendency that needs to be adopted for the study of world politics. It is of some interest that the term first gained currency during the Copernican Revolution, when the geocentric conception of the universe was abandoned in favor of the heliocentric position (replaced in turn, by the galactocentric world view, early in this century).

Howard Perlmutter has applied this notion to the study of international corporations, and the same question could also be raised in relation to other organizations. Perlmutter has argued that enterprises of global range—that is, those maintaining worldwide operations—cannot remain ethnocentric in character; they will have to become geocentric, if they wish to cope successfully with the demands of the contemporary world. He indicated in particular that geocentric organizations are those that take as their point of reference the world market, as well as global standards of quality and skill, and which are particularly responsible to the universal demands of modern science.[20] He might have added that they also need to have a positive orientation toward world order and the global political process.

These strictures about ethnocentricity may also be laid at the door of the social sciences, for these may be regarded as networks of interactions, the outputs of which have important consequences for human values. They too—if they are to retain relevance for a worldwide audience, if they are to cope with mounting global problems, and if they are to remain faithful to the universal imperatives of scientific inquiry—will have to make a turn in the direction of geocentricity. Some branches of the social sciences—such as the theory of international trade, which is still posited upon the quaint notion that trade occurs between "countries" —are now little more than simple adaptations of the nation-state system paradigm.

While such criticism holds true for all the social sciences, nowhere is it more applicable than in Political Science and the study of International Relations. If the spell of conventional wisdom is to be broken, the following changes may be specified as minimal.

First, a geocentric approach to politics will abandon the nation-state as the sole mode or model of political organization. This is in no sense a call for "abolition," because world societies need nation-states as constituent parts of their political order; but it is a recognition of the fundamental point that a world society that overemphasizes one form of organization at the expense of all others cannot hope to flourish. There is a need to abandon the conception of the nation and the state as natural formations, parts of an inexorable and unalterable order of nature, which is beyond and above human control. Nations are man-made constructs; like other social artifacts, they need from time to time to be reviewed, revised and reconstructed. Within the edifice of world politics, there is room for all kinds of politics: national politics, local politics and global politics.

Second, the basic concepts of politics need rethinking in the light of the requirements of large, complex and worldwide societies. Such notions as conflict and violence, constituency and representation, taxation, separatism or expropriation, brain drain, revolution or coup d'état need to be reexamined; each has to be related to the conditions that now prevail in various parts of world society and to the requirements of world interest.

Third, in the study of politics, world politics will necessarily become the keystone of the entire program. How men should govern themselves on this planet, and how each man can govern himself—these are the basic questions of politics, They set the limits on all other political problems.

Notes to Chapter One

1. Not all students of the subject would accept this restrictive definition. "To understand international relations in their full extent involves not merely knowledge of the relations between states but also of the relations between peoples . . . (and) a knowledge of the peoples themselves" (Alfred Zimmern, *The League of Nations and the Rule of Law* (London: Macmillan, 1939), p. 5. But few have pursued this knowledge to the full extent.

2. Political Science is defined here as including the field of International Relations; hence, International Relations is basically used in the sense of international politics.

3. Raymond Aron, *Peace and War: A Theory of International Relations* (New York: Doubleday, 1965), Introduction.

4. For some evidence to the contrary, see Table 14:5, below, on the incidence of armed conflict in national societies.

5. C. A. W. Manning, *The Nature of International Society* (London: Bell 1962), pp. 182-3.

6. F. Meinecke, *Machiavellism: The Doctrine of Raison d'Etat in Modern History* (London: Routledge, 1957).

7. Hans Morgenthau and Kenneth Thompson, *Principles and Problems of International Politics* (New York: Knopf, 1950).

8. Stanley Hoffmann, "International Relations: The Long Road to Theory," *World Politics*, Vol. 11(3), April 1959, 346–377.

9. Alfred Vagts, "Balance of Power: Growth of an Idea" *World Politics* 1(1), October 1948, 82–101.

10. Rudolph Rummel, "Indicators of Cross-national and International Patterns," *American Political Science Review*, Vol. 63(1), March 1969, 128.

11. The total number of International Relations practitioners in the mid-nineteen-sixties could be put at about ½ of one per cent of the total number of the scholarly scientific community.

12. Martin Wight, "Why is there no international theory?" *International Relations*, Vol. 11(1) April 1960, 35–48, 62.

13. Talcott Parsons ("Order and Community in the International Social System" in J. Rosenau ed. *International Politics and Foreign Policy* New York: The Free Press 1961, p. 122) stressed the "Aristotelian concept of self-sufficiency" as the fundamental model for the concept of society. But, strictly speaking, no society is self-sufficient, and even world society depends on the sun for supplies of basic energy.

14. Manning (cited, p. 1) views mankind "taken as a whole" as a "cosmos, a social universe in itself" and its study, in its global dimension, as "social cosmology."

15. Max Weber, "Politics as a Vocation" in ed. Gerth & Mills, *From Max Weber* (New York: Oxford U. Press, 1946), p. 78.

16. David Easton, "Political Science" in *International Encyclopedia of the Social Sciences* (New York: Macmillan), Vol. 12, p. 285.

17. Chadwick Alger "Comparisons of Intranational and International Politics" *American Political Science Review*, Vol. 57(2), June 1963, 406–19.

18. A definition stressing "joint consumption" makes a public good one whose consumption by A does not reduce its availability to B.

19. The term "geopolitics" carries within it certain odious connotations, going back to Ratzel, Haushofer and the period between the two world wars. At that time it referred in particular to the study of earth features and the shape of the earth for purposes of strategic policy. Perhaps the time has come to revive the term in a new context, by associating it with concern for the whole earth.

20. H. Perlmutter, "The tortuous evolution of the multinational corporation," *Columbia Journal of World Business*, Vol. IV, January-February 1969, 9–18.

PART ONE

The
Evolution
of
World
Politics

This study is divided into three parts: The Evolution of World Politics, The Nation-State System, and The Principles of World Politics. These refer, respectively, to the past, the present and the future.

The centerpiece of the analysis is the nation-state system; as the constitution of world politics today, it calls for thoroughgoing attention. A necessary preliminary to such attention, however, is a perspective on the past; that is the aim of the present part of this volume.

"The Evolution of World Politics" singles out for analysis three features of the contemporary world and then asks how each came to have the shape it has. These features are: globalization—the fact that the world now operates as one political system; autonomy—the condition of independence that characterizes the constituent parts of that system; and the nationalization of the state—the property of nationality that lends so much color to modern politics. These three distinguishing characteristics of modern politics will be examined in the spirit of the social sciences against the background of mankind's entire evolution.

In a longer perspective, this historical emphasis is intended to be read, not as deterministic, but rather as providing clues of the shaping of future world politics. The structure of world politics is, at every point in time, susceptible to some modification and change. Analytically, however, change is always a matter for the future, and that future recedes endlessly in time. To cope with the future—that is, to be able to manage change—human beings need guides and principles of orientation. Some of these will be attempted in the third part of this volume.

It is one of the clichés of the age that the preeminent feature of contemporary life is the speed of change: the rate of change now exceeds anything so far known to man; it is significant enough to subject entire populations to the effects of what has recently been dubbed "future shock." Examples are legion, as the "explosions" of change multiply. In the life of ordinary men, the experience of thoroughgoing transformations in both the social and physical environment has been the norm rather than the exception, and extensive political change has been included in this experience.

The bulk of the conventional study of politics, however, proceeds on the basic premise that the structure of the world system is, for all practical purposes, to be taken as unchanging, that it is a given feature of the human condition, perhaps a manifestation of "constancies" in man's nature. World politics is thus seen as no more than a stage on which various actors appear, act their roles, and make their exits; yet it itself remains unchanged. The Realists were nearest to maintaining such views, coming close to the position that world politics is, in its essential features, fixed, or else changes so slowly that nothing can be done about it.

As any careful and realistic student of empirical evidence cannot help observing the political organization of the world does not change only with the ebb and flow of some political processes; in recent decades, it has changed radically, through the substantial and worldwide consolidation of the system of nation-states. Hence, any study of world politics that aims at developing an understanding of a world in a state of flux must pay considerable attention to sensitizing its students to this condition. Only if it is widely understood that world political structures are capable of change (even if this is not visible to the naked eye) can the understanding of such changes make some progress. Change, in turn, might then prove to be the most basic subject matter of world politics.

The best opportunity for such sensitivity training seems to be an effort to place problems of world politics within the totality of human life in the universe. In a narrow and technical sense, such a perspective might be labeled historical; yet, for purposes of world political analysis, the likely assistance to be secured from historians can be at best limited. In particular, the terms of reference of this inquiry are both wide and yet also specialized: they are not restricted in their range of observation to the preceding decades or the last hundred years; there is no imperative need to take the nineteenth century as the golden era of world diplomacy, or the ancient classics as unsurpassed sources of political wisdom. The field of analysis is nothing less than all of human experience in the governance of large societies on this planet.

2

The
Context
of.
World
Politics

To PLACE WORLD POLITICS WITHIN
the evolution of life on this earth is no mean task. A sketch of some of
the main problems involved falls into three parts: (1) the context of life
in space and time; (2) the long-drawn-out evolution of man, and the
possible effects of this heritage; and, at greatest length, (3) the record
and relevance of civilized agrarian societies and, especially, the role of
empires.

Life in the Universe

The basic fact about life on earth is its profound solitude in space. The
earth is probably the only part of the solar system that has life on it.
Outside the solar system—but still within the galaxy of the Milky Way,
which houses it—the stars have habitable planets, some of which may
even have forms of life. Yet even within this galaxy, distances—hence,
also the time and energy needed to conquer them—remain enormous.
Merely in terms of radio signals, the nearest foreign stellar system is six
light-years away; the exchange of a single message would take at least
twice that time. Travel to this neighbor would then take dozens of years,
since rocket speeds are nowhere near the speed of light.

Beyond the Milky Way, distances become truly overwhelming. The
nearest other galaxy, even though it still belongs to the same local cluster,
is so far away that a message dispatched from earth at the time when
humans were barely distinguishable from apes (perhaps two or three
million years ago) would only now have reached it. Even if living crea-

tures or habitable space did exist there, they could not have any meaningful relationship to life processes on earth. For these reasons, problems of extragalactic relations appear irrelevant, while those pertaining to intragalactic communication remain simply very remote. Unless some other civilization has mastered techniques of travel at the speed of light (which on present evidence seems unattainable), world politics will for all practical purposes continue to be earth politics.

If there is little prospect of habitable space or life outside earth, there cannot be any great expectations for significantly enlarging the geographical scope of world politics. The moon and Mars may offer an environment hospitable enough for travel and for the support of small groups of determined men—for example, scientists prepared to endure rugged and unfamiliar conditions—but they are unlikely to provide opportunities for extended settlement within the next few generations. Although this last is not inconceivable on technical grounds, the cost and energy that would be required for such projects, measured against the world product, will remain considerable for some time to come. Even if this planet were to become the base for expeditions into space (a process that would be more significant for the political changes it would bring about on earth than for the results it might achieve within the solar system), it would remain the center and the substantial focus of world political processes.

The other basic fact about life on earth is its finiteness in historical time. Life on earth is about four billion years old; animal life, at most one billion years; and life approximating to human forms, perhaps one to ten million years. Figure 2:1 is an attempt, on the basis of information presently available, to place world politics within the context of the growth of life on earth. The continuous line represents the evolution of life since the beginning of the Milky Way, more than ten billion years ago. To depict this time span in a meaningful form, a logarithmic scale has been used. Each individual segment along that scale stands for a time period ten times shorter than the preceding segment. Hence the last period, labeled "modern" and shown to be one hundred years long, covers a period ten times shorter than its predecessor, marked "globalization" and covering 1,000 years.

The origin of the universe is shrouded in obscurity; whether the formation of the Milky Way is really the opening of the process remains an unanswered question. It is the "life-on-earth" stage of Figure 2:1 that is particularly important, because it comprises the origin of the solar system, of earth, and of life on earth. Each succeeding and increasingly shorter time span can thus be identified with a signal stage in the evolution of life and man. These are, in the unfolding order of this scale: animal life, the age of mammals, man-apes, *homo erectus* or man walking upright (and evolving fire and speech), *homo sapiens* (the hunter), agri-

Figure 2:1
The Evolution of Life

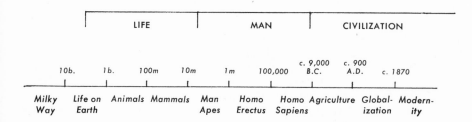

culture, globalization, and modernity (which could also be called the industrial system). Growth has been cumulative, in that in each successive stage the achievements of previous periods have been retained and put to use. Every one of these stages represents a fundamental departure in biological and cultural evolution, yet each was accomplished in a dramatically shorter time than the preceding one. The brief summary of the evolution of life projects a picture of accelerating progress: this fundamental process of growth has been gathering tremendous momentum; its ultimate destination is unclear and terrifying to contemplate.

The entire story divides itself into three major parts: the first is the origin of the earth and of life itself; the second, the evolution of man; the third, the rise of historical civilizations. For purposes of examining the historical experience of world politics, only the last—that of "civilization"—is, of course, relevant. This comprises the segments—identified as "agriculture," "globalization" and modernity—in relation to which problems of world order might be studied with some profit. After a brief glance at "primitive" society, the remainder of the present chapter will review the experience of agrarian world societies; the chapter that follows deals with globalization; and the remainder of Part One accounts for the evolution of the modern nation-state system. Yet it is salutary to bear in mind that in the pageant of life the entire known experience of world politics occupies no more than a minute place, perhaps less than one-hundred-thousandth part of the whole. That thought alone should inspire humility in those who take it upon themselves to arrange life on earth.

The Heritage of "Primitive" Society

The substance of the study of world politics conventionally coincides with the experience of historical or "civilized" world societies. These are societies about which historical records—in particular, written materials —are extant. They are large-scale societies which developed specialized means of social coordination; of these, writing and other forms of record-keeping were, of course, important instances. There is much justification in such procedure, inasmuch as world politics is, above all, large-scale politics.

Problems of scale render many comparisons between large and smaller societies redundant. But small-scale societies can afford lessons about the problems of managing total (that is "world") societies that cannot easily be perceived in other ways. Thus, preoccupation with agrarian societies excludes from the scope of inquiry the entire prehistorical record of man, which, as just demonstrated, is substantial in its time dimension and, for that reason, should not be ignored. An emphasis on settled societies also leaves out the "primitive" groups that have existed on the fringes of agrarian civilizations throughout the historical period; in diminishing numbers, these may still be found in various parts of the world. "Savage" or "barbarian" communities have never been without influence upon the societies they were in contact with.

The earlier discussion of the evolution of life was intended to establish precisely this continuity in the development of man, as well as the evident continuity between the development of life and animal life in general, and early forms of human society. The question is whether certain important traits of human behavior—such as aggressiveness—and forms of social organization—such as territoriality and social division of labor—as well as the general role of violence and war in human affairs, might be attributable to this heritage.

The long record of man's evolution bears evidence of preoccupation with sheer survival, along with testimony to the importance of hunting and other forms of aggressive behavior. This shows the continuity with forms of animal behavior, and also suggests that a natural selection of aggressive human types might have occurred as part of the high evaluation placed, in the struggle for survival, upon combativeness.[1] Aggressiveness has remained a characteristic of many large-scale political systems, right up to the contemporary period. The question therefore arises: what might have been the mechanisms by which aggressiveness became embedded in the system of world politics, beyond the degree that could be regarded as "normal" assertiveness?

The pressure of primitive upon civilized societies must have contributed toward setting up the inequalities that have since characterized all historical systems of world politics. Conquering barbarians (for instance, the Mongols in China, the Arabs or the Turks in the Near East) set up ruling systems, by seizing positions of power and living upon the spoils of war and occupation. All agrarian world orders needed military protection from the primitive but war-like tribes and had to pay a high price for it; the result was a system of internal inequalities. Parallel with this was a condition of external inequality: no civilization to date has brought within its fold the entire human race, though it did often include some outsiders who, with respect to that particular civilization, are "primitives" or "barbarians." This failure of the civilizing mission brought forth a constant pressure of barbarism—this has, in turn, been a steady influence toward violence in world politics; the rule of force and the reinforcement of behavior patterns built upon violence. Settled or civilized societies might be violence-prone because of the survival, outside their effective borders, of unassimilated, and perhaps unassimilable, "barbarians." In this sense, equality and inclusiveness could be regarded as requisites for the well-being of world society.

There may have been one other special mechanism for transmitting the influence of early primitive societies upon later civilized ones.[2] The importance of hunting in mankind's evolutionary history must have played a part in the sexual division of labor of society—that is, in the assignment of active, aggressive, protective and warlike functions to men, and the delegation to women of child-rearing, food-gathering and household functions. As the result of possibly several million years of such specialization, men are expected, even in our time, to be strong and aggressive, and women to be weak and submissive. But men's strength and aggressiveness is also linked to a monopoly of political leadership, and this would tend to give to politics an excessively aggressive character. Thus a rigid and monopolistic derivation of sexual roles from primitive ideals might also contribute to shaping the character of world politics.[3]

Thus far, the influence of primitive society upon civilized world politics has been seen as accentuating the factors of violence and threat. But primitive societies might also be viewed in another perspective, as offering structural analogies for the organization of world societies. The absence of formal government in most such societies has frequently been commented upon by anthropologists, and the expression *stateless societies* has been applied to them. "Statelessness" is also a feature of some systems of world politics and of the contemporary system in particular. Might then the contemporary system, for this reason, also be called "primitive"? [4]

It is doubtful whether anything would indeed be gained by calling modern world politics primitive. The feature that this system shares with primitive societies is lack of centralization, and from this proceed such other similarities as reliance on self-help in the enforcement of rights. But the class of non-centralized systems includes many others, besides primitive systems of government. An argument that maintained that non-centralization is somehow primitive would confound rather than clarify the issues. On the contrary, non-centralized systems are likely to be more highly developed, more complex than centralized (state) systems. Hence modern world society, by being non-centralized (or stateless—that is, lacking in world government), is not primitive but rather complex and highly developed. If, however, additional insights about the functioning of non-centralized societies can be gained by studying "primitive" experience, then so much the better. Historically, the assertiveness of "primitive" communities—for instance, the mountaineers of the Swiss cantons or of the Scottish highlands—has contributed greatly to the development of respect for political autonomy and individual freedom.

World Population

The basic data about the populations of civilized societies may be summarized as follows: [5] On the eve of the Agricultural Revolution, at about 10,000 B.C., the human species may have amounted to anything between two and twenty million people, distributed in hunting and food-gathering communities all over the globe. On the eve of the Industrial Revolution in England, by about A.D. 1750, the total world population ranged between 650 and 850 million people. By 1970, that population had reached the level of 3.5 billion and was still expanding; it could rise as high as 26 billion by 2070, if twentieth century growth rates continue unchecked.

The steeply rising curve of the world's population over the three most recent stages of the evolution of life is too well known to merit reproduction at this point. Humans have become the most prevalent and most powerful form of life on earth. Suffice it to note that modern world politics now occurs in the context of a world population of a size never previously experienced; hence, it also poses unprecedented problems of world order. Population size, therefore, serves to distinguish the modern world from the earlier stages of agriculture and globalization. Modern world politics also still occurs in the context of high rates of population growth. And some of its features are undoubtedly attributable to this fact.

Agrarian World Orders

The world societies that emerged in various parts of the globe in the wake of the Agricultural Revolution may be described simply as agrarian. It is now known that, in the Near East, some human groups practiced agriculture and domesticated animals around 7000 B.C.—in China, after 5000 B.C. —and that in time the practice spread to most parts of the world. Indeed, the Agricultural Revolution may be defined as the process whereby man came to control and enlarge the supply of disposable plants and animals.

The increased availability of energy from the use of these new biological converters (previously the only energy available to man was muscle energy) made possible the maintenance of larger populations and brought about the elaboration of more complex societies.

By today's standards, agrarian world societies were, nevertheless, still rather small. Their populations rarely exceeded one hundred million and were usually smaller. Globalization altered the operating scale of all agrarian societies, by gradually bringing them into closer contact and incorporating them into a worldwide system. It was based on the development of maritime technology, including extensive utilization of sails as inanimate energy converters, and of military technology based on gunpowder. The Industrial Revolution completed the process of globalization and was characterized by the large-scale exploitation of inanimate converters (coal, water, nuclear power) and hence by a tremendous enlargement of disposable energy.

The number of agrarian world societies found in history is rather limited; but some are quite well known. Much of ancient and general history, which is taught as the distillation of worldly wisdom, is in fact the experience of agrarian world societies, and in particular those of Greece, Rome and China.

None of the historical agrarian societies were, of course, global—that is, worldwide in extent. Their description as world societies is, to a degree, the conferring of a courtesy title, but in fact their experience is such as to be relevant to the study of all globalized politics. A significant part of the definition of world societies is relative self-sufficiency. On this score, all the agrarian systems reviewed here can be shown to have been largely—some completely—self-sufficient, that is, isolated from conscious or meaningful outside contact.

A basis for the classification of world orders is the degree of centralization found within them. Centralization is a property of systems of world order and it can range from zero to infinity: zero centralization obtains when such a system has no central authority; infinite centralization, when the central authority monopolizes all the power that is available within the system. These extreme positions are, of course, exceptional, but, for practical purposes, a distinction can most often be drawn between systems of high and low centralization.

The operationalization of this concept depends on the availability of data. Basic data have to do with the membership and the boundaries of the world system to be classified, and the distribution of authority and power within it. The latter could be indexed by computing the number of men under arms (the size of the standing army), or the financial resources that are available to members of the system. For most historical systems, this information is scarce. Nor are the systems as clearly discrete in time and space as the concept would require; in many cases, and in respect to the Mediterranean world in particular, the boundaries of various orders remain for the most part rather vague.

Table 2:1 shows a number of historical world orders, as a sample of the societies that might be drawn upon for a comparative study of world orders, but it contains all the more significant instances.

The criterion of centralization produces the basic distinction (illustrated in Table 2:1) between empires or centralized world orders (also known as world states) and systems of independence, or autonomy systems which are world orders of low centralization. Within these two broad classes, moreover, the examples have been arranged according to their imputed degree of centralization. Thus China's First Empire is known to have been more highly centralized than the Han Dynasty, which followed it; and the Roman Empire obviously ranks higher on this scale than the Holy Roman Empire of medieval Europe.

The distinction between empires and autonomy systems as types of world order is fundamental to the study of world politics. These are alternative solutions to problems of world order at the global level, and they differ substantially in the political problems they engender, and resolve.

In every known world order, military power has played a prominent role: in the empires, it has been the centralizing agent and the motor-force of power monopoly; in the autonomy systems, military power guaranteed independence, but it also brought about frequent engagement in wars. It cannot be argued that military force was dominant in empires alone and absent elsewhere. Rather it was that, in empires, military might served to organize one type of political system, a monopoly, while elsewhere it fostered more competitive, more diverse and in large part more creative systems.

The common denominator of historical autonomy systems has been

TABLE 2:1   Agrarian World Orders

Empires (centralized world orders)	Old Empire (Egypt) 2700–2100 B.C. First Empire (Ch'in Dynasty) 221–206 B.C. Alexander the Great 336–323 B.C. Roman Empire 30 B.C.–476 A.D. Persian Empire 550–330 B.C. Rule of Genghis Khan A.D. 1206–1227 Han Dynasty 206 B.C.–A.D. 221
	Holy Roman Empire (Europe, medieval) Dar-ul-Islam (Moslem world) ca. A.D. 1000
Systems of independence or autonomy (orders of low centralization)	Spring and Autumn (China) 722–481 B.C. Italian city states (A.D. 1250–1494) Greek city states (ca. 500 B.C.) Sumerian city states (3500–2500 B.C.) Maya (ca. A.D. 900)

their reliance upon moral resources. This has manifested itself, above all, in religion's providing a framework of common unity and also a commonality of intellectual and aesthetic values. Among the prominent instances that might be mentioned are: Sumer, the first agrarian world order, which consisted of a number of cities organized by a priestly class around temples that also were centers of scholarly and scientific endeavor, where the practice of writing and astronomy originated; the Mayan civilization, built around especially magnificent temples; the Greek world, whose sacred places and festivals gave it the consciousness of unity in relations with outsiders; and the Moslem world, which began as an empire but shortly dissolved into a number of independent jurisdictions, bound together only by common religious beliefs and practices.

The world orders of autonomy have also been notable for their compatibility with trade. The commercial achievements of the Greek cities, especially Athens; the far-flung trade routes of Medieval Islam, and the accomplishments of Venice and Genoa, Florence and Milan in banking and shipping and in organizing trade across the Mediterranean—these attest to the relationship between active trade and autonomy. Empires never promoted truly imaginative trade spanning wide areas; instead, they tended toward self-sufficiency. Extensive trading networks, on the other hand, depend on knowledge, mutual trust, and common languages, as well as on a wide acceptance of common rules and a freedom of movement—that is to say, they depend, basically upon an infrastructure of a moral kind and a climate of autonomy.

Empires as World Orders

Throughout history, empires have held a curious fascination for men. Political leaders have sought to build them; ordinary spectators have been awed by them, and historians have sung their praises. Aspirants to an imperial crown have always been many, and its contented holders few. The simplicities of the imperial structure, in which all power is demonstrably concentrated at one point and in one man, itself attracts attention and compels respect. Yet, its performance as a political system and as a structure of world order is imperfectly known: students of International Relations have for the most part ignored it, on the understanding that empires, like states, produced problems of "internal" rather than "foreign" or "external" politics.[6]

Yet empires have represented one solution to problems of order, and for that reason alone they cannot be ignored by the student of world politics. These include empires that, in their time, covered the most substantial part of their civilized world—for instance, the Persian, or the

Roman, or some of the Chinese empires. Some others, such as Byzantium (ca. A.D. 600), did not control an overwhelming part of their world; yet they were, at their height, the major political organization. No empire was ever free from boundary troubles; they all had frontier wars and contended with barbarians. None of them has shown an extraordinarily long life span, and some were quite short-lived. The Roman empire in the West, and the Chinese state in the East, in its various reincarnations, were long-lived, but never peaceful, orderly or intact for extended periods. Rome collapsed under the barbarians' pressure, and China was several times conquered by them. But empires undoubtedly represented, until quite recently, the major concentrations of power and wealth of the historical period, and they were the most spectacular structures of their time.

Yet while they must have seemed huge, masterful and overwhelming by contemporary standards, they do not appear so impressive today. The area they occupied was limited—at most semicontinental in scope (the rule of Genghis Khan being the widest in areal scope) and always subglobal. In population, they were not huge: Rome at the height of its power may have had a population no larger than that of France today; some others, such as the Inca rule, or the Persian empire, probably did not exceed ten million people. Finally, their resources were limited by the agricultural basis of their technology and their resistance to innovation, and were thus basically fixed. The resource base was also vulnerable to weather, epidemics and war-connected devastations.

The budget of Rome, the most formidable of empires, has been estimated, for the first century A.D., at about thirty million dollars; it was based largely on tribute payments from the provinces. That budget maintained an army that employed some 140,000 Roman citizens and 150,000 allies. On a population basis, this is roughly proportionate to the military forces of modern states, but it was also the greatest standing army until seventeenth-century Europe.[7]

Empires (like all agrarian world orders) were also simple in another dimension, in that they were, basically, a two-layered system of social organization [8]—that is, their degree of social complexity seemed to be adequately provided for by two levels of social interaction. Their world consisted, at the base, of numerous and isolated communities and settlements, each largely self-sufficient. But overlying this mosaic of villages was the network of the Great Tradition: the true seed bed and the substance of the culture of the age. The consolidation of that network amounted to what McNeill has called the emergence of the Great Society.[9] In the classical Chinese empire, this was shown in the illustrious tradition of Confucianism, the rules governing the conduct of the dominant Mandarin civil service, and the medium of communication among the governing classes. In the Roman world, it was the Graeco-Roman culture of the cosmopolis, and its emissaries, who manned the network of administrative and army posts throughout the empire. The Great Tradition was the unifying element of the empire, and its viability a condition of its survival; but it was also quite distinct from the little traditions of the villages and the habits of the underlying populations.

The chief product of the imperial political structure was order. The empires originated in violent disorders, through either gradual or sudden conquest. The First Chinese Empire, for example, grew out of the turmoil of the era of the Warring States, a period of two hundred years of nearly continuous warfare. The hallmark of Rome's rule, too, was order, backed up by stern law. That empire excelled in orderly administration, backed by a superbly organized army, and moving over first-class roads built especially for its use. Empires strove for order by creating large organizations, both military and civil. These were the world's first successful large-scale organizations, the builders of pyramids and other impressive engineering works; they were also the begetters of bureaucracy and enormous consumers of ink, paper and miscellaneous writing talent.

The empire assumed a stance of omnipotence; in fact, however, its rule was lax and shallow, except at times of war, precisely because it was so strongly preoccupied with order. The scope of government was severely limited. In the Roman budget, close to two-thirds of the revenue had to be allotted to keeping up the legions and to ancillary expenditures, such as roads. Much of the rest of the political organization was occupied with raising the funds and collecting the taxes to maintain this army. In all empires, outside the court and the emperor himself, the bulk of the organization of politics had to do with the military and with ways of raising revenue to supply the court and the army.

The price of order was the depreciation and destruction of autonomy. By monopolizing power, the empire could (but did not always) confer large benefits upon those who controlled that power: sometimes, this could be just one man and his entourage: in China, it was the ruling clan or family or conquering tribe; in Rome, the Senatorial families and, in time, the citizens of Rome. No rival concentration of power was tolerated, within or without. The imperial state discouraged or suppressed the emergence of potentially competitive large-scale organizations, especially economic enterprises. None ever emerged that could compare with the huge bureaucracies of the empire. Such economic or industrial activity as was needed was often undertaken by the state. Outside powers were either conquered or kept at a distance. Yet, as the consequence of seeking to preserve a power monopoly based on military force, the empire was always liable to dissension among the power wielders, especially among the controllers of military power. The Roman empire was repeatedly at the mercy of its generals, dissident legions and disaffected pre-torians.

Predictably, the price of law and order was the discouragement of innovation and a general decline in creativity and imagination. Thus, the culture of Rome derived from that of the Greek cities, that in a brief burst of creativity fanned by a climate of autonomy, brought forth the basis of modern science and philosophy, brilliant works of art and litera-ture. The China of the Spring and Autumn period and of the era of the Warring States was also a time of economic innovation, growth of tech-nology and cultural invigoration, when all the philosophical schools China has known originated. Indeed, for the one and perhaps only time in Chi-nese history, "one hundred flowers bloomed." The Renaissance, sparked by the interplay of the Italian cities at the close of the Middle Ages, was another of these glorious ages. These periods of flourishing of autonomy were among the most seminal and productive eras of human history.

Compared with the cultural and political riches of the autonomy systems, empires do not shine at all. It is not really surprising if, after experiencing a season of violent turmoil, men turn for a time away from freedom and choose to put a high value upon order. The difficulty about empires is that even order proves hard to maintain within them; but they always succeed in keeping freedom at bay.

Empires as Power Monopolies

Empires maximize order through monopolizing power (more precisely, through monopolizing the means of violence). As a first approximation, order may be defined as keeping violence and illegal acts within normal bounds. If the index of disorder rises above this normal level—for in-stance, through an increase in crime rates, in incidents of riot and dis-turbances, or in interstate wars—then the society experiences a lack of order; any political system that restores that society to an acceptable or normal rate of violence may, in that situation, be said to be productive of order. Empires base their value on such minimization of violence even while resorting to official terror. As a second approximation, the ques-tions must also be asked: Is such order just? Who benefits from it? Who controls the means of violence? Such second-order questions come to the fore as soon as order is imposed and violence reduced, for unless the dis-tribution of the benefits of order is just, disorder is likely to emerge once again. But if order has been brought about by means of monopolizing power, the conditions of a just order have been seriously compromised, because justice flourishes best in conditions of equality. In a power mo-nopoly, justice may not be attainable in the face of the power organization, and in other situations, it may be at best unpredictable. Justice has a better chance when claimants to justice pursue their claims in full autonomy within a framework of agreed procedures.

For these reasons, it is hard to accept the claim that a power monopoly is a condition of order. Yet this proposition has a following among political scientists, some of whom see such a monopoly as a normal condition of domestic order, by contrast with the international scene, which lacks such a monopoly and is consequently beset by disorder. Max Weber's definition of the state, referred to above, as the organization wielding the monopoly of legitimate means of violence, has been particularly influential in this regard. By this means, the imperial conception of order has been brought directly into the modern idea of the state, and of the nation-state. By a notable, if dubious, transformation, the empire has become the ideal state. The entrenchment of the imperial idea as the modal type of political order must be attributed to the influence of classical education throughout the Western world during the eighteenth and nineteenth centuries. Not only did the leaders of the French Revolution model their political reforms after the institutions of the Roman Republic; the architects of the British empire, too, let themselves be guided by the lessons of Rome, as depicted in Gibbon's classical *Decline and Fall*.

A monopoly prevails when a product market has only one seller (or one producer). In a competitive situation, with a number of sellers, the price at which the product changes hands is set by the market. It is the distinguishing feature of a monopoly that the price for the product is set by the monopolistic seller alone. The seller may not control the quantity of the product sold (for that will depend on the price he sets), but he is free to adjust his price in such a way as to maximize his revenue. Monopoly distorts the distribution of resources and allows the monopolist to appropriate an unduly large share of the social product through his pricing policies. In other words, monopolies produce less at a higher price.

A world empire may be regarded as the producer of order. The monopoly situation permits it to produce less order than the general interest would require. But power monopoly also permits it to set taxes at a level that would maximize public revenue, rather than at the level called for by the public interest.

Conditions of monopolization occur when: (1) production conditions favor large units, and new producers cannot enter the market; and (2) consumers cannot shift their demand to substitutes (that is, demand is inelastic). Such conditions may frequently be found in political systems.

Governments tend toward monopoly because, in their respective jurisdictions, they do not permit competition from rival producers of political goods and services. Being large organizations, they are, in any event, hard to compete with, and the costs of entry for a competitor are high. Elective and democratic systems develop devices for "dividing" power and allow for choice among alternative management teams to run the monopoly, but they do not change the nature of the monopoly itself. Commanding the means of violence, governments can keep out rival organizations, except when the situation has deteriorated to the point of rebellion. At the local level of politics, a consumer might move from one jurisdiction to another. But in a world empire he has no choice. Hence the monopoly is complete, and the stakes and the profits of imperial power run high. "Ordinary" monopolies can be controlled by "the government"; but who can control the world empire?

In a fundamental and compelling sense, there is no substitute for order: violence or anarchy endangers the foundations of social and individual life, and thus the demand for order is likely to be inelastic. This condition appears to have been particularly strong in relation to agrarian world orders. An agricultural society is peculiarly vulnerable to complete disruption (for instance, through destruction of seed or at harvest time); it places a high value upon order and is willing to forgo much to secure it. Empires have therefore been successful among agricultural populations and for considerable periods they have been able to control rivals. Yet their record in keeping order has not really been satisfactory, and their achievements as harbingers of peace and prosperity have been notable more often as aspirations than as experiences of mankind.

The Cost of Establishing a World State: An Example

World history records only a few instances of political orders that were true world states—that is, centralized empires, controlling most if not all of their worlds. The Persian Empire, the rule of Alexander the Great, possibly the Roman and the Chinese Empires—they came close to this condition, yet they never fully attained it. Nevertheless, the ideal persists in the unconscious of mankind and men continue to pay tribute to it.

The reality of agrarian world states is less prepossessing than the ideal image would suggest. The costs of establishing and maintaining world states have usually been heavy. A good and also unique example of the problems arising in the setting up of a world state by conquest, and the drastic measures that are required to put it on a firm footing, is the experience of China's "First Emperor," Shih Huang Ti. This Emperor died in 210 B.C., after only eleven years of imperial rule, but his reign left an indelible mark upon the course of Chinese history.

In the fourth and third centuries B.C., the system of seven major independent states then constituting the core of the Chinese world was engaged in continuous warfare. One of the seven, the Kingdom of Ch'in, succeeded in gaining an upper hand in these contests; its advantage lay in its centralized administration, specialized for waging war. By 221 B.C., the ruler of Ch'in had eliminated all his rivals and made himself Emperor of China.

In itself, this feat was not strikingly different from the achievement of several other conquerors of the agrarian era, and the reasons for the breakdown of the system of Warring States appear to be not unlike those that prompted the collapse of Greek independence. What makes the reign of Shih Huang Ti remarkable is the speed and the thoroughness of his measures for the destruction of all traces and memories of the independent states, as well as the compelling force of the framework of unity he established. The unity he so forcefully imposed upon China has remained to this day.[10]

In a series of draconian measures, the First Emperor proceeded to annihilate the states he had defeated in battle. The territory of the new empire was divided into prefectures and military districts, each in the charge of military officers under his command and responsible to him. The noblemen and ruling houses of the old kingdoms—that is, the bulk of the political class of the former states and its political layer, some 120,000 in all—were rounded up and exiled to the heartland of the empire. The armies of the states were disbanded and the populace was ordered to surrender all weapons of war. These were collected, shipped to the capital and melted down. Even the memory of the states was extinguished in the great burning of the books, in which much of China's historical and philosophical literature perished.

The emperor took equally strong measures to weld his new realm into a highly centralized political system. The laws of Ch'in were enforced in all parts of the empire. Writing was standardized and, being based on ideographs (that is, on pictures), became a medium of communication even in the absence of common speech, and thenceforth the principal means of achieving not only organizational effectiveness in the new bureaucracy, but also cultural unity at large. A road and postal network guaranteed speedy communications (even the length of axles was standardized). At enormous cost in human lives, the attention of the empire was focused upon the building of the Great Wall, a project that served as a means of absorbing both the surplus energy and the manpower that was left over from the wars. It also set an example of the great works (and of the instruments for keeping order and maintaining security from the barbarians) that the new political system was capable of achieving.

It might be irrelevant to ask whether the founding of an enduring world state in contemporary conditions would entail comparable costs and sacrifices. But it is a commentary upon the strengths and weaknesses of empires that even so imposing a structure as that headed by Shih Huang Ti collapsed from internal strain only a few years after the death of its founder. A period of civil wars ensued, and after severe turmoil the empire was reconstituted, though in a less centralized form, under the Han Dynasty. For the next two millennia the idea of empire held sway in China. Although dynasties came and went, empires rose and then collapsed, and, for long periods, China was even divided among a number of independent sovereignties, the idea of empire as the ideal political organization maintained its hold on the popular imagination and especially on the imaginations of educated people. It may not be too far-fetched to suggest that underlying the divergence in Chinese and European political and social development has been the dominance of empire in Chinese political practice, as contrasted with Europe's success in overcoming the legacy of Rome.

To conclude this digression into Chinese history, here is a passage from a near-contemporary historian, vividly describing the fortunes of the Ch'in Dynasty. In capsule form, this is not only an apt account of the rise and fall of a brilliant rule but also a paradigm of the processes of empire: how the initial achievements of order are soon inevitably offset by the pressures of power monopoly—how absolute power corrupts absolutely.

When Ch'in faced south and ruled over the empire, there was once more a Son of Heaven. Immediately the innumerable multitude of the people began to hope for the peace to which they are inclined by nature. There was not one that did not give Ch'in their allegiance and regard him with respect. In this was the true principle of security, of enduring glory and the elimination of danger.

But the King of Ch'in was of a base and greedy character. He relied upon his own judgment, did not trust ministers of proven ability, and was not willing to conciliate the nobility and the people. He multiplied the tortures and made the punishments more terrible. His officers governed with the greatest severity. The rewards and penalties were unjust. The taxes and levies were unbearable. The empire was crushed under forced labor, the officials could not maintain order, the people were in the last extremity of misery and the sovereign had no pity for them and gave them no help. Then crime broke out in every place and the Emperor and his subjects deceived each other mutually . . . From the princes and ministers down to the humblest people every one was terrified and in fear of their lives. No man felt secure in his office; all were easily degraded.

So Ch'en She (the leader of the revolt against Ch'in), without needing to be a sage like T'ang or Wu (founders of the Shang and Chu dynasties), without having any high rank such as Duke or Marquis, had only to wave his arms for the whole empire to answer like an echo.[11]

The Relevance of History

Empires were not, of course, the sole political expression of agrarian world societies. Numerous communities throughout the civilized world also served as examples of the success and the persistence of autonomous modes of political expression. But as a general rule, it was the empire that held the fascination of the historian, and of the gentlemen whose vocation it was to rule.

The chief purpose of this chapter has been to elucidate the limitation of the experience of these empires, and to differentiate clearly between empires and autonomy systems as alternative modes of world organization. The contemporary world does not offer the experience of world empire, but only of one type of system of independent states. The record of historical world societies demonstrates, in a way which hypothetical speculation cannot do as conclusively, the risk and the costs of an imperial world order (a theme to be taken up again in Chapter Four).

The lessons to be drawn from historical empires are mainly negative but still relevant for organizing military power in conditions where a world monopoly of weapons of mass destruction is technically feasible. They show the dangers of monopolizing power, and they also highlight the contextual conditions that should make this experience irrelevant to the future. None offer solutions for organizing global societies; none have develped successful political techniques that combine order with a range of freedoms allowing for creativity and change. They offer little else but the false ideal of a society that is ruled from one center by absolute power.

Notes to Chapter Two

1. Continuity with animal behavior patterns is a subject pursued by the ethologists. Recent research on the structure of the brain pursues similar themes.

2. In addition to influencing civilized life, such warfare did, of course, have considerable regulatory and other functions for primitive societies. There is considerable anthropological literature on this point.

3. Lionel Tiger, *Men in Groups* (New York: Random House, 1969).

4. R. Masters, "World Politics as a Primitive Political System," *World Politics* 16(4), July 1964, 595–619.

5. Carlo M. Cipolla, *The Economic History of World Population* (Harmondsworth: Penguin, 1964) p. 98 ff.

6. One recent exception is L. Wesson, *The Imperial Order* (Berkeley: University of California Press, 1967).

7. Tenney Frank, *An Economic Survey of Ancient Rome*, vol. 5. *Rome and Italy of the Empire* (Paterson, N.J.: Pageant, 1959), p. 4.

8. For the concept of "layers," see Chapter 13.

9. W. H. McNeill, *The Rise of the West: A History of the Human Community* (Chicago: University of Chicago Press, 1963), p. 71.

10. This account follows C. P. Fitzgerald's *China: A Short Cultural History*, rev. ed. (London: Cresset, 1950), Ch. 6.

11. From Chia I's "The Faults of Ch'in," as reported by Ssu-ma Ch'ien and quoted in Fitzgerald, *ibid.*, pp. 149–150.

3
Globalization

IN CLEAR CONTRAST WITH ALL OTHER historical societies, the contemporary world society is global. The process by which a number of historical world societies were brought together into one global system might be referred to as globalization. The nature and the shape assumed as a result of that process remain even today one of the basic factors of world politics.

Throughout recorded history, a trend can be observed toward the enlargement of the geographical scope of human communities; it has been one aspect of the increasing scale of social organization. Six thousand years ago, when a Great Society began to take form among the city states of Mesopotamia, the effective radius of its area may have been two or three hundred miles; two thousand years ago, when the Roman Empire dominated the Mediterranean basin, the radius of its control may have been one thousand miles or more (for a time it included Mesopotamia). The spread and enlargement of areas of civilization were at the same time occurring in the Chinese and Indian realms, so much so that what McNeill calls the "closure of the Eurasian ecumene" occurred between 500 B.C. and 200 A.D.,[1] some two millennia ago. Within that time span, Hellenic culture reached India, while the Han Empire established a degree of contact with India and its missions established the existence of the Roman Empire. The epidemics that swept the ancient world around that time may have been the first practical consequence of the establishment of some pattern of interaction in the Old World. Generally, however, these interactions remained for a long time intermittent, indirect, nonpolitical, and not yet truly global.

The Moslem World

At the opening of the period of globalization, at about 1000 A.D., the nearest approximation to a worldwide political order was the Moslem world. Its origins lay in the Arab conquests of the seventh century, and its binding force was Islam. At that time it ranged from Spain and Morocco, through Damascus, Cairo and Baghdad, to Persia and the North of India; in the centuries that followed, it reached as far as the Indonesian islands, and Central and East Africa. Even by comparison with medieval Europe, it was a prosperous, productive and culturally rich world. Its cities, Baghdad and Cairo, were cosmopolitan and populous (Cairo had more than one million inhabitants during the medieval period), as well as being centers of artistic and literary creation. Its scholars and scientists were the true successors of Greek learning, while its universities predated Europe's by at least a century.

The Moslem world, moreover, was then functioning on a politically decentralized basis. After the exit of the Ummayad dynasty (755 A.D.), the political unity of the original caliphate was effectively broken; by the end of the Abbasid rule (884), Islam became a system of states; each acknowledged the spiritual authority of the caliph and obeyed the precepts of Islam, but for all practical purposes they were independent. Within this world the most effective process, other than war, was trade; it ranged as far as China and fully covered the Indian Ocean. The language of this trade was Arabic; its lubricant, the common cultural heritage of Islam.

For several hundred years, the Moslem world was the true seat of civilization. In relation to it medieval Europe was for a long time not only politically on the defensive, but also economically and culturally inferior. Indeed, by occupying a central position in the Eurasian-African landmass and using it for their far-flung trade, the Moslems had already brought together the major centers of world civilization. Only the New World eluded them, and interoceanic shipping. Why was it that the final achievement of globalization escaped them, and that eventually they ceded their place on the world stage to the Europeans?

This is not the place for an extensive analysis of that problem. The most important events sapping the strength of the Islamic world were probably the Mongol invasions of the thirteenth and fourteenth centuries by such famed and dreaded horsemen as Genghis Khan, Kublai Khan and Tamerlane. The rule of the Mongols did not last but, even though they adopted Islam, their depredations seriously weakened the Moslem world community. At the center of this world, power shifted to the Turks, whose Ottoman Empire created a military threat to Europe after the capture of Constantinople, but whose rulers and subjects lacked

Figure 3:1
The Onset of Globalization

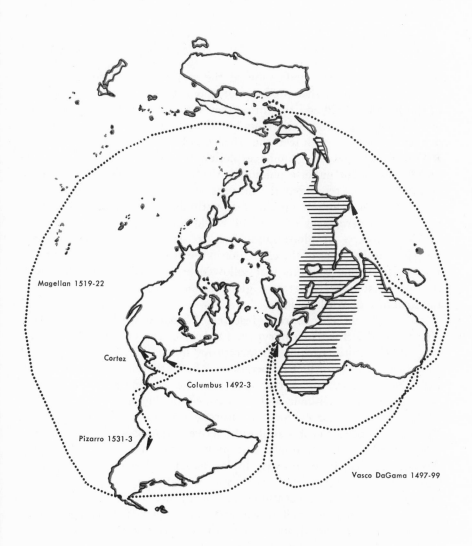

Magellan 1519-22

Cortez

Columbus 1492-3

Pizarro 1531-3

Vasco DaGama 1497-99

≡ Moslem World ca. 1500

••••• Spanish and Portuguese Expeditions 1492-1533

the vision of worldwide interdependence. After 1500, the Moslem world was strategically outflanked by European naval operations (see Figure 3:1), and its vitality continued to decline. While Islam continued to gain adherents in Asia and Africa, the brilliance of the Medieval period did not return.

The Expansion of Europe

The work of political unification of the world now fell to Europe. In one sense, the drive that produced it was a response to the prosperity of the Islamic world and the threat that was perceived to emanate from it. Leading that drive were the Portuguese and Spaniards, who had learned to respect and fear the Moslems during the centuries of the *Reconquista*. It was a genuine explosion of energy and vitality, of a breadth and scope hitherto unknown. Within a short space of time, soon after Copernicus reordered the heavens, men not only circumnavigated the globe, but followed up this feat with the establishment and maintenance of a permanent network of worldwide contacts.

The process of globalization was set in motion by people who lived in a small corner of the earth, not in the centers of world civilization. For the five hundred years that followed, it was they who determined the speed and the character of globalization; they also thereby shaped the structure of world politics.

By 1500, the characteristic features of modern world politics could already be discerned in embryo in Europe; in the course of globalization these features became characteristics of the entire global system. First was capacity for global operations. The European princes developed naval and military forces that were capable of long-range navigation —in particular, well-built and well-armed oceangoing fleets, superior to Arabic or Chinese competitors. Europe was but a far corner of the Eurasian landmass, but it was already active, vigorous and self-confident. The Crusades had accustomed Europeans to the idea of overseas expeditions; they had been an early display of self-confidence, indeed, arrogance. The Portuguese and the Castilians had been testing themselves against the Moslems for centuries, and were now ready to push ahead. Europe was militant, well-armed and well-organized, and aggressive; it was also well-educated, and through its new printing presses, both well-informed and capable of a global outlook.

Second was independence. Europe was not an empire and its activities were not directed from any one center. The Holy Roman Empire, which might never have supported expansion, had lost political authority by the thirteenth century; the Papacy, while still exercising spiritual leadership, never became involved to the degree that it did in the Crusades. Europe was an assemblage of autonomous political entities, of princes, prelates and nobles, of merchants, guilds and universities; it was by the action of each and all, in varying degrees and depending on the occasion, that the adventure of globalization was pushed forward.

Third was nationality. Within Europe, a few political authorities— and in particular, the Portuguese, Spanish, French and English mon- archies—came into the position of being able to generate strong loyalties among their subjects. Incipient nationalism strengthened their hand; the process of globalization and the contacts with the outside world that it generated strengthened such loyalties. The beginnings of the nation- state may already be observed during this period.

The "Age of Discoveries" (1450-1550) was based almost entirely on the Iberian Peninsula. But right from the start the effort was decentral- ized: the Portuguese monarchy organized and financed explorations of the route to India, while Spain, through the accident of support for Columbus' project (he had previously been turned down by Portugal), developed the route to the West and acquired large possessions in the Americas. A series of Papal Bulls, the most important one being the *Inter Caetera* of 1493, divided the uninhabited and heathen world between the Spaniards and the Portuguese.

By the middle of the sixteenth century, the basic framework of world communications had been established. English, Dutch and French merchants and mariners soon entered the field, and began to encroach upon the lucrative preserves of the Spanish Crown in the Americas and of the Portuguese monarchy in Asia. Conflicts ranged far and wide; but the stakes were mostly trade and exploitation in a few selected areas, such as bullion mining and sugar in the Americas, spices in the East, and slaves from Africa. With the exception of some areas in the Americas, including the Caribbean and the maritime regions of North America, the impact of Europe was confined to a number of coastal enclaves in various parts of the world. The reason for the thinness of this achieve- men was the basic military weakness of the European effort and the continued viability of the established civilizations of Islam, India and China (in striking contrast to the exceptionally sudden and quite unex- pected collapse of the Aztec and Inca societies, in the face of Spanish invasion).

Large-scale settlement and territorial control of the colonial type came only in the nineteenth century. As population figures surged in Europe and the volume of world trade rose sharply, a great wave of migrations flowed out, bringing continental areas in the Americas and in Australasia under European settlement. At the same time, Europe was pacified following the end of the Napoleonic wars in 1815; furthermore, it greatly strengthened its military position vis-à-vis the rest of the world, by advances in industrial and military technology (for instance, the development of rapid-loading guns). In quick succession, the remaining non-European civilizations experienced a political collapse: Mogul rule in India broke down in 1858; the Manchu empire in China disintegrated in 1911, following a series of rebellions, and the Ottoman Empire disappeared in 1918. Each of these areas then fell for a time under European domination. The Partition of Africa (formalized at Berlin in 1875) had completed the process by which most of the world had been brought under direct control of the European powers. Nevertheless, this stage did not prove to be truly lasting and, by 1960, colonization was completely reversed. Throughout the Americas, in Southern Africa and in Australasia, the new settlers retained power; but in the rest of Africa and Asia, indigenous nationalist leadership came to the fore.

Political Structure of Globalization

As noted, agrarian world societies were generally characterized by a twofold system of social layering: a top layer of the Great Society, and a bottom layer of the Little Tradition in the countryside (see Chapter Two, above), with little in between. One notable feature of European growth between A.D. 1000 and 1500 has been the emergence of the potential for such an intermediate layer of political and social organization. Like other agrarian societies, medieval Europe had a top layer of Roman tradition, of Church and empire. There was also a plethora of forms of parochial and local life: feudal princes, town and village committees, guilds, councils, congregations. But after A.D. 1000, a new level of political organization began to show here and there, especially in Portugal, Castile, Aragon and France. One set of princes in each of these areas began to assume a superior position, and around them there slowly grew a new, national layer of interaction, even while local and universal levels remained in vigor.

Sensing the vigor that was developing in Europe, and in an effort to project this energy outward rather than see it dissipated in internecine conflict, the Papacy set in motion a series of crusades against the Moslem world and for the conquest of the Holy Land. These were on the whole a failure. The overseas expansion into which some of Europe's energies were ultimately channeled became an enterprise not of the imperial and universal forces, but of the newly emerging intermediate or state layer of political organization. It is of considerable importance that the success achieved in globalization fed back to the strengthening of state authority in Europe.

Expansion produced a vast increase in the scale of European society, inasmuch as the whole of the world was gradually being incorporated into what was originally a European agrarian system. This increase in the scale of social organization came at a time of evolving social complexity, and helped both to foster and to promote it. Without such an increase in scale, the evolving complexity might have been smothered by an empire.

The growth of complexity could be viewed as an increase in the number of levels of social interaction and politics. After A.D. 1500, the intermediate layer, which represented the forces of the states, expanded at a rate higher than that of the other layers. Thus globalization brought about not an immediate strengthening of the global layer but rather a consolidation of the states—that is, of the forces of autonomy, but also of diversity and conflict.

On encountering agrarian societies during the course of their expansion overseas, the Europeans destroyed their Great Traditions and overthrew the top layers of social organization. In the Americas in the sixteenth century, they quickly dismantled the rule of the Aztecs and the Incas, and replaced it with their own royal administrations. In the East, they first destroyed the Moslem trading network and then, in the nineteenth century, replaced the historic imperial structures of Asia with European-administered or -advised governments. The former Great Societies were thus merged and absorbed into the political and social networks of a number of European states, without ever having any influence at the global level. Only one of the former Great Traditions—the European, in fact—emerged as the tradition of the global layer.

The nature and constitution of the global layer during process of globalization deserves more detailed scrutiny. While a global system of power and communications soon came into existence, it was weak and, to a large degree, separated from the politics of Europe. A few European states dominated the global structure, while the European community itself proceeded along virtually autonomous lines until well into the nineteenth century.

During the first two centuries of globalization, the dominant influence was that of the Spanish Crown. The conquests of Cortez in Mexico and Pizarro in Peru gave it a firm hold in the Americas, and the proceeds of these conquests soon gave it a large income. For a time, the Hapsburg King of Spain, Charles V, was also Holy Roman Emperor; in his person he combined the global involvements of his Spanish dominions with the German and European concerns of the empire. After his abdication, the two systems separated, but the Spanish line of the Hapsburg family remained the senior one and continued a world outlook. Philip II put Spanish resources into the vanguard of the Counter-Reformation. Even after his designs failed, the Spanish possessions in the Americas continued to be a solid asset, unmatched for a time by any other aspirants to overseas glory. The cities of Spanish America—Havana, Mexico, or Caracas—prospered and flourished culturally, long before anything comparable had yet grown in North America. Until about 1650, the Iberian monarchies dominated the global system of world politics.

That pattern did not last. The global monopolies of the Iberians were challenged by the Dutch and by the English. While the contest lasted at least a century and ended without a clear-cut decision, an early symbolic turning point was the Battle of the Spanish Armada (1588). From then onward, Spanish naval power gradually eroded. The Dutch East India Company succeeded the Portuguese in the control of the spice trade with the East, and the Dutch West India Company mustered a strong challenge to Spanish possessions in the Americas. The seventeenth century thus became the golden era of Dutch influence. Amsterdam was the central place of a trading network that was truly global: feeding supplies to it were colonial outposts on all continents. This meant, however, that the global network it sustained was primarily commercial and oriented to profit.

In the eighteenth century, English influence rose to ascendancy. The English East India Company was carving out for itself an empire in India, as well as exercising strong influence in English politics. The British West Indies became a source of great wealth in the Caribbean, on the basis of trade in sugar and slaves. France lost its first overseas empire in the eighteenth century and when the Spanish colonies declared their independence, during the turmoil produced by Napoleon, British naval power gave them military and political protection. And the growth of the English-speaking United States soon dwarfed the earlier prosperity of Spanish America. London established itself as the leading commercial center and both the Netherlands and Portugal, and their overseas domains, became dependent on it. Thus, while France dominated the affairs of continental Europe, English influence organized the rest of the world as true successor to Iberian rule.

The ruling pattern of the nineteenth century was the dominance of the global layer by the British Navy and by London, as the center of world trade, finance, and industry. This pattern withstood the challenge of the German High Sea Fleet during the First World War and defeated another German challenge in 1939-45. As the Second World War closed, a close alliance had been forged with the United States, the British role in global politics being replaced by an American-British partnership in the Great Power institution. By the nineteen-sixties, the Soviet Navy began to develop a pattern of global operations that, in its scope resembled the earlier German challenge. In an age that has raised air transport to a level equal with that of ocean shipping, such a challenge is no longer quite so compelling; it could yet lead to mutual accommodation, within a broader and more institutionalized framework of world authority.

In its earlier period, the global layer was, in flavor and complexion, Iberian and Catholic; in its later periods, it was at first Dutch-English and Protestant, then English and Anglo-American. In a formal sense, and until the advent of general international organizations in the twentieth century, the world has not known any government throughout these centuries. Britannia never claimed to rule anything but the waves; two-thirds of the earth's surface is, however, covered by water; those who controlled the oceans also controlled world communications and world trade, even if they were unwilling to become entangled in the details of the fratricidal politics of one small part of the globe.

Paradoxically, the principal consequence of the age of globalization has been the growth of the state-oriented, not the global layer of world politics. The weakness of the twentieth-century network of global interactions is not of recent origin, but rather the result of long-standing processes. The world has been organized for the past few centuries for the principal purpose of furthering European trade, and this single-purpose orientation cannot but have warped world development.[2] The world has lacked a governmental structure that would give equal, not to speak of higher priority to a rounded concern for all aspects of the welfare of the human race.

Some Other Features

One striking feature of the process of globalization has been the quality of arrogance and violence that fueled it. William McNeill notes the "deeprooted pugnacity and recklessness" which, in combination with advanced military technology and acquired immunity to a variety of diseases within a brief space of time, gave the Europeans of the Atlantic Seaboard the command of the oceans.[3] European warlikeness (even of the merchants who on the high seas easily assumed the role of pirates) was most pronounced when compared with the attitudes and aptitudes of all the other major world civilizations (except for the Moslems, another "community of will"). None of them could match the naked, if well-organized, force of their ruthless opponents. In the process of globalization, European warlikeness might well have become a dominant feature of the entire system of world politics.

There is no need to exaggerate the amount of force that was, in fact, deployed by European states for overseas conquests. Cortez conquered Mexico, in a legendary sweep, with a force of 508 men and 16 horses; a few years later Pizarro destroyed the Inca empire with 105 infantry and 60 cavalrymen. Major military operations for overseas expansion were virtually unknown. In most cases, small forces, many of them locally recruited, were used to capture and secure valuable colonial prizes. The employment of "native troops" for keeping order has been the characteristic feature of colonial administrations.

Yet, when security or profit demanded it, force was applied sharply and unhesitatingly. A striking instance was the decisive action taken by the Portuguese government in 1509 to destroy by force of arms the Moslem trade in the Indian Ocean. Their admiral had found that he could not compete with the Arabs on commercial terms and decided to use instead his superiority at sea. After defeating a Moslem fleet that had been organized against him, he set out to establish a string of naval bases, as strongpoints for the conduct of his operations. Within a few years, he was able to gain for the Portuguese Crown a monopoly of the spice trade, and to deal a decisive blow to the Moslem system of oceanic commerce. From this crucial naval campaign dates the beginning of European control of world trade.[4]

The small absolute quantity of force was, of course, multiplied by technological superiority—in the initial period, especially, by excellence in naval architecture and naval artillery, both of them tested in the rough waters of the North Atlantic. Added to this was unlimited arrogance and self-righteousness. The arrogance fed upon the early successes in Mexico, Peru and the East; fortified by legend—fanned by best-selling accounts of these exploits—it grew into a myth of European invincibility, not seriously challenged until the twentieth century. Before this myth, everything crumbled: not only empires, but also the defense mechanisms of the individual psyche. The most damaging effect of European expansion must have been the challenge to self-confidence and the loss of nerve experienced by large segments of the world's population. This was a victory for lifemanship, but a defeat for life.

Another striking feature of globalization was the importance of the role that naval matters played in it. The global network that had been so easily erected by the early explorers was naval; it remained virtually unchanged until the twentieth century. Maritime enterprise, which can command worldwide traffic lanes, with only minimal investments for harbor and some engineering facilities, had been able to unify the world even in the sixteenth century. This network bypassed the landmasses and the great land-oriented civilizations built upon them; it outflanked and surrounded them, clogging and severing their communications arteries, until they collapsed of heart failure. Conversely also, during most of this time, the direct and constructive influence of the naval network was chiefly marginal. Most of the world's peoples were not under its rule, but merely exposed to its indirect sway. In the earlier, Iberian period, the missionary impulse was strong and its effects have been lasting, in the Americas and even in the East; but during the Anglo-Dutch period, religious activities assumed a place that was secondary to commercial and financial enterprise. Even so, trade itself began to assume substantial proportions only in the nineteenth century. Globalization was thus combined with only minimum socialization toward wider values. The maritime network was far-flung and flexible, but it was also light in positive impact. It is no real prototype for modern world politics.

Third, by enlarging the scale of world society, globalization created the demand for organizations that would be capable of operating on such a scale. All the basic organization types of modern society—the modern state, modern corporate enterprise, and modern science—were shaped by it and benefited greatly from it.

A great expansion in state activity and efficiency may well have been the most profound influence of globalization. Royal governments in Portugal, Spain, England and France organized and reaped the fruits of discovery and exploitation. In this, they learnt much from the Italian city states, Venice, Genoa and Florence: during the late medieval period, these were models of administrative organization and efficiency. But they soon had to expand their organization greatly in order to govern their newly acquired posts and territories—that is, efficiently to conduct higher-level administration at a distance. The Spanish Crown was the first to develop an elaborate machinery for the government of its American possessions; it thus gave employment to the rising number of graduates of law schools and universities. In turn, strong bureaucracies undermined tendencies toward popular rule, created a steady flow of revenue, and made the rulers independent of the control of assemblies, which had been so prominent in the earlier period. "Bureaucracy, like absolutism, strengthened its grip upon the kingdoms of Europe, in part at least as the consequence of the needs experienced and experiments conducted overseas." [5]

In military governmental operations, globalization was peculiarly favorable to, as well as dependent upon, the development of the navy. Effective naval operations over long distances require not only technology, but above all a sound political organization: a steady tax base, because they are expensive; a shipbuilding and supplies industry, geared to governmental demand; a manpower base that might be relatively small, but had to be loyal and well-trained; and a governmental system that would be capable of coordinating these elements toward long-term goals. Governments that were capable of equipping fleets for sailing the world would also, as a rule, be efficient and strong governments, and it was they who set the tone of political organization.

Good navies were, for their part, closely dependent on the organization of commerce. The first Portuguese explorations were organized and financed by the Royal government; the monopoly of the spice trade that flowed from them was conducted entirely for the benefit of the King. This fusion of political and commercial activities probably contributed to the early decline of the trade. Spanish trade with the Americas was conducted by a monopoly of the merchants of Seville, with the financial backing of Italian and German houses, but it was less lucrative. It was the injection of Dutch and English enterprise, based on the long commercial experience of the cities of the Netherlands, that led to the development of specialized, corporate trade enterprises. The Dutch and English East Indies Companies became particularly famous, but there were many others. They all began as devices for pooling efforts to equip and supply fleets that sailed long distances. Voyages to the East, for instance, could last several years, and their profits were far from certain, although they could be spectacular. The organization, forethought, trust and care that were required for launching such expeditions were of a high order. Practices evolved in the organization and management of long-distance, hence higher-layered, trade and production activities became the bases of modern corporate organization.[6]

Finally, none of this wide-ranging activity would have been possible without a technological and scientific base. Superior shipbuilding technology, combined with the development of naval artillery, assured naval supremacy to European globalizers. Portuguese and Spanish successes in this were based on the application of trial and error to techniques that had been evolved by the arsenals of Venice and Genoa. But there was also the conscious application of contemporary scientific thought, resting upon the base provided by the growth of the medieval universities.

The Portuguese exploration that spearheaded this process of globalization was founded upon solid scientific research, one important field being the application of astronomy to problems of navigation. Astronomers have had a long association with governments; but it is known that in 1484 the King of Portugal convened a commission of mathematicians for the purpose of devising practical methods of finding latitude by solar observation. The result was the first European manual of navigation and naval almanac.[7] Equally important was the demand for charts and maps, especially for world maps and globes. Thus this became the golden age of geography. The first permanent scientific societies, such as the British Academy, which was formed in the seventeenth century, had close links with research on naval matters. Modern science grew

up in close partnership with the state, and the needs of exploration, chart-
ing, and prospecting—set up by globalization—were powerful.

The original burst of globalization coincided in time with a high
point in the growth curve of Europe's universities. By about 1460, when
some 40 universities were in existence (their numbers had been doubled
every hundred years for the previous four centuries), had acquired a
solid educational foundation for the launching of new enterprises. After
1460, the rate of growth of universities slowed down, only to pick up
again after the repercussions of globalization began to feed back into
the system. This latter trend, with a doubling rate of 66 years, continued until the nineteenth century, when even faster growth was set
in motion. Globalization rested on medieval university development and
stimulated in turn the even higher growth of science and of education.[8]

An Appraisal

The way in which the world has been brought together was a spectacular enterprise, with a magnificence all its own. Its role in shaping human
destiny has not often enough been appreciated, even though the tales
of exploration and adventure have long held the fascination of European audiences. But the spectacle and the splendor also had their shadows,
and some of these have been dark and long.

A most important characteristic of globalization was its marvelously
uncontrolled character. Despite the force and impetus of the process,
this was not an organized expansion of a centralized system, as were
the contemporaneous Chinese expeditions to Africa. This was not an
expansion of one entity, called Europe, seizing overseas territory; it
was rather the spilling over of a multitude of enterprises from Europe
onto the world. In turn, the impact of the process also changed Europe.
No one empire emerged but rather a series of imperial domains, each
in competition with the others. Despite attempts at monopolization, no
one rule attained overwhelming superiority; conversely, no single empire
gave its ruler sufficient power to establish dominion over the whole of
Europe.

The enlargement of the scale of the political system and the resources
tapped through globalization in turn helped to prevent the consolidation
of Europe under one imperial rule, or a regression in the steady growth
of its politics. The attempts of essentially continentally-oriented European
great states, under Napoleon or Hitler, to bring Europe under such rule
failed—in part because of the extra-European resources mobilized for
their containment.

Globalization helped to consolidate the system of independent states for Europe, and ultimately also for the world, by fostering the growth of a diversity of organizations, each one of which served as the seed-bed of new autonomy and diversity. But above all, this process strengthened the state, and by doing so it markedly affected the course of future political development.

Who benefited from globalization? In a broad sense, the Western community did. During the past few centuries, the share of the European stock in the world's population has risen substantially.[9] In part, this is attributable to an earlier burst of population growth in Europe; but this early growth had also made possible large-scale migrations and the settlement of some of the world's most fertile and productive lands, in the attractive temperate zones, by people of European descent. The abundant lands and waters of North America, southern South America, South Africa and Australia became extensions of Europe, and their exploitation significantly altered the distribution of global wealth in favor of the European groups. As the result of globalization, the Europeans and their descendants today control the major part of cultivable land and the most productive sources of food, and they could also control the resources of the seas.[10]

Within Europe, those who benefited the most were those governments and states, and their subjects, that led and controlled the process. At first, the Iberian monarchies grew powerful on its proceeds, then the Dutch, the English and the French. Globalization altered the distribution of power away from Central Europe—including the cities of Northern Italy, the German lands and the Baltic area—to the coastlands of the North Atlantic. The process of growth redounded in the first place to the benefit of those who organized it.

Side by side with the benefits of globalization must be put its considerable costs and its range of adverse, indeed disintegrative effects. With regard to a number of human societies, its impact has been deadly, both in terms of social organization and for individual members of such societies, for whom the prospects of life declined tragically as the result of European impact. The societies of Mexico and Peru disintegrated, and in the century following the conquest the population of Central America declined catastrophically, through violence, disease and depression.[11] Similar disasters befell the Indian populations of North America, the inhabitants of many Pacific islands and the aboriginal populations of Australia.

A major element in the intercontinental exchange of the seventeenth and eighteenth centuries was the African slave trade. Prompted originally by the manpower needs of mines and plantations in various parts of the New World, its effects upon the societies of the Americas was clearly detrimental; but the effect on Africa must have been devastating. It kept in being a continuous demand for slaves, to be secured by endemic warfare throughout the continent. It supported predatory rulers, whose only function was to manage the supply of slaves, as well as predatory traders, who pandered to such demands in the West and in the Near East.

The established non-European civilizations in the Moslem, Indian and Chinese realms reacted more slowly, but in the end they too experienced the effects of sea-borne influences emanating from Europe. They all collapsed by the end of the nineteenth century, when a loss of nerve occurred throughout the non-Western world, and brought in its train a disintegration of established political structures. This breakdown in turn influenced world income distribution. In 1860, the economic superiority of Europe was already in evidence; yet it was also within reasonable measure. There is some reason to believe that during preceding centuries the standard of living both in China and in India had been lower than it was in Europe, because of the higher population densities, supported by irrigation agriculture. But as the nineteenth century progressed, China and India fell behind further and further; by mid-twentieth century they were nearly out of sight. While Europe and North America forged ahead, Asia, Africa and Latin America fell behind. The consequent inequalities are evident not only in income, but also in basic differences in nutrition and health patterns. In time, these differences could assume a biological basis. In brief, globalization has also been profoundly divisive and the effects of this divisiveness are yet to be fully experienced.

The earth is the basic territorial unit of analysis for the study of world politics. The processes by which it has reached political unification have lasted for a long time and are still uncompleted. Overall, there has been a certain inevitability to this process: it is difficult to imagine it not occurring at some point in the world's development. Man was bound to persist in exploring and crossing the entire planet, and his exploration and settlement had to assume a certain more or less orderly pattern. To the extent that globalization has been accompanied by an expansion of man's horizons, by a broadening of knowledge and an enlargement of the limits of empathy, the process redounded to the general advantage.

But the precise path described by the entire experience need not have been the one that actually did occur, and the process might yet be channeled in new directions. How does man go about enlarging the bounds of community? How fast can he proceed in doing so? How far can he go without damaging it, or disrupting it beyond repair?

Most of the time globalization was a process of incorporating external parts into the ongoing fabric of Western-centered world politics. Those governments, societies, individuals that proved adept and adaptable enough were brought within the mainstream by means of cooptation.

The great majority were either dominated, controlled, ignored or isolated. An alternative mode of adaptation—that of adjusting Western-type life patterns to the requirements of the rest of the world—has not been adequately considered. Cooptation certainly has been neither deep, rapid nor sufficiently extensive. Complementary adaptation is yet to be explored—for instance, through the selective slowing down of growth rates. The work of globalization could yet be carried to completion in unsuspected ways.

Globalization ultimately raises the problem of whether the large community, indeed the community of mankind, can be a good community. Renowned political thinkers have consistently opted for an ideal community that is small and intimate. By and large, contemporary political thought points to the lack of community in large-scale organizations.

The historical experience of globalization does not permit us to make any optimistic or easy conclusion. It offers no grounds for the opinion that the large community must, of necessity, create wide benefits; indeed, there are reasons for thinking that it may instead create opportunities for great dangers. But it also discloses no theoretical or practical considerations that show that the large community is inherently unable to be good. The large community is here and can no longer be avoided; perhaps it can be made better.

Notes to Chapter Three

1. W. M. McNeill, *op. cit.*, Chapter VII.

2. In an exaggerated but telling expression, Buckminster Fuller (in *Operating Manual for Spaceship Earth* [New York: Simon and Schuster, 1969]) argues that until the First World War the world was ruled by the "Great Pirates"—the seafarers who conceived of it as a unit and managed its destinies, after a fashion, without directly ruling any territory.

3. McNeill, *op. cit.*, pp. 623–4.

4. J. H. Parry, *The Age of Reconnaissance* (New York: New American Library, 1964), pp. 159–162.

5. *Ibid.*, p. 320.

6. The prominence of corporate organization in the economic development of the United States may have had its orgins in the early influence of such commercial corporations. Virginia was founded by an English chartered company; New York was a trading post of the Dutch West India Company; the Hudson Bay Company had been prominent in Canadian history for centuries.

7. Parry, *op. cit.*, pp. 110–111.

8. Derek de Solla Price, *Big Science, Little Science* (New York: Columbia University Press, 1963), p. 27.

9. Cipolla, *op. cit.*, pp. 102–4, quoting Kuczynski, according to whom the white population of the earth was about 22 per cent of the human species

in 1800 and about 35 per cent in 1930; more recently, this proportion may have been declining.

10. According to G. Borgstrom (*The Hungry Planet*, New York: Collier, 1965, p. 29), "the privileged nations of the world"—which include the United States and account for some 450 million people—dispose of as many food calories per year as 1,300 million people at the bottom of the scale, who live in the least developed countries. "We like to think that we owe our abundance to our greater skill and ingenuity, completely forgetting that we owe it equally or maybe even to a greater extent to our good fortune in the great lottery of mankind, which has given us a disproportionate share of the world's agricultural resources."

11. Central Mexico had a population of 11 million in 1519 and one of 2.5 million in 1597 (quoted by Parry, *op. cit.*, p. 246).

4
Autonomy

I₋ₙ CHAPTER TWO, HISTORICAL WORLD societies were classified according to the degree of autonomy they exhibited; the distinction was drawn between empires, which allow no autonomy, and systems of independent states, which may display different degrees of autonomy. The contemporary global system is, of course, a system of independent states, and belongs in the category of autonomy systems.

In man's historical experience, systems of independence have been neither characteristically stable nor singularly long-lived, even though some of them have been brilliantly productive. The dominant and steadily recurring political formations of agrarian world societies have been empires, or power monopolies; the compulsions and attractions of empire have been great throughout history. To this day, empire remains one of the alternative models of world order.

Given the strength of the imperial idea, what requires explanation is the persistence of a high level of autonomy, as a property of the world system, throughout the period of globalization and into the present day. What are the conditions favoring the maintenance of independence systems? What are the conditions of stability for autonomy systems? How have Europe and the world been saved from universal empire?

Wars of the Balance of Power

The simplest answer to the question of why a system of independent states has been preserved for the past five hundred years is that all attempts to establish an empire have been defeated. It was not for want of trying that universal rule was avoided, but for lack of effective actors and because of the absence of favorable conditions. Yet the price of independence has been war. The lure of empire and the attempts to dispel it have been like a red thread running through the history of modern Europe and the global system, and the wars that make up this story have been the major element in the system of world politics; furthermore, they have imposed upon it a logic all their own. In the past, the preservation of independence became associated with the idea of the Balance of Power. The wars that it has entailed have thwarted all would-be empire builders; they have also been the decisive events and the major watersheds of the entire era.

The stage was set during the Middle Ages, when political practice and political thought lived off the lingering memories of Rome. Charlemagne was the first to revive the imperial cult, and the Holy Roman Empire remained for centuries the rallying point of the imperial idea. The Bishops of Rome drew upon the prestige of that city to build up the Western Church into a powerful organization under their own leadership. The Holy Roman Empire soon exhausted itself in a contest with the Papacy; while the latter held sway for a while (mainly during the fourteenth century), it could never aspire to the position of a true empire (without undergoing basic organizational changes that would give it major military forces). Medieval Europe thus had already witnessed one kind of balance—that between a large political and a large religious organization.[1] This showed that autonomy can be the result not only of a purely political balance, but also of generally interorganizational ones. The maintenance of that balance, too, entailed considerable conflict. But the fourteenth century, the time of greatest Papal strength, saw in Italy the growth of a system of independent city states, within which balance-of-power processes were also activated.

By 1500, therefore, both the condition of autonomy and the possibility of defending it against imperial designs were well established in the European community. During the centuries that followed, the increasingly wider and more complex autonomy system sustained repeated challenges. These imperial challenges which inevitably assumed the form of great wars, were usually associated with a striking personality, who was aspiring to imperial dignity or glory: Charles V and Philip II, Louis XIV and Napoleon, Wilhelm II, Hitler. In a broader sense, the challenges also had important organizational bases, at first dynastic, and later national: Hapsburg in the sixteenth and seventeenth, and French and German in later centuries. Each deserves some notice.[2]

The first modern aspirant to universal rule was Charles V. A Hapsburg and a Prince of Burgundy, he succeeded to the throne of Spain in

1516; three years later, he was elected Holy Roman Emperor. During his reign, Cortez and Pizarro added rich possessions to his dominions in the New World. In a memorandum written just after his election to the imperial throne, he was told by his Grand Chancellor, "God . . . has set you on the way towards a world monarchy, towards the uniting of all Christendom under a single shepherd." [3] Though he possessed great assets and good fortune, Charles failed in his goal of a world monarchy. When he abdicated, some fifteen wars later, his great dynastic designs remained uncompleted. Christendom had been deeply divided by the Reformation. All the while the King of France, his chief opponent, had been steadily gaining strength.

Against ever greater opposition, the Hapsburg design for universal monarchy was continued by Philip II, Charles' son and his successor to the Spanish throne. As a leader of the Counter-reformation, Philip saw his mission partly in religious terms. He achieved dynastic union with Portugal, uniting under one crown the far-flung possessions of the two Iberian leaders of globalization. But the zenith of Iberian power was already passing. The long fight against Dutch independence had sapped Spanish strength in Europe, and the exhausting war against England, of which the destruction of the Great Armada was only one incident, marked the beginning of the decline of Philip's power overseas.

The Thirty Years War (1618-1648) may be regarded as a transition between Hapsburg predominance and the European ascendancy of France. In the first phase of that war, the Austrian Hapsburgs were coming out ahead in a campaign against Protestant Germany; but then the King of Sweden intervened and, with the support of France, he restored the balance. By the end of this devastating conflict, at the Peace of Westphalia, France had become the leading power in Europe.

The English Crown and the cities of United Netherlands had also been prominent in fighting "Spanish pretensions" and the Papacy; on the whole, however, they pursued their ambitions in the world at large. The French monarchy, on the other hand, while not entirely ignoring overseas possibilities, developed its European interests most of all. A prosperous country and now the most populous in Europe, France (under Louis XIV) became a strong centralized state. This state achieved Europe's first true standing army, the most powerful since Roman times; it reached some four hundred thousand men, supplied and equipped by an efficient ministry of war, and protected by a system of fortifications that drew on the best in contemporary science and engineering.

Once again, Europe's suspicions were aroused and cries of "universal monarchy" were sounded—especially during the crisis of 1683, when the Ottoman Turks besieged Vienna and Louis XIV used his powerful army to carry out a series of piecemeal annexations. While these extended the boundaries of his state toward the east, that was not his only objective. Until 1688, he had reasons to hope that he or one of his sons might be elected German emperor; the imperial crown was exerting a new fascination. But after three major coalition wars, French power was contained; the Treaty of Utrecht (1713) marked the first public recognition of the Balance of Power.

French power surged forward once again under Napoleon. The French Revolution had modernized the political system; it had also placed strong armies in the field, and had backed them up with ideological fervor. As it was beginning to lose its impetus, Bonaparte, one of its generals, seized power in a classic coup d'état. At first he took the title of First Consul; but soon he crowned himself Napoleon I, Emperor of the French. In brilliant military campaigns, he put himself in control of most of Europe, dissolved what remained of the Holy Roman Empire, and placed his relatives and his generals on several of the thrones he had created or had made vacant. In the manner of many ancient conquerors who sought legitimacy, he took as his bride a Hapsburg princess, and titled his son King of Rome. But he could not conquer all; England fought him doggedly throughout his career, and Russia proved to be his doom. By 1815 he was no longer a threat, but Europe had by then endured more than two decades of near-continuous warfare. The Congress of Vienna marked the beginning of a new age.

The unification of Germany, marked by the defeat of another Napoleon, rekindled memories of imperial glory. Bismarck's German Empire became a major European power, building its strength on rapid industrialization, scientific research and scholarly and cultural excellence. For a while Germany held a dominant position on the continent of Europe, while Bismarck's policies were basically conservative. His successors were less sure of themselves, yet also more ambitious. By embarking upon a naval armament race, they steered themselves into a collision course with Britain. German *Weltpolitik* was the first important challenge to Britain's predominant influence in the extra-European world, which had been won through centuries of naval warfare, trade and settlement. Whatever the precise causes of the First World War, Emperor Wilhelm's erratic personality and German war aims (developed once the fighting broke out) conspired to project the picture of a state that was out to achieve world dominion.

The Second World War was but a repeat performance of the challenges of World War I; taken together, however, they were the greatest armed conflicts waged in human history and they profoundly affected the structure of the world. Hitler's Reich had a nostalgic air, part of the memories of the Empire of a Thousand Years. His conception of world order, such as it was, was close to the ideas of the geo-politicians and based upon "Pan-Regions": in a system of three or four such regions, including Pan-America and the Greater East Asian Co-Prosperity Sphere, the German Reich would lead "Pan-Europa" (which was also to include Africa) and presumably dominate the rest.[4] At the height of the war, Hitler's "New Order" in Europe resembled Napoleon's, but it was even more ephemeral. He was brought to naught by the same coalition that had won the First World War and had still earlier defeated Napoleon.

The Cold War

Almost without exception the major military conflicts of modern world history have been wars of the Balance of Power: wars to promote imperial ambitions and to protect the system of independent states. The maintenance of autonomy has been a costly process for mankind. Strik-ingly, too, the ambitions involved in these struggles have in each instance been, actually and literally, "imperial" and "Roman."

The "Cold War," if it is understood as the Stalinist attempt to control Europe in the years after 1945, may be regarded as another in the series of great challenges to European independence. It was certainly so regarded, for instance by Winston Churchill. Conditions favoring it included the weakness of Europe after 1945, and the possibility that the United States might precipitately withdraw its forces from the continent. But the American forces did not withdraw, and Europe got over Soviet threats and pressures, while at the same time the scale of world politics continued to expand to the point where the Cold War in Europe, and even a hot war in Korea, were no more than incidents in a global pat-tern of Great Power and superpower relations.

In contrast with all the earlier cases, however, a great war has so far been avoided. The old symbols of empire have been almost com-pletely subdued, whatever their indirect influence (if any).[5] The Stalinist conception of world order is now cast in the contemporary idiom of the international system. It is a world of nation-states, controlled by Communist Parties, each of which holds an internal monopoly of power, but accepts the direction of the Soviet Party. In practical terms, this has been embodied in the structure of the Third International, and in more recent operations of the world communist movement. On a limited scale, it operates in Eastern Europe, where Soviet will is ultimately backed by overwhelming military power. This is empire in miniature, but so far untested on a wider scale. It is unacceptable to those Communist Parties that securely control large and powerful states, such as China. Hence, the Communist system is susceptible to the same problems of limiting claims to the monopoly of power and authority as are met in any other nation-state system.

The Legitimacy of Autonomy

So far, this has been an account of when and how rulers have acted to defeat empire and to defend autonomy. In explaining why they have so acted, first place belongs to the quality of public and scholarly discussion about the Balance of Power. This discussion helped to bring about a climate of opinion in which autonomy attained a high degree of legitimacy and threats to it were censured.

Quite early in modern history, recourse to the Balance of Power came to be regarded as the legitimate and correct manner in which to manage the affairs of Europe and, after prolonged wars, to rearrange them. In the seventeenth century, it had already become a commonplace of public discussions; by 1713, a major peace treaty, that of Utrecht, mentioned it explicitly as a principle of the European order "specifying the conditions whereby the Peace and Tranquility of the Christian world may be ordered and stabilized." It became the essential element of the Constitution of Europe; public and scholarly debate became the means by which the legitimacy of that constitution was assured.

The legitimacy of the Balance of Power in Europe stands in sharp contrasts with the situation prevailing in China after the founding of the First Empire. The rule of the Ch'in Dynasty, as all empires are wont to do, collapsed in short order; but it was soon replaced by another dynasty, which continued the empire. As time went on, empires were followed by periods of greater autonomy, but the idea of empire lingered on as a myth that had taken hold of the imagination. Most influential in this process were the scholars, and in particular Confucian scholars, whose philosophy became the official doctrine. The scholars were at first repelled by the harshness of military methods; but once the Han Dynasty had established itself securely in power, they were brought within the sphere of political power, and became part of its administrative structure— sometimes even its rulers. Training in the classics became the accepted route to power, and scholars served as the gatekeepers of that process. The empire co-opted the scholars and they, in turn, became its legitimizers and its mythmakers. They made it certain that after the collapse of each empire a new one would take its place.

Not so in Europe. The basic difference is that an empire never had a chance to establish itself there, and to capture the European world of learning. While the Stoics of the late Roman period were influential, Rome never did develop a civil service on the basis of scholarly training. Moreover, it left to the Greeks all matters of instruction and learning. From the medieval period onward, the currents of intellectual life have been predominantly anti-imperial. Thus, the evolution of an explicit doctrine of autonomy (the Balance of Power) ranks as a significant contribution to the maintenance of independence in the emerging world system. Although the operations of the Balance of Power were frequently subjected to criticism, the principle of independence and the value of autonomy have endured without any serious challenge.

The intellectual origins of the doctrine of Balance of Power have been traced to fifteenth-century Italy, where the prosperity of a number of great trading cities created conditions favoring the growth of independence. Writing during the following century about the relations among these city-states, both Guicciardini and Machiavelli used expressions that were suggestive of the notion of balance. Sustained by the familiar mechanical and accounting analogies that were implied in it, the term became part of the political literature of the times, and soon the best minds of Europe came to share in and to develop its tradition. Francis Bacon, Fénelon, Viscount Bolingbroke, David Hume, Edward Gibbon, Jean-Jacques Rousseau, Leopold von Ranke and Winston Churchill are some of the better-known names associated with the Balance of Power.[6] It came to pass after a while that this principle became part of the conventional wisdom of European politics, and the very essence of European international relations. Such intellectual respectability offset the imaginative appeal of empire and religion; as a result, none of the great minds of Europe became imperial apologists or ideologists.

The classical writings on the Balance of Power are the true antecedents of the theory of International Relations; they also provided much of the analytical framework for eighteenth- and nineteenth-century diplomatic and international history. Thus, for instance, Friedrich von Gentz, who was later to serve as the Secretary-General of the Congress of Vienna, writing during the Napoleonic Wars defined the Balance of Power as "that constitution subsisting among neighbouring states more or less connected with one another, by virtue of which no one among them can injure the independence or the essential rights of another, without meeting with effectual resistance on some side, and consequently exposing itself to danger." [7]

Gentz went on to state four maxims that together composed "the only intelligible theory of the balance of power":

That if the states system of Europe is to exist and be maintained by common exertions, no one of its members must ever become so powerful as to be able to coerce all the rest put together;

That if that system is . . . to be maintained without constant perils . . . each member which infringes it must be in a condition to be coerced, not only by the collective strength of the other members but by any majority of them, if not by one individual;

But that to escape the alternate danger of an uninterrupted series of wars . . . *the fear* of awakening common opposition or of drawing down common vengeance, must of itself be sufficient to keep every one within the bounds of moderation;

That if ever a European state attempted by unlawful enterprises to attain to a degree of power . . . which enabled it to defy the danger of a union of several of its neighbours . . . such a state should be treated as a common enemy . . ." [8]

The chief thrust of the historical Balance of Power doctrine was unambiguous: maintaining independence by limiting the strong. When this failed (as in the destruction of Polish independence in the eighteenth century, which was effected without any protest), the efficacy of the doctrine naturally came under attack. But its meaning remained clear.

Some confusion still arises from the difficulty of determining what distribution of power could properly be described as "balanced." Gentz rightly denied that stability required every state member of the system to be equal to every other in power. [9] But it cannot be maintained that the degree of power inequality that is characteristic of a system is irrelevant to its persistence.

The extent to which the value distributions of a system diverge from the norm of equality can now be measured with some precision, with the help of the Gini coefficient (provided the necessary data are available). This index ranges from zero to unity; those values that approach unity indicate increasingly higher inequality. Further research might thus show that the optimum power distributions for a system of states might be found within a Gini index range of 0.2–0.4; degrees of inequality extending beyond 0.5 could be conducive to instability or injustice. [10]

Ideas that were characteristic of balance-of-power doctrines were also in evidence in other phases of political thought. There is a line of writing, extending from Aristotle through Harrington and Montesquieu to modern pluralists, that applies balance-of-power thinking to "domestic" politics. [11] It holds that the state too can be seen to rest upon a balance of internal forces, and that power monopolies are unnecessary for its operation. This important strand needs to be reintegrated into a theory of world politics, as one way of narrowing down the gap between "domestic" and "foreign" affairs.

The generally favorable reception accorded to balance-of-power thinking is also linked with concurrent but supportive developments in fields of thought other than political theory. Of importance has been the withdrawal of intellectual approval for the practice and theory of monopoly, both in economics and with respect to religion and all fields of intellectual inquiry that had previously been limited by dogma. Arguments were developed in favor of free trade and a free movement of resources, in defense of freedom of thought and information, and for a free press and for freedom of scientific inquiry. Further, ideological support for balance-of-power practices also derived from the fact that the size and strength of the intellectual community was rapidly rising. In a number of ways, therefore, the scholarly community has replaced certain dogmas concerning politics and authority with a symbol system that pragmatically but effectively conferred legitimacy on autonomy.

Benefits of Autonomy Systems

Underlying the argument so far has been the proposition that autonomy is good. Autonomy systems of world politics are those that are not world empires, or power monopolies. The costs of empires and political monopoly have already been discussed in Chapter Two. The category of autonomy systems is a residual one; it includes all those systems that are not monopolies. Autonomy systems are composed of a diversity of organizations, each of which, or significant numbers of which, have substantial autonomy. The nation-state system belongs to the class of autonomy systems; all other systems of independent states are also autonomy systems.

Among the advantages of autonomy systems of world order are the following: [12] (1) a more perfect market for political goods; (2) opportunities for experimentation and for the diffusion of innovation; (3) lesser danger from the failure of one component.

The basic advantage of autonomy systems is, in fact, the obverse of the case against monopolies. Autonomy systems offer the possibility of a more perfect market for political services, and a better deal for order and justice. Free markets depend on mobility and information and, despite some tendencies to the contrary, autonomy systems are more likely to satisfy these conditions than empires and other monopolistic systems. Large monopolistic states, such as Russia and China, have traditionally restricted individual movement and controlled internal migration through a system of personal passports. Nor have they been known for the freedom accorded to information media.

Among world societies, the Islamic world has been notable for the encouragement it has offered to travel—hence, to equalization of knowledge and of political opportunity—through such devices as the religious obligation, incumbent on every member of the faith, to undertake a pilgrimage to the Holy Cities at least once in his lifetime. Indeed, all historical autonomy systems have been known for their encouragement of trade (see Chapter Two). The Greek world had regular Olympic Games and temples as centers of religious traffic. Traveling scholars, too, and not merely merchants, have been the elements that for a long time supplied mobility and information for world systems; they have flourished more in autonomy systems than in empires.

Autonomy systems, moreover, allow a remarkable range of opportunities for social and political experimentation. Political reforms that are undertaken in one state can be freely taken up by others, or they may be rejected by them. Within the historical balance-of-power system, improvements in organization, military tactics and technology have been speedily diffused throughout. Thus, the eighteenth century was notable for widespread bureaucratic reforms in the machinery of government; the nineteenth, for the diffusion of industrial technology, and the twentieth, for the worldwide dissemination of the nation-state and of methods of economic planning and control. The pressure that guaranteed this diffusion arose out of competitiveness: those who fell behind were liable also to fall behind in military ranking, and to find themselves at a disadvantage in every other way as well. Thus, competition diffused most speedily matters of military importance, such as: techniques of gunnery or fortifications; the standing army, as a worldwide institution; conscription as a duty to the nation-state; railways as a method of troop mobilization, the institution of the General Staff. This also extended to innovations other than military—to such features of the nation-state system as diplomatic machinery, fiscal administration, and public education. The mechanisms for the diffusion of innovations included the circulation of knowledge and the mobility of people. Hierarchical systems as a rule have difficulty in innovation, because changes have to be centrally authorized, and the prestige of the center is attached to the success or failure of the proposed reform. Autonomy systems are therefore more innovative and more adaptable, hence also more flexible.

Finally, in an autonomy system, failures in the functioning of one organization do not endanger the survival of the whole; they do, in a hierarchical structure.[13] An empire either subsists or falls to pieces. This is seen particularly in its requirements for loyalty, which are high. A failure of loyalty—for instance, a mutiny or local rebellion—threatens to disrupt the entire structure. An autonomy system, by contrast, is not so greatly affected by breakdown in any of its parts. Civil or violent dislocations in an important sector—such as, for instance, China—can be contained and isolated. A global system of independent states can tolerate quite a few civil wars, coups, assassinations and riots, without suffering major disruptions itself. The areas of infection, provided they are not allowed to spread, may in effect be quarantined.

Autonomy systems are, in general, cheaper and more flexible. They are cheaper because they require less overhead for centralized administration than empires do, and they rely more on individual mobility and information; they are also more adaptable to challenges in the environment and more flexible in meeting them. But the beneficiaries of autonomy systems are not only citizens at large but, in particular, those states or other individual organizations that are members of autonomy systems. Most importantly of all, each individual autonomy—and all organizations strive to maximize their autonomy—is dependent upon the maintenance of such a system. Inasmuch as all independent states benefit from the existence of the system, all are to be expected to contribute to its maintenance. This implication has been spelled out with especial clarity in Gentz's maxims, just quoted. Hence states are interested in helping each other in various ways, and especially in emergencies, in recognition of their common stake in the survival of the whole system. This applies above all to preserving independence: loss of independence by one is held to be a threat to the independence of all. A system that treats independence lightly, by ignoring cases of aggression and annexation, courts disaster: it invites the conquest of all by one. The particular merit of the historical balance-of-power system has been the avoidance of that contingency.

Several of the historical world societies discussed in Chapter Two gave rise to autonomy systems, only to see them collapse into empires. Rome and Imperial China are the standard and significant cases. The modern system of independent states has also survived a number of dangerous crises: the cases discussed earlier in the present chapter were all attempts at empire that did not succeed. At this point in time, it is hard to say how realistic these policies were and how close to realization in fact was the goal of empire. Perhaps none of these attempts could have succeeded. The Hapsburgs gathered great power, in dominions over which the sun never set; but the political and religious forces they encountered proved to be even greater. Napoleon came close to ruling over Europe, yet even he did not have the means with which to control the seas and embark upon a global career. In the twentieth century, in retrospect, Germany never came close to sustaining a world empire, again for lack of global instruments. Perhaps the world has never been really close to global rule, however loud the clamor of its proponents;

it may be that such a goal has never been a realistic one in the modern period. But that would be placing too much weight on hindsight and on historical contingency.

Costs of the Balance of Power

The advantages of autonomy systems are undeniable; set against these are the observed costs of the historical Balance of Power. These are also major elements in the costs of the nation-state system.

Most observers agree on the close link between the Balance of Power and war: seemingly, armed conflict has proved, in the past, the only practicable method of balancing power. The system of independent states has been preserved, ultimately, by the willingness to fight for it— that is, by wars. The Balance of Power places a higher priority on autonomy, independence and freedom than it does on peace. The history of the modern system, therefore, is a history of modern war.

As outlined, for instance, in Gentz's maxims, the Balance of Power is a "constitution" that works better on paper than it does in reality. It has not proven to be sufficiently reliable to be self-enforcing, except through recourse to war. It has been self-enforcing—and that is an important point—but costly. Upon further analysis, the Balance of Power system suffers from tendencies to malfunction in two different dimensions, each of these malfunctions being associated with war.

First, there has been a tendency toward disintegration and anarchy (toward "infinite decentralization"). Combativeness and simple conflict are second nature to autonomy systems. State systems, being aggregates of military power (and paying scant attention to moral authority), are particularly liable to it. But an autonomy system depends for its survival also upon moral resources: adherence to rules and the fostering of institutions that are protective of the moral order. Conversely, disturbances in the moral order and in the social vision of the future disrupt it. If the moral order collapses and a climate of cynicism takes over— in which "anything goes" and the "market" dissolves into a "free-for-all"—then the inherent warlikeness of the system does the rest. The periods of great wars have been preceded by a weakening of bonds and institutions; they have been eras of spiritual vacuum and moral disarray.

The other malfunction of the Balance of Power leads, as it were, in the opposite direction, toward hegemonic dominance (or "re-centralization"). While it does not quite reach the point of empire, it comes close to it. The mechanisms here are the pressures of war, which bring about a concentration of military power, and thereby conditions that are favorable to power monopoly. A hegemonic system is one that is imposed by a few strong military powers, each commanding a portion of the total system as a "subempire." The "perfect market" model of autonomy dissolves here into monopolistic competition between a few oligarchic giants.

The most important example of hegemonic rule is the historical Great Power institution, which emerged from the Balance of Power system (it is reviewed in detail in Chapter Nine, below); one of its variants is the bipolar structure of superpower authority. Here the chief danger is collusion ("price-fixing" or "market-sharing"), of which the Partitions of Poland are the classical illustration. Another danger is the creation of zones of special prerogative, such as the British command of the seas during the nineteenth century, the dominant position assumed by some powers in some periods (for instance, by Austria in Central Europe after the Congress of Vienna), the spheres of influence in colonial Africa and Asia, or "regions" and "camps" of more recent vintage. These become in effect local monopolies; by virtue of that fact, they tend to disrupt the orderly functioning of the world system. Contrary to prevalent impressions, this is not a "normal" development of autonomy systems, but rather a malfunction that is characteristic only of the Balance of Power and of the nation-state system that grew out of it.

Maintaining Autonomy Systems

There is no reason for believing that world autonomy systems are any less stable than world empires or, in more general terms, that autonomy systems (what Chester Barnard called "lateral organizations" or "systems of free agreement") are any more prone to self-destruction than are hierarchical (or "scalar") organizations. "After much study I cannot find any general conclusion in this matter, except that there seems to be no justification for assuming that lateral organization is less stable than scalar organization . . . The essential question for this way of organization is whether the moral and cultural controls of the disruptive tendencies are sufficient to keep them within bounds so that they do not offset the positive accomplishments." [14]

The question may be put: to what extent was the historical Balance of Power system maintained by means other than war? How were its disruptive tendencies, which resided especially in the resort to war for purposes of system preservation, kept in check? To be sure, they were not kept in check firmly enough; but it might be argued that the danger could have been even greater—for example, if the entire world had collapsed into chaos or else into permanently warring camps.

The states system has relied above all on the crude balance of organizational power within states themselves. But in addition to organizational power, the system also used, and benefited from, the emergence and the operation of a number of cohesion- and solidarity-building networks. Some of the more important of these will now be dealt with.

The major early element of coherence for Europe was Christianity, and the organizational and social framework of the Church. After the Reformation, it became pluralistic Christianity of many Churches. Indeed, the first crisis of the Balance of Power sprang from attempts to reinstitute unitary control over Christianity. While the Reformation created religious pluralism, it did not destroy the feeling of cultural identity, which was being reinforced at the same time by rising contact with other civilizations. At first the defining edge of outside contacts was Islam, but the range of interaction widened as new areas were penetrated and explored. By the nineteenth century, Europe's political identity was still significantly Christian; but this ruling conception was then beginning to lose its religious tones and to acquire the secular qualities of a superior civilization—one that in the twentieth century was to forge the more neutral vocabulary of development and modernity. The conceptions of Christianity and later of secular modernity, both of which were pluralist in their makeup, might be credited with providing the overriding framework of unity within which the system of independent states could operate: they adequately defined the goals of public and private behavior, and institutionalized a value system that was compatible with power plurality, elementary predictability of action and basic solidarity.

Within this large framework, certain more specialized networks can be distinguished. One was afforded by the political solidarity of the rulers—the royal houses, which were interconnected by ties of marriage and by involvement in the same system of interaction (of which the churches, learning and the sciences constituted one part). Royal marriages and the conventions governing the rights of succession made up the substance of diplomacy; they also had a central place in alliance politics and in the process of amalgamating political entities. The best-known example is that of the happy marriages of Hapsburg dynasty, which were themselves intended as instruments of a dynastic design for an imperial world order. Figure 4:1 shows, at about 1550, all the major royal houses of Europe linked by an intricate system of family alignments. These intermarriages were absorbed by the states system and did much to reinforce it. Monogamy emphasized equality in the contribution of each partner to the common enterprise, and was thus compatible with other balances. Reinforced by consanguinity, the network of personal relationships among rulers institutionalized some aspects of family life at

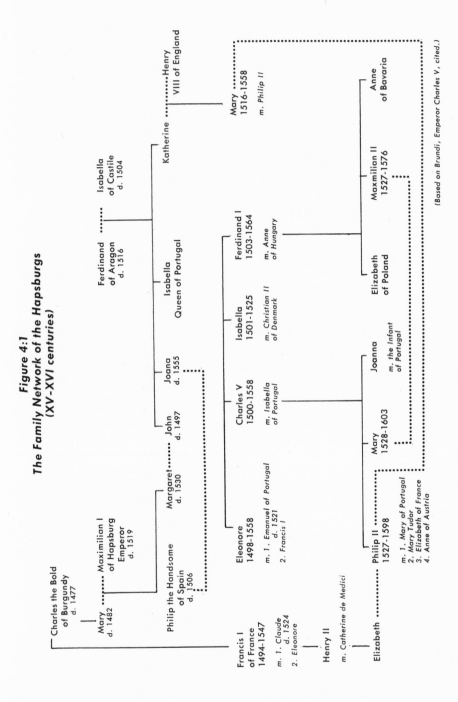

Figure 4:1
The Family Network of the Hapsburgs
(XV-XVI centuries)

(Based on Brundi, Emperor Charles V, cited.)

the global level and thereby helped to soften some of the hard edges of power competition.

Two other types of networks might be mentioned: those arising from the world of learning and scholarship, and those based on the world of trade and industry. The world of learning which grew out of the medieval church continued the early traditions of close communication, while the invention of printing provided the means for speedy communication. The world of commerce, too, had vitality and considerable independence. The merchant bankers were particularly important in facilitating far-flung trade and system-wide transactions. In the nineteenth century, the house of Rothschild, which had branches in the major capitals of Europe, acquired fame as a commercial banking dynasty that was on a par with royalty.

This would tend to show that a world order needs not only balanced power, but also a web of interdependence to stop the power centers from either colliding with each other or flying away in all directions. While it is true that the driving force of individual autonomies must be balanced by the strength of the rules restraining them, the awesome agglomerations of force that today constitute states need also to be enmeshed by the civilizing influence of networks of personal relations; their power needs to be balanced, in short, by organizations that offer resources of a moral order.

As the system of organizations develops strength, one would also expect the web of networks to grow thicker and more closely interwoven. Yet the general statement that would best describe the age of the Balance of Power would be one about the growth of the power of the state alone, while in terms of relative strengths network cohesion has been weakening. (One example is the disintegration of the "Monarchical International" in 1918, and the inability to replace it.) The fall in the binding properties of system networks was the result of the nationalization of the state (to be taken up in Chapter Six); it was the exact opposite of what needed to happen, in order to soften the impact of power concentrations. In other words, as the Balance of Power was becoming more effective in its military component, it was losing the restraining forces of the rules governing it. Hence the rising curve of costs and drain on life that it now entails.

Simple and Complex Autonomy

The weaknesses of the Balance of Power system might therefore be attributed to its increasing "simplicity." The pressures of war and the demands of military organization and technology have converted the

TABLE 4:1   Types of Autonomy Systems

Type of System	Composition	World Systems
Simple	States only (state-dominant)	Nation-state system
Complex	Balanced variety of organizations and networks	Multiple autonomy system

richness and variety of the medieval and post-medieval society into a larger but increasingly "simple"—that is, standardized and uniform—system. The autonomy of organizations within it has been reduced and they have moreover been subordinated to the state. The vitality of networks has declined and their role in the functioning of the Balance of Power has been diminished. Indeed, the name itself, Balance of Power, has proven to be misleading, in that it neglects to draw attention to the role of rules and their observance in the functioning of the system.

In line with this argument, a distinction arises between simple and complex autonomy systems (Table 4:1). A simple world autonomy system is one that is composed of states only; whatever other organizations are part of it are subordinate to the the states. Such systems might be called "state-dominant." In simple systems, the operation of networks is restricted. The anarchical and hegemonic disruptions that characterize these systems and are responsible for their costliness can be attributed in the long run to simplicity. They are additionally aggravated by the fact that the organizations in regard to which the system has become "simplified" are closely associated with military power.

The undeniable benefits and fundamental value of autonomy systems can be preserved if they are maintained in a complex state. Complex world autonomy systems are those that support a balanced variety of organizations and networks. The preservation of complexity is a matter of attending to the structure of world society, and in particular to the nature, control and distribution of organizational power within it, as well as the vitality of the web of networks that makes this huge inter-organizational universe a fit place to live in. Such problems will be taken up in Part Three of this work.

Notes to Chapter Four

1. The idea of a balance of power may have found their earliest expression in fifteenth-century illustrations showing the Pope in a state of equipoise with the Emperor. Cf. Alfred Vagts, "Balance of Power," *cited.*
2. See L. Dehio, *The Precarious Balance* (New York: Knopf, 1962).

3. Karl Brandi, *The Emperor Charles V: The Growth and Destiny of a Man and of a World Empire* (London: Jonathan Cape, 1939), p. 112.

4. Derwent Whittlesey, "Haushofer: The Geopoliticians" in E. M. Earle, ed., *Makers of Modern Strategy* (Princeton, N.J.: Princeton University Press, 1941), pp. 400–404.

5. Some observers of Communism point to the links between traditional Russian and historical Byzantium (Eastern Rome), to Moscow's early claims to be a "Third Rome," to the Tsar's assumption of the title of Emperor of the Russians in 1721, and to the role of the Greek Orthodox Church in that country.

6. H. Butterfield, "The Balance of Power" in Butterfield & Wight, eds., *Diplomatic Investigations* (London: George Allen & Unwin, 1966), pp. 132–148.

7. Friedrich von Gentz, *Fragments Upon the Balance of Power in Europe* (London: Peltier, 1806), p. 55.

8. *Ibid.*, pp. 61–63.

9. *Ibid.*, pp. 56, 63.

10. The Gini coefficient for the world distribution of military power (as indexed by military expenditures) ca. 1965 was in the region of 0.6. For a description of the Gini index see Hayward Alker, *Mathematics and Politics* (New York: Macmillan, 1965), Chapter 3.

11. Robert Dahl, *Modern Political Analysis* (Englewood Cliffs, N.J.: Prentice-Hall, 1963), pp. 84–87.

12. In general, the larger a system, the more services are demanded of it and the greater the pressure for participation; hence also, the more modern the system, the greater will be the demand for decentralization. See M. Kochen and K. Deutsch, "Toward a Rational Theory of Decentralization: Some Implications of a Mathematical Approach," *American Political Science Review* 63(3), September 1969, 734–749.

13. Chester Barnard, "On Planning for World Government," in *Organization and Management: Selected Papers* (Cambridge, Mass: Harvard University Press, 1949), p. 156.

14. *Ibid.*, pp. 158–9.

5

The

State

as

an

Organization

FIRST WITH REGARD TO EUROPE, THEN for the world at large, the Balance of Power explains the emergence and the persistence of a system of autonomy that is the dominant form of politics today. It also provides a clue as to why the principal units of autonomy have been states, and why states have continued to play such a key role in world politics. It is obvious that states remain among the principal units of analysis in academic discussions of the subject.

The predominance of states is not a "fact of life" nor a "law of nature"; nor is it an immutable condition of world order. It needs further explanation and must not be taken as given. Why does the contemporary system allocate such a large share of world authority to states? Why does it give a much more limited role to other organizations, to international institutions, to churches or to corporations, to mention only some of the possibilities? Why does it minimize the role of global networks as factors in the preservation of world order?

There is nothing in the nature or character of world politics that explains why states are singled out for a special position. The fact is that independent states are not, by any standard, the best agents for the conduct of world politics. Anyone who gives a moment's reflection to the matter must come to the conclusion that states, being devices for governing partial or limited portions of the globe, and being responsible at best only to partial and limited constituencies, are hardly the most efficient organizations for giving attention to world problems, to world order and justice. The situation in which they are so regarded seems basically absurd, and therefore calls for further elucidation, raising a question that did not arise in the traditional study of International Relations, which took it for granted that states were "the actors" of world politics.

The State Viewed as as Organization

The elementary fact about the state is that it is an organization, no more and no less. This puts it on the same level as other organizations: churches, corporations, world agencies, universities, city halls and village councils. It shares with these the basic properties of all organizations.

Organizations are devices for the attainment of some purpose; they are stable coordinations of human and material resources directed toward the production of certain determinate results. All organizations are instrumental toward a larger goal outside themselves; no organization exists for its own sake, and neither does the state.

The state shares this instrumental quality with all other organizations. Like them, it is a claimant on human and other resources for the pursuit of programmes that are relevant to larger goals. Broadly speaking, all organizations pursue important social goals, so that none can be ruled out *a priori* as a claimant on human resources, or elevated to a position above all others.

From one point of view, the world might be seen as a set of organizations. Each year world society produces a world income of certain finite proportions, and the organizational set makes claims upon it. There is no reason to suppose that some organizations are inherently entitled to a larger share of it than others. This fact alone serves to make all organizations interdependent: the standing and prosperity of each depends, to some degree, on the success of all the others.

States share with other organizations certain characteristic traits: all organizations have a full-time staff and other assets; a budget; an identity, and a clientele or public.

First, all organizations have bureaucracies. Bureaucracy is as old as the art of writing and of recording. The two basic sub-components of state bureaucracies have been the civilians (the clerks, the wielders of the pen) and the military (the soldiers and sailors, the wielders of the sword). These two types of full-time staff could be said to reflect the commitments of the political organization to justice and to order. They are not mutually exclusive, however, for the roles are to a considerable degree interchangeable; they are also mutually supportive. One could not function without the other.[1] The staffs need not be all or even mainly permanent; but there must be a permanent nucleus (and this distinguishes the organization from a group). As the organization grows larger, the permanent staff also grows and becomes embedded in procedures for recruitment, retirement and maintaining loyalty.

Second, organizations have budgets. These are a tangible expression of the links between the organization and its public, a way of summarizing its inputs and its outputs. Organizations need to mobilize resources in order to be able to maintain their staffs and other assets. A state budget raises revenue through taxation—which entails a machinery of tax collection. For every organization, revenue-raising is a central operation. A major function of the civil branches of the state is to raise taxes; the way in which taxes are levied, and the injustices arising in the collection and distribution of revenue, have traditionally been a major preoccupation of politics. But a budget also implies looking toward the future and planning future activity—hence, faith in organizational continuity.

Both staffs and budgets represent aggregations of power; inasmuch as all organizations must have both, they all possess power to some degree. Power, in turn, is the foundation of autonomy. A world society of a given population size and a given world income can support only so many organizations and not any more, because the staffs and the budgets of each comprise some fraction of the whole and they therefore cannot grow beyond the total of available resources. Organizations then must compete for what is available. The number of possible organizations is finite; but as population and income rise in the world society, the number of organizations that can be supported goes up too.

Third, all organizations have identities if only because they have names. Early names of states were frequently dynastic: they referred to the person of the ruler; more recent states have had names relating to geographical expressions. All names tell a great deal about the origin and character of the state: "United States of America" recalls the process of federation and the continental frame of its aspirations; "Hashemite Kingdom of Jordan" harks back to the dynastic theme; "Union of Soviet Socialist Republics" is strong in ideological emphasis. To names, organizations generally add other symbols of identity, and states have excelled in this; if they have not invented them, they have certainly used to great advantage such symbolic means as flags, anthems, buildings and monuments, history and historians, even postage stamps and passports. It is not only the organization that acquires identity and attributes but also the membership. Around this symbolic center there develop activities, systems of knowledge and clusters of sentiments; while its members acquire a means of identification, the organization is ensured of a continuity that extends beyond the contributions or even the life-cycle of any one leader or individual. Such "personification" alone does not guarantee continuity, but it does help to establish a presumption in its favor; it distinguishes the organization from its environment, clarifies its autonomy and is a necessary device for thinking about large-scale social processes.[2]

Finally, all organizations have memberships, a clientele, a constituency or a public. No organization is wholly private, nor is it involved with world society to an equal degree with all others. Between the nucleus of permanent staff and the outer bounds of world society, there are points along a descending scale of intensity of concern and identification that define the different degrees of membership. Despite this relative imprecision, however, an important component of organization is present. Except for the limiting case of an entirely self-serving organization, the clientele defines the goals of the organization and is its justification; it also supplies the wherewithal to carry on its business. In the final analysis, the organization's prospects of support and survival depend on how well it serves that public.

In agrarian civilizations, the citizenry of a state by no means coincided with its entire population: in Athens or in Rome, citizens with full rights formed only a small portion of the entire population; the larger proportion consisted of slaves. The idea that the community of a state normally coincides with the population that is resident in its territory is a modern one but not really illuminating. More interesting is an inquiry into the degree to which various segments and sections of that population identify with it and are represented in its functioning. Such different cases as South Africa, Malaysia, Canada, Spain, East Germany and the Soviet Union disclose a differential distribution of publics.

In the final analysis, organizations exist for people and because of people. Yet organizations, and most of all states, easily shed this instrumental stance. They become ends in themselves, assume a life of their own and detach themselves from wider social needs; or, if they have the power, they misshape the society so as to suit their particular purposes. States have in the past been notable for having precisely this power, and for being most adept in using it.

The state is, of course, only one among a variety of possible organizations. From the standpoint of world politics, it is of interest because it is an organization that is predominantly concerned with the production of order and justice, which is what makes it a political organization. The state is also preeminently an organization of the intermediate, or state, level of politics; it is less concerned with problems at the local and global levels. But it is also relevant to add that all organizations (most obviously, all large organizations) produce some order and some justice, and that all of them exhibit similar tendencies, common to organizations as a class, such as: the drive for autonomy; competition for social resources; the tendency for self-perpetuation; and the tendency to view themselves as ends in themselves. A good deal of state behavior is organizational behavior and needs no special political explanations.

In one other respect, however, states are also more than merely political organizations. During the past few centuries, states have become probably the most successful, the most widely influential and imitated, and also the most powerful organizations known to man. States have divided the surface of the globe among themselves, and they have organized expeditions into space. Some have grown to immense size, dwarfing all other contemporary or historically known organizations. Some states are giant organizations of global proportions, so powerful and so omnipresent that observers tend to forget their essential qualities as organizations, and hence their merely instrumental character.

In the nineteen-sixties, the United States federal government employed some five million citizens and was the largest single employer in the country (even the biggest corporate enterprises had payrolls of fewer than one million). The federal budget passed the one hundred billion dollar range; inclusive of all the funds channeled through the federal system, it was responsible for between five and ten per cent of world income. The federal armed forces had at their disposal the most awesome powers of destruction.

The Soviet Union was even more of a "successful" state. Here, virtually the entire population was in one way or another on the state payroll. Even the collectivized peasants, who had long been resistant to state authority, and were now theoretically partners in a collective enterprise, were in actuality, little more than state employees. The same could be said of most other Communist countries: far from having "withered away," their state was an ever-present, omniscient reality, having grown to its absolute limits and having attained, both domestically and in its sphere of influence abroad, the plenitude of a monopoly of power.

As a result of its being so successful, the state has become the dominant organizational form of contemporary world politics. By virtue of its success, however, its actual nature as an organization, and hence the limited scope of its purposes and the inherent limitations of its instrumentalities, have become obscured. No problem is regarded as being too large or too complex or unsuitable to be handled by it. Most common is the misconception that confuses the state with the public or the "country" it is supposed to serve. In common parlance, "France" can mean the French state, or the French nation, or both. States are supposed to serve nations, but they cannot serve them well if their essential purpose disappears in the myths surrounding them.

The question then is: why has the state become so powerful both among political organizations, and also by comparison with all other organizations? Answers to this question might be sought along two interrelated lines of inquiry: first, the relative growth of the state could be explained in terms of a high demand for its services; second, its growth could be explained as the result of its successful adaptation to the requirements of large-scale organization. One aspect of this adaptation, its nationalization, will be raised in the next chapter.

War and the Demand for State Services

The chief factor that has generated a demand for the services of the state in modern times had been war, and those conditions and circumstances that have contributed to the expectation of war.

Wars have been, in two respects, the salient feature of the age of state consolidation. As already indicated, globalization was accomplished by the projection of European armed might overseas. Even though the forces involved were small, they were always armed and never hesitated to use their weapons. Large-scale war was for the most part avoided, but the need to maintain forces in readiness at long distance imposed severe organizational strains on the state. The process of balancing power in Europe, together with the necessity that it created for fighting lengthy and exhaustive wars, put a premium on war machines and on those state organizations that were most adept at putting them together. The possibility of a "return engagement" was ever-present in a system in which available military power was distributed among several independent centers.

As long as they do not actually bring down the entire system, wars build the state. In peacetime, the expectation of war is the single most persuasive influence in bringing about this result. It leads to armament expenditures, military service, a build-up of war industry, military research and other preparations for combat. In war time, entire populations put their energy into the collective enterprise of inflicting violent injury on their neighbors and, by so doing, place themselves at the direct disposal of the political leadership. Protection from the disasters of war was doubly valued in Europe, which proved to be strikingly prone to violence: its disputes, which were carried on among self-righteous and vindictive parties, took extreme and threatening forms. In a system in which force played such a large part, the state and its armed forces offered the protection needed. Both civil wars and disturbances and system-wide international wars have had this effect.

Our previous account of the Balance of Power has already shown that wars have been the dominant events of the global systems over the past half millennium. The same trend may be demonstrated in another way, with the help of some statistical material showing the number and frequency of wars.[3] In the four-and-a-half centuries between 1480 and 1941, states recognized as members of the European (the then world) system participated in 278 wars. Of these, two-thirds, or 187, were fought mainly in Europe, the remainder chiefly outside. The data do not show any real trend in the frequency of wars, beyond confirming the idea that wars had indeed been frequent. The sixteenth and seventeenth centuries had some 60 wars each; the eighteenth century had 38 wars, and the nineteenth century, 89, of which 60 were fought outside Europe. There is also good evidence for an increasing intensity of wars. The number of important battles fought rose from about 100 in the sixteenth century to some 650 during the relatively peaceful nineteenth century. The number of estimated casualties also rose drastically, despite and hand in hand with, parallel increases in population—from about 10 per 1,000 population in the sixteenth century, to 54 per 1,000 in the first quarter of the twentieth. If anything, the need for protection must have risen in the last century, in spite of all the effort put into the military area.

Particularly important was the role of the great military states, which later in the period became the Great Powers. Their participation in war was the most intense. Between 1600 and 1945, fifteen wars may be singled out as major: they include all those described as Balance of Power wars in the previous chapter. France was involved in all fifteen of these; England, Austria and Prussia, in all but one. Russia and Italy joined in all but two. Generally, non-participation in such wars was a sign of having abandoned aspirations to an international military status. On the average, the major military states were at war at least one quarter of the time: over the period 1450–1900, France was at war 23.5 percent; England, 25 percent; Austria, 27.5 percent, and Russia 30 percent of the time In other words, the leader of a great state could expect to be at war at least one out of every four years. The pressures toward war were particularly acute for the major powers.

Two important stages may be distinguished in the rise of the demand for military power, and the consequent enlargement of the role of the state: (1) the wars of the seventeenth century, which led up to the creation of standing armies and of permanent civilian bureaucracies to maintain them; and (2) the two world wars of the twentieth century, which brought immense new accretions of power and consolidated the nation-state system on a global basis.

During the first period, the point of crystallization was the wars of Louis XIV, which had in part been prompted by his successes in building the first effective standing army in Europe (permanent navies had been achieved somewhat earlier in the maritime states in relation to globalization). One historian has summarized this period and its political effects as follows:

Two hundred years of warfare, commerce and political reorganization had been furthering the identification of prince and kingdom, but it was not until the era of world wars, beginning with the Turkish siege of Vienna (1683), that the process of history became accelerated enough to define clearly the political forms prevalent in the eighteenth and the nineteenth centuries. When the smoke cleared from the battlefields of those great wars (1683-1721), a new political organization stood out in clear relief . . . what had emerged was a Europe governed by a balance of power between great military states. Kings by divine right, who ruled within limits set by medieval constitutions, had been replaced by princes who were the chiefs, or at any rate the titular chiefs, of great military and civil bureaucracies. Princes had become identified with their states, and the time was not far off when the people too would become an integral part of the sovereign power.[4]

In 1680, France was the only great military power in Europe; but within a generation England, the Hapsburg Monarchy, and Russia had all reached this status, and fundamental alterations had taken place in the structure of most other European states. It would be an exaggeration to ascribe this development solely to the three decades of warfare that filled this period, for the process had begun even before 1500. But, continued the historian, "nonetheless, it is true that these wars, with their incessant demands for the mobilization of power, accelerated the process and at the same time fixed the form of the new states system."[5]

The next stage of this process was reached only in the twentieth century, when two successive world wars gave a new vitality to the state, changing it first into a nation-state and then into a worldwide institution. The hallmark of this period has been the successful integration of national life into the purposes of the state: the mobilization of newly powerful industry as a supporting arm of the war organization, and the involvement of the scientific establishment in large-scale armaments and operations research. Both these aspects are well illustrated in the massive effort for the development of nuclear weapons, in close cooperation between the military, the business and the academic worlds. Striking too, as compared with earlier times, has been the nearly effortless way in which major operations have been financed by efficient tax collections; the widespread introduction of income taxes, at the beginning of the twentieth century (after their invention in Britain during the Napoleonic wars), gave the state an unusually effective method of raising money. The easy availability of immense revenues may be the single most important factor in the contemporary ascendancy of the state.

In all such cases, the growth of the state took place in part at the expense of local autonomies. This process could be observed at its clearest in the federal political system of the United States, in which constitutional provisions allocate separate and distinct spheres of authority to federal and state authorities. One measure of shifting relationships is the index of centralization, which indicates the relative weight of federal (central) and state (local) expenditures for the system as a whole. Table 5:1 gives the information for a few selected years.

The United States' participation in major wars decisively shifted the balance between its central and local authorities. The initial establishment of federal authority had derived from the experience of the War of Inde-

TABLE 5:1   Central–Local Balance in the United States, Selected Years

1800 ca.	0.1
1902	0.4
1922	0.7
1940	0.9
1960	1.5

pendence, but it had functioned on a minimal scale only. The next great increment of federal power followed the Civil War. Then came World War I and World War II, following which the superiority of the national functions was clearly established. Each war has successively enlarged the share of governmental funds accruing to the national function. What is more, these increments have been nearly irreversible. Once an accretion has occurred, it has seemed difficult, if not impossible, to restore the "normal" ante-bellum situation. Wars have set in motion major new patterns of government functions.

The high incidence of wars has created a demand for state services, and in turn each successive war has increased the capabilities with which states could conduct wars, as well as creating new demands and raising the intensity of the battles and the extent of preparedness in the next period. A vicious circle was thus set in motion.

One result of the role of war in the consolidation of the state was a heightened degree of competitiveness in the whole system, both among states, and between states and other organizations, as well as among individuals. The system became dangerous to those who were unable or unwilling to adapt to the steadily increasing demands of war. Frequent violent conflict weeded out those political organizations that proved to be incapable of standing this strain and favored others that were innovative in administrative and military skills. Thus, Prussia survived and prospered because of its bureaucratic capacity and the size and quality of its armies, both of which had been raised to a high pitch of efficiency by the reforms of the seventeenth and early eighteenth century; by contrast, Poland became the battlefield of contending foreign armies, and was partitioned late in the eighteenth century, because its constitution, while favoring various of its components with a generous dose of autonomy, failed to sustain a central authority and a strong army. A natural selection of the strong and the warlike put a premium on innovative capacity, and eliminated those states that were tradition-bound, slow to respond, or merely patient.

In its first surge of power, in the sixteenth century, the state (specifically, the French monarchy, under capable leadership) defeated the challenge of a universal church. Had the Christian world not experienced a Reformation, or if religion had been allied effectively with Spanish-Hapsburg power, the Church might conceivably have become an alternative dominant organization. Another possibility might have been some form of urban-mercantile organization, for which the trading towns of Northern Italy or Northern Europe could have provided the model. In both cases, however, the organizations in question proved unequal to the task, unable to withstand the challenge of the large and well-armed forces of the states: the Church, because of its inherent weakness as an order-maintaining instrumentality, and its inability to muster sufficient forces on a continental, not to speak of a global scale. If the Papacy could be conceived to be operating at the global level, not so the cities, which were essentially local in scope and thus defenseless. The Dutch provinces federated upon attaining their independence; they formed a state and exerted considerable power in the seventeenth century. But they were too vulnerable to French pressure and needed English protection. Despite the excellence of their communications (both by sea and over river and canal routes) and the mobility afforded by their navies, the cities could not fight large wars and they succumbed one by one to the state unifiers, Venice being the last important city-state to fall (to Napoleon in 1797). In one way or another, war proved the downfall of them all. Given war, they could not win.

The states that did survive this competition were invested with all the glories and perquisites of victory. First, having successfully met the demands for security and order, having early reached a point of complexity where responsiveness was institutionalized, they developed a degree of accord with popular demand that outpaced that of other competitive organizations. Devices for representation and responsiveness developed by the state (leading up to its nationalization, which will be discussed in the next chapter) gave it an immense advantage over all competitors. Secondly, having proved successful in war and capable of managing ever larger organizational tasks, states also increasingly assumed other important social tasks. In the eighteenth and nineteenth centuries, European states moved into education, industrial and railway development and even social welfare, unemployment, health insurance, etc. Like all successful organizations, they responded with a range of services that were not directly related to their central purposes.

The State as Modern Organization

The growth of the modern state antedated, but in its basic outline proceeded along the same lines as, that of the business enterprise whose most prominent modern form is the corporation. The most important organizational development in the economic sphere was the transformation of what, for most of past history, had been family concerns, into corporate entities, wherein a much larger and more diverse association than a family could cooperate in organizing, financing and managing a large enterprise, and in which ownership might be entirely separated from management. But, despite auspicious beginnings in the process of globalization, in which chartered companies played a conspicuous role, this form experienced setbacks in the eighteenth century; it did not really take firm root until mid-nineteenth century, and did not reach extensive development until the twentieth.

In the field of politics, too, the family-concern type of organization gradually gave way to forms that were more attuned to the exigencies of warfare and to the demands of large social systems. Yet the change away from the dynastic state was slow. The proclamation of the United States of America as a Republic was an early and important breach in the monarchical front, and other American republics followed early in the nineteenth century; yet, by the middle of the century, the issue was still in doubt, and in 1865 the majority of states in Europe and Asia would still be described as formally dynastic. For at least a century, however, the role of the prince continued to become more and more that of a figurehead; by the end of the First World War, the issue was no longer in doubt.

Early in modern European politics, the state has been identified with the person of the ruler; in fact, in most cases the state was identical with the ruler (and his family and retainers). That situation was enshrined in Louis XIV's memorable dictum "l'état, c'est moi"; yet, even as he was speaking, he was at the same time organizing the huge civilian and military bureaucracies that in due course would undermine the power of the monarchy. The consolidation of these bureaucracies gave notice that states had an existence outside the person of the ruler; the personality of the ruler thus gradually became detached from the identity of the organization he was leading.

The great bureaucracies became the testing-grounds and the seedbeds of modern administrative and organizational development. The ruler's court gave way to a permanent establishment commonly associated with a capital city in which the departments of state would find their headquarters. It was a large-scale application of concepts of staff-line differentiation, and it exerted particular impact upon the formation of military staffs and naval boards. The general staffs gradually took over the command of the forces from the royal personages. The evolution of a foreign affairs department as the headquarters of a far-flung diplomatic service transformed what had earlier been the correspondence between rulers into interorganizational exchanges. The rationalization of finances brought about the differentiation of the private purse of the monarch from the public purse of the political organization, and laid the foundations for sound budgetary management (a process that in some states—such as Saudi Arabia—was still uncompleted in mid-twentieth century). No longer a simple exercise of royal discretion, executive decision-making became a process of interaction and bargaining among the sub-components of the state organization, each mindful of its own interest and its special clientele.[6]

Just as the state was changing from a family concern into a public organization, the nature of its leadership (or management) requirements was changing, too. The great bureaucracies became too powerful to be contained by one fragile network of family connections that held together the political system of Europe. They were loath to expose themselves to the risks inherent in family succession and in outside recruitment; in the course of time, the system was gradually changed. In some monarchies, executive leadership of the state organization was separated from symbolic and affective functions, and the result was a constitutional monarchy—for instance, in Britain or the Scandinavian countries. Real political power, or effective government, shifted to the Cabinet (a committee of leaders of the major departments of state responsible to the House of Commons); the Crown became the "dignified element of government," meeting the need for a unifying symbol and for the pomp and circumstance of ceremonial occasions. Elsewhere monarchies proved less adaptable and were gradually replaced by a republican form of government frequently through coups, revolutions or usurpations. Republics showed that the "royal family" could be dispensed with as a source of executive recruitment. The growing power of the state bureaucracies now compelled the recruitment of political leaders from within the political organization itself, rather than through the family network.

For world politics, this was an important change. It is true that organizational rationale has no rules according to which leaders recruited from within a large organization are always preferable to those recruited from without. Yet, in the nation-state system, the occupancy of high government office has come to be strictly regulated and to be restricted to "insiders." By mid-twentieth century, not one head of state or head of government was a non-national, or in any sense "recruited" from elsewhere in the global system. This limitation, unusual in its thoroughness and rarely observed with such strictness in the business world, tended to build up pressures for organizational autonomy, and ultimately to lead toward parochialism. Another result was the atrophy of system-wide political connections.

In summary, organizational growth has been characteristic of the large states and the great military powers. These great organizations have come to dominate first Europe and then the world. Their dominance is thus organizational dominance. Because it was states that first fashioned effective means of large-scale political organization and because these large-scale political organizations were the first to grow so strikingly, they have given lasting shape and character to world politics. The leaders of organizational development thus became the leaders of world politics.

Organizations and Networks

The behavior of states—that is, organizational behavior—looms large in much of conventional International Relations. Inasmuch as organizations are, above all, aggregates of power (although some organizations are less power-conscious than others), power considerations must rank high in any study of state behavior.

Organizations, too, are inevitably hierarchical. They are designed to implement specialized goals, to which all activities must be subordinated; for such purposes, they can be most effective. But they also suffer from some clear disabilities. Among the most important of these are the tendency to exaggerate the demands on loyalty that they create, as well as the difficulty they experience in fitting individual interests into organizational objectives. They are societies of status and great efforts are absorbed by them in the achievement of mere survival.[7]

In other words, organizations are the building-blocks of a society, but they cannot be the only building blocks. They need to be supplemented by other forms of patterned interaction that are less power-bound and less status-oriented. In the most general terms, these other needs are met by networks. Organizations and networks may be seen as polar forms of social organization.

Networks are patterns of interaction that are entered into and departed from by mutual and free agreement. As contrasted with organizational hierarchy, they are systems of equal-status relationships. They certainly have membership, but they are more open in relation to it; they may have identity, but they are less concerned with establishing it. Normally, they do not have budgets or full-time staffs, although they may benefit from the organizational resources of some of their members. By contrast with organizations, for which staffs and budgets are so important, networks claim few scarce resources, carry few overheads and therefore are inexpensive to maintain; they set few limits on extension and membership, and their number is therefore potentially infinite.

Examples of networks important to world politics are: diplomacy, a well-known, exceedingly elaborate and by now somewhat over-crystallized network; and the world financial community, which is sustained by relations of confidence among central bankers and leading financiers. Other networks include: markets, families, elites, audiences, nations, communications structures, professions.[8]

Important features of networks are the personal (rather than organizational) contacts they involve, and the value-regulating and norm-setting functions they fulfill. They achieve this through the pressures and rewards of personal relationships and the judgmental qualities that are inherent in them. The precise functioning of networks is yet to be clearly understood, but they probably have a critical role in stabilizing multi-organizational social systems and in creating communities within them.

Hierarchical organizations break up the wider society into segmented publics. This has been precisely the effect of the rise of the state in the world society. The weakness of the networks that now bind world society is an inevitable consequence of the organizational dominance of the state.

Notes to Chapter Five

1. Differentiation and specialization of military and civilian roles may be as much a matter of "balancing" these two aspects of political administration, as it is the result of the inherent requirements of these functions—in any event, in earlier times.

2. E. H. Carr, *The Twenty Years Crisis 1919-1939*, 2nd ed. (London: Macmillan, 1946), p. 148.

3. Data in this and the following paragraph based on Quincy Wright, *A Study of War*, 2nd ed. (Chicago: Chicago University Press, 1965), App. XX, XXI.

4. John B. Wolf, *The Emergence of the Great Powers 1685-1715* (New York: Harper and Row, 1951), p. 1.

5. *Ibid.*, p. 97.

6. Graham Allison's "organizational process" and "bureaucratic politics" paradigms successfully apply insights of organization theory to the understanding of these processes ("Conceptual Models and the Cuban Missile Crisis," *American Political Science Review*, 63[3], September 1969, 689–718).

7. Barnard, "On Planning for World Government," *cited*, pp. 155–160.

8. On the concept of network in sociology and anthropology see, for example, Clyde Mitchell, ed., *Social Networks in Urban Situations* (Manchester: Manchester University Press, 1969).

6

The
Nationalization
of
the
State

THE FACT THAT THE STATE IS AN
organization, no less and no more, has now been established. It was demonstrated at some length in order to counterbalance the emphasis that
is usually placed, in political and comparative analysis, upon the uniqueness of particular states. Viewing the state as one important organizational
type among several—that is, as one among the several necessary servants
of society—explains a great deal about it; it also minimizes the dangers
of misreading its place in the world.

As seen in the previous chapter, moreover, the state has been the most
notably successful organization of the age of globalization. Tested in the
harsh conditions of the wars of the Balance of Power, it grew in numbers
and strength and outdistanced all competing forms. In its latest stages,
however—that is, in the most recent time-span of the telescoped earth-
history (shown in Figure 2:1 as modernity)—it also assumed the particular form of the nation-state.

The question is: why has the state become so strongly tied to one
particular type of network (or complex of networks)—that is, to the
nation? how and why has the independent state, which was produced by
the Balance of Power, been nationalized?

No Foregone Conclusion

The universal nationalization of the state cannot be regarded as a fore-
gone conclusion, an inevitable result of preordained processes. Several of
the large states that shaped European and world history were not nation-

states, but rather dynastic and monarchical states or else non-national—
that is to say, imperial—states. The Hapsburg Monarchy, for example,
played a major part in the organization of Europe and the world for
about seven centuries. At the onset of globalization, its links with Spain
made it the nucleus of a world empire and, as Austria-Hungary, it lasted
until 1918. At no point was it a German nation-state, but rather a non-
national political structure, based on family links. The great colonial
empires of the age of globalization, such as those of Spain or Britain,
could not be described as nation-states, either. Spain lost its last colonies
in the Americas and in Asia only at the beginning of the twentieth century, and it was only after the middle of the century that Britain assumed
a character approximating the model of the modern state. For hundreds
of years, the colonial powers have also been complex political structures;
only in their truly metropolitan areas did they approach the character
of nation-states. The nation-state is, in fact, the product of the disintegration of the empires; Table 7:1 documents this proposition in some
detail.

    The nation-state cannot, therefore, be regarded as the only possible
form of world organization. Viewed against the rise of the great military
states in the seventeenth and eighteenth centuries, however, its emergence
is less surprising. For the pressures of absolutism and autocracy that these
military states created became increasingly felt, to be relieved only in
the nineteenth and twentieth centuries by way of nationalism. Such large
organizations could not survive without broadening their political base
and opening themselves to new demands. Some powers, such as the British
Empire, shrank to their metropolitan core, because they could not feasibly
broaden their base in this way; others, such as Austria-Hungary, which
would not or could not adjust, disappeared. The first state to have accomplished this transformation was the foremost military power, France,
which thus became the model nation-state to the world. In due course,
the model came to be nearly universal, but in the process the whole
system was also fixed in a particularly rigid mold.

Interplay of Network and Organization

The essence of the distinction between network and organization lies
along the specificity-diffuseness continuum. Organizations represent coordinations of effort directed toward specific purposes.[1] These purposes
are specific—in part, to those whose effort is being coordinated and in
part to the wider framework in which the organization operates, inasmuch as no organization is self-sufficient or operates in a vacuum. That
wider framework in turn is a network—for instance, a market—or a set

of networks; in general, it is a collectivity, in terms of which the related organizational activity makes sense. But it is also diffuse in its make-up, in that no single organization can fully satisfy the variety of purposes such networks encompass.

Two lines of interdependence might be postulated: (1) where network creates (or causes) organization, and (2) where organization creates (or causes) network.

The type (1) process is the common conception of the relationship between network and organization, with the latter being viewed as the result of a demand for a "good" to be produced by it. When a problem arises, or a task needs to be performed (say in the field of pollution), an organization is set up to deal with it—for example, an "environmental agency." Those who set up the organization may be supposed to be part of a network through which the organization will be made effective. Some network clusters (or social layers) are so obvious and so stable that the effort of tracing when and how they were first created never seems worthwhile: they simply exist. When networks bring forth a variety of organizations, they do not seem particularly dependent on any single one.

More interesting however is the type (2) process for, once it has been created, an organization takes on a life all its own. It no longer merely *serves* networks and social layers, but *shapes* them to conform to its own particular requirements. All organizations need continuous inputs, as well as a steady demand for its outputs. The larger an organization, the costlier its overhead installations and its permanent staff, and the more certainty it requires in the structure of its supplies and in the volume and composition of the demand. For these reasons, large organizations devote much of their attention to guaranteeing their supplies and controlling their markets. As organizations grow, therefore, they also build and rebuild their own networks; they develop new sources of supplies and revenue, and they also stimulate and create demand for their goods. Organizations that begin as creatures of the networks that envelop them can also become the masters of these networks, layers, associations and communities.

One example of such a relationship might be adduced from population theory. It can be shown that large-scale organizations themselves create a demand for population growth. Population theorists have analyzed this problem in attempting to answer the question: what is the optimum population for a given society? Their models specify different prescriptions, depending on the objectives to be pursued; they distinguish between economic objectives (in particular, the standard of living) and collective and organizational objectives, which may be identified as power. The interesting conclusion of optimum population theories is that "the population that is optimum for maximizing collective power is always larger than the population that is optimum from the economic point of view."

Thus, in particular, "the effect of any military or other collective burden is to raise the size of a country's optimum population." More generally, all systems that carry large overheads—hence, all large-scale organizations—benefit from increases in population, inasmuch as such an increase tends to spread the burden of fixed costs over larger numbers. As long as the organization can enforce a standard of living that is equal with or just above the subsistence level, all social output over and above the subsistence level of a layer population can be "allocated" to collective power.[2]

These are important conclusions: they confirm the suspicion that population growth rates are closely linked with forms of social and political organization. More interestingly, they represent some evidence for the relationship just suggested. Control of the population explosion might depend on changes in the structure of world politics. In other words, large organizations must not be allowed to shape their populations to the extent that they have in the past.

Neither type (1) nor type (2) process seems to have logical or empirical priority. Most probably, this is a circular process, as in (3):

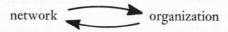

network ⟷ organization

where the two elements interact over time, and both undergo continuous change. So much is clear from a general analysis; yet the tendency of the social sciences has been to take networks (principally the community, or society, or political system) as fixed or given, and to single out for attention changes in organization. For the sake of restoring the balance, but also because world politics is frequently concerned with large-scale processes of network formation, special heed must be given to type (2) processes.

All organizations have a tendency to control their environment, including the networks in which they are embedded: they develop inclinations toward monopoly. The more stable and predictable the environment, the less energy they need to expend upon it; the more uncertain, disturbed and turbulent that same environment, the more complex the policies that must be deployed toward it. Some of these policies might involve centralization, absorption and expansion; others involve thorough-going value changes, to be achieved by way of institutionalization.[3]

Some degree of control by an organization over its environment might be regarded as "normal." But the problem must be so conceptualized that deviant cases of excessive or dysfunctional control can also be distinguished. The classic analysis of this process is probably Philip Selznick's field investigation of the Tennessee Valley Authority, which was based on the concept of cooptation.[4] By "cooptation" Selznick means the fact that organizations in difficult environments adjust through the assimilation and absorption into their leadership structure of hostile and potentially troublesome elements. In this process, however, they also bring about fundamental revisions in organizational objectives; in Robert Merton's terms, there occurs an unanticipated displacement of goals. "Cooptation" is a principle of wide application to political organization.

State and Nation

So much for a theoretical underpinning of the analysis of nationalization of the state. The relationships between state and nation may now be understood as a problem arising between the organization and the network (or network complex) that sustains it and which it seeks to control.

The mere emergence of the state as a separate unit of political organization is not, by itself, surprising. Large and populous societies tend to greater complexity and to more than the two layers found in the historical empires. The gradual emergence of an intermediate level of organization, based on the state, was a case of successful response to the needs of an expanding system (see Chapter Three). The rise of the state as a powerful political organization antedates the emergence of nations as foci of political orientation, as has already been established. The core of the European states system was built around rulers. Only gradually were some of these family concerns transformed into large-scale and increasingly impersonal organizations, which had to seek equally stable and extensive markets.

In turn, the growth of a variety of networks carrying these large organizations and benefiting from their strength could also be predicted from general propositions of network-organization interplay; they should not be surprising, either. If the intermediary level of world organization and the networks it carries are to be labeled "national," then nations of some form could be expected to emerge. This would undoubtedly be a complex process, destined to proceed along a tortuous and convoluted road. The problems that would be encountered in that progress would undoubtedly be varied and, often, unanticipated. But the existence of nations, at this general level, would be "normal" and non-surprising.

Thus, as a general rule, states made nations, rather than the other way around. This needs to be qualified by the observation that those states have proven successful, and have survived the tribulations of incessant wars, that have found themselves in conditions favoring the formation of nations—namely, where geographical, politico-historical and cultural circumstances have made it relatively easy to organize and consolidate a national layer of interaction. The growth of the French nation occurred under such circumstances; but the previous consolidation, under one political authority, of major parts of what is contemporary France was decisive in lending impetus to the process. Geographical and cultural predispositions do not suffice, however, to explain the rise of the French nation-state; conditions in Italy were in some respects even more favorable than in France, but they did not bring about a nation-state until much later.

Cases where nations made states are few and hard to define without ambiguity. Perhaps it is of some advantage to note that there was a Finnish nation before there was a Finnish nation-state. Was there also a Venezuelan nation before there was a Venezuela? Some commentators attribute to nations certain "natural," as though immanent characteristics, by contrast with the man-made features of the state. This is not really a defensible procedure; nations are also "made," only the process usually takes longer. In the Finnish and Venezuelan cases, the rise of these new nations derived from a feeling of discontent with the existing political arrangements, and the conviction that some people were not "sold on" the existing political networks. Those who were concerned about this used linguistic and religious differences, supplemented by appropriate historical justifications, to set up networks of relationships that in due course demanded to be served by their own independent state organizations. The rise of most of the "new nations" in the twentieth century can be explained in this way—except that, in the great majority of cases, even the initial linguistic, cultural and religious differences were not really pertinent. The new rulers simply took over the languages and the cultures, and occasionally also the religions, of the colonial authorities they were displacing. "Independence" often meant little more than a change in the occupancy of "Government House."

The factor of dissatisfaction with the performance of an existing intermediate-level political structure is, nevertheless, an important element in the nationalization of the state. The enormous and rising power of the state made it important that it be responsive to a large population. Only in a few cases of constitutional development did the dynastic state have this capacity for change toward democratization—that is, toward greater responsiveness to its markets. Elsewhere, responsiveness was obtained by way of costly and prolonged turmoil, in which the idea of the nation was a necessary part of the process. The modern democratic state has also been a nation-state.

Analysis discloses some close and unavoidable links between nation and state. The nation cannot be adequately defined without reference to the state. One such handy definition would describe the nation as a complex of social interactions (a network or networks), which now has, has had in the past, or aspires to having in the future, a state associated with it. This covers in one expression contemporary nationhood, historical nationalism (that is, a demand for independence that is based on memories of earlier self-government—for instance in Armenia, Scotland or the Basque country), and incipient or emergent nationalism, or a demand for a new state that cannot be explained on the grounds of such memories.

All this is really to be expected. The growth of nations can be accounted for as part of the expansion of world society, and needs no further treatment. But some features of the process are not so obvious; they appear to be abnormal and therefore to call for a separate explanation.

What needs explaining is the intensity of the association between state and nation, the capture of the nation by the state and the capture of the state by a simplistic and holistic concept of the nation. The latter idea is that, in a nation-state, the national network (however conceived) is entitled to dominance and to superiority over all other networks, no matter what instabilities this might cause to the state in question or to the world at large. No amount of nation-building will suffice if it is based on misconceptions of the ideal national community.

What needs explaining is the myths surrounding the nation and the nation-state, the intolerance toward minorities associated with these myths, and the excesses that have been committed in their name. Somewhere along the line, the nation-state has been deformed. The term "nationaliation of the state" is intended to account for these "abnormal" features.

The Fallacy of Community

Underlying much of the thinking about the nation is the idea that the nation is a community.[5] The images invoked here almost always hark back to primordial memories of tribal togetherness, of happy cave-dwelling in the warm comfort of a small group of family and intimates, united against the hostile and unhospitable world outside. They often come back to the ideal of the small village or neighborhood, where all know each other. Is the close community, the extended family, or the tribe a proper analogue for the modern nation? It is argued that the processes and techniques of identification that operate in small-scale groups may be immensely magnified through contemporary mass media, so that members of a large community can "identify" with one another in the same way and for the same reasons as do the members of a small community.[6]

This seems a false analogy and a mistaken concept. A large aggregate of millions of people cannot be just a small community writ large. There is no electronic substitute for personal contact and face-to-face communication. Modern techniques considerably extend the range of such contacts (for instance, by means of the telephone network or, with the help of the automobile, via the road network). But the securities, the intimacies and the certainties (of love and hate) that are provided by personal relationships cannot be reproduced by some miracle of mass media manipulation. The large community is an impossibility; it is a mirage or a sham.

Another variant of the same idea is the analogy between the nation and the neighborhood, the latter being conceived as a small territorially-based community, making for close cohesion. Here again the recall of primitive drives for territorial control is obvious; the claim is made that, in some significant way, the "territorial behavior" of small communities, or even of some types of animals,[7] is a valid analogue for the forces shaping a nation. But it is doubtful whether the local self-governing community is a proper model for larger society, and "territoriality" is by no means decisive in the formation of cooperative enterprises.

The weakness in these arguments rests upon the fact that a nation is not a community, but a network or a system of networks. It is a complex of networks activating and operating the national layers of a larger society. The national network never extends fully to the local level to the extent of smothering or swallowing up local life and imposing total uniformity. It never can do this, and it never should be made to. If it did, harm would ensue, because no single national arrangement can accommodate the variety of local circumstances. The nation is a system of relationships that copes with national problems, not with local problems.

The fact that the nation is a network may be seen in the role that language has played in national development and in nationalist movements. Language has been the basic tool of national communication; in an age that was dominated by the printed word (the growth of the state coincided with the invention of printing and the development of printed communications), the association between language, state and nation became significant and value-laden. It came to be claimed—and believed —that speakers of the same language formed a unique community, that such a language community was the national community, and that each such national language community required its own state.

In some instances, language (and the literature based upon it) came to have a significant impact in the fashioning of the identity of important states. In the sixteenth and seventeenth centuries, during the struggle against the Hapsburgs, French became the language of the French state; within two or three generations, the grammarians had fashioned the language into an instrument of precision and beauty, but also of rigid uniformity. Modern French flowered into literature and scholarship; it was part of the glory of the "Sun-king," Louis XIV, and it was strongly supported by the state and such state-initiated institutions as the Academy. Its excellence and the cultural treasures it unlocked became part of France's claim to superior political status in Europe. The development of the King's English played a parallel, though less ambitious, role in England. But in neither country did all the inhabitants of the land speak or use the national language. Rather, a number of local languages continued in use, and remain alive to this day (Basque, Breton, Provençal, Gaelic, Welsh, etc.). In these two cases, the creation of a national language helped to consolidate the state and the national layer of activities. But in Germany, Luther's Reformation and his Bible did not have the same results; they only divided the country. Not until three centuries later did the desire to emulate France and England grow strong enough to provide political expression for the idea that German speakers must be united in one state.

The important fact about languages is not their part in state-building but the circumstance that there are many languages, and that of these only a few are chosen to serve global and national functions. The language of the contemporary global layer is English, which has supplanted the French of classical diplomacy. It is also the language of world commerce, industry and science. National languages are more numerous but, interestingly, a mere few of them serve as official and commercial languages for a high proportion of nation-states. Some thirty use English as an official language, nearly as many use French. About twenty each use Spanish and Arabic (see Table 7:1). In all countries—although more obviously so in the larger ones—the official language of the state exists side by side with numerous local languages and dialects. India, for example, offers a most complex pattern of linguistic diversity.

In his studies of nationalism and social communication, Karl Deutsch popularized the idea that a people are a "larger group of persons linked by . . . complementary habits and facilities of communication." [8] This serves as a reminder that language is only one of the communication facilities that are available in a given system, and that the development of new habits and instruments of communication may change the relative importance of the written and spoken word. The printed message has now been supplemented by the image (photo, film and television); by contrast with the written word, this is fundamentally universal. Specialized networks (such as science) also have their own specialized languages.

Language therefore need not be seen as a special feature of nation-states, but rather as an interesting property of networks. Each network has its own language and changes it continuously, though slowly. Those who wish to participate in a particular network must often take some pains to learn its language.

Homogenization of the People

The nationalization of the state assumed two main forms: nationalization of political management, and homogenization of the people. The first occurred through the displacement of royalty from positions of political leadership and from its functions in system-wide communications, and has earlier been commented upon (in Chapters Four and Five). For the population at large, the significant thrust of the nationalization of the state has been toward homogeneity (at the expense of local life and local diversity), and also toward a clear-cut differentiation against "the outsider."

For maximum productivity and efficiency, organizations require homogeneous inputs and standardized outputs. The state regards a population in part as a source of inputs and it accordingly exerts an influence in the direction of standardization. (1) One type of uniformity required is linguistic; messages and communications are handled more easily if they are uniform as to language, style and symbolic content, and if the receiver shares this same language. (2) The need for conscripts and other military personnel who are suitable for rapid incorporation into the armed forces calls for people who share a common background of communication, education and experience. To meet such requirements, states pay much attention to "making" citizens: just as all organizations "socialize" their members—that is, transmit to them their values, and shape them according to organizational needs—so states see it as one of their important functions to educate the young. The growth of popular education since the end of the eighteenth century has been coincident with the real growth of nation-states. The basic character of future citizens is shaped in schools; national service in peacetime, or conscription, has been advocated on the grounds of imparting feelings of national loyalty.

The operating doctrine for "the making of citizens" [9] is patriotism. The celebrated toast of a seventeenth-century English Ambassador, "My country, right or wrong," is still the operational rule of patriotism, as it is a restatement of the universal demand for organizational loyalty. Pressures for loyalty are characteristic of hierarchical organizations. At an early stage, the state achieved an emotional identification with "the country," and thus became invested with the attributes of close community and the local neighborhood. In the name of the country, the state asked for unconditional loyalty, while from its side it offered the warmth of affectively secure and family-like relationships. Noble deeds were committed in the name of patriotism—but also some inexcusable horrors. Wars were commonly justified in its defense. As time went on, patriotism became nationalism, which was keyed in with ethnic characteristics as well, and brought to political prominence the differences between people. Organization theory indeed predicts that large-scale organizations undermine and divide the networks of society, because they lead to the growth of "innumerable secondary informal organizations, with customs and languages of their own." [10]

Concern for homogeneity thus led to nationalism and homogeneity in turn became a test of loyalty, the underlying supposition being that a society is strong or rich or fruitful only if it is homogeneous. Once examined, such a supposition must be immediately discarded. Organizations do require homogeneity and place heavy reliance upon loyalty, the maintenance of which becomes a major task of its leaders; moreover, failures of loyalty do indeed threaten the entire organization with disintegration. But societies need complexity above all, in order to be adaptable to the variety of contingencies that confront them; hence, they also need organizational variety. When the whole society becomes identified with the state, then the requirements of the state organization become confused with the needs of society, and disaster ensues. This is one reason why the organizational dominance of the state is dysfunctional for the wider society and undermines its long-term viability. In any event, even a large-scale organization needs diversity for maximum adaptability.

Yet uniformity, once it was invested with the halo of patriotism, became the hallmark of the nation-state. In Western Europe, the process occurred so long ago that it has already been forgotten and only the results of it remain. The United States, Central and Eastern Europe, Japan and Thailand experienced it in the nineteenth century, and large parts of the rest of the world were introduced only within living memory to such appurtenances as the flag and the anthem, national holidays, parades and spectacles, the glorification of national heroes—and the search for the "disloyal."

The quest for uniformity as an absolute goal is futile, because states serve a constituency that is too large to admit of extensive homogenization, especially through short-term policies. Large population aggregates, such as the states of the nineteenth and twentieth centuries, cannot be effectively and quickly homogenized merely by the fiat of a new state organization. The experiences of Germany after 1870, Yugoslavia after 1919, India and Pakistan after 1947 or Nigeria after 1960 suggest that political unity brings in its wake profound strains on the body social, and that prolonged efforts and much accommodation with organizations and networks at all levels have been required in order to cope with such shocks. By imposing uniformity on territorial and functional groupings of lesser scope, of diverse ethnic, religious and occupational character, the state has challenged and frequently injured them. In so doing, it has undermined its own stability.

Among the Great Powers of Europe, the Hapsburg Empire collapsed in 1918 because of its inability to accommodate to the forces of nationalism and the strains of the wars; similarly, the great colonial empires were dismantled in response to nationalist pressures. But some political constructions have managed to sustain a considerable degree of diversity —for example, the Soviet Union, after the restructuring of the erstwhile Empire of the Russians, and India, after its granting of considerable autonomy to provincial governments. This is not to mention numerous new states, whose national unity derived from accidents of colonial administration and boundary-making rather than from any prior national identity. For these latter, "national identity" in the European sense seemed hardly attainable in any reasonable time perspective, and could only be a troublesome mirage.

Seen as the drive for the homogenization of the state's clientele, nationalism is essentially disruptive and dysfunctional. Proceeding as it does from a concept of close community, it smothers, depreciates, disables or destroys the local and partial networks, and the political layers on which the health and the viability of the whole depend. Abuses and mischief follow when leaders of a ruling minority take it upon themselves to assimilate others to their ways. Misdeeds and crimes have marked this history: the persecutions of the Jews, the massacres of the Armenians, deportations of entire populations, to mention but a few. In Spain, the achievement of political unity late in the fifteenth century was marked by the expulsion of the Jews (1492) and the Moors (1506), one of the early examples of political homogenization. France expelled the Protestants in the seventeenth century, and England withheld political rights from Catholics until the nineteenth century. In the twentieth century, political settlements were often followed by population movements, at great costs to individuals. Among these were the Greek-Turkish exchanges after World War I, movements of population in Eastern and Central Europe after World War II, and the disturbances, migrations and vast casualties that were consequent upon the drawing of the Indian-Pakistani boundaries in 1947.

The drive for homogeneity is also self-defeating insofar as it tends to disrupt even well-established states. Nationalism is a threat to all local or non-national networks; it is apt to transform political dissatisfaction into political disaffection. Local networks of every kind become nuclei of disruption and may themselves opt for a sort of counter-nationalism—that is, for a nation-state of their own making. Some are more susceptible than others, but the completion of the process of nationalizing the state (by about 1960) did not bring to an end nationalist and separatist movements. After 1945, the world saw a host of movements of other than the purely colonial variety, striving to create new nation-states. Some of the more spectacular were the Kurds in Iraq, the Nagas in India, the Karens of Burma, the Eritreans in Ethiopia, the Ibos of Nigeria, and the Southern Sudan movement (see also Table 14:5). Of interest too was the resurgence of nationalist sentiments in Western Europe, among the best-established and ancient of nation-states: the Basques of Spain, the Scots and the Welsh in Britain, and among the Flemish populations of Belgium. Conceived as a dominant organization, the nation-state thus may well contain a built-in tendency toward fragmentation. In anticipation of that danger, national authorities may turn to homogeneity as the universal recipe. A vicious circle is initiated, with results that are hardly consonant with the image of national community.

Nation-State as Cooptative Device

The nationalization of the state has thus proven to be dysfunctional and abnormal. In the light of the theoretical arguments advanced earlier in this chapter, it might be understood as a successful attempt, on the part of the state, to capture its potential clientele, a successful instance of cooptation.

In his *TVA at the Grassroots*, Philip Selznick argues that organizational behavior may be analyzed as a response to the need for security of the organization, in relation to the social forces in its environment. One such mechanism of response is cooptation, understood as "the process of absorbing new elements into the leadership or policy-determining structure of the organization as a means of averting threats to its stability or existence." (The other mechanism is ideology, which can be identified in the present context as nationalism.) Cooptation assumes two forms. The first is *formal* cooptation, which occurs when the need arises publicly to absorb new elements, by way of openly avowed and formally ordered relationships of participation and accessibility. Cooptation of this type runs the gamut from the democratic to the mass-manipulative end of the spectrum. The second is *informal* cooptation, which brings about adjustment to the pressures of specific centers of power in the community. Selznick shows how the TVA coopted into its structure a definable administrative constituency; this included, among others, the TVA agriculturalists and the land-grant college system. He also shows how this process, together with "grass-roots" ideology, had certain important, yet unanticipated consequences for its future activities. In brief, through cooptation, the Authority entered into a network of commitments that significantly narrowed its future choices, and diminished its ability to attain the goals for which it was originally devised.

Cooptation and ideology thus appear as organizational "defense mechanisms,'" in the face of an uncertain and even hostile environment. Since all environment is uncertain to some degree, and since much of it may always appear to be hostile, a certain amount of cooptation may be expected to occur in all organizations. In that sense, it may be no more than a natural response to organizational exigency. But cooptation can also be carried too far; this occurs when, in response to such exigencies, the mechanism either disrupts the community network, by identifying it too completely with one organization, or else subverts the organization, by diverting it from its true purposes. Cooptation thus has its normal limits, beyond which it becomes deviant behavior, with manifestly harmful consequences both for the organization itself and for its social environment.

The nationalization of the state, then, may have been the process by which the state coopted key sectors of its clientele and in the process became a nation-state. Cooptation was a defense mechanism, a response to the dangers and the instabilities of the international environment. The most important of these instabilities was, of course, war; but there were also all the other common causes of organizational instability: the uncertainties of supplies of revenue, manpower and war materials, and the instabilities of demand, among volatile and fickle populations. The strain was severe and the competition for survival fierce.

The states that led in this competition were also those that were most actively engaged in globalization, along with those that were most prominent in the struggle for the Balance of Power: Spain, France and England. In these three countries, the state had entrenched itself firmly by the end of the Middle Ages, so that, by the sixteenth century, the process of cooptation was well under way. In all three instances, the state absorbed within its structure those elements that were most likely to oppose it: the aristocracy, by bringing it into court ceremonial and royal pageantry; the Church, by converting it into a national institution; the military elements, by incorporating them into the standing army; and the towns, long recalcitrant, by offering them trading monopolies and privileges in colonial commerce. The English political system offers some good examples of this; these include the incorporation of the representatives of the aristocratic and landed forces and of the urban interest into the parliamentary system; the Establishment of the Church by Henry VIII;

favors for chartered companies, and the institution of "justices of the peace," whereby the local squire was converted into an agent of royal power. For France, on the other hand, examples include the evolution of Versailles into a center of cultural and artistic splendor in the seventeenth and eighteenth centuries, a function later assumed by Paris itself.

Cooptation extended beyond formal political arrangements; as time went on, these became progressively more participatory. In the nineteenth century, suffrage and eligibility for office assumed near universality, and democratic rights became the mechanism by which the state entrenched itself even more securely in the public consciousness. On the informal level, too, cooptation became all-pervasive; the strength and the dominance of the state discouraged the growth of autonomous centers of power in business and cultural affairs. Yet the state did succeed in absorbing them within its structure and operations, and became responsive to the variety of economic, agricultural, industrial and maritime interests of its coopted constituents. At times it appeared, as it did to nineteenth-century critics of European capitalism, that the state had become the captive of the bourgeoisie and a "front" for the great capitalists. While this observation did have some truth in it, it was no more than an instance of the general tendency of the state organization to be captured by its manifold yet demanding constituencies. Thus it happened that those states that had pushed cooptation the hardest and had become most thoroughly nationalized—France and Britain, especially—also turned out to be the most prestigious on the international scene, both in military and diplomatic exploits and in the splendor of their capitals and the riches of their citizens.

The universalization of the nation-state, or the near-universal adoption of this pattern of political organization the world over, can be explained by the proven success of cooptation in its original home. Nationalism is the pattern of cooptation that reached such wide currency. The process was one of imitation in conditions that were favorable to cooptation—that is, in conditions of environmental uncertainty. This also occurred despite the obvious and immediately apparent costs of cooptation. For, in spite of its worldly success, and perhaps even because of the thoroughness of that success, the universal nationalization of the state cannot be regarded as an achievement for world order. Some cooptation would inevitably have had to occur, but in the world at large, nationalization went too far: the state added too large a share of social wealth to its purposes; it undermined its own proper role, growing at the expense of local strength and world stability. It now incorporates too broad a coalition of interests to be able properly to perform its own main functions of striving for national order and justice. The state now lays claim to not only a monopoly of power, but also a monopoly of loyalty and attention.

Why Cooptation?

Instead of being a search for the elusive qualities of nationhood, the present chapter has traced the emergence of nation-states in response to the requirements and consequences of large-scale organizational behavior. Two processes explain the success of cooptation. (1) the need, on the part of large scale organizations, for a steady market, and (2) the exclusive privileges that a successful nation-state has been able to offer to its citizens. The pervasiveness of the nation-state could be accounted for by the power of the example given by the states of the North Atlantic area, which ensured its worldwide diffusion.

The state was the first large-scale organization known to man, and the states system has multiplied this type of organization throughout the world. An interesting feature of large modern organizations is their need for the elimination of market uncertainty.[11] This has been achieved by several forms of market control, or else by an increase in the size of the operating unit. But it also makes the large organization less flexible, insofar as it is dependent on large investments, which must preferably be obtained through internal savings. The risk involved in large investments explains the importance that is attached to controlling demand fluctuations, as well as a certain rigidity in responsiveness and in the consequent social arrangements. Among the commonly used responses to market uncertainty are monopoly control and demand management through "brand loyalty."

Monopoly control has been a consistent goal of the leadership of states. While it has proven to be beyond attainment in global proportions, the idea of the jurisdictional monopoly of the state in its territorial domain has been generally accepted. It is not only among the fundamental rules of International Law, but also one of the influential conceptions of Political Science and a prescription for new nation-building. Jurisdictional monopoly is in fact incompatible with world order.

Market control through nationalism has been the other approach commonly applied. The instillation of "brand loyalty" is now widely recognized as an important purpose of advertising. Once again an important insight can be derived from the practices of large corporations. Galbraith has shown that the general effect of sales effort is

to shift the locus of decision in the purchase of goods from the consumer, where it is beyond control, to the firm, where it is subject to control . . . The specific strategy . . . consists first in recruiting a loyal or automatic corps of customers. This is variously known as customer loyalty or brand recognition. To the extent that it is successful, it means that the firm has a stable body of custom which is secure against the mass defection which might follow from the freely exercised consumer choice.[12]

The cultivation of nationalism, and its elaboration in a number of nationalist ideologies, may now be seen as one of the earliest instances of marketing of a political "brand name" through multiple techniques of public relations. The principal techniques were those of the written word; during the nineteenth century, the press became the focal center of political campaigning. Conversely, linguistic and educational factors—those influencing literacy and its formation—also became the object of extended political attention. As the person of the ruler ceased to be the focus of personal loyalty, attention had to be directed to organizational symbols. This was achieved through the identification of the state with the nation. National advertising—that is, the attachment of loyalty to a particular brand of political production—became a part of every political undertaking. As is common in oligopolistic situations, there may not have been much to choose between the several brands in competition; but once loyalty was implanted and became part of ego-identifications and of personal identity, it was likely to last a lifetime.

In return for loyalty, the state was in a position to offer a variety of exclusive rights and privileges, by exercising and enforcing discrimination in favor of its nationals. Tariffs on imported goods; prohibitions on the immigration of competitive foreign labor; the exclusion of non-nationals from employment in the public services and military forces, and the generalization of such practices to all large organizations—these have been only some of the favorite devices for building up the position of nationals. They have been particularly effective in the age of industrialism. Since all states use them, these restrictions may not be of much advantage to nationals of the more prosperous countries. But since the productive capacities and wealth of the world are unequally distributed among the several national jurisdictions, and since the existing distributions strikingly favor a minority of peoples, the privileges of the nation-state are an obstacle toward a more equitable arrangement of world affairs.

The red thread running through "the evolution of world politics" is war and violence, along with efforts to control these forces in conformity with some wider purpose. Thus also, throughout this account, order as the preoccupation of politics and as a condition of world organization has appeared substantively to be much more important than world justice.

It was conquest that finally brought the world together and opened it to globalization. Globalization and war have maintained the balance-of-power system. It has been competitive and war-induced pressures of the Balance of Power that have brought into being the state in its modern form. The uncertainties of the world environment, together with the state's own organizational requirements (principally fueled by war), have propelled the latter toward nationalization. The tensions and rigidities of the nation-state system have raised war to even greater intensity, both actual and potential. War and war-organized politics have impelled the constant restructuring of the world; they still continue as a major source of instability. Industrialism, science and technology have been in some ways no more than incidental to the same process. The world has been remade in the image of the great war-making states.

The organizing ideas of this first part—which has been cast in the past tense, and hence is primarily historical in content, have not been descriptive, but analytical in intention. Their purpose has been to illuminate, in a historical context, some basic questions of world politics, questions of the concern for order and justice, and the forces of monopoly; of the influences that shape and maintain the global structure; of the dynamics of large-scale organizational behavior, as displayed by states, and of the role of global networks of communication and influence, and their relationship to national and local layers of activity.

Lest the argument appear too analytical, however, it should also be remembered that the object of analysis has been the world society of the past half-millennium—that is to say, a concrete historical system. The characteristics of that system cannot be exhausted by the analytical concepts just mentioned; these include not only such impersonal forces as organizational growth and war, but also identifiable men and personalities.

An additional dimension of the contemporary system of politics is the fact, alluded to at several points, that for the past few hundred years the world has been subject to acts and initiatives that have originated, in large part, from Europe and the North Atlantic area. This small part of the world has formed the peak of a great world structure, with the rest of the world having to find accommodation at various points along its slope. The global layer of world politics still retains this shape, and no analysis is complete that does not bring out this crucial characteristic.

But the most important purpose of this long excursion into the past has been to demonstrate the roots of the nation-state system. Contemporary world politics is, in an obvious sense, the product of centuries of growth. Imposing in their majesty though these phenomena of growth may be, they were also instances of identifiable and understandable social processes, the work of men and not of nature. The nation-state system is man-made, even if frequently made in a fit of absentmindedness; it can be changed by conscious and purposeful intervention.

Notes to Chapter Six

1. James March and Herbert Simon, with Harold Guetzkow, *Organizations* (New York: Wiley, 1958), p. 4. "The high specificity of structure and coordination within organizations—as contrasted with the diffuse and variable relations *among* organizations and among unorganized individuals—marks

off the individual organization as a sociological unit comparable in significance to the individual organism in biology."

2. Alfred Sauvy, "Population Theory," *International Encyclopedia of the Social Sciences*, 12, 351–4.

3. F. E. Emery and E. L. Trist, "The Causal Texture of Organizational Environments," *Human Relations*, 1964, 21–32.

4. Philip Selznick, *TVA and the Grass Roots: A Study in the Sociology of Formal Organizations* (New York: Harper and Row, 1966 ed.) (first published, 1949).

5. Rupert Emerson defines the nation as "a community of people who feel that they belong together" (*From Empire to Nation*, Boston: Beacon, 1962, p. 95).

6. C. W. Cassinelli, "The National Community," *Polity*, Vol. 2(1), September 1969, pp. 15–31.

7. Robert Ardrey, *The Territorial Imperative* (New York: Atheneum, 1966).

8. Karl Deutsch, *Nationalism and Social Communication*, 2nd ed. (Cambridge, Mass.: M.I.T. Press, 1964), p. 96.

9. Charles Merriam, *The Making of Citizens* (Chicago: University of Chicago Press, 1931).

10. Barnard, "On Planning for World Government," *cited*, p. 148.

11. John Galbraith, *The New Industrial State* (New York: Houghton Mifflin 1967), Chapter Three.

12. *Ibid.*, pp. 205–206.

PART TWO

The
Nation-State
System

The nation-state system is the fundamental political institution of our world and of our times. Ever-present and ever-dominant, it has assumed the characteristics of a natural phenomenon, a creation of nature, a landscape that is populated with nations as though with living creatures. It governs our lives and conditions our thoughts, yet is so pervasive that its most important features are largely unfamiliar and most often taken for granted.

The system and its future possibilities are also the very center of the modern study of world politics. Contemporary political scientists are busily engaged in exploring the innumerable nooks and crannies of the huge edifice that is the nation-state system. But few have stopped to look at it in its entirety, and fewer still have paused to wonder whether this edifice continues to serve the purposes for which it was erected, or whether it might not require additions, renovations, or perhaps even reconstruction. Among the branches of political science, world politics alone contemplates the entire structure, analyzes its strengths and weaknesses, and hopefully prescribes modifications. To chart a course for the future it is, however, essential first to understand the present; elucidation of the present is the task of Part Two of this volume.

In this spirit, the chapters that follow examine the essential features and the logic of the operation of the nation-state system from two perspectives. In part, notice is taken of an ideal type, a model of the system; the rules of this ideal-type nation-state system are then specified, and their implications spelled out in some detail. In addition, portions of the political and international experience of the nineteenth and twentieth centuries—and in particular, of the system as of 1945—are reviewed from time to time, to determine the degree to which the model fits the reality, or affords explanatory power, or needs to be qualified. There is no need, of course, for the world of the second half of the twentieth century to fit perfectly the rules of this model. Cases of "lack of fit" or of deviation from the rules may be roots of constructive tension, and may thus constitute a dynamic element in the system, and a source of change.

The discussion opens with a characterization of the nation-state system and an account of the distribution of power within it. Great Power authority, which is basic to this system, is then examined, and its influence traced upon the network of other intergovernmental institutions, including bilateral and multilateral diplomacy. The mechanisms through which world political decisions are made responsible, as well as responsive to world interests, are reviewed. Finally, questions are asked about the degree to which the social context of world politics—that is, world society—accords with the framework that the nation-state system is imposing upon it.

The major concepts of the study of world politics—world society and the structures of world authority; the distribution of world power and the mechanisms of world responsibility—are thus brought into relationship with the problems of the contemporary world. These will be the basis for highlighting the salient features of the nation-state system, its strengths, its weaknesses and its inherent instabilities.

7

Nation-State
Dominance

Nation-State System Defined

THE NATION-STATE SYSTEM IS A
system of world politics whose dominant organizational type is the nation-state. The definition clearly turns upon the notion of dominance. Implied in it is a taxonomic principle, according to which systems of world politics may be, organizationally, either balanced or dominant; in the latter case, dominance may assume a number of forms, depending on the type of organization that prevails within them.

In the first place, the character of a system of world politics varies according to the assortment of organizations that is contained by it. All social systems sustain a mixture of organizations, but the ingredients vary among systems, and certain salient features—systems-outputs, in particular—are associated with particular organizational assortments. The nation-state system contains a rich variety of organizations; but among them the most characteristic and the most powerful is unquestionably the nation-state.

Implied in the foregoing is the notion that the organizational assortment that constitutes a given social system may be, but need not be, dominated by a particular organizational type (although not necessarily by a single organization). The notion of dominance is familiar, for instance, in ecology, where one species or unit may exert an especially strong influence on a particular ecosystem. Thus, man may have emerged as the dominant species on earth. Somewhat analogically, one or another organizational species may come to assume a dominant position. In the organizational field, dominance might be diagnosed where one type of organization absorbs a disproportionate share of the resources of a social system. As shown below, on such grounds the nation-state system might be regarded as nation-state dominant (some explanations for this state of affairs have been suggested in the preceding two chapters).

The notion of organizational dominance implies the possibility of the absence of dominance—hence, of a system that harmoniously combines a variety of organizational types, with a maximum of autonomy accorded to each. In fact, dominance in this view constitutes something of an abnormal or extreme position, an aberration brought about by exceptional or emergency conditions; these having earlier wrought havoc with social priorities, have subsequently been formalized and even fossilized into unbalanced institutions. What constitutes absence of dominance remains to be investigated, and what conditions tend to bring about or foster a balanced world system will be the subject of discussion in Part Three. Suffice it to note here that this possibility is far from being unimportant, for it affords a yardstick by which to judge the degree of unbalance of particular systems. In any event, the nation-state system does not belong in the class of balanced world systems. It need not be supposed that balanced systems are entirely hypothetical; some traditional systems of the past (possibly those of ancient India), about which unfortunately not much information remains, may have been closer to such conditions than the contemporary world is.

Finally, the concept of dominance applies not only to organizational types but also to interorganizational networks—that is, not only as between political and non-political organizations, but also as between levels of politics, local, national and global. Thus, in a global system, 1) the nation-state, which is the political organization of the intermediate level, may dominate both the local and the global levels of politics; or 2) influence may be evenly distributed among the political networks of the various levels, thereby balancing the political weight of the nation-state by that of local communities, including cities, and that of the global network. Ways of ascertaining the state of relations among level of politics still remain to be fully operationalized; the topic will be further developed below and in Chapter Thirteen.

Rules of the Nation-State System

The basic rules of the nation-state system may be derived from the principle of nation-state dominance. They may be expressed as follows:

(1) The world's ideal basic political organization is the nation-

state (*not* the city state, or the colonial empire, etc.). The earth's surface is parceled out among a limited number of such states; this makes the basic political organization a sizable territorial unit. The rule denies legitimacy to non-national (e.g. colonial) states. The post-1945 world brought into existence scores of new states, all designed as nation-states, even though in many cases the appellation referred to an aspiration rather than to any actuality.

(2) Within the territory allotted to it, the nation-state exercises complete control and jurisdiction over organizations and individuals. Here the basic organization becomes the dominant organization. While this is not a claim to absolute power, in many states it is interpreted quite strictly and pursued vigorously as an expression of organizational dominance. The key to dominance is territorial control, based upon monopoly of legitimate force. The counterpart of jurisdictional monopoly is, however, sovereignty, independence, territorial autonomy: the exercise of jurisdictional monopoly over a given territory excludes other states from claiming jurisdiction in relation to it. Non-interference is a principle of the nation-state system.

(3) The nation-state is responsible, and accountable for its actions to the nation and to no other nation. The principle of national accountability is a counterpart of the rule of jurisdiction; in external relations, it leads to the single-minded pursuit of the "national interest" as the supreme guide of state action. The particularist nature of the dominant political identification (the nation-state) leaves no room for a concept of world interest.

(4) A further consequence of the monopoly of territorial control is a distinction between internal and external (or domestic and foreign; or, in international legal parlance, municipal and international) problems. Transactions that involve movement across territorial boundaries (which define the limits of territorial jurisdictions) are "external" problems. These include a wide variety of matters, such as trade, migration, scientific and cultural exchanges, tourism, etc. The territorial boundary gives the nation-state, in external affairs, monopoly of control over transnational transactions. Nation-states, moreover, recognize only each other as principals of international relations, thus reinforcing the "foreign affairs" monopoly; organizations and individuals of one nation-state communicate and deal with other nation-states only through, or with the consent of, their own state. Diplomacy's salience in the world system and its assumption of authority over global problems are expressions of the nation-state's "foreign affairs" monopoly.

(5) The nation-state system recognizes no authority superior to that of the nation-state; self-help is its motto. This is the final corollary of

the "internal and external affairs" monopoly; but another aspect of it is also a status of equality in this basic jurisdictional matter. While the nation-state system does establish a uniform and comprehensive system of jurisdiction at the national level, it stands in the way of attention to global problems, and lacks a consistent framework of authority for dealing with them.

Specification of the rules of the nation-state system will clarify the differences that separate it from the earlier European imperial and monarchical state system. All too frequently it is assumed that the nation-state system was either substantially identical with that of earlier systems or in fact originated at the close of the Middle Ages. Far from this being so, of the rules just spelled out only the second—that of internal jurisdictional monopoly—would have seemed essential to the monarchical system at its height. The others, and especially those of accountability (rule three), of denial of superior authority (rule five), and even that of territorial monopoly were substantially modified by the fact that they operated among family-operated states, responsive to family links and interests, small in scale and organizationally underdeveloped. The state organization had not yet reached the degree of maturity that later gave it national character and allowed it to exercise effective control and maintain full autonomy. The nation-state system represents the most complete development of the logic of dominance for the political organization at the intermediate level.

Yet that logic also fails in more than one respect. From the vantage point of world politics, it represents a design for maximizing the autonomy of the nation-state by ensuring its dominance; but this version is bought at the expense of other values. The maximization of the autonomy of one type of organization, the nation-state, diminishes, if not denies, freedom to a whole range of other organizations, and to individuals who have been thus subordinated to the nation-state; it also obstructs the establishment of universal institutions. The maximization of nation-state autonomy also reduces, if not eliminates altogether, opportunities for the pursuit of justice, and especially of those forms of justice that cannot be attained through nation-states on a world scale.

The glaring weakness of the nation-state system is, therefore, its failure to provide for world order and justice. As a category, these do not exist except as problems of "external relations." Yet since such problems do exist and have to be attended to, they must be sought for. In emergencies, this takes the form of reliance upon Great Power authority—an essential, albeit an uneasy, part of the system. But because Great Power authority flatly contradicts the rules of jurisdictional monopoly, denial of superior authority and equality (being the *intervention* of some nation-states in the affairs of other states), it is disruptive of this system. Insofar as it is accountable only to a national constituency, it is doubly subversive. Weaknesses such as these may be seen as possible mechanisms of system transformation.

Time-Boundaries of the Nation-State System

When did the global system become a nation-state system? (1) when the Great Powers became nation-states; (2) when a majority of the world's population began living in nation-states; (3) when the nation-state assumed dominance in world politics. Conversely, a system would cease to be a nation-state system when conditions (1) and (2) no longer obtained. Most importantly however, the system's character would be fundamentally altered if the condition of *dominance* no longer prevailed. Thus it is through changes in the condition of dominance that structural changes of world politics might be achieved.

The Great Powers in world politics function not only as a source of authority (a matter to be discussed at length in the next chapter); in the state system, they also serve as models of political organization. Thus, the make-up of the Great Power Institution is indicative of the state of the system and a signal to the lesser states as how to organize. In 1865, the Great Powers—still essentially European—were Britain, France, Austria, Prussia and the Russian Empire. Of these, none was a true nation-state, even though Britain and France, while maintaining large colonial empires, had developed cohesive national societies within their metropolitan territories. By 1965, both superpowers, the United States and the Soviet Union, were large, federally structured, nation-states. Britain and France had shed most of their colonial dependencies, and even China, whose status was uncertain, was organized as a nation-state (despite the aberration represented by the conquest of Tibet in 1949-50). The turning points were World War I, which brought the collapse of three empires in Europe, and World War II, which hastened the liquidation of colonial rule.

As for population, in 1865 some fifteen per cent of the world's people may have lived in nation-states, mostly in Western Europe, the United States and a few other areas; most of the others lived in empires. By 1965, only a very small proportion of world population, less than five per cent, did *not* live in nation-states. Once again, the turning point was World War I, when the percentage of people living in nation-states passed the 50 per cent mark; but it was not until the decades following the end of World War II that the nation-state became a universal institution, thus decisively altering the character of the system (Table 7:1). Hand in hand with the transformation of the state (and its modernization) went the precise delimitation of national boundaries and the final consolidation of national territory.

The processes of establishment of the nation-state as a worldwide system must be seen, in their basic thrust, as irreversible, so closely are they bound up with modernization and other essential qualities of contemporary life. So large and complex a society as the modern world cannot dispense with this level of political and social organization. But nation-state dominance is a characteristic of a different kind. If the ascendancy of the nation-state is recognized as a condition of excess (to the degree, in fact, that nationalization has gone too far), then a decline in that ascendancy would constitute a change in the character of the system. Thus the principal future source of transformation for the nation-state system would be changes in the condition of dominance.

Nation-State Dominance

The first approach to assessing nation-state dominance leads through an analysis of the share of world production that is controlled by national governments. Agreed that, in modern society, nation-state authorities must own *some* share of the world's output; and assume, for the purposes of this argument, that a share within the range of five to fifteen per cent of world production is considered normal. Bear in mind, too, that the normal (or optional) range might have to vary as the function of total income: the higher that income, the richer the world, the greater the share of its production that it *might* (though *need not*) wish to allocate to national governmental services. Then, if the normal level of allocation is known, anything in excess of that level would be an indication of nation-state dominance, expressed in budgetary terms as the over-financing of the nation-state.

The national political organization is thus seen as one of the rightful claimants on world income, but only one of several such claimants and not inherently the most privileged. Corporations and business organizations, churches and universities and, above all, households, together with political organizations at the local and the global levels, are among the other claimants, each entitled to its rightful share. The difficulty lies in determining the criteria of fair allocation or of the "normality" of a particular share. But it might be taken as axiomatic that no single type of organization should, by right, control all, or the lion's share, of world production.

Fortunately, there is some empirical evidence that can be reviewed at this point. In 1959, for 41 nation-states, comprising 46 per cent of the world population, the mean share of central government (that is,

TABLE 7:1   States of the World, 1967

Status in 1967	Status in 1900	Remarks	Official Language	U.N. Member since
United Kingdom of Great Britain and N. Ireland	independent		English	1945
Canada	British Empire	Self-governing since 1867	English/French	1945
India	British Empire		Hindu/English	1945
Australia	British Empire		English	1945
South Africa	British Empire		Afrikaans/English	1945
New Zealand	British Empire		English	1945
Pakistan	British Empire		Urdu/Bengali/ English	1947
Nigeria	British Empire		English	1960
Ireland	British Empire		English/Gaelic	1955
Malaysia	British Empire		Malay/English	1957
Burma	British Empire		Burmese	1948
Kuwait	British Empire	British Protectorate 1899–1961	Arabic/English	1963
Sudan	British Empire	Anglo-Egyptian condominium 1899–1955	Arabic	1956
Jamaica	British Empire		English	1962
Barbados	British Empire		English	1966
Botswana	British Empire		English	1966
Ceylon	British Empire		Sinhalese	1955
Cyprus	British Empire		Greek/Turkish	1960
Gambia	British Empire		English	1965
Ghana	British Empire		English	1957
Guyana	British Empire		English	1966
Kenya	British Empire		Bantu/English	1963
Lesotho	British Empire		Sethoto/English	1966
Malawi	British Empire		English	1964
Maldive Islands	British Empire		Maldivian	1965
Malta	British Empire		English/Maltese	1964
Sierra Leone	British Empire		English	1961
Singapore	British Empire		English/Chinese/ Malay	1965
Southern Yemen	British Empire		Arabic	1967
Trinidad and Tobago	British Empire		English	1962
Uganda	British Empire		English	1962
Zambia	British Empire		English	1964
Rhodesia	British Empire		English	
United States of America	independent	British Empire to 1776 (also Spanish, French Empire)	English	1945
Philippines	U.S. dependency	Spanish Empire to 1898	Tagalog/English/ Spanish	1945
Liberia	independent		English	1945

TABLE 7:1 (*Continued*)

Status in 1967	Status in 1900	Remarks	Official Language	U.N. Member since
France	independent		French	1945
Algeria	French Empire		Arabic/French	1962
Tunisia	French Empire		Arabic	1956
Cambodia	French Empire		Khmer	1955
Central African Republic	French Empire		French	1960
Chad	French Empire		French	1960
Congo (Brazzaville)	French Empire		French	1960
Dahomey	French Empire	conquered 1892–3	French	1960
Gabon	French Empire		French	1960
Guinea	French Empire		French	1958
Ivory Coast	French Empire		French	1960
Laos	French Empire	protectorate since 1890	Laotian	1955
Malagasy Republic	French Empire		Malagasy/French	1960
Mali	French Empire		French	1960
Mauretania	French Empire		Arabic/French	1961
Niger	French Empire		French	1960
Senegal	French Empire		French	1960
Upper Volta	French Empire		French	1960
Republic of Vietnam	French Empire		Vietnamese	
Democratic Republic of Vietnam	French Empire		Vietnamese	
Haiti	independent	French to 1804	French	1945
Morocco	independent	French protectorate 1912–1956	Arabic	1956
Union of Soviet Socialist Republics	Russian Empire	(including Ukraine and Byelorussia)	Russian etc.,	1945
Poland	Russian Empire	also German and Austro-Hungarian Empires	Polish	1945
Finland	Russian Empire		Finnish/Swedish	1955
German Federal Republic	German Empire		German	
German Democratic Republic	German Empire		German	
Burundi	German Empire	Belgian mandate (1919–1962)	Kirundi/French	1962
Cameroon	German Empire	French/British mandate 1919–1960	French/English	1960
Rwanda	German Empire	Belgian mandate 1919–1962	French/Kinyarwanda	1962

TABLE 7:1 (*Continued*)

Status in 1967	Status in 1900	Remarks	Official Language	U.N. Member since
Tanzania	German Empire	British mandate 1919–1961	Swahili	1961
Togo	German Empire	French mandate 1919–1960	French	1960
Denmark	independent		Danish	1945
Iceland	to Denmark	independent 1918	Icelandic	1946
Sweden	independent		Swedish	1946
Norway	to Sweden	independent 1905	Norwegian	1945
Netherlands	independent		Dutch	1945
Indonesia	Netherlands East Indies		Bahasa/Indonesian	1950
Luxembourg	independent		French/German	1945
Belgium	independent	since 1830	French/Flemish	1945
Congo, Democratic Republic of	Congo Free State	1885–1908	French	1955
Italy	independent		Italian	1955
Somalia	Italian-British Empire		Somali	1960
Austria	Austro-Hungarian Empire		German	1955
Hungary	Austro-Hungarian Empire		Hungarian	1955
Czechoslovakia	Austro-Hungarian Empire		Czech/Slovak/	1945
Switzerland	independent		German/French/ Italian	
Yugoslavia	Serbia, Montenegro	also parts of Austro-Hungarian and Ottoman Empires	Serbo-Croat/ Slovene/ Macedonian	1945
Turkey	Ottoman Empire		Turkish	1945
United Arab Republic	Ottoman Empire	(under effective British control 1883–1936)	Arabic	1945
Israel	Ottoman Empire		Hebrew/Arabic	1949
Iraq	Ottoman Empire		Arabic	1945
Saudi Arabia	Ottoman Empire		Arabic	1945
Syria	Ottoman Empire		Arabic	1945
Lebanon	Ottoman Empire		Arabic	1945
Albania	Ottoman Empire		Albanian	1955
Yemen	Ottoman Empire		Arabic	1947
Jordan	Ottoman Empire		Arabic	1955
Libya	Ottoman Empire		Arabic	1955
Greece	independent	Ottoman Empire until 1829	Greek	1945
Bulgaria	independent	Ottoman Empire until 1878	Bulgarian	1955

TABLE 7:1 (*Continued*)

Status in 1967	Status in 1900	Remarks	Official Language	U.N. Member since
Rumania	independent	Ottoman Empire until 1878	Rumanian	1955
Chinese People's Republic	Chinese (Manchu) Empire		Chinese	(1945)
Mongolia	Chinese (Manchu) Empire		Mongol	1961
Republic of China (Taiwan)		(Taiwan to Japan 1895–1945)	Chinese	
Japan	independent		Japanese	1955
Republic of Korea	independent	Japanese Empire 1907–1945	Korean	
People's Democratic Rep. of Korea	independent	Japanese Empire 1907–1945	Korean	
Afghanistan	independent	British Protectorate 1907–1921	Persian/Pushtu	1946
Ethiopia	independent		Amharic	1945
Iran	independent		Persian	1945
Nepal	independent		Nepalese	1955
Thailand	independent		Thai	1946
Portugal	independent		Portugese	1955
Brazil	independent	Portugese Empire to 1822	Portugese	1945
Spain	independent		Spanish	1955
Argentina	independent	formerly Spanish Empire	Spanish	1945
Mexico	independent	formerly Spanish Empire	Spanish	1945
Venezuela	independent	formerly Spanish Empire	Spanish	1945
Chile	independent	formerly Spanish Empire	Spanish	1945
Colombia	independent	formerly Spanish Empire	Spanish	1945
Panama	To Columbia until 1903	formerly Spanish Empire	Spanish	1945
Cuba	independent	formerly Spanish Empire	Spanish	1945
Uruguay	independent	formerly Spanish Empire	Spanish	1945
Peru	independent	formerly Spanish Empire	Spanish	1945
Ecuador	independent	formerly Spanish Empire	Spanish	1945
Bolivia	independent	formerly Spanish Empire	Spanish	1945
Costa Rica	independent	formerly Spanish Empire	Spanish	1945

TABLE 7:1 (*Continued*)

Status in 1967	Status in 1900	Remarks	Official Language	U.N. Member since
Dominican Republic	independent	formerly Spanish Empire	Spanish	1945
El Salvador	independent	formerly Spanish Empire	Spanish	1945
Guatemala	independent	formerly Spanish Empire	Spanish	1945
Honduras	independent	formerly Spanish Empire	Spanish	1945
Nicaragua	independent	formerly Spanish Empire	Spanish	1945
Paraguay	independent	formerly Spanish Empire	Spanish	1945

The table shows how the nation-state system evolved out of a small number of major empires; it gives all states members of the United Nations in 1967, and nine non-members (for a total of 130); but it omits certain states also contributing to some U.N. expenses in 1967: the Holy See, Liechtenstein, Monaco and San Marino.

national level) expenditures in GNP was 19.5 per cent.[1] If public enterprises and social security accounts are included, the share of the central government rose (for the same year, and for 41 countries, with 48 per cent of the world population) to 25.8 per cent.[2] This latter figure is probably the more adequate indicator of national governmental influence in those societies, and makes clear that, as a group, nation-states are the single most powerful organization in the world today—if such proof were indeed needed.

Contemporary data are reinforced by such information as comes to hand about historical trends during the century since the nationalization of the state. The previous chapter's argument is vindicated through an analysis of data collected by Quincy Wright for a related purpose—namely, that of demonstrating the small but rising share of production that is devoted to financing international organization. The Quincy Wright data show, over the hundred years following 1870, a striking trend toward increasing saliency of the nation-state function in world society (Table 7:2).

The trend evidenced above is startling in its decisiveness. The world's single growth industry has truly been the nation-state, and its promoters have had a field day for themselves. No other industry or major field of human endeavor has shown a comparable expansiveness—hence, a capacity for dominance. In this expansion, the two global wars of this

TABLE 7:2 Share of nation-state expenditures in world income, 1870–1964 (annual averages)

	World Income ($U.S. billions)	Expenditures of all national governments ($U.S. billions)	Share of national governments in World income (percentage)
1870–99	50	5	10
1900–20	100	12	12
1921–45	250	50	20
1946–55	600	200	33.1/3
1956–64	1,200	300	25

Source: Wright, *A Study of War*, p. 1561; see also Appendix XXII, 666–672. These data, also used in Tables 7:5 and 7:6, cannot be regarded as other than very rough estimates; unfortunately, better data, spanning the entire period, are not at hand.

century have been a major factor. It is still too early to determine whether the decline shown in the last line of the table, for the years 1956-64 (free of major conflict), indicates a lasting trend; but it may be that, the bounds of normality having long been exceeded, a halt in this runaway inflation of the state function is in sight.

A second approach toward operationalizing the concept of nation-state dominance leads through a comparison of the share of world production that is claimed by the national, as against the local and the global, levels of politics. Once again, political analysis is lacking in any criterion of normality or optimality. Intuitively, one feels that dominance should appear as a disproportionate appropriation of resources by one of these levels of government; a "rule-of-thumb" criterion—equal shares for every level—could be the fair one. It could, at any rate, serve as the start of a more sophisticated analysis of "equi-balance." [3]

Empirical material on the allocation of resources among the local, national and global levels of government is striking, too. Table 7:3 depicts the relationship between national- and local-level government expenditures in seven large federal states. In all cases but one, central government expenditures are higher than the total of all state and local government expenditures—that is, the index of centralization exceeds unity. Hence, the local level of government appears to be relatively underfinanced, even in these federal states. If it is remembered that in federal states the local level is considerably stronger than it is in centralized states, in which local government plays an even more subordinate role, the conclusion seems justified that on a world scale the national level of politics has a claim on larger resources than the local level does.

The picture becomes more complete if the global level of politics is taken into consideration. Here the disproportion is truly overwhelm-

TABLE 7:3   Index of centralization for seven federal states, 1965 *

	C
Brazil	1.83
India	1.57
Pakistan	1.51
United States	1.3
Nigeria	1.28
Australia	1.25
Yugoslavia	.94

* Except Nigeria 1963, Brazil 1964.
Calculated from data in *United Nations Statistical Yearbook 1966.*

$$\text{Index of centralization } C = \frac{\text{Central government expenditures}}{\text{total state and local government expenditures}}$$

ing. Thus, the United States contributes to all United Nations and other international agency activities an amount of less than two-tenths of one per cent of the total of governmental expenditures (Table 7:4). The amount would still be under one per cent if the total of foreign aid were to be included in that accounting. Even the relatively large outlays at the local level shown in the table could be misleading, for the basic unit of the local layer is the city, while in the United States the major unit of local financing is the state, so that the city has always tended to be underfinanced, as compared with non-city communities. The global layer, by contrast, appears to be completely neglected. The large share of the federal layer includes, however, large defense expenditures, which in some respects represent indirect support for global purposes.

There is no reason to believe that data for other states would negate the proposition that the national level of political organization is overdeveloped—most of all at the expense of the global layer, but also in part at the expense of local activities. The nation-state dominance hypothesis would thus seem to be well supported by available evidence. If the nation-state system has correctly been defined as a system that is characterized by the nation-state dominance, then a transformation of that system can (or will) occur not through the "demise of the nation-state"—for that indeed is hard to imagine—but rather through

TABLE 7:4   Expenditures at three levels of government: United States, 1965
   (*$U.S. billions*)

State and local	95.318
Federal	122.395
Global	.250

Source: *Statistical Abstract of the United States*, 1965.

such a shift in the balance of political influence that dominance will move to another type of social organization, or else a different balance will emerge between various types of organization. Granted the possibly fundamental consequences for the future that will result from such shifts, the continuous collection, study and review of the type of data just analyzed remain an urgent necessity.

Non-Centralization

Nation-state dominance has fundamental consequences for the structure of world politics. Above all, it is associated with the weakening of world order, as manifested in low institutionalization and excessive decentralization of global authority. Non-centralization in turn favors self-help, and therefore reliance upon power. Such reliance is associated with power inequalities and the concentration of power in a limited number of power centers. Despite concentration, the uses to which power can be put are few: while war and war preparedness are well cared for, other global purposes remain under strength; one consequence is that world society remains weak.

The role of power in a social system of self-help has been widely recognized. What needs pointing out is not so much the relationship of self-reliance to the lack of a global power-monopoly (states resort to self-help because there is no world state), as the association between the weakness of global structures (hence, lack of order), the insistent claims of nation-states to territorial monopoly of jurisdiction, and the lack of autonomy for other organizations. That is to say, the source of the crisis of authority is not the existence of independent power sources, but rather the nationalization of the state and the unidimensional politics that that produces.

In the remainder of this chapter, nation-state dominance will be examined in its association with: first, non-centralization and second, power-concentration; a third section will deal with the specificity of that power-concentration.

The degree of centralization (or non-centralization) is an important analytical property of organizations and of systems of organizations. In Chapter Two, this property was used to distinguish among systems of world politics. Thus, empires were recognized as centralized world orders, and Balance of Power Systems, as characteristically non-centralized. In the historical past, the degree of centralization that is appropriate to a particular organization or system has frequently been a matter of contention. In medieval and post-medieval church history, especially before and during the Reformation, the proper degree of centralization for the church organization was a subject of considerable debate. The gradual accretion of power to the powerful monarchies of seventeenth- and eighteenth-century Europe, away from imperial and church authority and at the expense of local ("feudal") elements, was a process of national centralization. The history of federalism, or the theory of anarchism, revolve around a critique of centralizing tendencies, and the feasibility and desirability of decentralization. Despite this, analytical studies of that macropolitical process remain rare. If a sweeping generalization might be added at this point, mainstream political science has favored the strong, hence centralized state; it has argued for the inevitability of centralization in the face of technology, and implicitly denied the order-maintaining capacity of systematically non-centralized systems.

Centralization may be defined as the distribution of authority between the central and non-central parts of an organization or a system, in such fashion that centralization obtains when the distribution favors the central parts, while non-centralization prevails when the distribution favors the non-central parts. It is important to note, however, that centralization is a continuous variable; real-world systems can exhibit a wide range of centralization, all the way from zero degree to infinity, and can thus adapt to their environment by steadily changing this property. A given system might be either overcentralized (as an empire would tend to be, or as some nation-state, perhaps France or Britain, could be), normally centralized (as a federation), normally non-centralized (conceivably, certain future types of world politics), or else excessively non-centralized (as the nation-state system). The essential questions are the appropriateness of a given degree of centralization to certain environmental conditions, and the relationship between centralization and other properties of the political system.

The notion of centralization implies that the parts of any given system can be segregated into two discrete categories: central and non-central. That is to say, some of its parts can be identified as playing system-wide regulative, etc. functions, while others are not so crucial. This seems to hold for larger and differentiated, although basically simple systems; but it may not be applicable to small and simple or large and truly complex ones. In the contemporary global system, which is large but still fairly simple, the central organs might be identified as the universal international organization and the specialized agencies associated with it; the non-central parts, as the nation-states.

One convenient method of determining the degree of centralization that prevails in a system or organization is budget analysis. As previously argued, a budget is a characteristic property of all organizations; it may be regarded as a statement of the authorized activities of an organization —authorized by virtue of being funded. Thus, a relationship between the central and non-central activities of an organization or a system might also be expressed in terms of the ratio of their budgets. Such a ratio might be used as a measure of centralization; in the global system, the degree of centralization could be expressed as the ratio of international organization expenditures to national government expenditures. Table 7:5 shows in rough outline the movements of this index over one hundred years.

The trend disclosed by Table 7:5 is exponential. It documents a rapidly rising rate of centralization for the world system—a trend that has already lasted about one hundred years, even though the starting point was a rather negligible amount of centralization. The average doubling rate of the exponential growth curve has been approximately twelve years (the rate at which world science has grown for the past three centuries [4]). That rate slowed down somewhat between the two world wars, but picked up strength again after 1945. All exponential trends can be projected into the future, and so can this one. The projection yields an index of centralization equal to that of contemporary United States by about the year 2080; but, at this stage, no rash conclusion needs be drawn from that.

The use of an index thus makes possible comparisons between the global system and contemporary and historical federal systems (for which budgetary calculations are fairly simple). In particular, an instructive comparison might be drawn between the contemporary global system and the index of centralization for the United States at the outset of the federalizing process, which was 0.1. (ca. 1800; see Table 5:1). On such evidence the global system of today may be about 100 times less centralized than the United States was at the beginning of the federation, and that was hardly an over-centralized system. The present world political system might therefore, in terms of this criterion, be declared to be excessively decentralized and, for that reason, weak and disorderly.

If emphasis is placed however, in the exponential growth trend

TABLE 7:5   Centralization in the global system, 1870–1964

	Total expenditures for international organizations (annual averages)	Expenditures of all national governments (annual averages)	Index of global centrali- zation
		($U.S. billions)	
1870–99	0.1	5,000	0.000 02
1900–20	1.0	12,000	0.000 08
1921–45	10.0	50,000	0.000 20
1946–55	100.0	200,000	0.000 50
1956–64	500.0	300,000	0.001 66

Index calculated from data in Wright, *A Study of War*, cited, p. 1561.

shown in Table 7:5, the matter assumes a somewhat different aspect. The trend is remarkable if only because it shows international organization expenditures rising at a rate faster than those of national government expenditures. These latter have now reached so conspicuous a proportion of world income (about one quarter), that their continued increase can no longer proceed without impediment—except in the not inconceivable but hopefully unlikely case of another world war. International organization expenditures, by contrast, are still relatively limited and show obvious scope for growth. Thus, if the recent growth rate is projected into the not-so-distant future—its continuation is not altogether unlikely —the global system might reach, by about the year 2000, a degree of centralization comparable to that of the early American experience (that, is an index of about 0.1). While this still represents non-centralization of a rather low order, it would also mean a considerable change in the context of world politics.

The index of centralization serves as a useful if approximate measure of the degree of political autonomy (seen as freedom from central control) to be found in a given world system, and information at hand shows autonomy in the nation-state system to be rather high—in fact, too high, and disorder-prone. On the other hand the index takes into account only those elements of continuous international authority that are represented by international organizations, and these have been notoriously weak. It does not account for the contingent and non-continuous authority of the Great Powers (to be discussed presently). Hence it cannot be regarded as a complete description of the authority structure of world politics, but merely as a guide to the distribution of authority between global and national organizations.

Militarization

The nation-state system is beset by excessive non-centralization. One predictable consequence of this property is strong reliance upon military power.

In one way or another, all systems of world politics organize power. Related as it is to the ability to achieve a desired result, the problem of power inheres in all organization. Every organization is an embodiment of power; they are the impressive monuments to man's propensity to accumulate and to multiply what he has accumulated. Modern society worships power and those organizations that are most adept at compounding it.

Military power, or force, is but one of the forms that power assumes in society; but it is a particularly strategic form of power. Other varieties of power can be converted to military forms: wealth can be used to hire men and buy weapons, and knowledge to train and organize them, but the process takes time. Readily available force is, in the short run, superior to all other forms of power, because its utilization can terminate life: there is an awful finality about the successful use of brute force.

All social systems pay attention, and devote some of their resources, to military power and its organization. Military power guards order by maintaining strength sufficient to deter attacks from the outside; it can disrupt a just order, but it can also be used for overthrowing an unjust one. Because of the close and unavoidable links between order, justice and power, the uses and abuses of power are among the key problems of politics in general, and of worldly politics in particular.

Systems of politics, and of world politics, differ, however, as to the place they accord to military power and to reliance upon threats to life and limb. The good society does not abolish military power, or create a disarmed world; but it does seek to minimize reliance upon it, and to reduce the claims that it has placed upon society's physical and moral resources.

The early philosophers of the state system, Hobbes, Locke and Rousseau, were unanimous in finding inter-state relations to be in a state of nature—that is, ruled by brute force. In the seventeenth and eighteenth centuries the degree of militarization, at least in Europe, was quite high, for this was the formative period of the great military states; but data at hand on the intensity of wars and the number of battles and of war casualties,[5] show the twentieth century with the highest scores, by far, in these regards. It is clear that the growth of the nation-state system has not had the effect of diminishing militarization, as we were led to believe by the nineteenth-century advocates of nationalism, nor has it held militarization at a constant level, as the early students of the state system had insisted. Rather, the nation-state system has been marked by pronounced and *rising* rates of militarization, as can be seen in Table 7:6.

The trend disclosed in this table is so strong that even substantial mistakes in the estimates upon which the table is constructed could not affect it. In Column 5, the table shows a particularly significant trend toward governmental militarization: there is a steadily rising proportion of national government expenditures being devoted to military purposes, from a low 17 percent late in the nineteenth century, to some 40 percent in the early nineteen-sixties. In other words, there has been at least a doubling in the share of nation-state resources allotted to military ends (it is worth bearing in mind, though, that the averages for each period include the war expenditures and not only the years of peace). This would suggest that the nationalization of the state has been

TABLE 7:6   Long-range trends in the index of militarization

	1. Armaments Expenditures	2. World Income	3. Global Militarization	4. Expenditures of all national Governments	5. Governmental Militarization
	(annual averages $U.S. billions)				
1870–99	0.84	50	1.68	5	16.8
1900–20	2.7	100	2.7	12	22.5
1921–45	16	250	6.2	50	32
1946–55	75	600	12.5	200	37.5
1956–64	120	1,200	10	300	40

Index calculated from data in Wright, *A Study of War*, cited, p. 1561.

Index of global militarization = percentage of armaments expenditures in world income; index of governmental militarization = percentage of armaments expenditures in the expenditures of all national governments.

associated, over the past century, with a militarization of state activity. Historically, the state has usually had an exceedingly strong stake in military matters; but in the absence of comparable data on earlier periods, it cannot be argued conclusively that the nation-state is more militarized than were earlier types of state. Table 7:6 shows, however, that the great relative and the enormous absolute increment in the resources available to the nation-state (hence also the welfare services it is capable of rendering, in some ways the most notable achievement of the modern age) has not been accompanied by a decline in the salience of force in world politics. If anything, the contemporary political organization, affluent though it may be—or perhaps because of its affluence is more deeply involved with military power than in the past century and absolutely, of course, more than at any time previously.

Table 7:6 also displays, in Column 3, a sharp (about five-fold) rise in global militarization, the share of world income that is allotted to military purposes.[6] Again, the precise percentages need not be taken as more than well-informed guesses. The next table, 7:7, presents more detailed information for six recent years (1964-69), during which the same global militarization index averaged at just over seven per cent. This indicates that the figures in the long-range table might have been somewhat overdrawn. It remains true, nevertheless, that during a century of increasing nationalization of the state the militarization of world society has proceeded apace. The growth of the nation-state system has coincided with a powerful reinforcement of those elements of politics that are rooted in force. Could it be that steadily rising amounts of force are needed to preserve the system?

Information from other sources confirms the general argument that

TABLE 7:7   Global militarization index, 1964–1969

	Military expenditures	Gross world Product	Global Militarization Index
		($U.S. billions current prices)	
1964	139	1,903	7.3
1965	143	2,087	6.9
1966	160	2,296	7.0
1967	181	2,481	7.3
1968 est.	191	2,689	7.1
1969 est.	200	2,930	6.8

Source: United States Arms Control and Disarmament Agency *World Military Expenditures 1969* (Washington: G.P.O. 1969), pp. 10, 17.

Note: Military expenditures and Gross World Product are not fully comparable, because of the use of special conversion rates for Warsaw Pact countries.

in the "1945 System" in particular, military expenditures have risen somewhat faster than world production. Long-range trends thus do not point to an imminent decline of militarization. Yet this might be added: a world that continues to add to its gross product at a steady rate of from three to five per cent per annum is capable over a period of a number of years of considerable adaptability. If during such a period military budgets were held constant, their overall share of world resources could decline quite rapidly. Modern society has considerable built-in flexibility; but is it capable of using it?

At all events, militarization is not a constant property of "anarchic" systems of independent states but a continuous variable. The subject deserves further study and analysis of trend data. Fluctuations in the militarization rate might have important associations with the character of world politics, and with such phenomena as the rate of military coups and the number of military regimes in the world. Just as global militarization rose between 1965 and 1967, so did the number of coups and military regimes.

The trend of armaments expenditures over the past one hundred years has been a rising one. Particular wars or crises (the world wars, the Korean war, the Vietnam war) show up as peaks on a curve that is moving steadily upward. Whereas in the past major wars were the occasions for militarization, more recently a local war in Indochina has had that effect, as well as an arms race or a period of major tension between the superpowers (the "missile gap" arms race, and the tensions over Berlin and Cuba in the early sixties). The upward trend of the armaments expenditure curve is due less to the number of men under arms than to the expense and complexity of weapons and equipment.[7]

An affluent society evidently can afford more complex and more expensive arms; but why should it have to buy them? Or is there a necessary link between the structure of the system and the weight of military expenses? The evidence would seem to support the latter conclusion.

Concentration

The reason why a nation-state system generates such strong tendencies toward militarization is this: the nationalization of the state has coopted the best of the energies of modern society on behalf of an organization for which war and the mobilization of force are the major interests. Militarization, however, is not a uniform property of the entire world system; rather, it is a property that is strikingly concentrated at a few points of that system.

The global review of military power in this and the preceding section has been conducted on the basis of data derived from national military budgets. The assumption is that budgeted military expenditures can serve as a reliable index of military power, the further assumption being the existence of a perfect world market for military manpower and equipment, such that one dollar of expenditure buys a roughly equal amount of military power the world over. Such a perfect market does not, of course, exist; the nearest to it are the markets for certain widely used items of equipment, such as aircraft, vehicles and guns. Thus true comparability obtains more nearly in the heavier types of equipment, which are important for global and regional types of force, but will be least convincing with regard to military manpower, the market for which the nation-state system has come close to making a true monopoly. In any event, much caution needs to be used in the interpretation of budget figures. Current expenditures tell little about accumulated stocks of skills and weapons, or about the assets of location or the liabilities of poor communications. Expenditures, moreover, do not necessarily record satisfaction obtained, and they assuredly conceal a good deal of waste. Despite all these caveats, however, there is no other way to make global propositions about military power without getting bogged down in technical issues of an intelligence character, including secrecy, "classified information" and comparisons of non-comparable weapon systems.

In summary form, Tables 7:8 and 7:9 answer the question: who wields military power in the nation-state system? The answer is, almost without exception, nation-states. The United Nations, in its peace-keeping operations, commands a small amount of such power; in terms of Table 7:9, it could therefore be classified as a "minor" military power. But

TABLE 7:8   Distribution of world military expenditures, 1965, 1967

($U.S. billions, current prices)

Population 1965 (millions)	National governmental forces	1965	percentage of total	1967	percentage of total
195	United States	51.844	35.6	75.484	41.8
232	Twelve other most affluent nations *	20.836	14.6	23.374	12.9
231	Soviet Union	46.000	31.5	52.000	28.1
100	Six Warsaw Pact Nations	4.650	3.4	5.070	2.8
700	China	6.000	4.2	7.000	3.9
483	India	2.077	1.4	1.486	0.8
1,300	105 other nations	12.030	8.3	16.278	9.0
		143.437		180.692	
	United Nations peace-keeping	0.100		0.040	
	Insurrectionary and revolutionary forces	† 0.100		0.200	

Source: For national forces: *World Military Expenditures 1969*, pp. 17–19.

* Those with GNP per capita in excess of $2,000 in 1967: United Kingdom, France, German Federal Republic, Canada, Australia, New Zealand, Sweden, Belgium, Switzerland, Denmark, Finland, Norway.

† Estimate (Vietnam, Laos, Near East, Southern Africa, etc.,).

the great bulk of force is in the hands of national authorities (and of insurrectionary and revolutionary movements intent upon overthrowing national authorities).

The tables also show, however, that military power is not at all distributed equally among nation-states; on the contrary, the distribution is strikingly unequal. For the system portrayed in these tables, the bulk of this power (some seventy percent of it) is concentrated in the two nation-states at the top of the pile: the United States and the Soviet Union. The remaining thirty per cent is shared out among the remaining one hundred and twenty-odd states. This is the type of power distribution that has prevailed for most of the years since 1945; it might, therefore, be regarded as a "typical" "1945 system" distribution.

Thus, thirteen per cent of the world's population (in the United States and the Soviet Union) are protected by 70 percent of the world's military power. In the same years, the 13 percent also commanded close to one half of the world's gross product (48 percent in 1965 and 46 percent in 1967), which shows that they could indeed afford this power. Wealth alone went a long way toward accounting for the distribution of military power, but not all the way; in other words, power inequalities

TABLE 7:9   Classes of military power, 1967

Class	Range of military expenditures (current $U.S.)	Number of States	Nation-states
I Super	10 billion or more	2	United States, Soviet Union
II Major	1–10 billion	11	Canada, United Kingdom, France, German F.R., Italy, Czechoslovakia, Poland, China, India, Japan, Australia.
III Medium	100 million– 1 billion	42	Belgium, Denmark, Greece, Netherlands, Norway, Portugal, Turkey, Bulgaria, German D.R., Rumania, Austria, Finland, Spain, Sweden, Switzerland, Yugoslavia, Argentina, Brazil, Chile, Cuba, Mexico, Peru, Venezuela, Burma, China (T), Indonesia, Korean P.D.R., R. of Korea, Malaysia, Philippines, Thailand, D.R. of Vietnam, R. of Vietnam, Pakistan, Iran, Iraq, Israel, Saudi Arabia, Syria, U.A.R., Algeria, South Africa, New Zealand.
IV Minor	10–100 million	38	Albania, Iceland, Bolivia, Colombia, Dominican R., Ecuador, El Salvador, Guatemala, Nicaragua, Paraguay, Uruguay, Cambodia, Laos, Mongolia, Afghanistan, Ceylon, Jordan, Kuwait, Lebanon, Yemen, Cameroon, Congo (K), Ethiopia, Ghana, Guinea, Ivory Coast, Kenya, Libya, Malagasy R., Morocco, Nigeria, Rhodesia, Senegal, Sudan, Tanzania, Tunisia, Uganda, Zambia.
V Mini	1–10 million	24	Luxembourg, Guyana, Haiti, Honduras, Jamaica, Panama, Trinidad & Tobago, Nepal, Cyprus, Central African R., Congo (B), Chad, Dahomey, Gabon, Liberia, Malawi, Mali, Mauretania, Niger, Sierra Leone, Somalia, Togo, Upper Volta, Singapore.
VI Mini-mini	Less than 1 million or none	11	Iceland, Costa Rica, Malta, Maldive Islands, West Samoa, Burundi, Rwanda, Gambia, South Yemen, Lesotho, Botswana.

Source: *World Military Expenditures 1969*, cited, pp. 17–19.

are even greater than the staggering inequalities of wealth. The immense military investment undertaken by the two super-powers must be explained above all in terms of their preoccupation with global authority.

Non-affluent nations do not share in the world's military power.

Over 100 nation-states, with close to 80 per cent of the world's population, have less than fifteen per cent of the world's military strength, but just over twenty-five per cent of the world product. Hence, they have less military power than they can afford, even on their low income. The poorer they are, the less power they have. Could the reverse relationship obtain at the same time—that is, the less powerful a nation-state, the less affluent its population?

Posing the problem as one of power inequality (or concentration) carries with it the implication that a more equal power distribution might be preferred to a more unequal one. This proposition is worth entertaining and carries with it some important principles for the organization of systems of world politics. A system with more equitable power distribution would also be expected to be less likely to experience other gross inequalities, such as those of wealth, and thus to be more just; it would more truly be a balanced system and hence more orderly.

Stark power inequalities are one of the basic characteristics of the "system of 1945." A similar condition prevailed also in the Interwar (or "Versailles") system (Table 7:10). In 1937, seven Great Powers accounted for the bulk of global military expenditures. Taking into account only the metropolitan populations of these states, 80 percent of world military power was then accounted for by 27 percent of the world's population—a situation not unlike that of the more recent system.

Evidence of comparable quality is not at hand for nineteenth-century or earlier global systems, but historical trends indicate that a considerable degree of power concentration has been a characteristic of the state system right from the introduction of peacetime standing armies in the seventeenth century. The concentration of military power therefore antedates the nation-state system. Indeed, at the basis of contemporary power inequality, there is still the European military ascendancy that was first achieved during the process of globalization and consolidated in the nineteenth century. But the nation-state system might have made this inequality even starker, possibly more pronounced.

TABLE 7:10   World military power, 1937

	Population (million)	per cent	Military Expenditures ($U.S. billions)	per cent
Seven Great Powers (home population only)	569	27	14.428	80
(including colonial territories)	(1,280)	(60)		
Other States	845	40	1.385	20

Source: Wright, *A Study of War*, cited, p. 672.

Before the nationalization of the state, the link between populations and the power-wielding apparatus was less close, and the implications of unequal power distributions therefore probably less painful and less far-reaching. The present-day nation-state system, is not, of course, a power monopoly. If one state were to acquire significantly more than one-half—that is, more than 50 per cent of disposable military power—the system would be moving toward such a monopoly, because the difficulties of mounting an effective counter-coalition might appear to be insurmountable. Nor is the system portrayed in the military budget accounts a tight duopoly, with the two superpowers absorbing, between themselves, 85 or more per cent of the world power; such a situation can conceivably occur after a world war and probably did occur in the late summer of 1945. Rather, it is a system of loose duopoly, with the two superpowers absorbing, between themselves 85 or more per cent of world power; such a situation can conceivably occur after a world war and probably did occur in the late summer of 1945. Rather, it is a system of loose duopoly, still rather unequal, but also one in which the two major power concentrations are approximately equal in strength, hence balanced. Such measure of autonomy as obtains within the system is the product of the balance between the duopolists; the entire system rests upon that relationship.

Representing world power distributions as shares of military expenditures recalls those calculations that are made by anti-trust economists with regards to the market shares of major firms in an oligopolistic industry. It recalls, too, that markets (organizational networks or systems) that are dominated by a few giant firms and thus in a condition of oligopolistic monopoly, tend to deteriorate into conditions of chronic instability and even cutthroat competition. As a result of the havoc that is liable to be wrought by the collapse of one of these giants, oligopolistic situations are less stable than those of either pure monopoly or perfect competition (with a large number of producers).[8] It would appear that the state system enshrines an organizational system that is inherently susceptible to violent upsets.

Table 7:8 shows, finally, power inequalities as another variable characterizing the state of the global system. Between 1965 and 1967, global military power purchased by the superpowers rose from 67 per cent to 70 per cent. During the same time period, the militarization rate also rose from 6.9 per cent to 7.3 per cent (Table 7:7). These data offer support for two hypotheses: (1) that increasing militarization of the global system is associated with rising power inequalities; and (2) that a rise in conflict intensity (in this case the Vietnam war in particular) tends to aggravate power inequalities.

Empirical evidence shows power distributions in the nation-state system to be strongly concentrated, thus strongly unequal. There are grounds for thinking that the nation-state system accentuates power inequalities. The dominance of the state—a phenomenon that entails the placing of high value on military considerations—accentuates competition for military power and the importance of power accumulation. The pressures of war associated with the system promote militarization, and thus also power inequality. The nation-state system, finally, has grossly simplified the structure of power in a global system; by making nation-states the only legitimate units of power, it is conducive to gargantuan and sometimes haphazard accumulations of strength. All this makes power equalization one of the most important problems of world politics.

Specificity of the Foreign Affairs Function

Students of foreign policy often comment upon the wide range of the "instruments of foreign policy" available to a modern decision-maker. An application of the budgetary analysis used throughout this chapter does not support such a view. In global perspective, the range of instruments available to national policy-makers in a nation-state system is extremely narrow and is restricted almost entirely to military means and resources. The nation-state system not only channels a major portion of its resources to the military function, hence directs most of its free resources to problems raised by war and the threat of war: it also starves other global problems of needed inputs, neglects them and underfinances them. Table 7:11 illustrates this state of affairs by means of some rather free-ranging estimates.

In the first place, the use and application of instruments of foreign policy is a luxury almost exclusively reserved for a few large states, in particular the Great Powers. For most of the nation-states, this game is almost entirely pointless.

TABLE 7:11   Relative Importance of Instruments of Foreign Policy, 1965
(*$U.S. billions*)

	United States	World
Military	48	140
Clandestine and intelligence	4	8–10
Economic aid	3.8	7.0
Propaganda	0.2	1–2
Diplomacy	0.3	2–3
	56.3	158.0–162.0

Sources: Table 7:8; *United States Statistical Abstract*; author's estimates.

In the second place, and more importantly, most of the resources allotted by governments to international purposes, close to 90 per cent on a world basis, relate to military affairs and war. Even the remaining few per cent are closely tied to and support military purposes. Clandestine and intelligence activities center upon the mutual surveillance of military forces, their equipment and their deployment. A large part of diplomacy has to do with making and maintaining alliances and information-gathering. Even economic aid is frequently used as a defense support or as an alliance builder. By feeding the bulk of foreign policy resources into military channels, the nation-state system restricts drastically the freedom of choice for decision-makers to the use or the threat of the use of force, or to the dispatch or control over the movement of military supplies.

Certain important consequences may be deduced from this evidence, also by way of summarizing much that has been said in this chapter. The total of resources devoted by the nation-state system to "foreign affairs" is quite large. But to the extent that national governments are at all capable of problem-solving or of exerting influence in foreign affairs, their means of doing so are extremely specialized, limited to narrow and specific purposes. The system feeds upon itself and is thus self-perpetuating. But it also structurally restricts the pursuit, at the global level, of purposes other than military. Therefore, as long as the nation-state is the dominant organization, the ability of the global system to deal with problems other than military will remain restricted. For even if national governments wanted to attack other problems (and were fitted to do so, which they are not), they lack the resources for doing it. A redirection of resources from military to other purposes and problems must await, and would bring about, basic changes in the system of world politics.

Notes to Chapter Seven

1. Bruce Russett *et al.*, *Handbook of World Political and Social Indicators*, (New Haven: Yale University Press, 1964), p. 60.
2. *Ibid.*, p. 65.
3. See also Chapter 13 below, including note 11.
4. See de Solla Price, *Big Science, Little Science*, cited.
5. Wright, *A Study of War, cited*, Appendix XXI, esp. pp. 655–657.
6. Information about recent trends in world expenditures on educational purposes is incomplete because of lack of reliable and comparable data. In the years 1964–69, these have been in the region of five per cent of world product, with no evidence for a rising trend and some contrary indications at the time of the Vietnam war.
7. See also SIPRI *Yearbook of World Armaments and Disarmament*, 1950-1968 (Yearbook for 1968-9), pp. 20, 27–8, 200–1, and *United Nations Statistical Yearbook* series on world output.
8. Kenneth Boulding, *The Organizational Revolution* (New York, 1953).

8

The
Great
Powers

SYSTEMS OF EXCLUSIVE JURISDICTIONS are particularly vulnerable to problems of disorder and injustice. Functioning by way of free agreement and "lateral cooperation," such systems lack their own formalized means of preventing friction, strife and disruptive action. They must be policed by each and every member, who, acting out of consideration for morality, custom, opinion, habit and a variety of social institutions, either refrains from disruptive behavior or restrains others from indulging in it.[1] For this type of organization, the important questions have to do with the motivation and readiness of individual units to act in a restraining or non-disruptive capacity, and the efficacy of the mechanisms of responsibility. In its basic rules, the nation-state system as such has no explicit solutions to these problems.

Systems of free agreement—that is, autonomy systems—are not by themselves inherently unstable, provided their institutional balance contains adequate provision for the restraint of disruptive behavior. But the nation-state system is short on such restraint, principally for reasons, discussed in the preceding chapter, of nation-state dominance. Problems of order therefore assume particular gravity; but, because of the unequal distribution of power, only a few mighty states command the resources that are needed to cope with them. It is upon these states that responsibility for order devolves; they, in turn, being intent upon contributing to world order, necessarily have to cultivate their military power.

The nation-state system must, therefore, place certain responsibilities on at least a few states that are capable of assuming the task. But the requirements of free agreement, as well as the rules of the system, prevent the permanent establishment of structures of authority. They prohibit the interference by some states in the exclusive jurisdiction of other states, by declaring that all states have equal rights, and enshrine the national interest as the supreme motivation of action. The resulting compromise between the requirements for order and the rules of the nation-state system (along with the demands for autonomy) is the Great Power institution.

Great Power authority is an ordering device of the nation-state system. Yet, because of its implicit contempt for some of the rules of the system, it has been largely unrecognized in the formal structure of international society. International Law, on the whole, tactfully ignores it in books on the law of peace, because it conflicts with norms of independence and equality. Diplomatic historians take it for granted but rarely describe it; students of world politics hardly ever analyze it, except for occasionally exulting in its power. Yet that authority itself is still the central fact of world politics today.

The Great Power Institution

The Great Power Institution is the basic authority structure of the nation-state system. It consists of offices of authority occupied by a small set of nation-states which, upon "acceding" assume the role and status of Great Powers. Once in office, their behavior is governed by certain well-understood but not often enough explicated rules and expectations. A complementary set of rules and expectations governs the behavior of the non-Great Powers, often called the "small powers."

The status of Great Power is sometimes confused with the conditions of being powerful. The office, as it is now known, did in fact evolve from the role played by the great military states in earlier periods; and powerful states have customarily arrogated to themselves special privileges. But the Great Power system institutionalizes the position of the powerful state in a web of rights and obligations. The institution itself may be imprecisely defined, imperfectly understood and weakly implanted in the social matrix; but it is there and it therefore needs to be analyzed.

The institutionalizing of the Great Powers may be dated from 1815 and the Congress of Vienna, which ushered in a century of peace, adjusted from time to time by the operation of the "Concert of Europe." The institution is not at all an inherent feature of all international politics, but rather a feature of fairly sophisticated political arrangements. Vienna was the first occasion on which the affairs of the entire continent, and much else besides, were settled by a committee of the representatives of the major states. The previous global settlement, that which followed upon the Treaty of Utrecht (1713), was still only bilateral British-French agreement, the basic terms of which were later incorporated into more than a dozen other bilateral treaties, although even here certain prototypic features of Great Power authority could be discerned: the framework of the debates and of the ultimate settlement was set by the initiative of two of the most powerful states; the principle of the Balance of Power, and hence concern for the state of the system, was expressly spelled out in the treaty. But this inchoate feeling of the unity of political fate had not yet translated itself into an institution. The Peace of Westphalia (1648) qualifies even less as an instance of the functioning of the Great Power institution; it established independence as a fundamental principle of the system of states, but what it inaugurated was only the first French bid for hegemony, rather than an era of Great Power authority.

The Great Power institution is not a single-power hegemony; instead, it assumes the co-functioning of at least two strong states in a joint authority structure. Earlier global systems did from time to time contain power structures involving two or more strong states: the Spring and Autumn, and the Warring States periods of Chinese history (VIII-III centuries B.C.); the relations between Athens and Sparta at the height of the Greek city state system (5th cent., B.C.); post-Alexandrine states in the Near East (3rd to 1st cent. B.C.); some aspects of Ottoman-Persian-Mogul relations in the Islamic world system of the fourteenth and fifteenth centuries, and a few others. In none of these cases was the system regularized to the point where a joint structure of authority may be said to have emerged. None of these systems had a degree of cohesion, or means of access and communication, including a diplomatic network, that was commensurate with those of the nineteenth- and twentieth-century worlds.

The term "Great Powers" entered into diplomatic language at the time of the formation of the institution in 1814-15.[2] Its formal adoption in a scholarly context may be traced to Leopold Ranke's seminal essay entitled, "The Great Powers," which was published in a semi-official Prussian journal in 1833.[3] The essay was a thumbnail sketch of the preceding century and a half of history, as shaped by French hegemonic aspirations under Louis XIV and Napoleon. While it did not offer any extensive analytical treatment of the Great Power system, it was notable in a number of respects: for giving wide currency to the concept of Great Powers; for its definition of a Great Power as a state that "must be able to maintain itself (in war) against all others, even when they are united" (a statement that was meant to establish the point at which Prussia acceded to that status (1756), but which has since been used as the basis of a definition of Great Powers in general).[4] The interesting aspect of this definition is the close link it reveals between Great Power status and wars and, in particular, *great* wars—those in which several powerful states participate. Finally, Ranke's analysis brought out the relationship between the emergence of the Great Powers in the century prior to the French Revolution and the working of the Balance of Power system: "the concept of the European Balance of Power was developed in order that the union of many other states might resist the pretensions of the exorbitant Court," which was the way in which there actually did emerge "the rise of the Great Powers in the defense of European independence." Ranke recognized even the nationalization of the state as part of this process, seeing "nationalities . . . rejuvenated, revived and developed . . . become a part of the state, for without them the state would not exist."

The term Great Powers signaled the emergence, in place of family monarchies, of the great military states that were soon to become ends-in-themselves, rather than merely means for the preservation of dynasties—a process enlarged upon earlier in this work. But this raised some difficulties for seeing the Powers as part of a European, and ultimately a worldwide system of authority. The difficulties revolve around the fact that the Great Power system is based on organizational authority: the office of authority is occupied not by individuals but by organizations—that is, by states. Yet in most of political life authority is personal.

The devolution of international authority from the person of monarch, emperor or pope, to an impersonal organization, the state, has been a source of confusion, of imprecision and of instability. Authority needs to be based on loyalty, and loyalty can be both personal and organizational. But if a nation-state is to be the object of loyalty, how is it to command loyalty from individuals other than its own nationals? Great political leaders of the global system—John F. Kennedy, Winston Churchill, Franklin Roosevelt, Woodrow Wilson—did in the past command a loyalty that was, indeed, personal but also facilitated the fulfillment of their leadership role in the Great Power system. But such personalities are few and far between, and a global authority system cannot depend on the accidental emergence of personalities at the right moment in the right place. On a continuous basis, the great nation-states are incapable of generating wide support for their authority.

Authority, moreover, needs also to be responsive. Yet a nation-state, by the rules of the system, is responsive first and foremost to the needs of its own organization and its own nation, defined as the national interest. How then is it to do justice to the claims and demands of all the other members of the global system? The nation-state, as a limited-purpose organization for the production of public services for a limited territorial jurisdiction, cannot be assigned global rights and obligations, without its purposes being confounded, its priorities deranged, both the nation and the global system grievously destabilized. Only robust structures can withstand the strains that ensue, and even they not for long.

The Great Powers

The basic list of the Great Powers for the period 1815-1970 is shown in Table 8:1. This is important to note, because it reveals that the world's experience of Great Powers has been rather limited. No amount of abstract speculation can surmount the fundamental fact that the world has so far known only nine Great Powers, in the sense in which the term is used in this chapter. Of these nine, perhaps only four or five have had a massive impact upon the institution. The generalizations presented below result from the confrontation of these limited, though suggestive, data with the model of the nation-state system.

The criteria for inclusion on the list of Great Powers have been formal ones, but they parallel the rules of eligibility for Great Power status (to be discussed below). They are, for the nineteenth century, participation in the processes and procedures of the Concert of Europe; for the Versailles system, permanent membership in the Council of the League of Nations; for the System of 1945, permanent membership in the Security Council of the United Nations. These are the states that have been publicly and formally recognized by other Great Powers, and by other members of the global system, as occupying that status and therefore bearing special responsibilities in world politics. All others have been no more than aspirants or claimants to that office, or else "influentials out of office";

TABLE 8:1   The Great Powers, 1815–1970

	Entry and exit	Thermonuclear weapon tested	Remarks
Austria-Hungary (The Hapsburg Monarchy)	1815–1918	—	The Dual Monarchy was dissolved in 1918.
Britain	1815–	1957	Permanent member, U.N. Security Council.
Prussia, Germany	1815–1945	—	Status uncertain 1918–25. Occupied after World War II.
Russia, U.S.S.R.	1815–	1953	Permanent member, U.N. Security Council. Status uncertain 1917–33.
France	1815–	1967	Status uncertain 1940–45. Permanent member, U.N. Security Council.
Italy	1870–1943	—	Occupied in World War II.
U.S.A.	1900–	1952	Permanent member, U.N. Security Council.
Japan	1900–1945	—	Occupied after World War II.
China	1945–	(1965)	Permanent member, U.N. Security Council. (Seat assumed by Peking government, 1971)

there is no doubt that they have been important at certain junctions of world affairs, but they have also been unable to clothe their international behavior in the formal dignity of the world's most important office.

The list shows that the truly important members of this cast were at first, Britain and France; then, for a time, Germany; and more recently, the United States and the Soviet Union (although Russia's status as a great state dates back to the eighteenth century). Britain alone among them can boast an uninterrupted tenure of close to two centuries—a fact that goes a long way toward explaining British diplomatic influence. The great states have been those with global interests; they have been mostly European or European-oriented states. The non-European world—that is, the Third World—has never been adequately represented within this system.

The list omits certain important actors of the European and world historical scene. Portugal, Spain and Sweden, for instance, were, along with the five powers named, also major participants in the Congress of Vienna and original signatories of its documents. But they were not members of the inner councils where the decisions were made, and that was the last occasion on which they appeared in a major conference among the principal powers. For Spain, it was the last act of a great global career. Others of the first rank in the European states system of the earlier era were Denmark, Holland (the Dutch States-General) and Poland. In the Versailles period, a number of states, including Brazil, Poland and Spain, contended for permanent representation on the Council of the League of Nations, but the League Covenant was never amended to that effect. Since 1945, the right to permanent membership on the Security Council has not been the subject of dispute, except in the case of China (and there it was other grounds). Japan has so far made the most persistent bid for such a position though at certain times India enjoyed considerable influence and undoubtedly had aspirations to the role.

Once again, emphasis must be laid upon the distinction between important, or strong, or powerful countries, and a Great Power. The distinction is one between informal influence (being the presumed effect of power, or skill, or persistence) and formal office. As an office, Great Power status carries with it certain rights and duties, individual privileges and some obligations to the entire system—all of which make it an official position, and one that is not necessarily commensurate with the influence exerted. The Ambassador of West Germany at the United Nations, for instance, wields considerable influence because of the substantial contributions made by his country to various international programs, and without even being a member of that organization. The representative of Nationalist China on the United Nations Security Council, on the other hand, was, for years, entitled to cast a veto and to exercise certain other privileges of Great Power status, but his influence was at best rather marginal.

The Superpowers

The formal institutions of the System of 1945 were designed for a five-power system. Both the United Nations and the Council of Foreign Ministers, agreed upon at the Potsdam conference and empowered to negotiate the peace treaties, were to be under the authority of the five powers who became the permanent members of the Security Council.

The course of events since 1945 has put this system into considerable disarray. The role of China soon became untenable on account of the civil war situation, and then became entangled in the question of recognition for the Chinese People's Republic, the result being the virtual removal of China from issues of global authority until 1971. The role of Britain and France also was put to question (though much more slowly than in the case of China) by virtue of the reduction in their global responsibilities, and the reduction of their commitments outside Europe, which followed the liquidation of their colonial empires. The United States and the Soviet Union were the only powers left in the field with truly global interests and resources.

Table 8:2 documents the process of the emergence of the superpowers and highlights certain of its characteristics. Three phases may be distinguished here. In Phase One (from Tehran to Potsdam) the leaders of the United States, Britain and the Soviet Union laid out the structure of the postwar world: in three major conferences they constructed the outlines of the System of 1945; their Foreign Ministers, together with the French, slowly negotiated the peace treaties with Italy, Hungary, Rumania and Bulgaria and, finally, with Austria (1955). This last agreement paved the way for Phase Two, the post-Stalin transition meetings at Geneva, and in Paris, the latter turning out to be a complete fiasco as the result of the U-2 plane incident. No new Four-Power summit meeting has even been attempted since Paris.

Phase Three overlaps Phase Two. In it the emphasis shifted completely to bilateral meetings. The trend was set by the Camp David meeting, in some ways perhaps the most critical of postwar encounters. Its subject was disarmament; among its consequences were the inauguration of semipermanent disarmament talks, and the discontinuation of Soviet nuclear weapons assistance to China (along with the onset of the Sino-Soviet conflict). Since Camp David the United States President normally has met (but no more than once) with his opposite number in the Kremlin. Such meetings have been marked by informality and by low institutionalization: they may serve as little more than "getting-to-know-you-better" occasions, and thus they make few authoritative decisions; but they inevitably have global significance and widely felt consequences.

TABLE 8:2 Summit meetings, System of 1945 (1943–1970) *

Participants	Place	Date	Foreign Ministers Present	Subjects
USA (Roosevelt) USSR (Stalin) UK (Churchill)	Tehran, Iran	November 1943	—	War strategy, postwar plans
USA (Roosevelt) USSR (Stalin) UK (Churchill)	Yalta, USSR	February 1945	Yes	Postwar settlement in Euope and Asia
USA (Truman) USSR (Stalin) UK (Churchill, Attlee)	Potsdam, Germany	July–August 1945	Yes	Postwar settlement
USA (Eisenhower) USSR (Bulganin, Khrushchev) UK (Eden) France (Faure)	Geneva, Switzerland	July 1955	Yes	Post-Stalin relaxation of tensions
USA (Eisenhower) USSR (Khrushchev)	Camp David, Md., USA	September 1959	No	Disarmament
USA (Eisenhower) USSR (Khrushchev) UK (Macmillan) France (de Gaulle)	Paris, France	May 1960	Yes	Aborted
USA (Kennedy) USSR (Khrushchev)	Vienna, Austria	June 1961	Yes	Laos, Germany
USA (Johnson) USSR (Kosygin)	Glassboro, N.J., USA	June 1967	No	Middle East

* Includes all multilateral Great Power head of government meetings and all bilateral American-Soviet meetings, but not other bilateral Great Power head of government meetings (such as American-British, French-Soviet, etc.).

They have been paralleled by bilateral talks among the leaders of the other Great Powers; the American-Soviet exchanges, however, appear to be the most important.

The preeminence of the United States and the Soviet Union has rested in the first place upon their superior position in the world's military pecking order. Since World War II they have borne by themselves most of the burdens of Great Power status (see Table 8:3, p. 162). They have maintained military establishments of Class I rank (see also Table 7:8), so that disarmament questions concerned them most of all. Their joint authority in this sphere has been symbolized, since 1959, by co-chairmanship of the world's major disarmament negotiating body in Geneva, known for years as the Eighteen-nations Disarmament Committee and, since 1969, as the Conference of the Committee on Disarmament. The Strategic Arms Limitation Talks (initiated at Helsinki and Vienna in 1969) have again demonstrated the special status of the two powers.

In recognition of the strong military position they have both occupied since 1945, the United States and the Soviet Union have, from about 1960, emerged with a new international status—one that, in ordinary language and increasingly in official pronouncements, is referred to as that of super-powers. It might be added that the transition was hastened by a form of electoral process among non-Great Power governments, particularly of the Third World. Some were skeptical about the Paris meeting even before it started and its swift debacle gave them added ammunition. When many of the world's leaders gathered for the 1960 session of the United Nations General Assembly, they were in effect holding their own universal summit conference. Acting on behalf of the non-aligned nations, the leaders of Ghana, Yugoslavia, India, Indonesia and the United Arab Republic sponsored a resolution urging the United States and the Soviet Union to resume the contact that had been broken off at Paris, but they pointedly ignored Britain and France. In the following year the Belgrade Conference of Non-Aligned Nations sent special missions to Washington and Moscow, but once again they ignored London and Paris. Lack of "electoral" global support thus diminished the Great Power standing of Britain and France, and eased the way for the superpowers.[5]

But the crystallization of superpower status, especially on questions of nuclear survival, has not disposed of the acquired rights of the remaining Great Powers. For United Nations purposes, Britain and France retain a Great Power status, and France's refusal to meet financial assessments for peace-keeping operations has shown the ease with which United Nations designs can be thwarted by non-cooperative Great Powers. For purposes of general nuclear disarmament the full set of five nuclear weapon states is obviously indispensable. For Middle Eastern affairs, Britain and France have joined, since 1969, with the United States and the Soviet Union in seeking ways of restoring and maintaining peace, thus asserting a measure of authority. For Far Eastern purposes, the full set of five Great Powers (including China, as represented by Peking) was brought into the settlement of the Korean and Indochinese (Geneva 1954) and the Laotian (Geneva 1961-2) questions.

The position of the superpowers is far from firmly grounded and lacks constitutional organization. France and China have not recognized it. Western Europe's resurgence, Britain's closer association with it, and China's return to global authority will all encourage tendencies toward a wider sharing of authority among all the Great Powers. The world is therefore missing a completely coherent structure of authority. In part, however, this incoherence derives from the nature of Great Power authority itself, which loses definition in the periods "between" the great peace settlements. It makes for a fluid and flexible system which might move in a number of alternative directions.

Recruitment to Great Power Status

Not all states, and not all nation-states, become Great Powers; in fact, only four have joined the ranks since the original group took shape in 1814-15. What factors, then, determine eligibility of states for this office? What are the recruitment procedures? What are the factors that lead to exclusion from this role?

The basic precondition for "Great Power timber" is the possession of military power. Great Powers are, above everything else, great military (and naval) states. They do not all command forces of equal standing, but, at least in principle, they must be capable of fighting a major war. By derivation, the economic and industrial capacity for raising, equipping and sustaining a strong military force is also essential. More recently, nuclear capability has been a test of Great Power status; all states that have been entitled to such status in the United Nations had, by 1967, completed tests of thermonuclear weapons (Table 8:1). It remains to be seen whether or how the promotion of additional states to nuclear status will affect the question of authority.

Ranke's definition of Great Power status as the capacity to stand off the assault of other powers still conveys adequately the flavor of the essential military qualification. Through the mechanism of nuclear deterrence, a well-prepared nuclear state is in fact protected from attack by any other atomic power. But a power that fails to maintain a credible military posture, as shown by its losing face in a military encounter or indeed losing a war (for instance, Russia in 1905 or 1917, or France in 1940), loses for a time its standing as a Great Power. Thence comes the unremitting preoccupation of the leaders of the military states with their military standing and the maintenance of a strong home base, and the ceaseless striving of their governments to maintain forces at a competitive level.

Alongside military power, the other qualifications pale into insignificance. But a political institution does need to be representative of the system it serves, if it is to function effectively, and the question might be asked about the degree to which considerations of representativeness have any influence on eligibility for Great Power status. Most of the historical Great Powers were European or, like the United States, affiliated with Europe. The Ottoman Empire was part of the European diplomatic system for centuries but it never entered that system on the authoritative and legitimate basis of a Great Power. The first outsider to penetrate the charmed circle was Japan, by dint of its victory over Russia in 1905. When defeat overtook it in 1945, it seemed appropriate that the ranks of the Great Powers be replenished by a representative of Asia and the Far East. This, together with the sheer size of her armies, promoted China's position at the expense of Japan's.

Many are qualified, but few are chosen. The basic fact about the Great Power institution is the process of self-selection by which it has organized itself. It is in fact a "club" (or "concert"), whose initial membership was the product of the anti-Napoleonic alliance that won the peace in 1814-15 and to which, in a spirit of far-sighted generosity, reconstructed Bourbon France was admitted without much delay. The nucleus of the institution was thus built upon the intensified personal and organizational contacts and the solidarities engendered by the Napoleonic wars, soon to be reinforced by the expansion of railways and trade throughout Europe and the world.

To this basic group, additions were made as time went on. The procedure of admission has been one of cooption; that is, existing members of the "concert" have reached agreement among themselves to let in a new member. Each entrance has usually entailed the services of a sponsor, in high standing, from among the sitting powers. Thus Bismarck sponsored Italy; Britain legitimized Japan's position by entering into an alliance with her; and in 1944-45 the United States successfully advanced the claims of Chiang Kai-shek, despite the shaky position of his government. On occasion, sponsorship has also taken the negative form of blackballing: thus, the question of recognition for Peking has entailed, after 1949, China's seat in the Security Council and her claim to Great Power status, while nonrecognition has carried with it the more important consequence of denial of status.

Just as a successful war serves as the initiation rite for a new Great Power (and stress needs to be put upon "successful"—that is, finishing the war as part of the winning coalition), so the exit procedures are closely tied to wars. Austria-Hungary lost status when the ancient monarchy broke up at the end of the First World War; Germany, Italy and Japan, having suffered defeat in the Second World War, ceased to count as Great Powers. The status of Britain and France, although weakened because of that war, was maintained because of their participation in the winning coalition. In the nineteenth century, France's defeats in 1814 and 1870 did not, on the other hand, affect her status, and Germany too was readmitted following the 1918 defeat.

Since 1945, the United Nations has played an increasing part in determining a country's status. Services to the organization and to the global community can now be rewarded by elevation to a permanent seat on the Security Council, and a general increment in status. Since this can occur only through a Charter amendment, requiring the consent of two-thirds of the membership, the process would be akin to an election, even though the consent of all the existing permanent members would still be required, thus maintaining the cooptative features of the traditional system. Sponsorship would no doubt, also be required in practice, and it is conceivable that Japan could be the first of such reelected, re-coopted members of the institution. China's position too, was being annually reappraised through closely watched votes in the General Assembly; her regaining her United Nations status therefore also depended in one sense on an election process. Finally, the role of Britain and France, as earlier pointed out, has been affected by their lack of support among the non-aligned states of the Third World.

Some analysts attach importance to the number of Great Powers in a global system.[6] The list of Great Powers answers this question for any given point of time. For the System of 1945, however, no simple answer is sufficient. If attention is restricted to the superpowers, the system would have to be called bipolar; if Security Council membership is taken into account, too, the system becomes multipolar. For purposes of classification, contemporary world politics might thus be seen as at least two-dimensional, depending upon the context and the issues. It is the increasing complexity that adds interest to this study because it could foreshadow some important changes. In a situation in which the Great Power Institution itself was losing validity, the number of powers calling themselves "Great" would become irrelevant.

Rights and Duties of Great Powers

The rights and duties of the Great Powers are the response of the nation-state system to the need for the authoritative resolution of certain problems. These problems are most often linked with war, or with crisis situations that threaten to bring about armed conflict. The Munich Conference of 1938 is a good example of Great Power decision-making called for by an escalating war crisis. While the rights and duties of Great Powers may be observed most clearly on occasions of authoritative decision, the expectations they engender are, of course, more pervasive, and affect much of general international behavior.

The exercise of Great Power prerogatives and obligations takes place in two types of situation: (1) within the context of joint decisions and (2) through individual action. Each needs to be examined in turn.

The crucial exercise of Great Power authority takes place at the conclusion of a major war. At that juncture, the winning coalition—with or without the cooperation of the losers—reconstructs the state system and lays down the framework of the ensuing peace. The fundamental and constitutive character of these occasions needs stressing, because they tend to be glossed over as part of the exceptional exigencies of war. Yet it is precisely in those emergency conditions of war and of the immediate post-war era that the structure of the succeeding peace period is determined.

The universe of cases from which these statements are derived is rather limited. The modern state system has known only five peace settlements of a general character: Westphalia (1648), Utrecht (1713–14), Vienna (1815), Versailles (1919) and Yalta-Potsdam (1945) (see also Table 14:1). The first was an international congress, meeting in two parts in the cities of Muenster and Osnabruck; the second was a series of bilateral settlements; only the last three can be called instances of the operation of the Great Power Institution. In Westphalia and Utrecht, individual strong states exercised preponderant influence over the terms of the settlement—France over the first, and Britain, with France, over the second—but the Institution itself had not yet taken shape.

When the Great Powers came together to put an end to a great war, on each of these occasions, the settlements were truly architectonic, both in intent and in actual fact. The men who drew them up worked on a huge canvas. They reconstructed old states and constituted new ones, redrew frontiers, installed and confirmed rulers and governments, shifted populations, regulated armies and fortifications, reassigned colonies and drew up new rules of international law and relations. Issues that at any other time would have taken years of intricate negotiations, replete with crises and misunderstandings, were sometimes settled in a few hours of discussion among the chiefs of government of the Great Powers. The status and the future disposition of large parts of the global system were suddenly free and under review. Great Power authority between great wars derives fundamentally from these postwar settlements.

At the conclusion of great wars the Great Powers have customarily exercised the right to build the edifice of peace. The general exhaustion that follows in the wake of great conflicts has given them this opportunity to clean-sweep established rights and institutions: a major war leaves behind it a devastated and enfeebled landscape; the losers have fled the battlefield, and have been replaced by more pliable personalities. The victorious Great Powers are never as close to holding the monopoly of power nor ever more unequally strong and overpowering than at the opening of peace. Flushed with the heat of victory, their triumphant forces extend over the entire system; they are ready to enforce joint decisions. No one dares resist them. Assured of overwhelming strength and unchallenged by competing authority, the Great Powers are the sole imaginable sources of decision-making. Thus, great wars and their aftermaths provide the opportunities and set the scene for the exercise of Great Power authority.

The thoroughness and comprehensiveness of such postwar settlements, together with their near-cataclysmic impact upon some areas and some peoples, precludes frequent recourse to drastic solutions because no society can tolerate perpetual turmoil. Of necessity, then, this essential occasion for Great Power authority must remain intermittent; such rights as the Powers do have remain restricted to great emergencies. An interval of at least one generation has thus marked these settlements; some have lasted as long as a century.

The argument might be advanced that a system as inflexible as the international state system, with its entrenched sovereignties, hallowed privileges and co-opted clienteles, stands in need, from time to time, of such drastic overhauls. The rigidity of the system and weakness of its system-wide institutions calls for an occasional letup, not only in a great war as an orgiastic outbreak of suppressed urges and inhibitions, but also in the sweeping character of the subsequent reconstruction. But is a nuclear cataclysm admissible as a method for correcting the accumulated rigidities and injustices of the system of '45? If the political system can no longer afford to cure its infirmities through such periodic shakeups, what alternative structure can be devised to take its place?

Intermittency (as contrasted with continuity) as a characteristic of Great Power authority is also the chief feature of the Great Power role in "interwar" periods. In these, lesser issues arise, together with complications that have been created by earlier decisions and the Great Powers take them up. Since 1945, for instance, they have been concerned continuously with the status of Germany and, especially, of Berlin. Whenever a crisis threatens international peace and stability (for instance, in May 1967, when President Nasser ordered the closing of the Straits of Tiran), the Powers must express concern; they are expected to assume responsibility, and sometimes they do succeed in calming the situation. But the Great Powers do not and cannot provide a continuous government: they may be in permanent diplomatic contact and, on occasion, engage in frequent and formal consultations; but most often they disagree (because the serious crises are usually of their own making). The chief reason why they do not constitute a continuous government is that they cannot make use of effective organs of common action.

The characteristic of "interwar" situations is lack of overwhelming physical and moral superiority. What the Powers are able to invoke is derivative claims to initiative, based on their responsibility for peace; on the strength of these, they seek to exploit their potential military influence at the locale of the crisis. Interventions of this kind tend to be less effective and less convincing. The back-up force for authoritative action is costly and risky, and it takes time to assemble. In May 1967, at a time when the United States was already fighting in Vietnam, it had one week in which to act, so as to secure for Israel guaranteed rights of access to the Red Sea; it did not act, and a war was on. Peace in the Middle East has eluded the Great Powers for more than two decades.

The other basic feature of Great Power authority is its limited scope: its exercise has been confined to the interlocking complex of territorial, military, and structural issues that constitute the staple diet of the nation-state system. The substance of these decisions has to do, first and foremost, with territorial questions: the boundaries, regimes and governments of individual states, and all the ways in which established boundaries and systems could be disturbed. The stability of the territorial settlement is a matter of concern, as is the stability and composition of individual governments. The production and distribution of weapons, including nuclear weapons, and questions of arms limitations and test bans also preeminently concern them. Finally, after each great war, the Great Powers have fashioned anew the constitutional structure of the global system; in effect, they were the architects of the nation-state system, and of its main institutional features: diplomacy and the various international organizations. The Great Power Institution is crucial to the functioning of the nation-state system, but it is not a general-purpose government (just as it is not a continuous government), able and willing to process the myriad issues that are capable of arousing the interest of members of the global system. It is not an institution that is responsive to all the potential demands of the world system, but only to a few.

Through the exercise of authority that is often only grudgingly conceded, the Great Powers are expected to uphold world order and to defend the general interest. This is commonly seen as the duty to maintain peace. "The special position which has been granted to the Great Powers for more than a century," said an official British Government commentary on the Charter of the United Nations, is due to them because upon them is placed "the main responsibility for the maintenance of international peace and security." [7] Keeping the peace does not exhaust the requirements of world interest, yet the Great Powers do not bear any special responsibilities or obligations for the many other issues that are likely to crowd the global agendas and that ultimately lie at the root of threats to peace and order.

Because of common duties of the Powers with respect to peace, the stability of the territorial order and the distribution of military power, the Powers share some important interests. But in certain other fields they might also clash. Students of international politics tend to emphasize the conflictual aspects of Great Power relations; they argue the existence of a fundamental conflict of interests, for instance, between the "satisfied" (status quo powers) and other (revolutionary) states, whose unsatisfied aspirations inevitably clash with the former's conservative aims.

Conflict—not merely competition—among the Great Powers is unquestionably strong. Some powers have, for significant periods, rejected meaningful participation in the international system, while demanding a larger allocation of its benefits. The Soviet Union in the revolutionary phases of its foreign policies since 1917; Germany, Italy and Japan after 1933; and China, in the mid-nineteen sixties—all these have authored antistatus quo and radical positions that set them clearly at variance with the other Great Powers. At such times and in such contexts, the Great Power institution has lost much of its usefulness and its validity.

But these instances, important though they may have been in shaping much of world politics, should not obscure the fact that, at other times and in other contexts, the Great Powers have shown themselves to have a number of interests in common. They have an important stake in peace, not only because their position of authority rests upon the ability to maintain peace, but also because, as the largest producers of military power, they are most likely to have to carry the unpredictable expenses of war and to suffer the punishing costs of its campaigns. In a nuclear exchange, for example, they would be the first to suffer devastating damage. As Great Powers, they also have interests that set them apart from non-great powers such as maintaining the Great Power Institution, keeping smaller powers "in their proper place," and, generally, preserving their own special prerogatives.

This "collusive" aspect of Great Power authority can assume an oppressive character and, on occasions in the past, it has attracted unfavorable notice. Some aspects of the post-Vienna "concert" came to be seen as an "unholy alliance," by means of which the Great Power governments undertook to repress liberal regimes throughout Europe, and even planned to extend such activity to South America (at which point Britain dissociated itself from the concert, and the United States proclaimed the Monroe Doctrine). Great Power cooperation—for instance, in the suppression of the Boxer Rebellion, or in quelling colonial disturbances—sometimes has a "world policeman" aspect to it, as has mutual acquiescence in claims to a sphere of influence.

Spheres of influence serve as reminders that Great Powers claim authority not only in joint but also in individual action. In the present context, individual action refers to governmental behavior that is appropriate to the Great Power role and is thus analytically distinguishable from action taken solely in pursuit of the national interest.

When states act in an authoritative or "official" capacity, that action derives its meaning from the functions that the Great Powers perform in the nation-state system. It must be action that is capable of being understood, explained and justified on grounds of maintenance of regional or world peace and order. The boundary between justified Great Power action and unilateral intervention, however, is hard to draw: does the landing of troops in support of a weak government (Lebanon 1958; the Eisenhower Doctrine) fall within the scope of legitimate activity? Does demanding the withdrawal of medium-range missiles from Cuba (1962)? Do worldwide nuclear test monitoring and satellite surveillance? or landing troops to protect the Suez Canal (Britain and France, 1956)? The last instance was most certainly not widely accepted as legitimate.

A "sphere of influence" might optimistically be defined as an area in which one Great Power assumes exclusive responsibility for the maintenance of peace. In terms of political analysis, it denotes a situation in which one power has acquired a monopoly or a near monopoly for its services to that area. Two sets of conditions interact to facilitate such monopoly: (1) high transport and communication costs for locally delivered military power, favoring one state over others (a natural regional monopoly); and (2) collusion, where the world is divided by agreement among the powers —a form of "market-sharing" that can offer stability in exchange for higher-priced security.

The historical political systems never did know a perfect market for military power and therefore supported local monopolies of all kinds. Globalization has been a process of perfecting markets; the growth of sea power drastically cut the cost of power transfer and eliminated the need for the far-flung and costly overheads of camps, stores, fortresses and forces in being that were required by immobile land armies. Sea power not only eliminated small local monopolies, however, it also created a large new monopoly. British naval supremacy in the nineteenth century created a series of British spheres of influence all over the world. The proximity of the United States to the Caribbean area lent some degree of substance to the Monroe Doctrine in the nineteenth and early twentieth centuries. In the contemporary world, however, global power is air- and missile-borne to every point of the earth at short notice; thanks to reconnaissance satellites, the entire earth surface can be continuously kept under surveillance by every major power. These factors drastically reduce the costs of resources, information, and decision-making with regard to military power delivery; they thus undermine the natural advantages that have traditionally been held by certain states in certain areas—for instance by China over Korea and Indochina.

There remains *collusion.* If Great Powers were to agree among themselves that spheres of influence are desirable as being conducive to peace [8] (also as making matters simpler for their political leaders), then such an arrangement might persist, even if its "natural" justification had disappeared. The term "sphere of influence" originally gained currency late in the nineteenth century, when Asia and Africa were being parceled out among competing European powers. In 1907, Britain and Russia reached a famous agreement for the delimitation of their respective spheres in Persia. The Molotov-Ribbentrop pact in August 1939 opened a contest for spheres of influence in Eastern Europe.[9] Japan's wartime "Co-Prosperity Sphere" was a crude attempt to do the same thing in East and Southeast Asia. In contemporary world politics, spheres of influence are no longer publicly delimited in explicit treaties. But Great Powers still reach agreement on such matters—sometimes verbally, sometimes tacitly. The classic example of such a deal, which is still relevant to the "System of 1945" was the understanding reached between Churchill and Stalin, in 1944, about the distribution of British and Soviet influence in the Balkans, once these areas had been reoccupied by Allied troops. In a spirit of almost light-hearted banter, Churchill drew a series of percentage distributions alongside a row of the names of Balkan countries—Greece: (Great Britain in accord with the U.S.A.) 90%, (Russia) 10%; Yugoslavia: 50% for each, and so forth. Stalin agreed without much discussion. In his memoirs, the then American Secretary of State, Cordell Hull, commented with apprehension upon this transaction.[10]

In the wake of the Soviet invasion of Czechoslovakia, a spokesman for the State Department asserted that "The United States has never entered into a sphere-of-interest agreement or understanding with anyone, anywhere in the world," and denied allegations of indifference to the Soviet operation.[11] This sounded, however, rather like a case of protesting too much. Technically, of course, the Monroe Doctrine was not an agreement; [12] but it had received the acquiescence of many powers, and of Britain in particular (before the claims were abandoned in favor of the Good Neighbor Policy). Well-modulated Soviet reactions to British and later American activities in Greece (1944-49), along with mild American reactions to Soviet activities in Hungary (1956) and Czechoslovakia (1968), suggest that some concept of spheres of influence was at work there on both sides. Despite later disclaimers to the contrary, the understandings at Yalta and Potsdam seem to have amounted to acquiescence in an effective zone of Soviet influence all over Eastern Europe.

The post-1945 arrangement that has been nearest to the sphere of influence is the exclusive military alliance. Such a defense system entails the exchange of military protection for the acceptance of hegemonic (Great or Superpower) status in intergovernmental dealings. Some alliances are more multilateral than others, and thus tend to dilute the effects of simple dependency—(for instance NATO, with three Great Powers); most have strong elements of Great Power dominance, and therefore some aspects of protection. In Eastern Europe, the Warsaw Pact has served to legitimize both the Hungarian and the Czechoslovak cases of Soviet intervention; it thus rivals Communist Party links in its importance as an instrument of Soviet control. A world that is marked by unequal power distribution and bipolar concentrations tends to produce spheres of influence.

As a principle of world politics, the idea of spheres of influence is incompatible with the rules of the nation-state system, especially if it is interpreted (like the "Brezhnev Doctrine," which was evolved in the aftermath of the Czechoslovak affair) to mean the right to interfere with national governmental functions. It has yet to be shown whether the demand for military protection will decline sufficiently for its price to fall, so that security will become easily accessible to all governments. Will collusion become for that reason more difficult in the future? Strong arguments might be advanced to the effect that, by acting individually, Great Powers are even more likely to abuse their rights than when they act collectively or by common consent. Historically, however, spheres-of-influence arrangements have outlived their usefulness, and the world would probably be a better place without them. They are no longer needed to feed either vainglorious conceptions of imperial greatness or false fears of military security. There are no parts of the world left where either governmental weakness or local irresponsibility make them unavoidable.

Legitimacy of Great Power Authority

The irrelevance of normative concerns to the behavior of Great Powers, as well as to international politics in general, has been a basic tenet of the theorists of the nation-state system. A frequently quoted dictum is the one reported in "The History of the Peloponnesian War" by Thucydides as having been part of a speech by Athenian envoys to the Melians: "The strong do what they can and the weak submit." [13] Another oft-quoted homily of the same genre is the observation that "The big fish eat the little fish." Small fry should take heart from the fact that, through the progress of civilization, man's intensive fishing of the larger species has made life distinctly uncomfortable for the bigger sea creatures, some of which are threatened with extinction at the very same time as the little fish continue to proliferate. In that regard, "Blessed are the meek, for they shall inherit the earth" [14] may be an injunction that is closer to the spirit of modern civilization than are the lessons of the Peloponnesian War.

The Athenian envoys had gone to Melos, a small settlement in the Sea of Crete, to request abandonment of the stance of neutrality in the war and submission to their hegemony. To the blunt formulation of a right of the strong (quoted above), the Melians replied "In our opinion, it is in your interest to maintain a principle which is for the good of all—that anyone in danger should have just and equitable treatment and any advantage, even if not strictly his due, that he can secure by persuasion. This is your interest as much as ours, for your fall would involve you in a crushing punishment that would be a lesson to the world." [15] But their arguments carried no weight and hostilities were soon commenced. After a year's siege, the Melians surrendered at the discretion of the Athenians, who put to death all the grown men they took, and sold the women and children into slavery. The war went on for years, until Athens' hegemony was destroyed.

Basic to this analysis of world authority is the view that the Great Power Institution, founded though it may be upon large power inequalities, is nevertheless more than a mere power structure or the application of brute force. Not only is it an institution that responds to certain needs of the nation-state system; it also reflects (it does not only determine) certain constellations of social and political values. Even the Athenian dictum about the Right of Might was predicated upon the observation that "The question of justice arises only between parties equal in strength." In some of its aspects, even the nation-state system brings about an equalization of strength, particularly in relations between the Great Powers and, by a process of generalization, also among other states—for instance, the friends and allies of the Great Powers. In a few respects, this process might even be found to extend to all states. Hence, on even the most minimal of assumptions, the processes of justice and some respect for common values and established principles cannot be excluded from the consideration of Great Power activities.

The underlying and legitimizing value of Great Power authority is the maintenance of peace and order in the midst of a welter of competing autonomies. Within this broad framework, two further sets of values—procedural and substantive—can be distinguished. Great Powers act legitimately if their authority conforms with both these values.

One reflection of the wide acceptance of Great Power authority among governments at large is the *procedural* expectation that it is right for certain states to exercise leadership in world affairs and to take the initiative in emergencies, whether within or outside the United Nations. In times of crisis, the eyes of the world—in particular, the eyes of every national leader—turn upon the Great Powers: their reaction and response, or else their failure to act, serve as clues to countless others. The nation-state system accords them maximum attention and the widest visibility; their use or abuse of this privileged position invariably has profound consequences.

A classical example of positive and procedurally satisfactory use of Great Power initiative was the launching of the Marshall Aid program by the United States in 1947-48. In the winter of 1946-47, Europe experienced a severe economic crisis: the economic and the political structures of the continent had not yet recovered from the strains of war; they were under severe stress. Alerted in good time to the seriousness of this situation, the makers of American foreign policy rose magnificently to the challenge. In a Harvard Commencement address, Secretary Marshall hinted broadly that the United States would be prepared to consider requests for extensive economic aid, provided the Europeans themselves would take matters in hand, adjust their requests among themselves and draw up a program of action. To make doubly sure that the hint would be understood, British and French correspondents in Washington were given the appropriate background information. Within hours, British Foreign Secretary Bevin was in touch with his French colleague, and the Europeans had "picked up the ball." After some brief sparring, Moscow declined to join and pulled its satellites out of the preliminary planning. Western Europe then organized itself; within a few years, it was back on the road to prosperity.

Points to be noted about the unfolding of this initiative are the constructiveness and promptness of the response to the crisis, the sensitive handling, the respect for national autonomy, and the maximizing of opportunity for all affected governments to become involved in the planning. The success of the European Recovery Program set the tone for many subsequent years of American leadership.

Great Power authority needs to be exercised in a manner that minimizes interference with the independence of states and holds in respect all legitimate interests. Connivance at the destruction of independent states, as in the annexations by Nazi Germany of Austria and Czechoslovakia in 1938–9, undermines not only the foundations of the nation-state system, but also the moral authority of the Powers. Correct procedures also call for the most extensive use of diplomatic consultation. Anticipatory consultation is always more effective than ex post facto attempts to secure "collective legitimization"—for instance, by having the United Nations pass approving resolutions *after* the decisions have been made. It is not really the function of international organizations to "rubber stamp" decisions that have been arrived at outside their own processes.

Substantively, Great Power decisions need to be attuned to the age's world values; in a broad sense, they must be capable of being seen as answers to the great public issues of the day. Each of the great peace settlements has been justified by, and has in fact embodied, a distinct value consensus. As a consequence, they have all been influential in shaping the future of the system, in addition to exercising influence by way of their contractual provisions. Westphalia enshrined the principle of sovereign independence; Utrecht proclaimed the principle of the Balance of Power; after a generation of revolutionary warfare, Vienna took a stand upon the principle of legitimacy (although, to its peril, it ignored nationality); Versailles made good on this deficiency and, in Wilson's eloquent elaboration, acclaimed national self-determination. Starting with the draft of the Atlantic Charter in 1941, democracy became the ruling model of the post-World War II world. The right to self-government, as formulated in the Atlantic Charter and incorporated in the United Nations, laid the moral foundation for the postwar surge of anti-colonial movements, as well as the worldwide abolition of colonialism in the two decades that followed. A mere listing of such principles shows them to be more than empty slogans; they were the constitutive principles that were expressive of global values formally endorsed by Great Power decisions.

Most importantly of all, perhaps, the quality of Great Power actions determines the moral quality of world politics. If their policies are cruel, selfish and short-sighted, they not only demean themselves, but also bring out the worst in governments and in men around the world. When they radiate a spirit of generosity, and stand for enduring values of order and justice, they have a chance of warming the spirit of the age. The quality of the ensuing world order is the ultimate test of Great Power authority.

The Costs and Burdens of Great Power Status

The burdens that the Great Power office imposes upon its holders are uniformly high and frequently oppressive. Yet insofar as the Powers also make up the centers of the world's social, cultural and economic activity, these burdens are shared by the entire world system.

The most obvious and easily ascertainable cost of status is the expenditure for armaments on the part of the governments and nations of the great states. The data presented in the previous chapter have strongly suggested that the burden of armaments has been rising steadily over the past century, and that the major part of this burden has been carried by the Great Powers. The cost of armaments, moreover, is carried largely through the internal financing of the organizations within their jurisdictions (thereby creating the need for complete jurisdictional control over, and absolute security of the economic and financial home base). Contemporary Great Powers do not receive tribute or subventions from their smaller allies or protected states; hence, they all bear a disproportionately heavy burden. The costs of maintaining the system of 1945 have been borne preponderantly by the United States and the Soviet Union (Table 8:3).

This is not to suggest that, either in a national or a global perspective, armaments represent a complete waste of resources. Some weapons and armed forces are needed to maintain order in all societies. But the nation-state system, through the Great Power institution, absorbs an unnecessarily large proportion of resources, and in that sense wastes some of them. The most obvious result of this waste is the underfinancing, in

Table 8:3
United States, Soviet-Russian military expenditures as share of all Great Power expenditures, 1870-1967

the richest and most powerful states of the world, of other necessary public and private functions, and hence the drastic weakening, in the name of world order, of certain essential functions of the social and political system that purports to be devoted to maintaining that order.

The nation-state, and its fullest embodiment, the Great Power, here confronts a challenge of its own making. To cope with the uncertainties of the international environment, the state turned itself into a nation-state; in so doing, it also coopted a varied and increasingly vocal public. The more nationalized or "politicised" a state, the more it experiences the urgent demands of the public for a variety of services, some of which it is inherently incapable of satisfying—e.g. "the good life"—while others it can meet only by abandoning or curtailing its military commitments.

Harold and Margaret Sprout have illustrated the dilemma of "rising demands and insufficient resources" in their study of British public expenditures.[16] Successive British governments have found it "politically inexpedient to dampen private spending severely, or to cut back governmental spending for the social services." Between 1953 and 1966, expenditures for military purposes therefore declined from a peak of nearly 30 per cent of the total to less than 17 per cent. Britain simply found it increasingly difficult to support the military establishment at the level to which it had become accustomed through centuries of Great Power status.

The British dilemma is, of course, the dilemma faced by all Great Powers. Their strength and their status derive from popular support, domestic tranquility and productivity; yet the price of support and of tranquility and productivity is public services. As a result of their Great Power involvement, however, domestic purposes suffer, while conquest and other such obvious returns on military investment are no longer sufficient to constitute acceptable behavior, in the eyes of their own people. The nation thus has to be appeased by appeals to grandeur, moral superiority, and its sense of global mission. Athens required its allies, for example, to share in the expenses of the navy and of the empire; but, in so doing, it stirred resentment and rebellion among them. Rome, by contrast, coopted, incorporated and absorbed her allies, and then collapsed under the weight of the superstructure thus created. Neither of these examples presents a satisfactory solution, yet a tendency to each inheres in the Great Power system.

Military appropriations and the continuing burden of war debts represent a large and continuing drain on conventional economic resources. Less obvious and more insidious is the drain on what might be an even scarcer resource—the time and attention of national leaders. The time cost of Great Power involvement is usually staggering, yet the time that is available to a political leader is finite: whatever part of it is expended on designs and explorations at the global level cannot be redirected to national or private concerns, however urgent these may be. But the duties of national leaders are first and foremost at home: the nation-state is not designed to be an organization for governing the world. The nations that indulge in this luxury do so at the peril of straining the political fabric; the leader who spends a large part of his time planning foreign-affairs strategies is doing his own direct constituents a disservice. That task, if it takes more than a modicum of time should be delegated to other agencies, global in nature. One might argue that "design-wise" the Great Power institution was to function only intermittently—which is also a way of minimizing its time-cost aspect. In recent times, however, this feature has been disappearing from view, despite the paucity of the results that have been associated with Great Power activity.

Yet just such careful attention is truly needed, inasmuch as the foreign enterprises of a Great Power are far flung and frequently expose it to high risks. The larger the military forces that are being maintained, the greater (presumably) the services rendered by them, but also the greater are the risks that they create. Protection of the military forces thus becomes an end in itself, with a momentum all its own. The role of war in both initiating and terminating the Great Power role adds to these risks. Steps to ward off hypothetical and sometimes imaginary dangers to these forces through the contingencies of war turn into necessities, demanded by the canons of "national security."

The basic list (8:1) shows that the role of Great Power is anything but a comfortable one. It is hardly a guarantee of either external peace or domestic tranquility. As to the nine states that are identifiable as such powers, all of them have frequently and exhaustingly been entangled in wars. One (Austria-Hungary) disintegrated in the heat of World War I, which it had had the major share in precipitating; three others (Germany, Italy, Japan) lost that status as the result of the Second World War, at the cost of personal destruction to governmental leaders and of untold suffering to their nations. At the conclusion of the First World War, all three of them had already been shaken by political upheavals. The Emperor of Russia and his governing class also paid dearly for indulging in the sport of kings; their rule was shaken twice in a half-century by unsuccessful wars (Crimean and Japanese), and finally collapsed in 1917, under the unbearable pressures of a third. It was some time before the Soviet Union reemerged on the world scene. China's status and example hardly deserve emulation, either: her successful campaigns in Korea (1950-53) and India (1962) earned her respect as a military power; but the earlier convulsions of the civil war, inextricably intertwined with World War II and its aftermath, and later the Cultural Revolution, along with the turmoil of the Vietnam war, hardly testify to political solidity as a concomitant of Great Power status or aspirations. In the eighteenth and nineteenth centuries, the stability of French governments was repeatedly shaken by the exertions that had been imposed by external ambitions. Ranke pointed out that, among the conditions responsible for the French Revolution, was the "deep discredit" that France's deteriorating international position had brought upon the Royal government.[17] In the twentieth century, neither France nor Britain proved truly capable of filling a Great Power role, for their weakness in both World Wars had to be shored up by the virgin resources of the United States. Even the seemingly inexhaustible capacities of the United States have proved to be severely, if not dangerously, strained by the Vietnam war.

On the record, therefore, no Great Power can be judged to have been consistently successful in the fulfillment of its role; in every case, the costs at some point became unbearable. By way of projection, no greater success can therefore be expected in the future. Yet such risks are not merely historical or statistical; they inhere in the logic of the institution, in the functioning of the nation-state system. That system concentrates the risks and strains of war and crisis at a few points and with tremendous force; it dramatically exaggerates the destructive tendencies that are characteristic of all hierarchical structures and become tremendously magnified in states, the world's most powerful and most dangerous organizations. In Chester Barnard's terms, all "scalar"—that is, hierarchical—organizations have "a persistent tendency to the exaggeration of the needs of hierarchy and of internal political activity." They also develop, through the pressures of centralization, an internal need for organizational devotion, which in turn implies a "general superiority to others." [18]

The traditional vices of nationalism—excessive devotion; exclusive superiority; exaggeration of national needs, and consuming absorption in domestic politics,—now stand revealed as characteristic of hierarchical organizations under stress. All nation-states display these flaws, not because of some features of what is presumed to be their "national character," but simply because they are huge and domineering organizations. The Great Powers are the most powerful and the most prominent of the nation-states. For all of them, the pressures of the last war, complete with the anticipated demands of the next war, have led to excessive centralization of government and the emasculation of local and functional activity; they have imposed a state-dominant hierarchy upon the social order, and this has brought with it internal disorder—dissent and its suppression. Thus the Great Powers and their striving for status have served to bring out the worst features of the nation-state system.

Spain is an early and generally ignored example of the debilitating effect that the striving for global hegemony has upon the fabric of society. In the period of the Reconquest (ca. 1000-1492), the Iberian peninsula accommodated many flourishing autonomous and only loosely federated communities; the Kingdoms of Aragon and Castile were themselves a federal structure that accorded large autonomy to their several parts. Then came the discoveries of Columbus; the conquest of Mexico and Peru; entanglement with the Hapsburg politics of the Holy Roman Empire, and competition with the Portuguese on the world's oceans. The first generation of global power did bring immense riches; yet the escalation of political ambitions in Europe brought overconfidence, demands for loyalty, the Inquisition and intolerance, as well as a large-scale persecution and expulsion of subversives at home. Soon the glory of the conquests faded and the reality of an exceedingly centralized political system remained. While the proud Spaniards stood unshaken in the conviction of their enduring superiority, soon no one remained who was willing to accept them at their own valuation. They rose high—and they fell hard.

The strains and stresses of Great Power authority not only impose costs upon particular national societies, but also unbalance the entire global system—principally for the reason that other, smaller powers insist upon avidly attempting to imitate them. The hypertrophy of the national political function, strikingly represented by the Great Power is a source of deadly strain for all of world politics.

Motivation for Great Power Status

If the price is so exorbitant, why do states and their leaders aspire to this rank? Some undoubtedly do not. There have been instances of states that were eligible for this role yet adopted policies of isolation and withdrawal. The United States, in its relations with Europe after 1920 (but not in the Far East and the Americas), abandoned a position of leadership that had been won in the closing stages of the War. China in the Cultural Revolution has been curiously self-encapsulated.

In the global perspective, the withdrawal of one Great Power does not either change the system or improve it. In any event, an attitude of self-effacement has, in the past, proven rare. The mores of the states system have promoted the position and built up its value in the eyes of political leaders. While the turnover of occupants has not really been great, the intramural competition for status, along with the pressures of the office, have been considerable, so that the participants have displayed both a strong motivation and a sometimes unreasonable dedication.

The first set of conditions of such motivation has to do with individual satisfactions. As a rule, national politicians enjoy filling the role of world leaders; some even exult in it. To most, it gives more than a sense of power: some relish the sense of "mission," or the chance to make history; others experience awe at its responsibilities which, in the nuclear age, are truly extraordinary, encompassing not only world order but perhaps even the survival of the human race. The exhilaration that is bound up with fulfilling such exacting duties exudes from Dean Acheson's autobiographical account of war-time and post-war foreign policy; entitled *Present at the Creation*,[19] his book is a fitting monument to his role in forging the foundations of the system of 1945.

This sense of pride and self-importance, the consciousness of filling a global mission, has pervaded the foreign-policy organizations of all the Great Powers. Their diplomats expect preferred treatment; in the small world of the local diplomatic corps, they assume the position of superiority that their nation-state is seen holding in the world at large. (Much of their attention will be devoted to preserving the symbols of such status—for instance, by decorating the official limousine with a highly-prized license plate, say DC-1). At the smaller capitals and in the lesser countries, a Great Power Ambassador may be the most powerful man in the land—a "proconsul" in the best Roman style, who can visit painful retribution upon his hosts (for instance, by instigating and controlling a foreign invasion, as the Soviet Ambassador did in Prague in 1968), but also bestow large bounties of economic and military aid. The military leaders attain an enhanced sense of responsibility, and actively participate in the making of world order. They enjoy overseas assignments and the manifold relations of superiority with regard to foreign armies and nationals that these entail. Great Power status entitles them to ask for the latest in military equipment, to be equal if not better than that of their competitors, while the defense industry stands ready to back them up on this, as do the veterans of earlier wars.

National legislators and local government leaders, on the other hand, together with tax collectors and the keepers of the purse, tend to be more restrained in their enthusiasms. Responsive as they must be to narrower constituencies, they derive less satisfaction from global responsibilities (except when on foreign tours), and are the first to feel the impact of expensive foreign moves on the home front. Sometimes they even develop hostility toward "foreign entanglements"; at other times, however, they also exert an influence in the direction of a narrower and more selfish implementation of foreign policies than would have been undertaken by the executive leaders alone.

Most intriguing of all is the process whereby nation-state rank— that is, Great Power rank—devolves to some degree upon individuals and organizations who are nationals of that state. The national of a Great Power acquires high status in the global system solely by virtue of his nationality. This may not matter as long as he remains among his conationals; but when he steps outside the national boundaries (or encounters non-nationals on home grounds), then status superiority comes into play. It might take such trifling forms as especially attentive treatment from border guards, hotel clerks or taxicab drivers; but it also might elicit preferred treatment in economic and financial matters, and in all the innumerable ways in which governments confer favors upon individuals and organizations—employment vouchers, business licenses, or investment permits. (The reverse effects of this condition also come into play, when a decline or fall from Great Power status has disastrous consequences for individual lives and careers.)

In the global system, nationality is still basically an ascriptive status (even though it may at times be "achieved" through migration and naturalization); as such, it is on a par with other ascriptive characteristics: sex, age, race, etc. Modern society tends toward reducing the importance of such criteria in the allocation of positions and the distribution of rewards. Nationality runs counter to this tendency, in that it sets itself up as the criterion of discrimination in some relevant and many irrelevant matters. Great Power rank compounds this discrimination, for it accords preference to some non-nationals over others, sometimes even to Great Power nationals over co-nationals (for instance, to foreign advisers occupying positions of power in governmental administrations). Preference for Great Power nationals might be tolerable in situations of minimum contact: as long as only a few individuals or organizations move across frontiers and venture into the world, such discrimination can have no great import. In situations of high interdependence and much trade, traffic and population movement, however, it flies in the face of the needs of modern world society for an achievement orientation, for equality and fair treatment, and instead brings in its wake friction and resentment.

In earlier times—and not really so very long ago—land acquisition and territorial annexation were a recognized reward, or at any rate a concomitant, of high political status. Conquest and annexation constituted both an enlargement of the range of political authority and also an opportunity for booty and personal enrichment on the part of rulers and followers alike. The nation-state system has reached a degree of stability that discourages and indeed prohibits conquest, and in modern society land tends to play a lesser role as a source of wealth and power. Since 1945, the Great Powers have, if anything, lost territory (in the colonies); but they have received incidental territorial favors, in such forms as military bases, the right to station troops or to make calls at friendly ports, rights of overflight, and radio and radar facilities for missile and satellite guidance.

Three Great Power Decisions

To elucidate further certain aspects of Great Power authority, three decisions will be examined in somewhat richer detail; these are the Munich Conference (1938), the Yalta decisions in respect to China (1945), and certain aspects of the Geneva conference on Indochina (1954). This is not a representative sampling of the universe of Great Power decisions, but rather the choice of a few, so as to highlight some inherent problems of the institution.

Munich is now part of the language, as a symbol of cowardly appeasement. Yet it is well to remember that Munich also is a textbook case of the exercise of Great Power authority, for it was on that occasion that four Great Powers—Britain, France, Italy and Germany—took it upon themselves to "save the peace of Europe" by destroying Czechoslovakia.

The stage was set by Hitler's campaign against the Versailles settle-

ment of 1919, and specifically by his demands for the annexation of the
Sudetenland, on the grounds of mistreatment of ethnic Germans in that
part of Czechoslovakia. The ostensible issue was nationalism and self-
determination. A few months earlier, the world had acquiesced in the
annexation of Austria in the name of the same principle; a second such
conquest was now under way.

Hitler backed his demands by troop movements and war preparations. For the governments of Europe, this was a crisis of major proportions: Czechoslavakia had a military alliance with France and with the
Soviet Union, and Britain was committed to the defense of France; a
German attack on Czechoslovakia would therefore lead to a European
and a world war.

The leaders of the four powers (Chamberlain, Daladier, Mussolini
and Hitler) met and, following the British lead, agreed to accede to the
German demands for the Sudetenland. Confronted with Great Power
collusion, the Prague government submitted and, for the moment, the
peace of Europe was preserved. When Chamberlain returned to London,
he said that he was bringing "peace in our time." But in the name of peace
—the value justifying the settlement—an independent state had been
destroyed (word having previously gone out that Czechoslovakia was
not a "real" nation-state, and hence needed dismembering). Six months
later, German troops occupied Prague and established a protectorate; even
the Czechs were deprived of self-government. In any event, arguments
about national self-determination for ethnic Germans were thus seen to
have been little more than window-dressing for large-scale expansion.

In the slightly longer run it was plain for everyone to see that the
decision had been a disaster. Not only had peace been purchased at an
exorbitant price; it had lasted for less than a year. War had not been
averted; its postponement only put the Western powers in a worse position, twelve months later, both physically and morally than they were in
1938. Shortsighted acquiescence in the violation of principles of world
order proved, in the perspective of history, to be extremely costly. Echoes
of Munich could be heard in Prague in 1948, and again in 1968.

Yet the right of Great Powers to make important decisions is not
easily contested. For it is they who are faced with the awesome responsibility of plunging the world into a war that might only make everyone
worse off. It was the Czechoslovak state, however, that paid for it, to
begin with—and in "spot cash." All too often the smaller states are forced
to provide the wherewithal to meet the short-term obligations incurred
by the Great Powers. No wonder they dread such occasions.

At *Yalta* (February 1945), the conditions influencing the Far Eastern
decisions of the three Great Powers (United States, Soviet Union and
Britain) were: the dogged resistance of the Japanese forces on Okinawa;

the military estimate that the hostilities with Japan might be prolonged for another 18 months; recent Soviet military successes in Eastern Europe. The tactical situation seemed to indicate the urgency of bringing the Soviet Union into the war against Japan without delay. The atom bomb was as yet untested.

Proceeding from a faulty intelligence estimate, the United States accepted the necessity of paying a good price in exchange for firm agreement on the date of Soviet entry into the war in the Far East. Little thought was given to the possibility that the Soviet Union might in fact be eager to enter the battle as soon as possible after the close of the European campaign.

The matter was raised in military staff meetings between Roosevelt and Stalin, in the absence of any State Department representatives. Stalin played his hand well and Roosevelt made considerable concessions. The Soviet Union gained railway rights in Manchuria (Chinese, but at that time Japanese-occupied), bases in Port Arthur and Darien (Chinese, but Japanese-occupied), concessions in Mongolia (over which China claimed suzerainty), and territory in Kuriles (Japanese). Told about the agreement, Churchill accepted it without question, since he regarded the United States, on account of its military stake in the North Pacific theater, as fully entitled to take the lead. On the grounds of guarding against "security leaks," the decisions were kept from the Chinese government for several months.

Once again, the assembled wisdom of the Great Powers proved wanting. The concessions to the Soviet Union were granted at the expense of China, and they were probably unnecessary. The war against Japan ended within a week of the date agreed upon for the Soviet entry, yet the agreement still gave the Soviet Union the right to occupy Manchuria and its industrial centers, and opportunity to help the Chinese Communist forces to establish themselves in that strategic area. This shortsighted decision did little to lift the low morale of the Chungking government; the flimsy historical foundations of the Soviet claims were soon exposed when, in 1955, all the Manchurian rights were handed back to China.

The value justifying this decision was, once again, peace: the importance of cutting short the duration of hostilities and reducing the number of casualties. Once again, the military exertions of the Powers put them in the position of making such decisions. But these were anything but good decisions, even if viewed only in terms of short-term expediency. For they were procedurally wrong (China was neither consulted nor informed), and they violated China's territorial rights. The final irony was that the same meeting confirmed plans for the establishment of the United Nations, as one part of which China was to be promoted to the position of a Great Power in the Security Council. This was hardly a way to build up either the status of a new member of the institution or the effectiveness of the new organization itself.

Early in 1954, the Berlin meeting of the Big Four Foreign Ministers resolved to convene a conference with the object of bringing to a close the war then in progress in Indochina. This was to be the first occasion on which China was to be represented in a Great Power role by the Peking government. The conference assembled in *Geneva* in May, on the morrow of the Viet Minh victory at Dien Bien Phu. Officially taking part in it, in addition to China, were the Great Powers of France (a major participant in the conflict), the United States, Britain and the Soviet Union, and the regional parties to the conflict: the Democratic Republic of Vietnam, the Republic of Vietnam, and the Royal Governments of Cambodia and Laos. As the conference went on, representatives of India took part in the discussions; later, they assumed the chairmanship of the International Control Commission in Indochina.

At this point, attention will be focused on two issues whose handling by the conference throws light on typical Great Power attitudes: (1) the fate of Cambodia and Laos; and (2) the determination of the boundary line between North and South Vietnam.

The major adversaries in Indochina had been: France, the Saigon government, the royal governments at Pnom Penh and Vientiane, on the one hand, and, on the other, the Democratic Republic of Vietnam (D.R.V., led by Ho Chi Minh), whose major strength lay in Northern Vietnam but which also controlled large areas in the Central and Southern parts of the country. Moreover, during the years of hostilities, this basically Vietnamese movement had also developed links with, and sponsored similar movements in Cambodia and Laos. In 1950, an alliance of the three Indochinese movements had been formally established, and on the basis of Vietnamese military support organizations were soon set up claiming the status of revolutionary governments of Cambodia and Laos.

As an opener, the Democratic Republic delegation in Geneva demanded that these two revolutionary groups be admitted to the conference with a status identical with their own. The issue was not merely procedural, for such an act would set up expectations of equal treatment on other, substantive questions before the conference, above all on the allocation of territory. Paralleling the partition of Vietnam there might have been partitions in Cambodia and Laos.

France, Britain and the United States demanded separate treatment for the two countries, and opposed the seating of the Khmer Issarak and Pathet Lao delegations. Maintaining that the delegations were little more than the stooges of the Vietnamese, they argued that the political position and the cultural background of the two countries was completely different from that of Vietnam, and required separate treatment. With neither side willing to budge, the entire conference was stalled. Finally, on June 16th, Chou En–lai publicly came out in favor of the withdrawal of Viet Minh troops from Cambodia and Laos as part of the process of neutralization; in effect, he conceded to the Western demand for separate treatment for the two countries. This important concession was the first break in the negotiations.[20]

In the present context, it is significant that the concession was announced by Chou En-lai. Circumstances suggest that the abandonment of Vietnamese aspirations in the two other Indochinese states reflected above all China's interest in the neutralization of the whole of Indochina area—that is, in creating a regime that would prevent the possible introduction of American forces into this security-sensitive area. In exchange for guarantees of neutralization, mediated by Krishna Menon and confirmed by Nehru, Eden and Mendès–France, China agreed to the withdrawal of Viet Minh troops from Cambodia and Laos,[21] and the abandonment of the claims of the insurgent movements in those countries. It might be supposed that neutralization was of greater interest to China than to the Vietnam Democratic Republic; the status and position of the Khmer Issaraks and the Pathet Lao, both of which were heavily dependent upon Vietnamese troop backing, was of greater interest to the Viet Minh. Thus it is possible to argue that, on this occasion, China traded some established Viet Minh advantages for the benefits of neutralization.

The other issue arose in the closing stages of the conference, when the line had to be drawn dividing North and South Vietnam. The opening negotiating position of the D.R.V. delegation on July 9th was the 13th parallel; it became the 14th parallel on July 11th and, apparently under Chou En-Lai's pressure, the 16th parallel on July 13th. The fact that the political organizations and military units of the Democratic Republic of Vietnam already controlled most of the countryside between the 14th and the 17th parallels was a strong argument in favor of their starting bid; but the French held out for the 18th parallel, and it was literally in the closing hours of the conference, on July 20th, that, at Molotov's initiative, agreement was finally reached on a line slightly south of the 17th parallel.[22]

The crucial territorial element of the Geneva settlement of 1954 was thus directly influenced by the two Communist Great Powers. Twice they extracted concessions from their reluctant Vietnamese allies, in the interests of bringing the conference to a close and effectively neutralizing Indochina. China's interests in this matter have already been reviewed; it has been suggested that Molotov's arbitral position was, on the other hand, influenced by the desire to kill the European Defence Community project, then before the French Parliament and a matter of great concern to the Soviet government.[23] By cooperating with Mendès-France in

Geneva and helping France to get "an honorable peace," Molotov was working for a *quid pro quo*. A few weeks later, the French Parliament indeed voted to shelve the defense treaty. Concessions wrung from the Vietnamese Communists thus served to accommodate general Chinese interests in Asia and Soviet interests in Europe. In retrospect, the decisions reached do not appear wise nor do they seem to be productive of stability. Despite its favorable military position, the Democratic Republic of Vietnam provided the wherewithal for concessions accruing to the Communist Great Powers. No wonder it has since become wary of multilateral negotiations.

These are only some of the cases that might be studied to illuminate the exercise of Great Power authority. They suggest the following:

(1) Effective Great Power decisions occur within the context of war and war emergencies—both at the point of possible entry into, and exit from, a war in which the Great Powers are or may become involved.

(2) The Great Power decisions that have just been examined were characteristically shortsighted. A foreshortened perspective is generally a feature of decisions taken under stress.[24] Crisis situations tend to foreclose alternatives and direct attention to military matters, at the expense of long-range considerations favoring world order. Fore-shortened perspective thus becomes an inherent characteristic of war and war-related decisions, and therefore also of major Great Power decisions. The shortsightedness of these decisions is attributable to the exigencies of war; yet, inasmuch as war is linked directly to Great Power status and to its exercise, it also becomes an element of structural weakness in the entire system.

(3) The immediate costs of Great Power decisions are usually borne by the smaller states that are affected by them rather than by the Great Powers themselves. In some cases, the latter even turn such occasions to their own advantage. The tendency to shortsightedness that appears to be inherent in emergencies is reinforced by pressures for self-seeking and ill-considered action. As long as the concessions could be made at the expense of others, the Great Powers have tended to slide into poorly conceived settlements that are generally also unjust.

Criticism of Great Power Authority

The structure and the logic of Great Power authority have now been set forth in detail. Even though much has already been said by way of criticism of it, a reappraisal is indicated. The institution is a necessary feature of the nation-state system; it is logically required by it: the nation-state system needs Great Power authority, just as the Great Powers need the nation-state as the base of their operations. Each reinforces the other, and their mutual interactions tend to be self-perpetuating.

But, that is not all. The institution also contains features that make for instability and tend to undermine the nation-state system. Most important, the institution is incompatible with modern world society.

The most basic criticism of the Great Power Institution as a source of world authority is its *irresponsibility*. It puts world order in the trust of national authorities that are ill-designed and ill-adapted to carry out this responsibility, because they are inherently unfit for it. While the institution entrusts world order to national governments, the only public to which such governments are responsible is their respective national constituencies. Even in the best governed states, matters of "foreign" affairs have customarily been subject only to minimal degrees of responsibility and responsiveness. On the pleas of secrecy, confidentiality, security and urgency, Great Power administrations most often "get away with" a large degree of non-responsibility in their "external" dealings; such authority as they do exercise, especially in emergencies, is in effect arbitrary.

There is, of course, some degree of responsiveness provided by the system of diplomatic representation, by the network of alliances, traditional friendships and customary understandings, and even by the institution of diplomatic protest. Friendly governments in particular do not embark upon authoritative departures from customary relations with each other, without first making preliminary soundings and extensive consultations. Even Great Power authority does not operate in a vacuum of arbitrary power. But the diplomatic network, too, has its inherent limitations. It is solely an intergovernmental network, so that world problems are treated by it only to the extent that they are filtered through national-governmental perceptions. It responds primarily to the interests and problems of governments, rather than to world opinion. Diplomacy has no specialized structure of action for Great Power decisions; instead, momentous problems of world order are handled in the same manner as the stream of routine bilateral and mostly intergovernmental business. Diplomacy promptly responds only to military emergencies; it has few resources for the continuous monitoring of world problems.

Great Power authority is also unrepresentative. The majority of the world's population has never been represented in it; at most, the institution stands for the European cultural area. But it is also doubtful whether the world would be much better off if some other section were to be exclusively represented in it. Neither Japan's nor China's previous experience as members of the institution has shown promise of more enlightened solutions. Between 1895 and 1945, Japan's governmental conduct in Asia was hardly exemplary; it reached a low point in the design for the

"Co-prosperity Sphere." Those who would "give" China a sphere of influence in Southeast Asia are, in effect, asking for similar results.

Fundamentally, what the Great Power Institution "represents" is military power, and not people. It would be more representative if military power were distributed in a more equal fashion; yet the equalization of military power might also mean the end of the Great Powers.

A significant correlate of irresponsibility is resource misallocation, for an irresponsible system also lacks mechanisms for allocating resources: (1) The Great Power institution consumes too many resources in military power, and in the support of nation-state dominance. (2) The burden of world order is unequally distributed among nation-states. (3) The benefits of world order are unequally distributed, too, and not all countries have a stake in maintaining peace. (4) Despite conspicuous waste on military matters, global needs and problems are generally underfinanced.

The other basic weakness of the Great Power system arises from its intimate connection with wars—that is, from its inherent *instability*. The authority of the powers is brought into play by wars or warlike emergencies; it therefore needs wars and emergencies in order to maintain itself. The Great Powers use war as a legitimizing principle; without war, there would be no need for them. But the cost of modern war is reaching astronomical and excessive levels, and a third world war, leading to another Great Power "settlement," cannot be anticipated calmly. Does this mean that there is no longer any need for Great Powers, or that the present-day powers will maintain their position forever, justifying their authority by the need to avert the final catastrophe?

In the meantime, the inconceivability of global nuclear war detracts from the credibility of Great Power authority. For in regard to those emergencies that might eventuate in wars, the commitment to waging wars is now uncertain and impractical, and a basic prop of that authority is missing. For this reason, such authority might be basically superfluous; moreover, in times of peace, it is also unworkable. The fragile structure of agreement that may be erected during crises never lasts long; the Great Power consensus dissolves into conflicts over "spheres of influence" —over which government should swear fealty to which other government.

The search for intergovernmental influence, which the Institution injects into world politics and of which diplomacy is the chief instrument, may possibly be that one factor that is most subversive of world order. The stable nation-state system demands non-interference, inasmuch as that is a condition of independence, and it is hostile to spheres of influence, which for that reason can neither be clearly delimited nor publicly and consistently maintained.

In the nuclear age, the only proper objects of Great Power authority are arguably the Great Powers themselves, for they alone possess the capacity for total destruction. Self-regulation, rather than the government of other nations, might thus be the path of modernization for this well-entrenched institution. The rest of the global political processes need to be accommodated through other channels.

For, as a type of authority, the Great Power institution must be characterized as fundamentally *pre-modern* or, in Johan Galtung's term, "feudal." A feudal system is one in which "rankings have a tendency to be concordant, in the sense that a nation that ranks high on one dimension has a tendency also to rank high on other dimensions." [25] Robert Dahl was referring to this same phenomenon when he wrote of "cumulative inequalities"—a condition in which "greater control over one resource, such as wealth, is closely related to greater control over most other resources, such as knowledge, social standing, military prowess and the like." [26] Feudalism and agricultural societies in general are examples of cumulative inequality, whereas modern America, along with other industrialized societies, tends toward non-cumulative, dispersed inequalities. An Emperor of Rome or a King of Tudor England would also likely be the major owner of land, and command the greatest respect, if not the highest religious standing. Modern society, through its processes of pluralization, tends to disperse values: the holders of political power need not be those who have the greatest wealth, social standing or knowledge.[27]

It is tempting to argue that the Great Power institution is an example of pre-modern tendency toward the cumulation of values (or rank concordance). The Great Powers dispose of political authority by virtue of their military power; but they also attract economic wealth, industrial potential and organizational capacity of the highest order, and they command the intellectual resources of the great universities and of world science. The cumulative effect of these inequalities tends to make the global system underdeveloped and pre-modern, even though the association is not absolute. In the system of cumulation, political authority and military power occupy crucial positions; hence, the dispersion of authority and power might be a necessary condition for the modernization of world society. The bulk of the world will remain underdeveloped unless decumulation of political and military power is as much part of development programs as "economic growth." A modernized world politics, on the other hand, would not need a Great Power Institution.

One pronouncedly pre-modern feature of the Institution is the concern for power hierarchies that it imparts to the entire system. In strict accounting, the world only has a few Great Powers; all the other nation-states, more than a hundred of them, are equal in being non-Great Powers. But in practice this is not really so: the enthronement of military power as the dominant hierarchical principle creates a series of "non-official" but real subsidiary hierarchies, all the way down the pyramid of world power. While a certain usefulness and legitimacy cannot be denied to the Great Power institution, the subsidiary hierarchies it induces are petty, futile, and unsettling.

Just as a great tyrant begets a host of little tyrants, who ape his manners and his aspirations, so the Great Powers produce a host of second-rate and second-string imitators. If the Soviet Union can attempt to impose its will upon Czechoslovakia or Yugoslavia, then perhaps Yugoslavia can try to push Albania around. If in the world as a whole Indonesia or Egypt rates as an underdeveloped country, yet perhaps in respect to Malaysia or Yemen, they may rank as big brothers. Even Saigon can feel and act superior to Cambodia. International politics has been enlivened by many such frustrated aspirations to "greatness." Whenever a strong leader builds up some self-confidence and waxes ambitious, talk begins about "leadership": France as the spokesman for Europe; Brazil as the leader of South America; Australia as the power of the South Pacific; Ghana (or Nigeria, or the Congo) as the leader of Africa. The ideas behind such schemes are vain and empty, and nothing is more calculated to provoke animosity and friction than such tinsel glory. Yet the fashions in this regard are set at the center, and imitation must be expected to occur in a system that rates high the exercise of intergovernmental influence.

The Great Power Institution is profoundly non-egalitarian in two other important respects. By basing authority upon the national exercise of military power, it establishes protection as the service that is provided by the Great Powers to their client governments, and the concomitant obligation to service in arms (in the form of military alliances) that is owing to the protecting power; in this sense, again, it is strictly feudal. Second, reliance upon national military power promotes and requires strong feelings of superiority by nationals of one state with regard to those of others. The institution reinforces the ever-present tendencies toward ethnocentric nationalism and helps to escalate the spiral of resulting tensions.

In brief, the Great Power institution fails to meet the tests of modern world society. For one, it is a system that boosts order yet diminishes justice. It neglects the rights of the small states and weak governments, and it ignores the great issues of international justice, such as the relations between rich and poor nations; these remain outside its purview. More pertinently, it is too simple to function as a continuous governmental institution. The issues that arise today—including development, overpopulation, the environment, urbanization, the young and the aged, and the emergent world culture—demand continuous attention by a host of specialized institutions, such as the Great Powers are unable to provide.

None of the Great Powers, indeed no nation-state, excels in handling world issues; the financial and the normative strains it would encounter in attempting to handle these would be too severe. Fundamentally, nation-states are not devices for ruling other nation-states. In the long run, what right has any one nation to govern another? This basic incompatibility lies at the root of the dilemmas of Great Power authority; on all these grounds, the institution stands revealed as a superfluous and basically outmoded structure of an evolving world society.

Notes to Chapter Eight

1. Chester Barnard, "On planning for world government," *cited*, p. 150 ff.

2. A contemporary diplomat, Count Muenster, wrote in August 1815 in a dispatch to the British Prince Regent about the expression "quatre *grandes Puissances* alliées": "C'est une appellation, qui a commencé à s'introduire dans la diplomatie, depuis la paix de Paris" (1814); he added, ironically, that this was a period when people professed respect for the rights of the weakest and a wish to arrest the destructive surge of brute domination. (In C. K. Webster, *The Foreign Policy of Castlereagh 1812-1815* [London: Bell, 1931], p. 562); see also p. 229 where Webster dates the emergence of the distinction between the Great Powers and the others from the Four-Power Treaty of Chaumont (March 1814), wherein the signatories promised in Art. V. "to concert together . . . as to the means best adapted to guarantee . . . the continuance of the peace."

3. English translation in Theodore H. von Laue, *Leopold Ranke: The formative years* (Princeton: Princeton University Press, 1950), pp. 181–218.

4. Cf. Martin Wight, *Power Politics* (London: Royal Institute of International Affairs, 1946), p. 18; "A Great Power is one that can afford to take on any other Power whatever in single combat."

5. Another set of influences contributing to the segregation of France at this time revolved around the question of a NATO Directorate of the Three Great Powers; this was proposed by President de Gaulle in 1958, but not acted upon either by Presidents Eisenhower or Kennedy.

6. Cf. Morton Kaplan, *System and Process in International Politics* (New York: Wiley, 1957), p. 22.

7. *A Commentary on the Charter of the United Nations* (London: H.M.S.O., 1945), p. 16.

8. Hans J. Morgenthau, *In Defence of the National Interest: A critical examination of American Foreign Policy* (New York: Knopf, 1951), Ch. V(2), "Another Untenable Argument—Opposition to Spheres of Influence."

9. G. L. Weinberg, *Germany and the Soviet Union 1939-1941* (Leiden: Brill, 1954), pp. 47–8.

10. Cordell Hull, *Memoirs* (New York: Macmillan, 1948), p. 1458; Winston Churchill, *Triumph & Tragedy* (Boston: Houghton Mifflin, 1953), p. 227–8. Describing this, Churchill adds ". . . there was a long silence . . . At length I said, 'Might it not be thought rather cynical if it seemed we had disposed of these issues, so fateful to millions of people, in such an off-hand manner? Let us burn the paper.' 'No, you keep it,' said Stalin."

11. Robert McCloskey, quoted in *New York Times*, August 24, 1968;

he described as "malicious and totally without foundation" the intimation that the Soviet Union had been given to understand that the United States was indifferent to the Czechoslovak invasion.

12. The Covenant of the League of Nations, included, at President Wilson's insistence, in Article 21, a reference to the Monroe Doctrine, there described as a "regional understanding."

13. Thucydides, *The History of the Peloponnesian War* (ed. Sir Richard Livingstone) (New York: Oxford University Press, 1960), p. 267. Thucydides' "History" has had a strong influence on the theorists of the nation-state system; Hobbes translated it into English, and Ranke wrote his dissertation on it.

14. *St. Matthew*, 5(5).

15. Thucydides, *ibid*.

16. H. & M. Sprout, "The Dilemma of Rising Demands and Insufficient Resources," *World Politics*, 20(4), July 1968, pp. 660–93.

17. Ranke, in von Laue, *cited*, p. 208.

18. Barnard, "On planning for world government," *cited*, p. 159.

19. New York: W. W. Norton, 1969.

20. J. Lacouture & Ph. Devillers, *La Fin D'une Guerre*, (Paris: Editions De Seuil, 1960), pp. 184, 186–7, 217–8.

21. George Modelski, *SEATO: Six Studies* (Melbourne: Cheshire, 1962), pp. 142–3, 208–10.

22. Lacouture & Devillers, *cited*, pp. 252 ff, 267–8.

23. Donald Lancaster, *The Emancipation of French Indochine* (London: Oxford University Press, 1961).

24. K. J. Holsti, *International Politics: A framework of analysis*, (Englewood Cliffs, New Jersey: Prentice Hall), 1967, p. 357–8; "Individual and organizational decision-making processes tend to become less effective with compression of decision-time. . . . When decision time is short, estimates of multiple outcomes from a given decision are likely to be reduced, and concern for short-run consequences of decisions increases."

25. J. Galtung, "East-West Interaction Patterns," *Journal of Peace Research*, 1966, No. 2, pp. 146–176.

26. Robert A. Dahl, *Modern Political Analysis*, *cited*, p. 33.

27. Kaare Svalastoga, *Social Differentiation* (New York: McKay, 1965), p. 39, is less confident of such a tendency: "The positive correlations generally found among major stratification variables may be a condition for the stability of the system."

9
Diplomacy

DIPLOMACY IS THE PRINCIPAL
political institution of the contemporary global system; it expresses the
dominance of the nation-state in world politics. Diplomacy assumes two
forms: classical bilateral diplomacy, whose characteristic unit is the resident mission (a number of these can be found in every national capital,
where they make up the local "diplomatic corps"); and modern multilateral diplomacy, whose characteristic units are the intergovernmental
conference, and its direct descendant, the intergovernmental organization.
The common denominator of both forms of diplomacy is governmental
control, for both are the arms, agencies and extensions of the state
and serve as channels of intergovernmental relations.

Classical and multilateral diplomacy are both, moreover, intimately
linked with the Great Power institution. Although multilateral diplomacy
did evolve from classical diplomacy, and despite the fact that intergovernmental organization has indeed introduced new practices into
world politics that might evolve still further, both are nonetheless firmly
rooted in the nation-state system.

Global Institutions

International non-governmental organizations alone bring a new element
into the global system; the basic distinction among global institutions lies
between governmental (or diplomatic) and non-governmental institutions. In the nation-state system, non-governmental organizations occupy
a marginal or a subordinate role, and are subject to the overriding

authority of the state. Yet every addition of resources and autonomy reduces this subordination, and any appreciable growth of non-governmental institutions would serve to alter the character of the global system.

Table 9:1 illustrates this distinction and elaborates it further by bringing out the contrast between relatively centralized units (chiefly organizations, but also individuals, to the extent that men or women might be so regarded, irrespective of their organizational affiliations—for instance, the late Bertrand Russell) and networks, which are relatively non-centralized systems, most often patterns of interorganizational or interpersonal relations, such as assemblies, markets or elite patterns. This parallels Chester Barnard's distinction between "scalar" and "lateral" organizations, previously referred to [1] and brings out the contrast between hierarchy, which is characteristic of the former, and the requirements of status equalization, which distinguishes the latter. A complete society needs both types of arrangement; what makes a difference is the ratio in which they are combined.

For purposes of convenience and clarity, a distinction is also drawn between predominantly political and predominantly non-political institutions. Organizations, individuals and associative networks that are chiefly involved in questions of world order and justice, and specifically concerned with incidents of disorder and injustice, will be labeled "political"; all others will be put into the residual category of "nonpolitical." This is for the most part a matter of emphasis, for in some respects all global institutions, in their constitutive aspects, delimit both the character and the possibilities of order and justice in the world. The character of the world constitution, in the sense of the structure and interrelationship of all the world's institutions, is the most basic of all political questions today. All organizations, moreover, are invariably multifunctional;

TABLE 9:1   Global Institutions

	GOVERNMENTAL		NON-GOVERNMENTAL	
	Predominantly political	*Predominantly nonpolitical*	*Predominantly political*	*Predominantly nonpolitical*
Organizations (Relatively Centralized)	Nation-states (esp. Great Powers)		Amnesty International	World corporations Ford Foundation
	U.N. Secretariat	World Bank	Institute for Strategic Studies	Global Universities
Networks (Relatively Non-centralized)	U.N. General Assembly The Diplomatic Corps	World monetary system	World Parties The European Movement	Olympic Games World Science

further, all of them produce political goods in some quantity. But, with regard to their possible effects on world order and justice, some are more important, more strategic, than others, and the distinction made above is intended to bring this out. In any event, it is well to bear in mind that (national) governmental institutions do not monopolize, either conceptually or in practice, the world's political functions. Only in the nation-state system is world politics identical with governmental activity.

The table of Global Institutions throws some light upon the so-called problem of the "actors" in world politics.[2] Traditionally, the study of International Relations has treated states as the only such actors, although more recently international organizations have also been put into this category. As a rule laying down research priorities was little more than a methodological expression of nation-state dominance in world politics. In International Law, it took the form of the principle that states are the only subjects of that law, and thus the only entities to which rights and duties could until recently be ascribed under International Law (since 1945, international organizations have also acquired an international legal personality). This meant that the states reserved to themselves the monopoly on raising and disposing of world problems.

Actors of world politics are all those whose actions can affect the character of world order and the quality of world justice. As has just been pointed out, all global institutions belong in this category, except that some belong in it more than others (and in this sense are more "political"). The student of world politics therefore needs to sample a variety of actors; the actors he chooses for his attention will depend both on the nature of the problem he is raising and the system he is researching.

In the study of world politics, however, the problem of "actors" has also been taken to mean that fruitful explanations or predictions about global political processes must be framed in such a way that the units of the proposed theories are made up of states or other "actors." The view that International Relations Theory *must* be constructed out of such terms as "states," "international organizations," "blocs" has been the reason for much fruitless endeavor.

Methodologists of science point out that fruitful theories are built "about the properties of things rather than about the things themselves"; theories are focused upon "selected characteristics of objects rather than upon the objects" as such.[3] The assignment of each new property provides opportunities for testing relationships with other properties. In world politics, the basic concept is that of world society or global political system; but real insights will not come forth until theories begin to be built upon such properties of the global systems as inequality, nation-state dominance or centralization. Some of these units of theory, such as power inequality, are ways of summing up characteristics of nation-states; others, such as nation-state dominance, are relational properties of the entire global system. New properties of the global system are yet to be constructed; but there is no law restricting students of world politics to any particular type of theoretical unit. It may be that the really powerful explanations will draw upon units that are both "political" and "non-political," and at all levels: "global," "national" and "local." Hence the problem of "actors" will be dismissed as being only a pointer toward the need to invent new theoretical "units" of world politics.

The present chapter discusses some of the salient characteristics of the two major national-governmental components of the global system: classical diplomacy and multilateral diplomacy and, in particular, the United Nations. Non-governmental global institutions give rise to problems that go beyond the scope of the nation-state system model of world politics. They may be regarded as agents of change and, for this reason, their discussion will be deferred to Part Three of this volume.

Classical Diplomacy

In the nation-state system, every member is entitled to dispatch a diplomatic representative to the head of every other (duly recognized) member of the system. Each nation-state member of the system has a corresponding obligation to receive such missions in its capital and to grant them direct access to the head of state. The rule is founded on reciprocity and derives from the ground rules of the nation-state system. It applies only between states that recognize each other as such, and the process of recognition therefore entails the establishment of diplomatic relations. The "actors" of diplomacy are states exchanging among themselves authorized diplomatic agents.

The practice of sending and receiving missions creates a worldwide network of diplomatic representation The chief characteristic of this network of representation is bilaterality. Any two points within it are either connected by a direct link in the form of an embassy, or else they are not connected at all. There are no separate points or "exchanges" facilitating the transmission of messages, although the absence of direct diplomatic relations (between A and D) might be compensated for by contacts in a third capital (of C).

As part of the diplomatic network, every national capital accommodates a political system known as "the diplomatic corps." This consists of the Foreign Ministry, as the host organization, and all the diplomatic missions that are formally accredited to it. As a political system it is loosely structured. The most important occasions on which it functions as an entity are symbolic and ceremonial: they are either national events in which the corps participates—such as national day parades, inaugurations of the head of state, state visits and state receptions—or else ceremonial events of the corps itself—such as arrivals or departures of heads of missions, or national day receptions. The corps is headed by a dean, commonly the ambassador with the longest accreditation; but his duties too are for the most part ceremonial—except on occasions when the rights and privileges of the corps need to be protected. Most of the political business is dispatched in direct bilateral relations between the mission and the host foreign ministry. But the ceremonial operations of the corps replicate at each national capital the structure of the nation-state system; they serve as the symbolic representation or dramatic validation of the meaning and the functions of that system. The prominence of the corps at each capital and the privileges enjoyed by diplomats are the direct consequences of nation-state dominance in the world at large.

The diplomatic corps is the mechanism by which every national capital is switched directly into a global network. Each such capital is not only the center of national life, the hub of the national layer of politics and society, but also a part of the global system. Diplomats who move into and out of it all the time circulate on a worldwide scale, and keep meeting each other at different capitals. At small capitals, with little life of their own, the diplomatic corps can overwhelm the national society; its role can become dysfunctional, the global system having fused with the national layer.

The practice of sending messages between powerful organizations, and the employment of messengers for carrying them is, of course, an age-old one. Immunity for messengers is well-established, too. But the institution of permanent missions is much more recent: it dates back only to the fifteenth century, among the city states of Renaissance Italy. Machiavelli was a distinguished Florentine Ambassador, and Venice set the standards of diplomatic practice. The rise of independent states in Europe gave a boost to diplomacy, so that by the eighteenth century, the institution was well established in numerous manuals of diplomatic behavior. The evolution of the diplomatic method was paralleled by the growth within existing state organizations, beginning in France in the sixteenth century, of separate departments for the handling of diplomats and diplomatic correspondence. The Congress of Vienna rationalized the system by inventing devices for minimizing conflicts over precedence (such as the practice of alphabetic ordering); the Vienna *"règlement"* still provides, with only slight amendments, the basic framework of diplomatic intercourse.

Throughout its career, the diplomatic system has been closely associated with the Great Power Institution: missions exchanged among the major states have customarily formed the nucleus of the network and the Great Powers set the tone and the conventions of diplomatic practice. Interestingly, though, the role of the Great Powers has not been crystallized in a formal ranking system. The Balance of Power originally prevented the crystallization of rank in diplomatic procedures; an attempt to assign permanent ranks to all states failed at the Congress of Vienna, as a result of opposition of the British Foreign Secretary.[4] It was then decided to rank envoys rather than states and to restrict the title of Ambassador to the representatives of the Great Powers, but the rule could not be enforced and it became meaningless toward the end of the nineteenth century. To this day, however, the Great Powers maintain the largest diplomatic services, receive the largest number of missions at their capitals, and commonly generate the greatest part of the bulk of diplomatic business.

In 1963-4, the four largest diplomatic services were those of the United States, Britain, the Soviet Union and France, in that order. Together these four states (out of 119) accounted for 28.5 per cent of all the diplomats sent out and for 18 per cent of all diplomats received. Theirs were also the biggest embassies—the mean for all United States missions, for example being nearly 28 diplomats, as contrasted with the median for the whole system: four diplomats.[5] Their status is formally no different from that of the others, but it shows in a number of ways and is manifested most clearly in the amount of influence exerted with the host government.

Since the mid-nineteenth century, most diplomatic missions have included military attachés, who serve as liaison officers with the host armed forces, as channels of military intelligence, and as expediters of arms deals. The military attaché symbolizes (but does not exhaust) the close and traditional link between diplomacy and strategy, or the "strategic-diplomatic complex" that Raymond Aron sees as the essence of international politics[6] but which should more properly be regarded as the essence of the nation-state system.

The principal function of diplomacy is intergovernmental communication. Diplomacy evolved at a time of slow and insecure communication, and it soon became the preferred channel for the exchange of messages between states. Yet it was never purely or solely a technical device for the transfer of information. The medium was also a message: the diplomatic network was also built as a system of political representation. By means of it, the interests of one government were injected into the decision-making processes of other governments. Even the elementary processes of recognition and accreditation established foreign states as entities whose interests could not be entirely ignored; the rights of access to the head of state and the state organization assured opportunities for the representation of issues and for the registration of protests.

A parliament is a well-tried multilateral device of political representation. Diplomacy, too, is a representational device—but within a bilateral context. Diplomats may be regarded as the delegates of their constituencies, defending the interests of their constituents before a distant executive, yet never really escaping the status of delegates. Just as the parliamentary system has shaped the political process of many states, so diplomacy has fashioned the nation-state system.

In that system, however, diplomacy has gone beyond communication and representation and has assumed control over "foreign affairs" and, in some states, a monopoly control. The medium has now become the entire message—and there is nothing else to the message. Foreign Ministries now habitually claim, as a matter of governmental "efficiency," the dominant voice with regard to all governmental matters concerning relations with other states.[7] They lay claim to superior status on inter-departmental coordinating committees; they insist on seeing and trans-mitting all intergovernmental correspondence, and they pass on military aid plans and operations, economic aid questions, propaganda and intelli-gence programs. Through the issuance of passports and visas, they control the movement of all individuals in transnational relations; through their influence over trade controls, currency regulation and tariff talks, they shape international trade. They even arrange for and, in many countries, conduct cultural and intellectual exchanges. As a rule, the stronger the nation-state in national society, the greater control it exerts through its diplomatic machinery over "foreign relations." Where the state holds monopoly power, such control is total; what is more, the nation-state system sanctions it.

The prominence and the prerogatives of diplomacy in the global system are quite extraordinary. Their most obvious external manifesta-tions are the pointless and now non-functional rights that diplomats enjoy in all capitals, and which make them a privileged caste, above the law. Is it necessary that they should have immunity from arrest and prosecution, so that they might ignore parking rules, or habitually indulge in speeding, inflict injury or forget all about their traffic vio-lations? Most often, too, diplomats are the elite corps of the national public service, and diplomatic appointments are among the most eagerly sought-after favors. They are also the best paid and most liberally rewarded of all governmental servants, and in their overseas posts they often enjoy comforts they could not claim or attain at home. In addi-tion, of course, these privileges bestow high social standing. In occupational prestige ratings, ambassadors consistently score close to the top among all occupations. The extraordinary rights of diplomats reinforce the nation-state system. But are they justified in terms of the criteria of world interest, or of the contributions that diplomacy makes to world welfare?

In Criticism of Diplomacy

Contemporary diplomacy provides neither adequate communication nor faithful or reliable representation; it is (1) technologically redundant; (2) uneconomical and (3) politically harmful to world society.

The practice of resident diplomatic missions was instituted at a time when communication, even over short European distances, was unreliable and expensive. Diplomacy served a real need because horse riders and horse-drawn carriages or sailing ships were the speediest means for transmitting messages, and occasional merchants, pilgrims or scholars therefore the only source of information about developments even in neighboring areas. But today communications are instant, worldwide, cheap and secure. No government needs the services of hundreds or thousands of people merely in order to communicate with other governments. Depending on the degree of the urgency, it can use the ordinary mails, cables, radio, telephone or even a satellite hook-up. Yet even today governments only rarely use such commonsense devices. Are diplomats still filling a real need?

As a century-old and tradition-bound institution, diplomacy has been consistently resistant to technological innovation. The typewriter, for instance, encountered resistance in the great offices of state, where the belief in the efficacy of finely penned notes persisted long after the speed and efficiency of the typewriter had been demonstrated beyond any doubt in commerce and industry. To this day, the telephone remains almost totally unutilized in interstate relations, despite the fact that international telephone communication has been an accomplished fact for over a generation. Vital and expensive business deals are daily transacted by way of electronic devices, yet foreign offices continue to ignore this medium on the grounds of the lack of security and the dangers of vital information being intercepted.

Most messages between governments still proceed along the traditional and tortuous route of the "diplomatic note" (why not "letter"?): from the Foreign Ministry of A, in language A, to the Embassy of B in A, to be translated into Language B, encoded and transmitted to Foreign Ministry B (by its own radio, diplomatic pouch or even occasionally by courier), where it is then decoded and finally conveyed to its proper destination.

The installation of "hot lines" (a scrambled teletype link-up) between Great Power capitals in recent years was hailed as a breakthrough in intergovernmental communications. What is striking however, is not the act itself but its late occurrence and the lines' infrequent use.[8] Can it be that the adoption of the telephone and of other modern communication techniques might make diplomacy itself redundant as a communications channel? Diplomacy's tradition-hallowed ways, as well as the nation-state system, raise serious doubts about its compatibility with advancing technology.

Both as a form of communication and as a representational system, diplomacy is uneconomical and unnecessarily complex. It is as though, in a telephone network, all subscribers were linked to each other by separate lines; this might be practicable in a network that comprised five subscribers, but it becomes ridiculous in one involving hundreds or thousands of users, for whom exchanges become imperative. Yet the theory of diplomacy continues to insist that each recognized nation-state be linked, by a special line all its own, with every other member of the system. Those that do not keep up such lines suffer some notable disadvantages.

In practice, the network displays considerable gaps. Table 9:2 shows how incomplete the coverage that is provided by the diplomatic network really is. Contemporaneously, only about one quarter of the possible—and needed—linkages are in existence. A few states maintain fairly extensive coverage: the Great Powers already mentioned, and some other diplomatically ambitious or interested states, such as India, Japan, the United Arab Republic, Israel and West Germany. Most other states restrict their representation to a few major capitals and to their own region. The unequal coverage of the diplomatic network mirrors the general inequalities of the nation-state system, even though

TABLE 9:2 Diplomatic Coverage, 1920, 1963–4

	States N	Needed Links (N^2-N)	Actual links (Number of missions)	Coverage (Actual as percent of needed links)	Total number of diplomats sent out
1920	50	2,450	1,100	45	
1963–4	119	14,161	3,712	26	23,356

Adapted from Ch. Alger and S. Brams, "Patterns of Representation in National Capitals and Intergovernmental Organizations," *World Politics*, 19 (4), July 1967, pp. 647–8, 651; also C. de Witt M. Poole, *The Conduct of Foreign Relations under Modern Democratic Conditions* (New Haven, 1924), pp. 21–22.

the diplomatic inequalities are less pronounced than the far more important power inequalities.

Further, completeness of coverage has declined during the twentieth century. Despite a considerable increase in the number of missions, the degree of coverage, which approached (and probably exceeded) one-half during the interwar period, has more recently declined to just about one-quarter. This is due, above all, to the creation of a large number of new states, most of which are small and impecunious, and find the burden of maintaining a large number of missions excessive. For Cambodia, for instance, which is by no means one of the world's smallest countries (1965 population: 6 million) but has a state budget (1965) of only about $U.S. 60 million, the maintenance of a large number of embassies would obviously impose a crippling expense. The annual cost of keeping one small mission is at least $100,000; in order to maintain complete coverage, a state such as Cambodia would have to devote a major proportion of its revenue merely to the upkeep of embassies. Some do it, nevertheless, as a form of outdoor relief and foreign travel for national elites and as a way of keeping potential troublemakers, including ambitious military officers, well out of the country. Moreover, in a system of 130 members, the creation and recognition of one new state calls, in principle, for the establishment of 258 new embassies and thus imposes a tremendous burden upon the capacity of the entire network. The larger the diplomatic network—beyond an optimal size of no more than two or three dozen—the less efficient it becomes, and the more it tends toward fractionation and inequality.

The nation-state system is the only interorganizational system known to have such an elaborate and costly communications and representational machinery. Certain other large organizations in modern society—among them, corporations, professional and business associations, universities and labor unions—have evolved some rudimentary forms of "diplomacy" and maintain, for instance, "liaison offices" of "lobbyists" in national capitals, or even at the headquarters of international agencies. The chief executive of every organization engages in a good many activities involving external relations, contacts, negotiations and general public relations. But there is no effort to institutionalize bilateral relations with bodies of the same type, and even the largest corporations have no system of representation with other corporations in the same industry. A number of separate institutions—including professional associations, industrial organizations, private clubs, and the legal profession as such—serve as generalized exchanges, providing services to smooth the operation of a number of interorganizational systems. What is special about international diplomacy is the extraordinary length to which relations between organizations of the same type, level and purpose have been fixed, formalized and even fossilized in one particular manner, how inbred and self-centered this system has become, and how impervious it is to the general social environment.

The most serious criticism of diplomacy has to do with the harm it inflicts on world society. To grasp this point, it must be remembered that the diplomatic system was originally instituted not so much to improve communications, but rather to replace one intimate communications system with another more impersonal system. The Middle Ages constituted, in Europe, a period of great "togetherness." The high point of the period, the Crusades, was an occasion on which rulers of many lands joined together in exacting enterprises, sometimes extending over years and giving rise to prolonged absences from home. Other Church-sponsored events, such as councils and congresses, also brought rulers and their subjects, too, frequently together. Given the poor state of communications, travel by political leaders was relatively common. The evolution of the modern state, involving claims of equality along with the concurrent Reformation, which destroyed religious unity and thus constricted the communication function of the Church organization, called for new forms of political communication and representation, such as would reduce the previously high degree of intimacy.

The new system of diplomatic representation therefore grew out of the need to *keep political leaders apart*. It instituted the barrier of intermediaries, behind which rulers who were conscious of their new status could take shelter, while attending to the needs of the "home front." By reducing the need for and indeed hindering personal outside contact, diplomacy undoubtedly contributed to the gradual stabilization and ultimate nationalization of the state. By the same token it has never become, and cannot be expected ever to become, a device for facilitating general contact and communication. It is rather a well-tried system for *minimizing* interaction, and for keeping people apart, instead of bringing them together. It is a system that thrives upon, that indeed maximizes differences and distinctions. It cannot cope with a large quantity of contacts, for these would, *inter alia*, tend to reduce distinctions. Its operative assumptions are predispositions to be ready for antagonism and to expect the worst.

Probably the single most important disservice rendered by diplomacy has been the discords it has engendered over matters of "influence." The contests that the Great Powers engage in often have to do with their relative influence in or over certain frequently weak, countries. Looked at more closely, influence commonly turns out to be the influence that the Embassy, with its civil and military advisers has over the host government, as compared with that exercised by other embassies. A status competition among embassies can thus turn into a Great Power conflict; the organizational needs of an embassy, having been transmuted into security interests, thereby gain the halo of national issues. The prerequisite of nation-state system stability is the independence and autonomy of its members—that is, the absence of influence by other states; diplomacy is inherently constituted to undo that condition.

As a communication function, diplomacy today is without any importance. The world's press is fully adequate to the task of reporting general political and economic developments in all areas. Specialized organizations need specialized reporting, but that could easily be arranged without the paraphernalia of diplomacy. The general information purveyed by diplomacy is of two kinds: reports on the political situation and the stability of the host government, and military and intelligence data. Much of the information gathered is, however, trivial—malicious gossip about political personalities and the "what-did-he-really-mean-when-he-said . . ."-type of analyses of the obvious; some of it is, however, dangerous—particularly when it is devoted to fanning suspicions and building speculative structures of hypothetical disasters. Characteristic of the distrustful spirit of diplomacy is the story, probably apocryphal, that is attributed to Metternich, the master diplomat: upon being told of the death of the Russian Ambassador at the Congress of Vienna, he exlaimed, "Ah, is that true? What could have been his motive?" Diplomats, like intelligence organizations, see the world as composed of fragments only; they never see the world as one, and they lack either the incentive or even the conceptual equipment to develop ideas of world interest.

As a system of political representation, diplomacy is similarly deficient. The interests it represents are first and foremost those of the national state organizations, which in turn reflect the priority that is consistently given to military concerns. Other interests are represented secondarily and derivatively; despite that fact, a monopoly of the representation with regard to even these secondary interests is tenaciously maintained and jealously protected in international legal practice. Yet the sum of national interests never does add up to the world interest; for this reason, the interests that are aired and legitimized by diplomats, like the information they assemble, are inherently fragmentary. Diplomats are by their nature incapable of looking after world interests.

Finally, both as a communication and a representational system, the diplomatic network is greatly overloaded at some points and underemployed at others. For instance, in the mid-nineteen-sixties, the State Department was receiving some 1,300 cables each working day, of which the Secretary saw only about twenty or thirty. Every day, once again, 1,000 cables were also sent out, and of these the Secretary saw six and the White House perhaps one or two.[9] Thus the great mass of information, incoming requests for action and outgoing instructions, remained in effect inaccessible to the top political leadership, despite the fact that the real responsibility for action on every cable rests with the Secretary, and in the end, with the President. Such a system must be described as suffering from information overload, basically traceable to the attempt to convert some Foreign Ministries into agencies for overseeing the entire world's political development (why should the Secretary be roused from bed every time there is a new coup in Patagonia?). At the same time, other Foreign Ministries "twiddle their thumbs," while away their time—for instance, worrying about stranded tourists—and generally waste the scarce resources of national brainpower, which they consume so voraciously.

Hans Morgenthau has argued that, while "not good enough" [because it has failed to prevent many wars] "diplomacy is the best means of preserving peace which a society of sovereign nations has to offer"! [10] Perhaps it is but it may be that the nation-state system itself is not good enough. Diplomacy is the most glittering and spectacular part of that system; but it owes its living to divisions and distinctions and is no longer functional in world society. Its glitter now hides little more than outworn privilege.

Multilateral Diplomacy

The flaws of traditional diplomacy have been so patent that, ever since the end of the First World War, determined efforts have been made to devise better means of safeguarding world order and organizing world politics. The main development has been toward multilateral diplomacy, of which two principal types may be distinguished: conference (or committee) diplomacy and parliamentary diplomacy. As the name itself implies, however, multilateral diplomacy is not a radical or complete departure from established forms; it is an adaptation of classical diplomacy to the needs of a more complex international system, so that it remains an instrument of intergovernmental relations and thus intimately bound up with the nation-state system.

The reason why multilateral diplomacy arises is that some issues cannot be treated in a "two-only-at-a-time" fashion. The great peace settlements and the Great Power meetings that were discussed in the previous chapter were early and influential examples of multilateral diplomacy, as was the practice of international conferences; the United Nations evolved out of these, and to this day the bulk of its activities may still be described as those of a large diplomatic conference in permanent session.

Basic to the character of multilateralism (and the source of its difference from bilateral relations) is, of course, the number of parties (or organizations) that are involved in the relationship. A two-unit system (which can be a bipolar system) cannot and need not distinguish between bilateral issues and systemic problems; it treats both in the same way. That may be one reason why bipolar (and polarized) systems have difficulty in evolving a systemic perspective, and why systems of bilateral relations have trouble in conceptualizing world interests. A three-unit system distinguishes between three sets of dyads and the systemic issue of the triadic relationship; a system of four units contains six dyads, four triads and several types of systemic relationships. Hence, the larger a system (in terms of units, such as organizations), the greater the salience of non-dyadic (non-bilateral) relationships, but the greater also the number of possible dyads and the greater the possible confusion. Classical diplomacy and most of conventional thinking about International Relations (including the name itself) are based upon the dyad as the modal form. While Great Power contacts (e.g., among the superpowers) can still be visualized mainly in dyadic relationships, the increasing visibility of non-Great Powers and the establishment of many new states have created the demand for institutions that are based upon multilateral formations and upon systematic and universal conceptions. Yet the singular importance of certain pairs of global relationships—such as the American–Soviet, or the Chinese–Soviet—continues to influence the perceptions of world politics with regard to the dyadic model.

No system utilizes all the relationships that are open to it; it may indeed systematically discourage some. Diplomacy uses only about one-quarter of the dyads that are open to it. Thus the type and the relative frequency of relationships supplies important clues to the character of the global system. The earlier discussion about centralization showed that the rate at which international organizations were growing (Table 7:5) was rising exponentially; this would suggest a continuous strengthening of multilateralism. Most of recent quantitative research on international relations, however, has focused on dyadic relations and said little about the relative weight of each. If the way in which national political leaders (heads of state and government and foreign ministers) allocate their time between bilateral and multilateral travel can be taken as an index of multilateralism in the global system at large, then recent data show multilateral travel to be quite significant. In 1965, 52 percent of all the country-visits made by Foreign Ministers were prompted by multilateral occasions (including both general and regional conferences), as were 42 percent of the country-visits of all political leaders.[11] If extrapolation were justified, it could be argued that the contemporary global system is being progressively multilateralized, even at the intergovernmental level. The change is even more striking if it is viewed in a lengthier time perspective; one hundred years previously, high-level multilateralism was almost completely nonexistent.

The growth of institutions that are capable of coping with multi-lateral exchanges is of especial benefit to the smaller, the less powerful and the less wealthy states. It affords inexpensive ways of conducting diplomatic business, even of a bilateral character, and in that sense is a substitute for the elaborate structures and formalized procedures of classical diplomacy. It is not surprising that states with weak diplomatic services compensate for that fact by extended memberships in international organizations.[12] Multilateralism offsets certain of the weaknesses of the Great Power system: it is more nearly representative, in that it gives a voice and a role to the smaller states, and thus is closer to the mores of the nation-state system. If it were to be established on a permanent basis, it could process a great variety of issues more legitimately and in a continuous fashion.

The most important form of multilateral diplomacy is the international organization. Beginning with 1815 and the establishment of the Central Commission for the Navigation of the Rhine, the number of intergovernmental organizations has been rising exponentially at a doubling rate of about twenty years; by 1965 the figure reached 192.[13] Much of this increase is attributable, however, to regional organizations. As Table 9:3 demonstrates, about one third of the world's intergovernmental organizations are universal in scope, and the remainder are regional. The great majority of these organizations are predominantly nonpolitical; most of the predominantly political organizations are regional, and only one political organization is universal—the United Nations.

Diplomacy at international organization sites has certain features that distinguish it from the behavior that is customary in the diplomatic corps at national capitals.[14] In the first place, each national mission repre-

TABLE 9:3 Intergovernmental Organizations, January 1, 1965

	Predominantly Political		Predominantly Nonpolitical	
Global	1		67 *	
Regional	15		110	
W. European		4		32
Inter-American		3		27
African		3		25
Others		5		26
Total	16		177	

Derived from M. Wallace and D. Singer, "Intergovernmental Organizations in the Global System, 1815–1964" *International Organization*, 24 (2) Spring 1970, pp. 250–256.
* Includes twelve specialized agencies of the United Nations (of Table 9:4).

sents the nation to all other nations represented at the site, and is involved in practically uninterrupted informal contacts and negotiations. Second, such sites have certain non-national features that are not present at other locales, inasmuch as Secretariat officials who assume non-national roles are likely to be more numerous than diplomats. The physical context of buildings and facilities is likely to have a more neutral character, too. There are opportunities for unscheduled contact and thus for extensive communication and learning experiences. Third, the nonpolitical inter-governmental organizations bring together large numbers of government officials other than diplomats, who find themselves as a result in a minority. Finally, the regular meetings of assemblies of multilateral organizations are occasions for the evolution of parliamentary diplomacy. This brand of diplomacy, which involves both public debate and lobbying, along with other private parliamentary activities, has established itself most prominently in the global political forum of the United Nations; but it also makes its appearance regularly at most of the regular meetings of the nonpolitical international organizations.

Parliamentary Diplomacy

The growth of parliamentary diplomacy may be traced to the two Hague Peace Conferences (1899, 1907), the practice of international congresses of a technical nature, and the experience of the League of Nations and the United Nations. Although it is still part of the diplo-matic complex of the nation-state system, parliamentary diplomacy brought a number of new features into international relations.[15] It is a representational system that is much closer to the parliamentary model than classical diplomacy is.

Parliamentary diplomacy thrives in large gatherings—especially general-purpose meetings, lasting some length of time. Short confer-ences with only a few participants develop different styles; but even ad hoc gatherings of some size tend to drift into parliamentary-type situations.

For students of world politics, the most interesting feature of parliamentary situations is the opportunity they present for power equalization. In bilateral intergovernment contact, the relative power of the parties largely determines the outcome of every encounter. In parliamentary conditions, the ability to determine the agenda or to secure priority for certain resolutions, the timely move to adjourn—in other words, the ability to manipulate the rules of procedure—confers advan-tages upon those who wield parliamentary skills, and not only upon the powerful.

An important postwar experience in the application of the rules of parliamentary procedure took place at the San Francisco signing of the Japanese Peace Treaty in 1951. Through the device of agreeing, at the opening of the conference, on precise rules of restricted debate, the conference was able to proceed smoothly on its course (despite Soviet attempts at delay), under the Chairmanship of Dean Acheson.[16] In the end the Soviet Union refused to sign the treaty, but most of the other participants did and the postwar status of Japan was placed upon a regular footing.

Election to office, too, becomes an important part of the political process. The occupancy of certain positions—for instance, the chairmanship of a meeting, or the question of which nation, in any given month, occupies the Presidency of the Security Council—comes to matter a good deal. Elections to seats in the Security Council have in the past been occasions for considerable lobbying and repeated ballots.

Another feature of parliamentary diplomacy is the practice of public debate and the frequent appeal that is thus made to world public opinion. Traditional diplomacy prided itself upon operating in conditions of confidence and even secrecy, and cultivated a disdain for the general public. That attitude has thus received an important correction, even if the significance of open debate is apt to be exaggerated, and if the public that is actually concerned with these debates is a narrow one. Nevertheless, the character of the political process is significantly affected by what is said and what is publicly declared to be official policy.

Finally, parliamentary diplomacy formulates and decides issues through resolutions and recommendations of a quasi-legislative character. In most cases, these cannot be compared to the regular activities of a legislative body, because their subsequent execution leaves something to be desired. The United Nations, however, did take, during its first two decades, a number of decisions of considerable importance, each of which was arrived at through the parliamentary process of canvassing, lobbying, tabling resolutions and, in some instances, dramatic voting. Among these might be mentioned the Assembly Resolutions on Palestine (1947) and on Uniting for Peace (1950); equally significant because public have been Security Council actions on Korea (1950) and on the Congo (1960), even if the forum itself was somewhat closer to committee diplomacy. Some more recent resolutions on African issues, including those on Rhodesia and South Africa, have also been important.

The fact of voting and the general observance of an ordinary or a qualified majority rule by most international assemblies need not be overemphasized, as long as the representative character of such assemblies is no greater than that of the nation-state system. The differences in population size among member nations militate against the attribution of compelling moral authority, let alone any great political significance, to decisions that are taken by bare majorities, or by numerical majorities of the smallest states. A certain inequality of representation is not un-known in parliamentary arrangements; even in equal-constitutency sys-tems, the population of constitutencies may differ by as much as a factor of two or three. In the United States Senate, states as unequal as New York (population 20 million) and Hawaii (population 200,000) have an equal number of votes, the factor of disparity in this case being 100. This does not prevent the Senate, however, from being the more power-ful of the two Houses of Congress. In the global system, inequalities are even more pronounced, and the factor of disparity approaches 10,000 (India 500 million, Maldive Islands 98,000).[17] The global system needs to be reapportioned before world parliamentary processes can reach a higher degree of authority.

The United Nations

The center of multilateral diplomacy is the United Nations Organiza-tion. It is, without doubt, the most important among all the intergovern-mental bodies; it sets the tone for all the rest, and is politically and morally preeminent among them. However, it is still no more than an organ of the states that are members of it—an instrument devised by them for the solution of their problems. It is not a world government or a superstate, but part and parcel of the nation-state system.

Associated in a "United Nations family" are a dozen "specialized agencies," which are the most important of the universal intergovern-mental organizations (Table 9:4). For certain purposes—for example, when computing global centralization, Table 7:5—the U.N. family may be regarded as a unit. It represents a global resource network spread over a dozen world cities and commanding organizational and financial resources of between one-half and one billion dollars in the late nineteen-sixties. The fact is that it is a system loosely coordinated through special agreements, made by each agency with the United Nations Economics and Social Council under Articles 57 and 63 of the Charter. The spe-cialized agencies resemble the functional departments of any government (the International Labor Organization is the equivalent of, and has strong working relations with, national departments of Labor, etc.), and most of these governmental functions are well represented at the global level (the only notable exception being the absence of a strong defense ministry). The desire of every Secretary-General of the United Nations is to strengthen his control over the agencies, which are each jealous of their autonomy, some of them having traditions that go back a century and each having their own separate world constituency.

TABLE 9:4   The United Nations family, 1967

Organization	Head-quarters	Budgeted * Expenditures ($U.S. millions)	Estab-lished
The United Nations	New York	140.4	1945
General Assembly	New York		
Security Council	New York		
Economic & Social Council	New York		
Trusteeship Council	New York		
International Court of Justice	The Hague	(1.4)	
Secretariat	New York		
Conference on Trade & Development	Geneva	(9.2)	1964
Development Program	New York	182.8	1965
Institute for Training & Research	New York		1965
Industrial Development Organization	Vienna	(8.2)	
Office of High Commissioner for Refugees		(3.5)	
Relief & Works Agency for Palestine Refugees in the Near East	Beirut	45.8	1949
Children's Fund	New York	39.9	1946
Force in Cyprus		15.0	1965
World Food Program		70.4	
World Health Organization	Geneva	56.1	1946
World Bank Group	Washington	34.0 ‡	
International Bank for Reconstruction & Development			1945
International Development Association			1960
International Finance Corporation			1956
United Nations Educational & Scientific Organization	Paris	30.1	1945
Food & Agriculture Organization	Rome	29.9	(1905) 1945
International Labor Organization	Geneva	25.7	1919
International Monetary Fund	Washington	22.1	1944
International Atomic Energy Agency	Vienna	10.5	1956
International Civil Aviation Organization	Montreal	7.0	1919
International Telecommunications Union	Geneva	7.0	1865
General Agreement on Tariffs and Trade Interim Commission	Geneva	3.2	1948
World Meteorological Organization	Geneva	2.5	1928
Universal Postal Union	Berne	2.0	1874
International Maritime Consultative Organization	London	0.9	1946

Source: *Yearbook of the United Nations 1967* (New York, 1969).

* Appropriations for 1968 or expenditures in 1967.

‡ Administrative expenses only for 1967; total loans granted in 1967: 670m; net income for 1967: 175.6m.

The executive heads of all the specialized agencies meet regularly to review common problems in the Administrative Committee on Co-ordination, but they are not to be regarded as a "Cabinet" or "Ministers in Council" of the U.N. Secretary-General, who presides over these meetings. There is no clear reason why the coordination of these agencies should be any greater or why centralization should be fostered within the U.N. family. On the contrary, decentralization at the global level might help to loosen up the high centralization now common in national governmental systems and help them to develop, too, into more loosely structured federations of governmental functional organizations. The recent tendency has been, however, to form new organs and divisions within the United Nations Organization itself, rather than create new specialized agencies.

The United Nations is part and parcel of the post-World War II settlement, whose basic outline was laid out in Tehran, Yalta and Pots-dam in 1943–5; it is within this framework that the world still basically operates. This also means that the United Nations has been designed, like other parts of that settlement, by the Great Powers; not unnaturally, the Great Powers have occupied and continue to occupy within it positions not only of influence but also of authority.

The reestablishment of a general international organization was first proclaimed as a war aim by the leaders of the United States and Britain in the Atlantic Charter (1941); it was endorsed by the Soviet Union at the Moscow Conference of 1943. The Great Powers wrote the working draft of the Charter at Dumbarton Oaks (1944), carried it further at Yalta, and finally obtained the acceptance of its main pro-visions at San Francisco (1945), despite some opposition by the smaller powers. The authority of the Great Powers is a fundamental principle, pervading all United Nations organs and activities. In the Security Coun-cil they bear "primary responsibility" for the maintenance of international peace and security, and hold a veto over substantive decisions by that body. By Charter right, they occupy permanent seats on the Security Council and the Trusteeship Council, and by custom they have been regularly reelected to the Economic and Social Council and represented on the executive organs of all the specialized agencies to which they belong. Decisions requiring Great Power unanimity include the appoint-ment of the Secretary-General, amendments to the Charter and the admission of new members. Certain senior staff positions are reserved for Great Power nationals (thus the Security Council Affairs Department of the Secretariat is customarily headed by a Soviet national). The Powers contribute the major part of the organization's budget—some two-thirds of it—and have a correspondingly large claim on all the staff appointments (for the filling of which, the national budgetary contribution is one of the relevant criteria). The power of the purse that they wield was demonstrated during the years following the Congo operation of 1960: the Soviet Union and France refused to support it, either politically or financially, and as a result of that opposition, the organization nearly ground to a halt in 1965. A Secretary-General who runs afoul of a Great Power—as Trygve Lie did with the Soviet Union over Korea, and Dag Hammarskjoeld over the Congo—loses much, if not most, of his usefulness to the organization.

In such fundamental respects, the United Nations as a whole, and not just the Security Council, is one more embodiment of the Great Power Institution. In a positive sense, the world's major aggregates of military power are thus linked to a permanent institutional network that is more broadly based and responsive to wider interests than the ad hoc consultations of the traditional variety. But this civilizing role of the organization is quite marginal. The comments and criticisms of the previous chapter fully apply in the present context. Such failures and weaknesses as have been attributed to the United Nations, in particular with regard to its record on peace and security, must therefore be laid at the door of the Great Powers. Attempts to remedy such weaknesses must begin with the overriding global authority system of the Powers, and not by tinkering with the United Nations.

Despite the primacy originally assigned to the Great Powers and to questions of security (the two are, of course, intimately linked), the evolution of the United Nations has proceeded in the direction of augmenting the weight of the non-Great Powers, and increasing the salience of issues other than those of peace and security. Accordingly, the center of gravity of the Organization has shifted away from the Security Council to the General Assembly and the Secretariat. The Assembly is the more representative body; it functions consistently in a parliamentary manner, and regularly processes a great variety of issues in general debate and through its dozens of committees. It is now more than a forum that the Great Powers can use for legitimizing their policies; since 1960, and Hammarskjoeld's repulse of the Soviet attack on the powers and position of the Secretary-General in the Congo crisis, the Assembly has been a source of comfort and support for the executive head of the organization; in return, the Secretariat has been able to render to the smaller powers services (including some aid) that were earlier obtainable only from the Great Powers, and at the cost of dependency.

The role of the smaller powers, along with the salience of global issues other than war, has been aided by the near trebling of United Nations membership since 1945, when it was 51, to 125 in 1970, by the significant contribution of such states as India, Canada, Japan or Sweden

and of their active and frequently articulate leaders, by their considerable role in peace-keeping and, most importantly of all, by the relatively
light incidence of major conflicts and conventional inter-state war. The
Great Powers dominate the times and the areas of major tension. The
absence of major conflicts allows a voice to the smaller powers, and to
all the other interests and issues of the global system that surface when
tensions ease and international life resumes its inherent diversity.

A most dynamic element of the United Nations could be the Secretariat. Built upon the independent executive responsibilities of the Secretary-General, the Secretariat has become a sizable organization, comparable in size and effectiveness to a nation-state of the medium rank.
Its regular budget was, in the sixties, larger than that of 70 to 80 states
in the global system; if the several special budgets and programs are
added to it, the figure approaches one-half billion dollars and begins to
represent considerable resources. The Secretariat has its headquarters in
New York, as well as substantial offices in Geneva, Bangkok, Addis
Ababa and Santiago; it is represented in most member states by what is
in effect its own diplomatic service (in part by "Information Offices"
and, in all countries receiving development aid, by "Resident Representatives" of the Development Program). This gives the Secretary-General
direct access to national governments; in emergencies, special representatives of the Secretary-General act as his political agents in various
trouble spots of the world (for example, the Middle East). The Organization has its own aid program (The Development Program, which
makes both technical assistance and capital investment grants); it ranks
among the world's ten largest assistance schemes, and could acquire some
influence over the large resources of the World Bank. Like all political
organizations, it even has its own military element; during its first two
decades, it has deployed a number of observer and emergency forces,
and has a staff headquarters in New York and a stock of experience
accumulated during the course of handling peacekeeping operations.

The qualities and the resources of the United Nations determine
the sort of function that it performs in the global system. Most obviously
and evidently, it is *not* an organization for waging wars—not even
defensive wars against aggression; its political and military resources, if
set against those of the world's major or even medium powers, would
not permit it even to try to do so. If marshaled against those of a Great
Power, these resources are completely insignificant. Added to those of
a major power, they do not make any difference, and thus do not allow
the United Nations as such to play any independent role. Without
resources, however, the role of leadership, or of the organizer of a
coalition, is unthinkable. That is why doctrines of collective security,
giving it the responsibility for organizing a league against aggression, are

completely misconceived. The first major experience of the Organization in Korea was in this respect not prototypical but rather an aberration, made possible by the fortuitous absence of the Soviet representative from a crucial Security Council meeting in June 1950 (a mistake unlikely to occur again); it showed, too, that in such a collective security operation, the organization itself has no autonomous role of its own to play. The most important point is, however, that a general international organization cannot function properly in a war system, nor can it function at all in a general war, which is rather like a civil war of the global system. Instead, as the League of Nations did in 1939-40, it must adjourn most of its activities and wait in hibernation for the outcome of the conflict over which it is unable to exercise any influence.

It should be obvious that the Organization cannot fight, or lead, wars of any but the most modest kind. In any event, its equipment is designed to cope with internation wars, whereas most of the troubles since 1945 have been national and subnational. The Congo operation was of this latter kind; but was it worth staking the survival of the Organization and risking bankruptcy to carry it through? Small peacekeeping operations of the Cyprus variety, or peace observations on the Kashmir model, are all that can rightly be expected in the near future.

If the United Nations cannot fight wars, it is just as doubtful whether it can do much to help prevent wars. It can do this indirectly by functioning effectively and helping to solve urgent world problems. But it is doubtful whether it can do this, directly, by helping to settle peaceably intergovernmental disputes—a task that loomed large in the mind of all international organization planners. The record of its first two decades has not really been impressive. There is no need at this point to go into the story of the cold war, China's relations with the world, or even the wars in Indo-China. The Israeli–Arab conflict in the Middle East is as good a case as can be found, and it affords little evidence of the usefulness of United Nations interventions. Despite the fact that all parties to the conflict belong to it, and that the organization's involvement has been profound right from the start, it cannot be argued convincingly that the United Nations has made a significant contribution to settling that situation or to averting further conflict. In some ways it may even have made it worse, by aggravating tensions and making the conflict more malignant. It is not so much the organization or its structure that are at fault as the idea that "settling disputes" or "stopping wars" is the proper task for that organization.

If this is in any way the function of the Great Power institution, primarily without the organization, and if the institution fails, surely the United Nations as a whole need not take the blame for it. Fundamentally, wars are too disruptive for a network as fragile as the nation-state system, or an organization with as circumscribed means as this one has. In any event, it is doubtful whether anything can be gained by focusing the world's attention on some local trouble spot or crisis. No one expects national parliaments or legislatures to settle civil wars, or other violent contests between constitutive elements of political society. If the nation-state system is prone to such conflicts, then a solution must be reached through changing that system, not through overloading the United Nations.

In the matter of keeping peace, the functions of the United Nations would seem to lie in serving as the world's symbolic expression of genuine concern for peace and in spotlighting the system's fatal proclivity for war. This much indeed is called for by the world interest—but no more than this.

Beyond the area of war, peace and dispute settlement, the functions of the organization are much wider; once again, they lie, first and above all, in giving focus and expression to the world interest—that is, to world problems and to various ways of solving them. The Secretary-General's asset here is his role as the world's greatest host, one who can bring together and offer facilities to those people who are willing to pay attention to global problems. He could exploit to the best advantage his position as the world's top master of ceremonies. It might be argued that the United Nations' greatest service has been to act in this capacity to myriad international conferences—from the annual sessions of the General Assembly, whose debates shape world opinion, to a host of important and unimportant meetings of a specialist character; from the Application of Science and Technology for the Benefit of the Less Developed Countries, to the Prevention of Crime and the Treatment of Offenders. The significance of the hundreds of gatherings it sponsors or accommodates each year is less instrumental or informational than it is symbolic, ceremonial and solidarity-building. Through such meetings, universal concerns are expressed and clarified, and the discourse is fashioned by way of which common values are argued and defended, and their acceptance, validity and legitimacy are demonstrated. Over the long haul, such activity creates networks and helps to shape a global consensus on matters of wide interest. Economic development has been one such problem that is substantially shaped by the United Nations' practices of research and debate; and relations between the races, as well as between rich and poor countries, could be others.

Specific activities and influences take a variety of forms. Delegates to the United Nations, all of whom rank high in national societies, are attuned to world problems and to world political processes. The legitimacy of certain types of regime is established, as well as the lack of legitimacy of others—for example, colonial regimes. World issues are aired and formulated through the General Assembly's parliamentary process; these include such questions as racial discrimination, control over the sea bed or the protection of the environment. Finally, the organization serves as the framework for the pursuit of a variety of global aims, which would perish for want of a hospitable climate—matters as diverse as research on desalination, concern over nuclear fallout, or simply the collection of global statistics. Fostering the habit of looking at the world as one, and systematically collecting and inspiring research about it constitutes a major service to the world interest, because conceptions of world interest cannot be operationalized without global information being available.

In the quarter-century of its existence, the United Nations has demonstrated its true worth, as well as its hardiness. By contrast with the League, which was plagued from the start by defections, the United Nations so far has lost no members and has several applicants still standing at the door. At the time of the financial crisis in 1965, Indonesia announced a decision to withdraw from the organization; but it meekly returned to the fold before the end of 1966. During that period, with Jakarta's aid, Peking broached the subject of an alternative world organization, designed to attract what President Soekarno called the "New Emerging Forces." [18] Premier Chou En-lai claimed the right to stage "rival" dramas on the world stage.[19] But the Afro-Asians stayed cool to the idea and, with the fall of Soekarno, it came to nothing. China then plunged into the turmoil of the Cultural Revolution. The United Nations weathered a severe financial storm, as well as an exacting test of loyalties; it proved its strength however, beyond what might have been expected.

The nation-state system enthrones power and implants strategic-diplomatic values in global concerns. Within such a system, the United Nations does its best not by repeating the patterns of diplomacy to which it is so closely bound, but evolving, in contrast with them, a role conception that stresses moral concerns and the promotion of the world interest.[20] Such a role would in time demand greater autonomy and a larger degree of functional separation from nation-state control.

"Vertical fusion"—the excessive control exercised over global problems by national organizations—is the main structural weakness of the nation-state system and of its political institutions in the global system. A degree of separation between the national and global layers of political activities, and with it a reduction in the role of diplomacy, may be a necessary condition for world order.

Notes to Chapter Nine

1. Barnard, "On planning for world government," *cited*, p. 149 ff.
2. Arnold Wolfers, *Discord and Collaboration: Essays on International Politics* (Baltimore: Johns Hopkins, 1962).
3. Robert Dubin, *Theory Building* (New York: The Free Press, 1969), p. 30.
4. Lord Castlereagh, reporting to his Prime Minister on proposals being considered to rank the Courts of Europe and "classify them," expressed a strong preference for a simple rule of ranking envoys instead of Courts. He suggested this latter course in a pragmatic fashion as the "least likely to give Umbrage, whilst it affords an adequate remedy to the existing Embarrassments" (Dispatch of January 22, 1815, *Public Record Office*, Foreign Office, 92/11). This disposed of the possibility that the Vienna Congress might introduce a system of fixed ranks for all states, and made possible the gradual evolution of the principle of formal equality, a crucial condition for a modern system.
5. Ch. Alger & S. Brams, "Patterns of Representation in National Capitals and Inter-governmental Organizations," *World Politics*, 19(4), July 1967, p. 651.
6. Aron, *Peace and War, cited*, Ch. 1: Strategy and Diplomacy, or On the Unity of Foreign Policy.
7. Hoover Commission Reports on the Organization of the executive branch of the Government, 1949: Task Force Report on Foreign Affairs.
8. As of 1970, the following dyadic Great Power relations had a "hot line" status:

	Agreement reached:	First reported use:
U.S.A.—U.S.S.R.	April 1963	June 1967
France—U.S.S.R.	July 1966	?
Britain—U.S.S.R.	February 1967	?

9. Testimony of Secretary Rusk, December 11, 1963 in *Administration of National Security*, Hearings of the Sub-Committee on National Security Staffing and Operations, Committee on Government Operations, United States Senate (Washington: G.P.O.) 1965, p. 388.
10. Hans Morgenthau, *Politics among Nations* (New York: Knopf) 2nd ed. 1959, p. 534.
11. George Modelski, "The World's Foreign Ministers: A Political Elite" *Journal of Conflict Resolution*, 14(2), June 1970, p. 155.
12. Alger & Brams, *cited*, p. M.
13. M. Wallace & D. Singer, "Inter-Governmental Organizations in the Global System 1815–1964," *International Organization*, 24(2), Spring 1970, p. 272. The number rose as follows: by January 1st 1865, to 3; 1915, to 49; and 1965, to 192. But the rate of formation of global international organizations alone did not show the same exponential trend:

Rate of formation of global intergovernmental organizations in existence on January 1st, 1965

1865-1884 : 5	1905-1924 : 18	1945-1964 : 25
1885-1904 7	1925-1944 13	

14. Chadwick Alger in H. C. Kelman, ed., *International Behavior* (New York: Holt, 1965), pp. 521–547.
15. Dean Rusk, "Parliamentary Diplomacy: Debate versus negotiation," *World Affairs Interpreter*, 1955, 24, 121–38.

16. Acheson, *Present at the Creation*, *cited*, Ch. 56.

17. The Gini index for the United States Senate approximates 0.3, but for the General Assembly and for most other international parliamentary bodies reaches 0.7.

18. George Modelski, *The New Emerging Forces* (Canberra: 1963), passim.

19. "In these circumstances, another United Nations, a rival one, will be set up so that rival dramas may be staged in competition with that body which calls itself the United Nations . . . How can it be that the United States is allowed to stage its own dramas while we are not?" Premier Chou En-lai, at banquet in honor of Dr. Subandrio. January 24, 1965, in *Peking Review*, 8(5); January 29, 1965, p. 6.

20. Cf. Conor Cruise O'Brien, *The United Nations: Sacred Drama* (New York: Simon & Schuster, 1968).

IO

Responsibility

Iₙ THE PRECEDING CHAPTERS, THE nation-state system has been defined as a network of institutions, of which classical and multilateral diplomacy are the most important forms, and in which the Great Powers play the most significant role. The question now arises whether or not this network processes the global political problems thrown up by world society.

Like all great social arrangements, the nation-state system proceeds, to a degree, on its own momentum. It is composed of large organizational structures, which often give the impression of being huge bodies that are firmly set upon predictable collision courses. There is an inertia about the great bureaucracies that sometimes makes for despair about the possibility of ever seeing them firmly linked to the pursuit of human purposes. Such inertia alone is able to convert instruments that were devised for noble ends into institutions seeking little else but their own self-preservation.

The nation-state system is not an end in itself. It is a global political system—that is, an institutional arrangement through which a number of ascertainable purposes are served. A global political system should respond to *some* of the demands and interests of *all* members of world society. The demands made upon the nation-state system are those of its effective constituency, but these demands should also be guided by a recognizable conception of the world interest. The course and the decisions of the nation-state system must be responsive, as well as accountable, to a global constituency; they must be informed by ideas of the world interest.

The questions that need to be asked about the nation-state system are basically: who uses it and who should use it? to what interests and demands does this political system respond? what are the mechanisms by which responsibility and accountability are achieved, and are they adequate? are these demands and these mechanisms adequate for the satisfaction of world interest?

The Constituency of the Nation-State System

Decisions on global problems call for a sense of world responsibility, along with the proper mechanisms through which to ensure that global interests are brought to bear upon them. Global decisions have worldwide effects, and everyone who is affected by them needs to have access to these mechanisms.

In the nation-state system, the most important decisions of world politics are made by nation-states; the most authoritative of all decisions are those taken by the Great Powers. These latter are, as it were, super-nation-states, and the organizations of multilateral diplomacy are, to the greatest extent, instruments of nation-states and of Great Powers.

Nation-states, moreover, are first and foremost responsible to their own nations. In specific instances, the national authorities might be responsible to an assembly of elected representatives, a congress or parliament; they might also be responsible to a single party embodying the national will, or perhaps only to their own conception of the nation's interest. But they are *not* responsible to supranational agencies, or to external ("foreign") interests. Does this mean that, in a nation-state system, all decisions about world politics (whether they be, for instance a Great Power decision on arms limitation, a Security Council resolution defining the conditions of an international settlement, or a governmental proposal for trade control or aid dispensation) can be responsive, and should be responsive, only to the national interest? Does the nation-state system *preclude* all broader responsibility or more inclusive interest?

At first blush this would appear to be so, inasmuch as the nation-state system enshrines the national interest of each member nation as the fundamental criterion of governmental action, even on world issues. This might be an improvement upon earlier systems, in which such problems were the concern of even narrower elites, unencumbered by any wider outlook or by any need to justify their actions to a larger audience. But the situation is still unsatisfactory.

The model of the nation-state system is here faced with the realities of world politics. That model is based upon the assumptions of: 1) minimum interdependence and 2) hostility, such contact as may exist being presumed to be either hostile or else purely instrumental. In conditions of physical self-sufficiency (minimum interdependence) and moral self-sufficiency (the consequence of hostility and an instrumental conception of the world outside), little heed needs to be given to world responsibility.

Some nations could conceivably go a long way by acting upon such assumptions. Generally, the more isolated a state and the less physically interdependent it is with other nations, the more attractive such a doctrine might seem to be. Protected by the Channel from armed intrusion, and secure in her supplies through the command of the sea-lanes, for example, Britain in the nineteenth century may well have fitted such a model in some respects. The larger the state, moreover, the more self-sufficient it is likely to appear; the less susceptible it is to outside influence, the more it can ignore or even sustain hostility. In the twentieth century, at various times, the United States in the period of isolation, the Soviet Union (and Russia before that), and more recently China, have fitted such a description: they have therefore tended to find basically "isolationist" conceptions of world order satisfactory. Thus, several of the world's Great Powers have been large and self-sufficient states. Military power in the nation-state system is, in fact, built on industrial and agricultural self-sufficiency, guaranteed supplies, and the capacity to withstand blockade; what is more, it rests on hostility and instrumental alliances—all of which are conditions that support the assumptions of the pure nation-state system. It might therefore be argued that, in this regard, the system operates in the interests of the Great Powers, and that the negative conceptions of world responsibility that are inherent in it serve the interests of the Great Powers better than they do those of less self-sufficient and smaller states.

A *system* of nation-states totally *without* interaction—that is to say, without interdependence—is, however, a contradiction in terms. A political system of pure, unadulterated hostility is likewise absurd. Hence the principles of responsibility that underlie the nation-state system are unworkable for the system as such, even if they appear to be relevant in special conditions and in particular relationships. Yet they do impose a certain order of priorities, structure the situation, and influence decisions in a variety of ways. They make certain, of course, that such mechanisms of world responsibility as do emerge within the system remain weak. Such responsibility as operates is primarily intergovernmental, its extreme form being the possibility of intergovernmental collusion *against their own constituents*. Conceptions of world interest take forms that tend to perpetuate the status quo.

The Nation-State System as Pressure Group Politics

In the nation-state system, world politics is pressure group politics. This is so because of low institutionalization—that is, excessive decentralization [1] and weakness of organizations articulating the general interest—and also because of the weaknesses of the prevailing conceptions and ideologies of world order and justice. When order is weak and claims need not be justified, when coalitions may not be capable of being mobilized through appeal to general principles, the pressure of the strongest prevails. World politics partakes of all those features that are familiar to political scientists from their study of national and local pressure-group politics.

In the nation-state system, the most potent pressure group is the nation-state itself, while the primary mechanism of responsibility is intergovernmental pressure. Governments that are active in world politics are, as a rule, sensitive above all to the opinions, judgments, reactions and interests of other governments. The instrument that transmits this sensitivity is the diplomatic network. Intergovernmental influence is the business of diplomacy, and diplomatic links may be among the major reasons for the existence of such governmental responsiveness as there is. The degree of sensitivity varies, but every government is sensitive to some other governments some of the time and on some issues. While the Great Powers tend to be exposed to a wider range of demands and to a wider spectrum of responsibility, the governments of the less powerful states are usually more vulnerable to pressures.

For analytical purposes, governments that make demands upon international decision-makers are pressure groups in world politics, just as much as international pressure groups pure and simple. Governmental demands tend to be focused upon nation-state preoccupations, and are frequently limited to strategic-military affairs; being specific and narrow in scope, they do not differ in character from the claims of other groups that are more conventionally identified with pressure-group activity.

An international pressure group is any organization (or collection of individuals) that makes demands upon global decision-makers. It is not really material whether or not that pressure group is of the same nationality as the decision-maker in question. What does matter is the right to be heard, which belongs to all members of the global system that are likely to be affected by the decision. It is the right to a hearing that establishes links of responsibility for all decisions on global problems.

Pressure-group activity attends each exercise of international authority. The peace settlements that have been made by the Great Powers have been occasions for vigorous pressures from a variety of groups. At Vienna, in 1815, for instance, British anti-slavery groups were influential in obtaining special treaty provisions putting limits on the slave trade for all signatories. Among those who were clamoring for the attention of President Wilson and the other leaders of Versailles in 1919 was Nguyen Ai Quoc, later to be known as Ho Chi Minh. As it was, no one in authority at the conference was willing to give him a hearing, to let him air his relatively modest program for greater political rights for the Vietnamese in Vietnam; the following year Nguyen Ai Quoc became a founding member of the French Communist Party and embarked upon a life-long career of revolutionary leadership.[2] Had he been even partially successful at that time, great miseries might possibly have been spared the world decades later. Unfortunately, the structure of a Great Power meeting alone ruled out the possibility of any attention being paid to conditions in the colonial territories of the victorious allies. In any event, the pressure that a Vietnamese exile leader could bring to bear upon such a conference was rather limited, despite attempts to mobilize support in the then French Socialist Party. The Versailles peace-makers, however, were guilty of an even greater fault when they refused to respect the rights of China in the face of the demands of Japan, one of the Allied Powers. Here, too, a direct link connects the abuse of Great Power responsibility with the May 1919 Shanghai disturbances and the origin of the Chinese Communisty Party.

Within the United Nations family, certain forms of pressure-group activity have been put on a regular footing. All the specialized agencies now provide a natural focus for the aggregation of interest groups. The World Health Organization crystallizes the opinions of the medical profession the world over, for example, while the International Civil Aviation Organization is particularly sensitive to the interests of the international airlines. The Economic and Social Council has instituted an elaborate system of lobbying activity, on the basis of Article 71 of the Charter; this provides for consultative arrangements with "non-governmental organizations which are concerned with matters within its competence." Such organizations could be both international and national in character; but the latter would be included in consultation with the member state concerned. Over 200 groups had official "consultative status" in 1968; this gave them the right to bring matters to the attention of the Council, attend meetings and, for some, to speak in debates. Major groups included the Rotary International, the Salvation Army, and international labor and religious organizations.

Despite this institutionalization at the United Nations, the vulnerability of many such groups to governmental displeasure is considerable. A large proportion of nongovernmental international organizations of a public character are located in the North Atlantic area and operate only sparsely in the Third World; this makes for a lack of political support among the non-Western majority of the United Nations. Organizations that had incurred displeasure for criticizing human-rights conditions in the Soviet Union found themselves, in 1968-70, subjected to official investigation, and faced with a threat of withdrawal of their privileges.

Pressure-group spokesmen (and this includes government representatives) may thus be found wherever decisions are made about world politics (the exceptions are wartime meetings, which are surrounded with secrecy and protected by security, even though pressure-group influence is still felt indirectly). Frequently, they perform useful functions: they bring to the point of decision pertinent, if one-sided, information and the strength of special pleading; their concern is with specific and specialized demands, which reflect narrow but often intensely felt interests and principles.

The proliferation of pressure groups at points of international decision, however, does not by itself assure the implementation of world interests. The world interest is not the *sum* of pressure-group demands (for this purpose, national interests are a species of pressure-group claim); it calls for the leavening of such activity with responsiveness to more *general* considerations. A system of strong pressure groups tends to slight the requirements of world order and justice; it also lends itself to a good deal of procrastination (that is, non-decision-making), where urgently needed action is forgone, for fear of offending vested interests.

The nation-state system is weakly institutionalized; within it, special interest groups of the hierarchical-manipulative type predominate (because a system of pressure group politics naturally gives special opportunities to groups that have a concentration of power). The two most prominent are nation-states and large corporations, which are sometimes at odds and sometimes in league with each other. The activities of oil companies in some parts of the world afford examples of spectacular and profitable arrangements, supported by a good deal of diplomatic flag-waving, yet falling short of the criteria of world interest. The growing numbers of such groups and their involvement in world politics are not necessarily indicators of world integration, but rather signs of a disorderly and unstructured political system, in which the highest bidder and the strongest pressure carry the issue, regardless of merits or of long-term consequences. Unadulterated pressure group politics, unrelieved by wider vision, is a sign of social disorganization.

Quasi-Parliamentary Factions

If pressure groups are special-pleading, particularist devices, for the purpose of maximizing parochial (and sometimes vested) interests, political parties represent a higher level of integration of activity and a concern for systemic and universal (as well as frequently ideological, hence value- and principle-based) modes of political action. Parties are mechanisms for the translation of the political preferences of large sections of a political system into organizational programs; they are broadening and generalizing agents, fusing a variety of individual and pressure-group claims into political platforms. They are mediating devices between the state (and also the corresponding political organizations, at the local and global levels) and the constituency; hence, they are fundamental levers of responsibility and responsiveness. Parties are also, of course, avenues for reaching positions of political power, both for groups and individuals; specifically, they are instruments for elections, or else for executing coups or promoting revolutions, or even for fighting civil wars. In so doing, however, parties also serve as mechanisms of responsibility. By appealing to and competing for support in the whole of the political system, parties tend to become a principal force shaping political systems into political communities. The growth of nationalism has coincided with the rise of the national political party.

The advent of parliamentary diplomacy, as previously discussed, poses the question of whether one of the chief institutions of parliamentarism, the political party, can also find a place in the nation-state system.[3] Modern parties are only a late development of the parliamentary system; they are not invariably associated with it. But even single-party and militarily controlled states, which commonly dispense with, or diminish the role of, parliamentary institutions, still need a party apparatus of a kind, in order not to lose touch with grass-root sentiment. There is no single compelling reason why parties should be found in contemporary world politics; yet the pressures of large-scale modern society suggest some disposition for the formation of intermediary and formalized devices of responsibility.

The nation-state system has failed to develop parliamentary world parties. The lack of institutional growth in this direction is due to the incompatibility of such organizations with the rules of the nation-state system, in regard to independence and control. Growth of world parties would mean basic changes in the organization of world politics. Yet the parliamentary conditions that prevail in international organizations (in particular, continuity of operations, general and public debate, and voting as the mechanism of decision-making) have given rise to groups that cannot be called parties, but may best be described as parliamentary factions (the term not being used here in a derogatory fashion). In the United Nations, they assume the forms of: (1) caucusing groups and (2) voting blocs.

The caucusing groups arise principally from regional loyalties; these in turn reflect underlying cultural and even linguistic affinities. What was probably the earliest group, dating back to the origins of the United Nations, was formed of delegates from Latin America, who were accustomed to meeting frequently in the Organization of American States, and using Spanish and a Spanish cultural background as a medium of exchange. The Commonwealth group soon followed, using English and a background of British culture and institutions. The Arabs utilized links they had earlier formed in the Arab League and, of course, Arabic as their language. The Communist bloc, too, had a common language, Russian. The largest of the more recent caucuses, the African group, still represents association on the basis of regional and cultural affinities. In each such caucus, delegates with some sort of affinity meet regularly, and exchange views on upcoming issues. Some caucuses are formal affairs, with chairmen, agendas and decisions taken by votes; but most caucuses do not impose uniformity of voting and are not universal voting blocs (except for the Communist bloc). Most often, however, they exhibit an underlying solidarity on certain issues—for instance, in the African group, on racial issues involving Rhodesia and South Africa. Most of all, they seem to respond to the need, on the part of delegates to a large assembly, to come together with others of like background. Regional similarities as factors of cohesion recall similar tendencies in early French national assemblies.[4]

The caucusing groups fall short of being parties. Their membership criteria are exclusive and particularist—for example, non-Arabs can never join the Arab caucus. They offer inward-looking places of retreat from the turmoil of the meeting place, rather than occasions for the formulation of global policy. They bring forth issues of regional urgency (witness the plethora of African issues dominating the General Assembly), but they tend to be lacking in any global outlook. Their prevalence is a sign of political immaturity. A true party would have to go beyond regional solidarities; it would have to construct a global platform and open its membership to all who were willing to support that program. In any event, United Nations seating arrangements, which are in alphabetical order and with assigned places, do not encourage spontaneous grouping; they thus resemble conference procedure more closely than they do parliamentary practice.

More recently, associations have arisen on the basis of more general programs and interests: these are the groups of non-aligned states, non-nuclear states and underdeveloped states. While they come somewhat closer to the party model, they are still a good distance away from it.

The group of non-aligned states had its origins in India's diplomacy in the Korean war and the Indochinese settlements of 1954, as well as in the concurrent questions of the organization of alliances in South and Southeast Asia. The stature of leaders such as Nehru, Tito and Nasser, and the links of personal understanding that they developed among themselves gained large attention for this group. High-level Conferences of Non-Aligned States in Belgrade (1961), Cairo (1964) and Lusaka (1970) have given it additional substance. The category of "non-aligned state" was incorporated into some features of international organization—for instance, in the structure of the Committee on Disarmament, since 1961—but not into the leadership of the United Nations Secretariat (the "troika" proposal of the Soviet Union, according to which the Secretary-General was to be replaced by a committee of three, representing the Western, the Eastern and the "neutralist nations" respectively, failed of acceptance in the same year). Nehru himself opposed the evolution of the non-aligned group into a voting bloc, and the non-aligned nations did not develop any parliamentary organization nor a notable voting cohesion. Divisions in the Third World, including notably Indian–Pakistani difficulties, seriously weakened it; as the salience of military alliances in the world at large receded, the significance of non-alignment as a principle of global association also diminished. The divergence of interest between the Great and the smaller powers, which had formed the basis for solidarity among the non-aligned states, was more recently crystallized in another form by the Treaty on Nuclear Proliferation, when a Conference of Non-Nuclear States met in 1968.

The underdeveloped states have been conscious for many years of a community of interests, but this feeling has not been paralleled by the growth of common institutions. The nearest to any such thing occurred within the context of the first meeting of the United Nations Conference on Trade and Development (Geneva, 1964), when a bloc of 77 developing states took a consistent stand in opposition to the developed countries. The paucity of results associated with this effort has militated so far against consolidating this nascent unity or generalizing it in other directions.

"Voting blocs" are a related though separate phenomenon in all large international organizations. Studies have shown that governmental delegates in such circumstances vote in a fairly predictable fashion, and frequently act in unison. Factors such as alliances, aid and common trade help to explain a large part of such commonality. The super-issues around which voting alignments have tended to cluster have been shown to be two: the East-West issue, in which rivalry between the two superpowers comes into play, and the North-South issues, in which the Great Powers tend to be opposed to the "non-great" powers and the "have-nots." Factor analytical studies for 1947, 1952, 1957 and 1961 show East-West issues to account for about two-thirds of the voting, and the share of North-South issues to have declined from about 20 per cent to 13 per cent during the same time span.[5] Questions arise, however, as to whether this evidence can be confidently extrapolated to other years or into the future.

Throughout the existence of the United Nations, the United States delegation has played a decisive role in its parliamentary proceedings and a number of delegations have habitually followed its leadership. NATO and O.A.S. states, along with some Asian countries, could regularly be counted upon to vote with the United States. In earlier Assemblies this was the ruling majority, and it still remains a substantial voting bloc. Could this American-led group, then, be regarded as a parliamentary party? At the United Nations, its members never caucused as such, its cohesion being assured by frequent diplomatic consultations and by the alliances, aid and trade that bound its members. Voting cohesion could be ascribed to intergovernmental contacts, the alliance systems and the prominence of the Great Power role in a given institution, but it is not characteristic of party loyalty that binds the representatives themselves.

Factional or party-like activity in intergovernmental organizations is severely constrained by the fact that those who engage in it are instructed governmental delegates, not elected representatives with a direct mandate from a constituency. All delegates are appointed by governments and serve at their pleasure. Personal loyalties among delegates may, and undoubtedly do, develop; but they cannot persist in the face of contrary instructions. Delegate collaboration, either in caucuses, in voting or in other contexts, directly reflects the interests of nation-states: not so much the interests of national voters, as of the state organizations that dispatched these delegates. Not having been elected by any constituency, delegates lack contact with the grass-root issues, as these might relate to world politics: they become, in effect, spokesmen in a system of pressure-group politics.

The weakness of parliamentary diplomacy, as of pressure-group politics, is its factionalism: the concern with narrow interests; the lack of perspective, and the lack of opportunity to work for global interests —all of which is aided and abetted by the fact that the immediate rewards of international parliamentarism are rather minute, despite the fact that the long-term consequences of inactivity can be disastrous. The strength of pressure groups in world politics is mirrored in the weakness of party political institutions.

Extra-Parliamentary World Movements

One condition for the effectiveness of parliamentary institutions, including parties, is a "normal" distribution of political preferences in the constituency that is served by such institutions.[6] Normality refers to the strong core of consensus that characterizes such a distribution, as well as to the weakness of political extremes. In other words, parliamentary institutions thrive in *non-polarized* political systems.

The nation-state system, by contrast, is particularly prone to polarization.[7] It fragments and isolates political activity, and is inherently antagonistic to the consensus-building activities of political parties. At times of tension, it polarizes around the Great Powers. The great wars have been occasions in which the entire system has been clearly and comprehensively divided into two warring camps. The "cold war" was one example of this process, at a lower level of tension, with the Iron Curtain decisively separating the world into two blocs.

The reason why the nation-state system tends towards polarization is that it is a "simple" system. Nation-state dominance guarantees that the entire world is parceled out among a number of structurally identical entities; the boundaries of these monopolistic entities are fissures along some of which the world can be arbitrarily redivided. The weakness of global institutions (and of local interests) augments the ease with which polarization can occur at times of war and war danger, through the process of alliances.

Polarization is a symptom of political malfunctioning. A more "complex" system would be less likely to slide down the conflict spiral. It would still allow for polarization, but would localize it to one part of the global system, rather than allowing it to dominate the entire structure.

Empirically, little is known about the present state of global consensus. The suspicion is that it is in bad shape, hardly adequate to provide a base for sound parliamentary activity. A fragmented, non-consensual or polarized system is, on the other hand, a fertile ground for extra-parliamentary and revolutionary political activity. Revolutionary movements are symptomatic of failures to cope with fundamental problems of order and justice: worldwide movements arise in response to global problems of this kind. The nation-state system's liability to polarization creates one particularly vicious circle, which is conducive to the fostering of revolutionary movements. Political polarization and the dislocation it engenders in wars and social turmoil breeds revolutionary and extremist movements, while these in turn reinforce the need for a nation-state system, as a means for maintaining order and fragmenting and compartmentalizing the trouble. Polarization, on the other hand, can be laid substantially at the door of that very system, and the emergence of revolutionary movements can be attributed to the system's failure to deal with existing disorders and injustices.

Revolutionary or radical movements may be distinguished according to their degree of centralization. Relatively centralized revolutionary movements are represented by nineteenth-century socialism or twentieth-century communism. During the Comintern period, Communism in particular went through a phase of excessive centralization: it became the world's first and so far only revolutionary world party, national member parties being formally and factually regarded as mere branches of the Moscow-based organization. The extraordinary degree of centralization, so much out of tune with other political aspects of the global system, proved obviously self-defeating, so that central control came to be some-what relaxed, particularly in the years since Stalin's death. Yet the move-ment has not been able to devise an effectively non-centralized structure, such as could accommodate a variety of autonomous organizations.

Examples of non-centralized movements include some religious move-ments, nineteenth-century nationalism and anarchism, and the contempo-rary youth unrest. The immediate effectiveness of non-centralized activity might well be small, but this agitation always signals important problems and in the long run it can prove to be quite significant.

The goal of world revolutionary movements is obviously revolution, but it is not always clear what kind of revolution this is to be. In the nation-state system, that question is not easily answered. Through several of its phases, for example, Communism has been associated with the idea of "world revolution," yet the precise meaning of that phrase is not obvious. It cannot be the seizure of power at the global level, because there is no power to be seized there: a non-centralized global system (lacking a world state) is immune to world revolution, in the sense of capture of the central organs of authority. In contemporary conditions, any attempt to stage a coup at the United Nations headquarters, or to replace the Secretary-General by force, would be a patent absurdity. World revolution can therefore mean only the conquest of power in a number of states and preferably in the Great Powers; but this immedi-ately becomes an arduous undertaking. Marxist theorists are inspired by the historical example of 1848, when a number of governments did col-lapse, in various parts of Europe, in an epidemic of organizational failure, and by the experiences of turmoil following the two great wars. Like the Great Powers, the revolutionary movements thrive on political upheaval; but like the Great Powers, too, they may succeed in doing little else than consolidate the nation-state system.

In the nation-state system, world revolutionary movements are likely to be swallowed up by the nation-state. When they seize power in na-tional politics, such movements tend to become absorbed in the tasks of administering that particular state and are soon coopted into the national community. Or else, if they maintain revolutionary interests in a number of different major states, they become inextricably linked with Great Power aspirations, and with the need to legitimize them and build external support for them. Soon the revolutionary component of foreign policy becomes indistinguishable from more commonplace hegemonic ambitions. The process could be observed with clarity in revolutionary French policy, which soon declined into Bonapartism—the chief preoccupation of which became the placing of family members and deserving marshals on the thrones of Europe. Soviet policy underwent a similar transforma-tion: within a few years after the October Revolution, the requirements of the orderly conduct of relations with foreign states imposed a separation of state functions from the operations of the Comintern. The Comintern became, first, a bone of contention in Stalin's struggle for total power, and, soon afterward, the docile instrument of his own ambitions. Chinese revolutionary principles during the years of their ideological break with the Soviet Union have been equally hard to distinguish from the requirements of Chinese foreign policy and the drive for superpower status.

Thus the nation-state system molds, absorbs and domesticates radical designs of the most varied kinds. It is an environment that is favorable to malignant disorder but essentially hostile to world revolution, just as the self-centered nation-state is an inadequate vehicle for a world revolutionary movement, even though it may harbor and protect national revolutionary regimes and movements of all hues. This built-in immunity to world revolution is an inherent feature of all autonomy-maintaining systems, of which the nation-state system is only one. But while revolutionary movements cannot expect total success in such systems, their existence does indicate the presence of grave structural and functional weaknesses in these systems; they must be regarded as signals, drawing attention to urgent problems of world politics—that is to say, as mechanisms of world responsibility. They are, in one sense, the product of the inequities and of the unrepresentative character of existing world political structures.

Global Elite Networks

World responsibility has so far been depicted as the product of interorganizational relations, of relations among governments, pressure groups, parties and organizations of various kinds. The same phenomenon may also be conceptualized as being the product of interpersonal relations—in particular, of relations among individuals of elite status. Membership in a global elite network carries with it an obligation of mutual responsiveness—especially, of sensitivity to each other's judgments.

Global elite networks may be primarily position-based—that is, binding officeholders (for example, diplomats) in similar positions in a number of states; or else they may serve to bind individuals who are of elite status but without strong organizational loyalties, such as writers or scientists. Elite networks rely either on personal acquaintance and friendship, or else on reputation; personal reputation is likely to be the currency of sanction and reward within that system. The operations of global elite networks still need to be better understood.[8]

The character and membership of elite networks is shaped by common cultural background—in particular, education—by a commonality of values, and by the frequency and intensity of the interaction they experience. A low-interaction system, such as that postulated for the model of the nation-state system, will have weak elite networks. Indeed, the system discourages, if it does not positively prohibit, transnational elite interaction, just as it discourages all other forms of interaction. Laws of some countries prohibit the acceptance of foreign titles, honors or decorations: the Soviet government, for example, prohibited Boris Pasternak from accepting the Nobel Prize. Diplomacy is an exception here, even though a built-in feature of its ethos is some degree of cynicism with regard to its own transactions, along with an acquired immunity to excessive sensitivity. Yet even diplomats have been known to become partisans of the interests of the countries they have been accredited to.

Nation-states assert control over global elite contacts; some, such as the Soviet Union, allow no communications without their surveillance. Networks that escape national control, such as those that are centered upon international organizations, are frowned upon in many places as suggestive of "cosmopolitanism" and other un-national aberrations. Yet modern society fosters a variety of professional and occupational commonalities the world over. These are the raw material of wider connections and, in favorable circumstances, the seedbeds of new networks. No stable world order would be even possible without them.

World Media

One precondition for global responsibility, and particularly for accountability, is the availability of information; an adequate system of world politics requires a high information content, and therefore a system of information media. In the modern world, the media have proliferated; they come in all sizes and to suit all tastes. Some are elaborate and expensive, but assure global coverage: the world press, radio and television; others are simple and cheap, and call for little expertise but illuminates only fragments of world experience: the telephone and the hand camera, the typewriter, the Xerox and other duplicating machines.

For maximum effectiveness, the large media systems need to be arranged in networks and require considerable autonomy. At various sites of world politics (for instance, in the major capitals, at the United Nations headquarters, or on such scenes of international crises as Saigon or Cairo) the media are represented by the world press, which supplies words and pictures to the world, through the efforts of a corps of journalists, reporters, photographers and film cameramen. The press corps is a late complement to the diplomatic corps. Evolved in the nineteenth century but grown to substantial strength only in the system of 1945, it shares some of the characteristics of the latter; but it is notable for its autonomy, and for the ability to make the product of its work available to the whole world (by contrast with the diplomatic corps, whose watchword is secrecy). In this respect of information equalization it is similar to science and learning in general.

The size of the global system makes the modern media peculiarly important. The larger the social system, the more elaborate and the more functionally autonomous are the media networks that it requires. The printing presses—that is to say, reading and writing, as well as language— have furnished the information basis of the nation-state. In small and medium countries, the printed word could be distributed nationally with great speed—on the day of publication, after the advent of the railways. Nationalism had to rely upon language as the principal information system.

Electronic media have now made possible instantaneous and global information systems. They convey not only words but other sounds and also images; that is how they make possible the dissociation of language from politics (yet they may at the same time open up an association between sounds, images and politics). "It is a principal aspect of the electronic age that it establishes a global network that has much of the character of our central nervous system. . . . With instant electronic technology, the globe itself can never again be more than a village . . ." [9] Technological advance creates the conditions for (although, by itself, it does not make inevitable) the formation of new political structures. For every audience is a rudimentary political system; an audience for a global feat, such as a moon landing, is the primitive matrix of a global society.

World media need to develop autonomously, even though all organizations—large organizations, in particular—have their own information systems: states have intelligence services, and business firms have marketing research services. Organizational information systems, however, tend to feed their output up the hierarchy and toward the center and to be weak on lateral distributions. Even Presidents, too, with access to the world's best information services, regularly consult several daily papers. A multi-organizational universe needs particularly strong media networks. If a free press has been the condition of democratic politics in a nation-state (and so guaranteed in the Constitution), free electronic media might be the condition of minimum world order. They are particularly important for individuals, small organizations and non-centralized systems that would otherwise be excluded from the world political arena, and therefore have no chance to accumulate support or to promote new ventures.

The importance of the world media is not to be assessed by their success in distributing mere facts, such as the names of political leaders.

If at any given time a large part of the population chooses to forget the name of such persons, or the political complexion of some foreign country, that in itself is not really important. What matters is common awareness of such perennial global problems and predicaments as war and peace, development or environment, and of the possibility of talking together about them.

World media promote accountability above all, however, by highlighting those occasions on which world values have either been promoted (for instance, through a discovery, an invention, or a daring feat) or else violated (the invasion of Czechoslovakia; executions in the streets of Saigon, or in the country lanes of Biafra). By doing so, the media in a sense also dispense rewards and sanctions, even though others too contribute to this process. Thus, it was world television that captured Chairman Khrushchev's famous shoe-banging episode at the United Nations, but it remained up to Soviet politicians to replace him four years later on the grounds of "uncultured" behavior.

The nation-state system offers a secure basis for a variety of media operations and thereby contributes toward developing conditions of media autonomy. The political autonomy produced by the nation-state also makes possible a large degree of media autonomy. At the very least, there is no single-channel world state television. But as a device for ensuring global accountability, the system does have some weaknesses. In many countries, the media are closely controlled by the state; where the latter holds the power monopoly, they are also monopolized. They thus serve as instruments of national policy and cannot have it as their objective to correct its shortcomings. In all countries, media are closely linked with national political institutions; they maximize exposure to national problems, at the expense of both local and global problems. Thus, despite technological advance, the emergence of a true world press or television is still far from being a reality. Only a few printed publications so far (such as the London *Economist* or *Time* magazine) are slowly evolving a global conception of their functions, and to some extent this might also be true of such daily papers as *Le Monde, The New York Times* and the *London Times.* But the world media are also characteristically oriented toward Western and developed countries; like other existing mechanisms of responsibility, they reflect and inform interests that are already well-informed.

World Opinion

The idea of world public opinion antedates the nation-state system. It flourished in the Age of European Enlightenment, during the eighteenth

century. The Encyclopedists, for example, saw the human race as form-
ing one great society, which obeyed the Laws of Nature. The signers of
the Declaration of Independence were paying "a decent respect to the
opinions of mankind" when they explained their reasons for breaking
with King George III. Immanuel Kant felt free to assume that a "community of the peoples of the world has developed so far that a violation
of the rights in one place is felt throughout the world." [10] In the nineteenth century, Jeremy Bentham and John Stuart Mill became exponents
of the power of public opinion. Woodrow Wilson's design for the League
of Nations was closely bound up with his faith in the efficacy of such
opinion.

World public opinion is, in a basic sense, the ultimate constituency
of world politics; its sanctions are information and publicity. Kant supplied the philosophical foundation for world opinion when he elaborated,
as the basic formula for judging the right or wrong of particular policies,
the criterion of publicity: "All actions relating to the right of other men
are unjust if their maxim is not consistent with publicity." In brief: "every
legal claim must be capable of publicity." [11] This was a corollary of the
categorical imperative, a central part of his moral philosophy and a fundamental element of his thought. Policies that had been laid open to the
scrutiny of world opinion were likely to be policies that were conducive
to public order and a state of perpetual peace.

In a large society, the operation of opinion depends upon the free
functioning of the media. Advances in media technology during the twentieth century might have made fully operational the injunctions of the
thinkers of the Enlightenment. As Kant himself had said, publicity is not
by itself enough because "no one who has decidedly superior power needs
to conceal his plans." [12] Superior power is not often certain in politics;
as a result, the states of the early European system delighted in secrecy,
and few of their diplomatic, let alone military, methods were open to
close examination. The diplomacy of the Italian Renaissance, during the
formative period of that craft, was replete with duplicity, deceit, bribery,
betrayal and political assassination. Publicity might have done a great
deal of good for manners and morals, in a society of more or less equal
states. Diplomacy did in fact mend its manners as time went on, and communications and the press became more effective.

As the mechanism through which public policy could yet come closer
to the public good, publicity is the key to the effectiveness of world
opinion, even though, like justice and because it bears on justice, it requires
conditions of power equality. But how does it function in the nation-
state system? Can it be, as Hans Morgenthau has argued, that "under
present world conditions . . . a world public opinion restraining the foreign
policies of national governments does not exist"? [13]

Writing shortly after the end of World War II, Morgenthau elaborated his views at considerable length: (1) in spite of the basic similarity of men all over the world and the "community of psychological traits and elementary aspirations" the lack of shared experience, universal moral convictions and common political objectives prove the impossibility of world public opinion; (2) the importance of the technological unification of the world is greatly exaggerated; (3) nation-states are the dominant molders of public opinion; (4) since a public opinion presupposes a society and a consensus, there cannot be any world public opinion, because "such a world society and such a universal morality do not exist."

Since the time of Morgenthau's writing, even technological conditions have changed drastically in nature and impact. The enormity of thermonuclear explosions, just as much as contemporary television reporting, provide that shared vision, that "identity of experience uniting mankind." [14] But in the main Morgenthau's is an argument cast within the nation-state framework. For that system has erected new barriers to world opinion such as its eighteenth- and even nineteenth-century exponents did not foresee. States have coopted nations while, cloaked in the mantle of national interest, they affect imperviousness to world opinion.

The contemporary nation-state system indeed offers only limited scope for world opinion. Debates in a United Nations forum at times distill a certain consensus and at other times make manifest existing differences; but the display of governmental opinions that such debates offer, while it is better than no debate at all, at best only approximates world opinion.

World public opinion; formulated in a variety of contexts (not only governmental, and perhaps not even primarily governmental), commanding wide support and conveyed and made known by the media, is the conscience of the world. Its primary function could be not so much to restrain shortsighted foreign policies as to direct attention to neglected world problems. For the greatest effectiveness, it needs to be informed by a convincing conception of the world interest.

The World Interest

"The end of Government is the good of Mankind," [15] wrote John Locke at the end of the seventeenth century. For thinkers of his time and before the ascendancy of the nation-state, the universal interest was a familiar concept. Since then, the national interest has moved to the center of the stage, and even the idea of a world interest has lapsed into darkness and desuetude.

Yet such a concept is necessary, even in the nation-state system. For unless some infinitely wise "invisible hand" is assumed to maintain order and justice among nation-states, explicit principles are indispensable—if only as guidelines for those (such as the leaders of the Great Powers) who cannot avoid acting, and whose actions could have irreparable consequences for the future of mankind. Such principles are also necessary as standards in terms of which to evaluate and criticize international conduct.

The world interest is more than the sum of pressures for world responsibility—that is, of the intergovernmental exchanges, the pressure-group politics, factional and revolutionary activity, the blaze of the media and the murmur of world opinion. The "good of Mankind" is more than the unavoidably self-centered and self-serving spokesmen for it have asserted it to be. Scholarship alone cannot define or legislate it, but it can help in clearing away some of the underbrush and sketching out the outlines of the problem.

Each individual system of world politics will promote its own conception of world interest. The nation-state system conception includes the maintenance of that system in its essential features: globalization, state autonomy, nation-state dominance and Great Power authority. Nation-building as the goal of world policy summarizes this conception of the world interest.

The maintenance of one particular political regime for mankind cannot possibly exhaust the content of world interest. Such a concept needs to have bolder bearings and keener horizons than that.

Three more fundamental elements of the world interest suggest themselves at this stage: (1) Survival of the earth as an oasis of life, in the black and inhospitable vastness of the universe, ranks as the highest and irreducible world interest. Nothing else can supersede this consideration. (2) In addition to the needs of survival, there has to be a maximum of varied and balanced autonomy for the inhabitants of the earth, as the guiding principle of order. (3) Within a framework of order based on autonomy, increased equality is the road to justice.

Such a wider conception of the world interest may not be realizable in the nation-state system. Not only is justice unattainable there, and autonomy strictly one-sided; even survival has come into question. Conceptions of world responsibility must therefore include the possibility of changes in global politics.

Notes to Chapter Ten

1. Compare Chapter 7, section on "Non-Centralization."
2. Bernard Fall, *The Two Vietnams* (New York: Praeger, 1963), pp. 88–90.
3. See also G. Modelski, "World Parties and World Order," in C. E.

Black and R. A. Falk (eds.), *The Future of the International Legal Order*, Vol. 1 (Princeton: Princeton University Press, 1969), pp. 183–225.

4. M. Duverger, *Political Parties* (New York: Wiley, 1963), pp. xxiv–xxv.

5. H. R. Alker and B. M. Russett, *World Politics in the General Assembly* (New Haven: Yale University Press, 1965), Ch. 7.

6. Modelski, "World Parties and World Order," *cited*, p. 209 ff.

7. J. Galtung, "East West Interaction Patterns," *cited*, p. 150: "With a feudal relationship between two blocs or systems, polarization is already built into the system. . . ."

8. For instance, G. Modelski, "The World's Foreign Ministers," *cited*.

9. Marshall McLuhan, *Understanding Media: The extension of Man* (New York: New American Library), pp. 298–302.

10. Immanuel Kant, *Perpetual Peace* (1795) (Third Definitive Article for a Perpetual Peace).

11. *Ibid*, Appendix II ("on the harmony which the transcendental concept of public right establishes between morality and politics").

12. *Ibid*.

13. Morgenthau, *Politics Among Nations, cited*, Ch. 17, World Public Opinion, pp. 235–245. See also E. H. Carr, *The Twenty Years Crisis 1919–1939, cited*, pp. 31–8. He points to a number of well-known cases of the flouting of world opinion in those years, such as the seizure of Manchuria, the conquest of Ethiopia and the final destruction of Czechoslovakia. It might be worth recalling that those responsible did not fare so well in the end, after all; in retrospect, it might have been wise for them to heed world opinion.

14. Morgenthau, *Politics among Nations, cited*, p. 239.

15. John Locke, *Second Treatise on Government*, Para. 229.

II

The
Reality
of
World
Society

THE RULES OF THE NATION-STATE
system exclude the possibility of a world society. These same rules have
blinded students of International Relations to facts and trends that point in
the opposite direction, and deny the validity of the nation-state system as
a general model for the study of world politics.

From Jean-Jacques Rousseau to Hans Morgenthau

Observers of the world scene have not always had this myopic view.
The dominant conceptions of the Age of Enlightenment, for instance,
assumed the unity of the human race and the existence of universal bonds
and obligations. Writing in the *Encyclopedia* in 1755, Denis Diderot
expounded such views as though he were reiterating the conventional
wisdom of the time. But the intellectual winds were even then beginning
to shift. In the same work, Jean-Jacques Rousseau came out against the
universal view, and later built upon this argument a structure that stands
to this day among the classics of the theory of the nation-state.

In what might be called an eighteenth-century Great Debate (later
to degenerate into a celebrated quarrel), Diderot held that the test of
morals and of government was the general will of the human race, as
embodied in the law and practices of civilized peoples. Rousseau strongly
dissented from this view; for him the society of the whole human race
was "a veritable chimera," in that race alone did not constitute a society:
mere likeness of kind or identity of psychological conditions creates no

real union. A society must be founded upon common possessions, such as a common language, an identity of experience, a *sensorium commune*, a common interest and well-being. Furthermore, reason by itself was never sufficient to bring men together; men's ideas even of self-interest are derived from the community in which they live. Finally, if there was any idea of a general human family, it arose from the little community in which men live instinctively; an international community is the end and not the beginning of the road. It is not really the most important of the communities at all.[1]

Rousseau's arguments prevailed and became the conventional wisdom of the age of the nation-state. Hans Morgenthau's dissection of world opinion, cited a few pages earlier, closely recalls Rousseau's reasoning and rests upon the same proposition that

such a world society and such a universal morality (as are required by world public opinion) do not exist. Between the elemental aspirations for life, freedom and power which united mankind, and which could provide the roots for a world society and universal morality, and the political philosophies, ethics, and objectives actually held by the human race, there intervenes the nation . . . Inevitably then, the members of the human race live and act politically, not as members of one world society applying standards of universal ethics, but as members of their respective national societies, guided by their national standards of morality. In politics, the nation and not humanity is the ultimate fact.[2]

The non-existence of world society and the fact that nation-state dominance is the "ultimate fact" of politics have consequences not only for the effectiveness of world opinion; they are also fatal to the prospects for peace. On Morgenthau's analysis, peace is possible only in the national society, because such society alone: (1) possesses suprasectional cross-cutting loyalties, (2) encourages the expectation of justice, and (3) brings overwhelming force to bear upon the violators of peace. In short, national societies have states and the states keep peace within. In the world at large, these conditions do not obtain; since there can be "no state without a society willing and able to support it, there can be no world state without a world community." Hence, there can be no lasting world peace.[3]

That peace depends in part upon society, and certain structural arrangements within it may be taken as self-evident. But the proposition that world peace is impossible without a world state must be vigorously contested. It may be the cliché of generations of complacent thought and argument, which has also penetrated the study of International Relations; yet the argument is extremely tenuous and will stand analysis.[4]

The establishment of a world state of "overwhelming" power is unlikely to bear out the pious hope that, contrary to historical experience, such an event will bring about lasting and beneficent peace. Such a power monopoly would either be an empire or would tend to deteriorate into one; on the basis of past performance (see Chapter Two), its prospects of success would be rather slim.

World power monopoly cannot be the precondition of world peace. Morgenthau's other conditions of social peace, the strength of cross-sectional loyalties, and the actuality of the expectation of justice, need to be empirically examined; the degree of their realization in the world at large will be reviewed later in this chapter. What is striking about Morgenthau's arguments, however, as about those of Rousseau, is the fact that they describe not the world as it is (for that, extensive research would have been required, since the information is far from being readily obtainable or unambiguous), but only the postulates of the nation-state system. If such a system is to work in the manner that has been specified in its rules, then world opinion *has* to be weak and the nation-state *must* be the "ultimate fact," the wielder of overwhelming force, the exclusive repository of justice and the sole claimant upon loyalties. If such postulates are not in fact being satisfied, then perhaps the nation-state system is not working as well as it should.

Even more startling is the conclusion that the postulates of the nation-state system not only deny the possibility of peace, but are in fact incompatible with it. If world politics were to be conducted in accordance with the rules of that system, war would need to be a certainty. A system that tolerates only a monopoly of loyalties, that centralizes great forces, and makes justice dependent on habitually weak support, indeed renders war inevitable. It is this theoretical necessity for war that should make scholars wary of the model of the nation-state system, as well as of its various ramifications.

If Hans Morgenthau's postulates are denied, however, then there is no logical next step to a theoretical inevitability of war, or to his consequent pessimism about the prospects for peace. Instead, such a denial would call for a close look at proofs for the existence of world society. For it would appear that the time has come to examine the conventional wisdom, and to pose once again the question of whether Diderot's position might not be the more fruitful one for today's student of world politics. The postulate of world society allows for the situation in which the nation-state system shapes it rather strongly, and even negatively; conversely, denying the existence of world society blinds observers to the great canvas of earthly life upon which any view of world politics has to be painted.

Models of World Society

As the central concept of a geocentric approach to world politics, world society needs careful elaboration and precise analysis. This task will be taken up in the remainder of the present chapter and once again in Part Three.

Three criteria may be laid down for establishing the existence of world society—that is, for determining whether a given population aggregate might be so called: (1) awareness; (2) interaction and interdependence, and (3) common values. They are necessary aspects of all social action and in specified degrees they must be present in a global social system. They are also, however, to some degree incremental, inasmuch as common values presuppose interaction and awareness, and interdependence presupposes awareness. Conceivably, radio contact could be established between stations on earth and in other stellar systems or other galaxies, without requiring interdependence. But even the mere exchange of messages and the sharing of a communications system already constitute interaction and also presuppose adherence to certain rules of communications—that is, to a rudimentary value system.

The world state, or power monopoly, is not a necessary condition for the existence of world society, although its presence would undoubtedly be significant. Morgenthau's other conditions of society, on the other hand, are aspects of interaction and commonality of values, and will be examined in due course. Cross-sectional loyalties are characteristic of interdependent social systems; the expectation of justice prevails in a system that shares the relevant values. Rousseau's *sine qua non* of a universal language, an identity of experience, or common interests, also belongs among the same, more general categories.

A conceptual clarification is in order before proceeding with the analysis. The question is: what is the most useful model for thinking about world society? Figure 11:1 introduces diagrams intended to bring out some elementary differences among four models or conceptions of world society.

Model I is a representation of the nation-state system, composed of large and small countries. The questions to be answered here are: Is this model satisfactory? How do contemporary world conditions diverge from this model of self-sufficient, self-responsible and basically noncommunicating communities? If such an ethnocentric model is inadequate, what can be put in its place?

Some who are dissatisfied with the ethnocentric conception of the world view mankind as one big undifferentiated mass, a universal "Family of Man" (Model II). Such is a fair rendering of the ideas of eighteenth-century Enlightenment, as represented, for instance, by Diderot (who

Figure 11:1
Models of World Society

I. Nation-State System:
   Ethnocentric

II. World Society
    Universal Family of Man

III. World Society
     Egocentric

IV. World Society
    Geocentric Layered Networks

    "The Layer Cake"

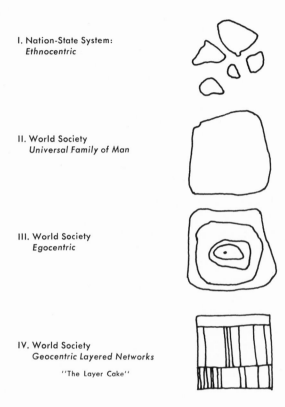

was however careful to distinguish between civilized and other peoples).
This is also the view that is being criticized by Morgenthau, when he
denies that the psychological unity of the world and universal aspirations
for life, liberty and happiness suffice as building blocks of world society.
What might be labeled "cosmopolitanism" takes insufficient notice of
the diversities that characterize the world, and the variety of strata of
all ages that make up its structures. It prompts the search for an illusory
and ever-receding community, a tightly-knit, affectively-bound small
group (a family, a tribe or a city) but writ large—which is a contradiction
in terms. And when the vision fails, such a universe, like the nation-state
system, lapses into polarization.

Replying to Diderot, Rousseau proposed an individualistic, or
egocentric view of the world (Model III). With each individual the

center of his own universe, smaller communities, beginning with the family, the village or the city, build up toward larger unities, including the nation and the world. Reasonable though this view may seem at first, it is not really adequate. The hierarchy of interest that it implies has nothing natural or logical about it; it says little about social as distinct from personal priorities. Must the city always take precedence over the nation? Rousseau's concept assumes, too, that wider communities (more correctly: more extensive networks) must be built up from smaller communities. This need not be so. Wider networks may give birth to smaller communities, and vice versa. There is no inevitability about the direction this process takes. The egocentric view of the world is too subjective to be of much service for political analysis.

The architecture of large social systems calls for fresh designs and new principles. The coziness of the small group cannot be duplicated by proportionate enlargement, for the same reason that a flea blown up a thousand times could not jump at all. The search for close intimacy has already caused disasters in the name of national unity; it can lead only to chaos, if it is made into a global imperative. Problems of scale in social systems demand novel solutions.

The blueprint underlying the present study is the geocentric model of layered networks, which can also be called the "layer-cake" model of world society (Model IV). It is designed to capture some of the complexity that is inherent in world society, at the same time as it emphasizes the elements of order in it. This will be gone into at greater length in Part Three; for the present, the pages that follow are intended to demonstrate only the non-applicability of Models I and II.

Awareness

Global awareness is the first condition of world society. Such awareness, however, is not anything new; it has been the product of globalization for several centuries. The travels of Marco Polo to China, the voyages of discovery, the regularization of international mails, and the laying of a worldwide cable network—each of these has been a milestone along the road to increasingly reliable knowledge about world conditions,

This ground was covered, in part, in the section above on world opinion. Two aspects of the communications revolution now need commenting on in more detail: the significance of the decline in the real cost of communications, and the growth of specifically global information and communication systems. The ramifications of these processes are extensive; they may become substantial enough, in due course, to serve as the matrix of functionally independent global processes.

Most important of all might be the continued decline in the *cost* of information, at a time when other basic resources—in particular, land, air and water—are becoming relatively scarce, principally because of population growth and concentration. All types of costs in the production, transmission and distribution of information have fallen: the costs of sending messages, of dispatching people and goods, of research, education and information storage. At the same time, these functions have come to occupy an increasingly important place in the world's scale of priorities.

In the three decades between 1940 and 1967, international cable and telegraph rates between New York and Tokyo were cut by over one-half; the price of basic three-minute person-to-person calls between the two cities fell from $19.50 to $12.00. Calls to London declined by even a larger factor.[5] At a time when other costs (as measured by the wholesale price index) have been nearly doubling, and gross world output probably trebling, the real cost of information transmission has been going down and the trend is still in progress. The sharp impact of earth satellites on telephone service and on television programming (including television broadcasting in developing countries) is yet to be fully felt. The cost of any "off-time" telephone call anywhere in the world might soon fall to as low as $1. The process that began in the nineteenth century in relation to letter mail—when, through the operation of the Universal Postal Union, the cost of sending a foreign letter became invariant with respect to distance—is now spreading to voice and image communications.

Similar developments have occurred in transportation and in education. Access to educational facilities is now available on a broad basis, and the expansion of educational activities has boosted the demand for information. Research, conceived as the purposeful production of information, is now an organized social function; in terms of its returns, it may still be a declining cost industry.

In any case, as the world has grown richer, the demand for information has risen, quite apart from its falling price. Accordingly, big strides have been made toward the evolution of specifically global communications, transportation, research and educational networks. Not all of these are international in management, but they all display a tendency to develop specialized organizational forms for the performance of global functions. The communications satellite corporation is a specifically international corporation of widely spread ownership and management, the first example of a world public utility. The airlines industry, while fiercely competitive (mostly along national lines), clearly differentiates between international carriers and, in larger countries, major domestic and local feeder lines. The international lines form a distinctive, world-spanning network of trunk routes; they make possible personal contact between most points in the world within 24 hours, and they facilitate an immense expansion in tourism, which is a form of global study and experience. Science and education at the quarternary level now form a functionally specific network, which is global in function if not in designation.

Broadly viewed, the modern communications industry is the central nervous system of the world body social. With ever-increasing efficiency, it supplies the common sensory experience that is necessary to guide its processes, to identify world problems and to devise solutions for them. Just as the Age of Discovery stood at the inception of the modern state system, an age that re-evaluated all accepted notions and political orders, so the modern communications revolution—whose high point so far has been the venture into space, and the first objective glimpse of the earth as a whole—may produce yet new visions of life on this planet and a reassessment of world politics. What is more, the spectacular growth in the fund of knowledge, combined with wider personal experience, may also help to build that trust upon which all social systems are ultimately based.

The Role of Trade

Trade has long been regarded as the cement of the international community, as an influence for peace. Adam Smith, John Stuart Mill and Richard Cobden and, more recently, Norman Angell were among those who have argued that free commercial competition augments wealth, and, internationally, through specialization and the division of labor, creates interdependent networks of mutual advantage that it would be too costly to break. Kant asserted flatly that "the spirit of commerce, which is incompatible with war, sooner or later gains the upper hand in every state." In this tendency he saw one of the guarantees of inevitable peace.

Contemporary students of global interdependence have continued to pay attention to international trade. Partial global data (Table 11:1) suggest that world trade (the sum total of world exports and world imports) indexed in the 1950's and 1960's at about 20 percent of world output. Since each shipment is counted twice, once as an export and again as an import, the actual share of world resources that is engaged in world trade comes to about 10 percent. But the higher figure may more accurately represent the weight of foreign trade in the world economy, because to each shipment corresponds, first, a set of exporters and second, a set of importers. On either account, whether it is reckoned at 20 per-

TABLE 11:1   Importance of International Trade
(*$U.S. billions*)

	1. World Exports	2. World Imports	3. World Trade (1 + 2)	4. World output (current prices)	5. World trade as percentage of world output
1938	24	25	49		
1953	83	84	167	770	21.7
1964	172	182	354	1,903	18.6
1965	186	199	385	2,087	18
1966	204	216	420	2,296	18.7
1967	215	227	442	2,482	17.8
1968	240	252	492	2,685	18.3

Sources: *United Nations Statistical Yearbook for 1966, 1970; World Military Expenditures 1969.*

cent of world economic activity, or 10 percent of real resources, the role of international trade in the world picture is quite substantial.

The series is incomplete because good data are lacking, and it cannot therefore be taken as conclusive; also, the estimates of world output are rather crude. For this reason, not much can be deduced from it about trends toward either a rise or a decline in the proportion of world output passing through international trade. But studies by Morgan of a number of developed and developing economies over a time span of some decades indicate a considerable stability in the foreign-trade ratio, at about the level indicated by global data shown in Figure 11:3. Morgan's research confirms, moreover, that the average involvement in world trade is about the same for the developed as it is for the less developed countries—in the region of 20 percent.[6] In other words, Morgan finds no evidence to support the thesis of the decline in the relative importance of international trade as the result of industralization.

International trade in the proportions just described is not incompatible with the rules of the nation-state system. Though undoubtedly significant, it is not so large as to overwhelm the system or to challenge it seriously. More particularly, the degree to which states participate in trade varies. Of the Great Powers, most show a below-average rate of involvement: the United States, seven percent; the U.S.S.R., five percent; France, 20 percent; China, nine percent. Britain alone among the traditional Great Powers (with a rate of 30 percent in 1959) has had a large stake in commerce and has traditionally been a spokesman for the merits of unhampered trade. By contrast, many non-Great Powers, both in the developed and in the developing world, greatly depend upon foreign trade—for instance, Egypt, 38 percent; Sweden,

41 percent; New Zealand, 43 percent; Norway, 51 percent; Denmark, 55 percent; Liberia, 71 percent; Libya, 79 percent. Hence, a world order arranged by the Great Powers will neither give particular prominence to international trade, nor will it favor its undue expansion. Great Power status, being a function of military power, is also a function of economic self-sufficiency, and is therefore directly opposed to any but marginal (non-strategic) flows of imports in particular.

The theory and practice of international trade, with emphasis on differential factor endowment and on currency exchange rates (both of which pit the residents of different areas and the users of different currency systems against one another), proceed within the nation-state system and serve only to enhance its assumptions and strengthen its institutional framework. With no provisions for factor mobility or a world currency, commerce is based on a system of strong reserve currencies (at first the pound sterling, and later the dollar); this is the equivalent of the Great Power system in the financial field.

In any event, world trade is only fictionally an exchange of goods between "countries." In reality, it is a resource-and-income-allocation network whose control has, in consequence of the development of world poliitcs over the past two to three centuries, come to reside in Northwest Europe, with England and the Low Countries as its centers. The functioning of this network is closely bound up with the operation of the nation-state system and reflects the distribution of power within it. The share of the underdeveloped countries in world trade is of the same order of magnitude as their share of world income (between 15 and 20 percent), and is not significantly larger than their share of world military power. All these phenomena seem to be closely interrelated.

The participation of developing areas in international trade is small (relatively to their populations, though not relatively to their income), and has been declining. Between 1953 and 1965 exports from developing countries as a proportion of all exports fell from 26.9 to 19.5 percent. Most of this trade, moreover, is controlled from outside their territory. The glaring example of this is oil. At a time when the over-all share of the developing countries in world trade was declining, the significance of oil among their exports rose from 21.2 percent in 1953 to 30.4 percent in 1965.[7] Certain governments in oil mining areas (including the King of Saudi Arabia and the Sheikhs of Kuwait, Bahrein and Abu Dhabi) reap substantial and unearned profits from oil royalties; but the control and disposition of oil production is entirely in the hands of a limited number of large international corporations (seven "majors" control three-quarters of non-Communist oil). The same thing holds for most of the primary products that are exported by developing "countries" to world markets.

The great bulk of international trade is controlled from, and also occurs within, a rather small portion of the globe, the Northwest Europe/North Atlantic area, with Japan only lately (although vigorously) joining in. The same kind of unevenness may be observed in regard to tourism (which takes in the export of travel and holiday facilities). The ten largest tourist-receiving countries, which accounted for between 80 and 90 percent of all tourists in 1965, were in Western Europe and North America.[8] In other words, international trade is not a source of coherence for the whole of world society; on the contrary, it starkly illustrates the lack of integration and the unevenness to be found in it. It is a process by which the rich and powerful countries are woven into a pattern of close, though not too close, interaction; for world society as a whole, this "clustering" has an unbalancing effect. The network of interdependence that emerges from it is too one-sided in the distribution of its benefits.

Despite the fact that the developing countries' share in world trade is small and falling, the impact of this share is great because it engages large segments of their economies. Many of the poorer and smaller economies depend on export for the bulk of their revenue; but price fluctuations frequently jeopardize their economic as well as political stability. Yet, because of their limited market power and influence in the global system, their ability to manage these vital matters (hence, also, to be meaningfully involved) is quite small.

World trade may be defined as an interorganizational exchange that takes place in a world market; in that sense, much of what conventionally passes for international trade does not really qualify, and the true share of world trade in the world economy is probably smaller than it was shown to be in Table 11:1. The market need not be perfectly competitive, but there must at least be some competitive pressure within it, to bring about price adjustments or resource shifts. Examples of such competitive markets are the gold market and the shipping and insurance markets (based on London), the market for passenger aircraft and large ships, and various agricultural and mining products markets. The trade in arms too is largely a world market. Movements of commodities such as these constitute world trade. By contrast, trade in bricks or gravel, in highly perishable items, in land or housing, is largely local, and will be influenced only indirectly by world trends. A shipment of bricks from Vancouver, B.C., to Seattle, Washington, does not constitute world trade. The shape and composition of world trade, along with its relationship to national and local trading patterns reflect the present character of world society.

Contrasting with interorganizational exchanges are intra-organizational transfers, such as: movements of parts from a manufacturing center to an assembly factory; shipments of oil from mining areas to processing plants to distribution centers; the transfer of liquid reserve funds between branches of a worldwide enterprise; transfers of know-how, patent rights, instructions and blueprints within a large corporation. Unlike traditional trade, this process knows no importers or exporters, it may not figure in trade statistics, and it may even elude governmental control. It is made possible by the existence of corporate and other world-spanning organizations. It has been argued [9] that the share of intra-organizational transfers in the world economy is rising, and that that rise is being accompanied by an increasing importance of intergovernmental exchanges (such as aid) which, though interorganizational, do not have the characteristics of trade. Whereas traditional international trade is easily accommodated within the nation-state system, the intra-organizational transfers of global enterprises pose entirely new problems for world society.

The traditional commodity-exchange type of international trade has been largely in the hands of Western Europe. Intra-organizational transfers, however, occur within the great corporations, and the world of the corporation is centered in the United States, with strong supporting centers in Western Europe and Japan.[10] The change in the character of world resource transfers also brings shifts in control patterns, even though the developing world is still entirely outside it.

International trade has customarily been explained by differences in the "endowment" of "nations," and has therefore been seen as the exploitation of these differences. The rise of the large and potentially geocentric corporations [11] and the intra-organizational transfers that have accompanied it have shifted the emphasis to processes of large-scale cooperation, to the utilization of economies of scale that transcend arbitrary and political boundaries. The natural limit for certain enterprises is now the whole earth, and some have already approached that limit. Thus the potential demand for large new airliners is limited, in part, by the size of the globe and the (fixed) distance between various points on it; development costs being extremely high, only three or four organizations in the world are capable of embarking on such a venture. Those that do are engaged in a global enterprise.

Modern Interdependencies

So much for economic interdependence, because it is undoubtedly fundamental to the daily concerns of mankind. The problem is, of course, wider. Science and the world of learning are in principle one large cooperative system. Knowledge is free (to all who can afford the expense of continuously updating costly library and information storage systems); once discovered, it is shared by all. The free interchange of findings has given rise to an extensive division of labor within science and the practice of narrow, although thorough, specialization. Such specialization makes possible worldwide attacks upon such problems of common concern as the weather, the geophysical properties of the earth, the structure of matter, or the nature of life. Economies of scale require the concentration of scarce resources at a few research sites; in particle physics, for example, three or four large research laboratories, are sufficient to serve the needs of all of world science. The same principles apply to educational specialization, especially at the university and graduate level, for the demand for specialists in certain fields is limited, even on a global scale. A rupture in this pattern of interdependence is a loss to all, although it is a long-term loss, the consequences of which are not experienced immediately. The wider interest of science lies in the lessons it offers as a model of decentralized interdependence.

Finally, there is political interdependence, which takes a number of forms. A remarkable feature of the nation-state system as a device for the maximization of independence is the uniformity with which the nation-state now covers the entire globe. Independence apparently does not extend to the freedom *not* to be politically organized into a nation-state. Uniform reliance upon a single and dominant organizational model makes the nation-state system as excessively interdependent, and as vulnerable to disasters as a prairie that has been converted to single-crop cultivation is to fire, pests and diseases. Despite the high productivity that may be achieved, a breakdown in one of the system's exemplars might be evidence of a structural weakness in the entire species, and the system could conceivably suffer from sudden panic or from an epidemic of low morale.

These are still unfamiliar metaphors. More commonly, war has been regarded as a mechanism of interaction, and also a symptom of interdependence. War has created the nation-state system, and the threat of war is the principal mechanism for maintaining it. The structure and operation of the system are, in themselves, a principal illustration of worldwide interdependence.

"Peace is indivisible" was one of the political slogans of the inter-war years in Europe, and a watchword of the League of Nations in its later years. Even at that time, peace was to some degree divisible; for although war, like all violence, is infectious and tends to spread into world wars, a war in the highlands of Bolivia need not necessarily be seen as a threat to the structure of world society.

True interdependence has been achieved only by the threat of nuclear annihilation. Nuclear fallout and the evident enormity of nuclear destructiveness pose the danger that the action of even one nuclear garrison may terminate life on earth. In other words, the future well-being of all is indissolubly intertwined with the decisions of those few who have power to set in motion the arsenal of mass killing. Defense, or security or protection from threats to life and limb, is now so huge and so demanding a task that the cooperation it demands is in some respects global in scope.

The reason why nuclear interdependence is so compelling is ulti-mately that the earth is small and there is no escape from it. The same thing applies to all the other aspects of global independence previously examined; political interdependence, the intricate honeycomb of science, and the structure of the world economy. They all rest, at bottom, upon constraints of size and on the necessity for cooperation—not in all re-spects, but in certain specifiable respects—because the earth has its limits and it has relatively few resources. The assumption of a moving or open frontier upon which the nation-state system may have rested earlier is no longer tenable.

Basic to global interdependence is the realization that mankind shares a common base of finite resources. The most recent apostles of this insight have been the ecologists, who have been keenly aware of the interplay of various life-cycles upon this planet; this concept is the basis for their alarm over global pollution of every kind, over the destruction of wildlife and of nature in general. But thoughtful observers of human affairs have assumed this all along as among the grounds of concern for the future of the human race. Kant, for instance, argued a "universal law of hospitality" on the grounds of a "right of association which all men have . . . by virtue of their common possession of the surface of the earth, where, as a globe, they cannot infinitely disperse and hence must finally tolerate the presence of each other." [12]

The true resources of earthly life—the globe itself and its surface, the water and the air—are all finite.[13] The size of the globe is fixed, which limits the amount of energy that the earth can absorb from the sun and the universe. This in turn determines the quantity and quality of life that is the biosphere. The finite nature of these basic resources sets an upper limit to the kind of life and politics that can develop on earth.

A good deal of political debate in earlier centuries had to do with property, and with the rights of men to appropriate it for their own personal use. Such debates concerned in particular territory, landed property and, by extension, the capital resources built upon land. But if land is divisible and apportionable, and if the fruits of it are exchange-able by trade, air and water are not. No one can claim to own a particular segment of air or to control all water, because of their capacity for worldwide circulation as part of the weather. No human being can exist without them, so that a doubling of the world population automatically cuts in half the quantity of air and water that is available to each. Hence the politics of air and water control open up problems that the territory (and property) oriented nation-state system is not prepared to cope with. Indeed, constructive utilization of air and water as the "commons" for mankind could lead to changes in world organization. The finiteness of world resources demonstrates the fact that the only self-sufficient unit of human organization is world society; all others fail this test and, in the age of global interactions, create interdependencies of every kind.

Finally, each instance of interdependence creates cross-cutting loyalties. All the processes just analyzed foster and maintain networks of personal and organizational relations, and these in their turn rely upon and create loyalties. Even international trade takes place within a framework of trust and mutual confidence, and cannot but generate loyalties, even if these do tend to be limited in scope. The cooperative properties of global organizations create cross-cutting loyalties of a stronger kind. The scientific community has long been known for the universality of its concerns—a tradition that goes back to the Republic of Letters of sixteenth- and seventeenth-century European scholarship. The need to look for solutions to the problems that are posed by the finiteness of human resources and the consequent threat to life sets in motion processes that lead to yet newer loyalties. An interdependent society, conscious of its problems, cannot help generating the loyalties that are necessary for their solution; in the process, it inevitably creates cross-loyalties. As it is doing so, it is at the same time chipping away at the conceptual foundations of the nation-state system, which locates a monopoly of loyalties in the state.

Common Values

Every society requires some value consensus, and world society is no exception.[14] The nation-state system rests upon the acceptance of certain rules, all of which have become rules of international law, and upon the high price that is placed on independence. But does the degree of consensus that is now found in world society go beyond the minimal requirements of the nation-state system? Does it promise support for a more comprehensive system of world order?

Some precision is needed in defining the scope of the sought-for consensus. There is no need to search for a global homogeneity of the populations at large; for the most part, it is sufficient to attain some minimum commonalities in regard to, for example, justice, hospitality to strangers or travelers, respect for human life, and agreement on what constitutes desirable human behavior. But some more specific consensus is required for the operation of the global networks: acceptance of rules of communication, including world languages; agreement on rules of interaction, both hostile and cooperative; and participation in rituals and ceremonies expressing such consensus, such as assemblies, fairs and exhibitions. In regard to the populations at large, and to the functioning of the global networks, value commonalities refer to both substantive and procedural agreement. Both are needed and both need to be considered; there is no need to exaggerate the role of substantive consensus at the expense of the procedural variety.[15]

Substantive consensus has in the past been associated with religious and political ideologies, and the evident worldwide diversity in this regard has been a source of concern. It might be argued, however, that some degree of ideological conflict must be expected in large-scale political systems. Ideologies that purport to define the shape of man's local community, or the constitution of the national authority, need not necessarily be relevant, however, to problems of the global system.

Ideologies undoubtedly divide. In so far as they concern global problems, however, they also help to define the nature of debate in the world system, and to structure it, even in a conflictual relationship. They are indispensable to the operation of world parties.

Even in substantive matters, however, elements of universal consensus may be discerned. Among these are respect for human life, the most elementary aspect of respect for individual and personal freedoms, and the bonds of sympathy that are evoked at times of natural disasters or man-made accidents. The International Red Cross and a host of welfare programs are witness to such sympathies. The suffering and the welfare of children everywhere evokes concern; that concern has been institutionalized in the Children's Fund, one of the reliably financed United Nations programs. Among the consensual values of the post-1945 nation-state system have been nation-building and economic development, both of which command strong and unquestioned support.

The case of colonialism is worth noting as an example of the adjustability of the world value consensus. During the nineteenth and early twentieth centuries, the possession of colonies was a mark of international status and colonialism an accepted political institution, in no way different from the imperial systems that have been known to mankind for centuries. By mid-twentieth century, this had changed. Now colonies were rapidly turned into liabilities and colonialism into a term of international opprobrium. The conviction that colonialism was bad soon acquired the force of a moral law, and this undoubtedly speeded up the process of decolonization; it helped people under colonial rule to achieve justice for their cause. The attainment of independence and the establishment of new nation-states in the formerly colonial areas may be regarded as an important instance of justice being expected and achieved substantially through both local and global activity; it was a case where world society itself generated a merited feeling of the expectation of justice.

Of interest too, is the unity manifested in the global currency of artistic values and art styles, in matters ranging all the way from pure art forms to popular music and designs for everyday living. It constitutes a consensus on what is to be regarded as beautiful. Arts whose medium of expression are other than language have been notable for tackling aesthetic problems and giving vent to feelings that seem to be universal. Architecture may be the most universal of these forms; it has produced in proliferation, in all the world cities, multitudes of uniform concrete and glass structures. Changing tastes in music, fashions in dress that appeal to the young and are part of a growing youth culture have been among the most intimate manifestations of these trends. If artists and the arts are the perceptual antennae of society, translating perceived needs and sentiments into art forms, and generally anticipating new trends, then the worldwide sweep of such art phenomena indicates the limitations of the nation-state as a framework of cultural expression. It may also forecast changes in the organization of world society.

Both awareness and interdependence rest upon a minimum of procedural agreement. Forms of communication (such as language) depend on certain rules of procedure (such as grammar and spelling). The nation-state is a community that is bound by the procedural commitment to the use of one language. World systems too have their languages, and a *lingua franca* has been part of every such known system. Latin, French and English have had varied careers as languages of diplomacy. Contemporary world society uses English as the major means of communications, with French a strong second language, especially in Africa. But it also benefits from several other shared symbol systems, including the Morse code, maritime signals, traffic signs, maps, mathematics, symbolic logic, computer programming, and film and television. The rules of all of these are universally understood and accepted.

Interaction requires rules for expediting it. International law is an array of widely shared procedures for intergovernmental relations, and included in the same tradition have been attempts to restrict the use of means of violence—for instance against civilians or prisoners of war, or in regard to certain armaments that are felt to be offensive to humanity, such as chemical, bacteriological and nuclear weapons. Viewed as the constellation of certain constitutive values of the nation-state system, international law has been successful in regularizing and legitimizing the state as a worldwide institution. In its emphasis on the state, international law has tended to de-emphasize the role of war as an agent of change. Efforts first to circumscribe and later even to abolish war through international legal action (in the Kellogg-Briand Pact of 1928, which was cited in the Nuremberg Trial of 1945-6, and in the United Nations Charter, whose signatories pledged themselves to abstain from the use or threat of force, except in self-defense) have tended to delegitimize war as an acceptable procedure for the settlement of disputes. Thus peace, universally accorded lip-service but less readily practiced, can be seen as an important, though negative, procedural principle of the global system: prohibition of the organized use of violence by nation-states against each other.

Peace is not incompatible with the rules of the nation-state system. But a sustained spell of peace is likely to alter the underlying structure of the system, because in the absence of war the dominance of the state in the global system would look less and less convincing. Problems other than war could seize hold of men's imagination and organizations and individuals better attuned to these problems would assume prominence. The nation-state system needs war for its self-justification; peace as a global value erodes its authority.

The common values of world society find expression in a variety of ceremonies and rituals. Each international congress, conference or assembly is, in the very act of foregathering, a ritual event of considerable potency. Each such act consecrates and illuminates values and emotions that are shared by wide portions of humanity. The United Nations itself is the supreme ritual of them all. Other world events of similar significance include the Olympic Games in the field of sports, and the great world fairs and exhibitions, which have been, ever since 1851, spectacular celebrations of man's latest industrial and technological achievements.

Conclusion

The nation-state seeks to mold world society in its own image. It fractionalizes and compartmentalizes life, which, without it, might be able to flow more freely. But the nation-state system cannot contain the forces of awareness, interdependence and common value that are at work in world society, even if these forces show as their major flaw a striking degree of unevenness. Cooperation due to the requirements of size and the pressures of finite resources gives rise to global enterprises that are made possible by cheap communications and a changing value system.

These positive developments put into question the ethnocentric model of world society, and undermine the preconditions of the nation-state system.

Notes to Chapter Eleven

1. In C. E. Vaughan, ed., *The Political Writings of Jean-Jacques Rousseau*, Vol. 1 (Cambridge, 1951), p. 415; George Sabine, *A History of Political Theory* 3rd ed. (New York: Holt, Rinehart & Winston, 1961), p. 582; Georges Lassudre-Duchene, *Jean-Jacques Rousseau et le droit des gens* (Paris: Henri Jouve, 1906), pp. 116–7.

2. Morgenthau, *Politics among Nations, cited,* pp. 244–5.

3. *Ibid.*, pp. 470–481.

4. For the contrary argument—that nature itself "guarantees" perpetual peace, and without requiring a world state—see esp. Kant's *Perpetual Peace* ("Of the guarantee for perpetual peace"), which was in part a reply to Rousseau's arguments in the *Social Contract*.

5. *Statistical Yearbook of the United States 1967*, p. 514.

6. Theodore Morgan, "Economic Relationships among Nations: The Pattern of Commodity Trade," in Bert F. Hoselitz, ed., *Economics and the Idea of Mankind* (New York: Columbia University Press, 1965), pp. 161–3.

7. *United Nations Statistical Yearbook for 1966*, p. 411.

8. *Ibid.*, pp. 468–481; in 1965, some 150 million people were counted as international tourists in various parts of the world; that was about 5 per cent of the world's population.

9. E. Benoit, "Interdependence on a Small Planet," *Columbia Journal of World Business*, Vol. I, 1966, 9–18.

10. G. Modelski, "The Corporation in World Society," *The Year Book of World Affairs 1968*, p. 69.

11. Perlmutter, "The tortuous evolution of the multinational corporation," *cited*.

12. Kant, *Perpetual Peace*, "Third Definitive Article for a Perpetual Peace."

13. G. Hardin, "The tragedy of the commons," *Science*, December 13, 1968, p. 1243.

14. Talcott Parsons, "Order and Community in the International Social System," in J. Rosenau, ed., *International Politics and Foreign Policy* (New York: Free Press, 1961), 120–129.

15. Herbert Spiro, *World Politics: The Global System* (Homewood, Ill., Dorsey, 1966), Chap. 9.

PART THREE

The
Principles
of
World
Politics

The test of a theory of world politics is its ability to come to grips with the future. A study of this important subject, if it is to be worthy of its name, cannot remain content merely with recitations of the past or with dissections of the present; it must also offer concepts and constructions, as well as some set of principles that is relevant to what, in the governance of mankind, is yet to be.

The social sciences do not, of course, engage in prophecy or crystal-gazing. They cannot and do not attempt to foretell single events, however important these might be. But they can do two other things in relation to the future: they can work on techniques for devising and improving the methods of forecasting world trends; and they can elaborate and perfect theoretical schemes and principles that produce an understanding of complex social processes and that, in favorable circumstances, can help to guide purposeful social policy.

Both these undertakings (the first, a more passive stance of observation; the other, possibly a more active stance of knowledge-seeking, with interventionary implications) can be helpful in encounters with the future. They are mutually exclusive, to the degree to which they rely on different methods and pursue different objectives, being narrow and technical in the case of forecasting and broad and theoretical in the case of understanding (their "payoffs" differ too). They are mutually complementary to the degree that the social sciences need both types of approach. Prediction can offer accurate information about likely trends in certain narrow respects, on the basis of some variant of the assumption that trends known to have occurred in the past are likely also to repeat themselves; understanding, by contrast, being based on explanatory models of social reality, offers comprehensive and possibly powerful systems of thought that may nevertheless be of little help in relation to specific trends and events.[1]

The present study is not concerned with prediction and the forecasting of world trends, in the sense just referred to. The correct description and accurate projection of some basic world trends is, without doubt, an important component of the study of politics. It includes, broadly, the field of political statistics; the collection, analysis and extrapolation of information on such matters as national populations; and all kinds of political, military and economic equations. Standard sources of reference, such as *The Statesman's Yearbook*,[2] have been performing some of these functions for a long time. More recent United Nations statistical services provide much basic information on such essential matters as world population, world trade, and world development.

These offer useful bases for anticipating certain essential future trends, although they have the handicap of relying on national sources of data collection. The development of forecasting procedures that will be pertinent to world trends may, by contrast, require both an improvement in methods of global information-gathering and also the refinement of predictive indicators. Consideration of the theory of world politics indicates the need for good information regarding trends in such features of the global system as centralization, militarization, and change in conference patterns or in the growth rate of international institutions. The data base to serve the predictive purposes of the field of world politics requires the collection of additional sets to serve as indicators for such theoretical concepts as nation-state dominance. Several such concepts might be suggested, but their use in future forecasting efforts will not attempted at this juncture.

The concluding part of the present study therefore leaves prediction and anticipation aside, and instead seeks to demonstrate concern for the future in a second, possibly more crucial way. Its aim is to explore the range of theoretical constructs that might be relevant to coping with the unknown world to come. In one way, this is a look at relevant utopias —utopias because they are blueprints of worldwide political arrangements as yet mostly untested, but also utopias that have been made relevant by the use and application of social science methods. Part One mapped out the past, Part Two explored the present; Part Three offers some guidelines for thinking about the future.

Analysis has so far found the nation-state system to be wanting in some important respects as the political system for humanity. Yet the system is now at its peak and strong forces may be discovered to be maintaining it. To move it in directions called for by the world interest, a deeper understanding is required of the pressures that keep it in its present form and the developments that might incline it toward more benign uses. First, therefore, comes an analysis of the processes that strengthen the system and aggravate its dangerous features: these will be summed up under the rubric of "the vicious circle." Their nature may be such, perhaps, that a break in that circle may not be outside the bounds of possibility.

Second comes a review of possibilities of change in the nation-state system—that is, of some alternative lines of development that might be reached through a process of "benign circularity." These alternatives will be reviewed principally from the standpoint of the criterion of complexity. The nation-state system must be criticized fundamentally as being exceedingly simple and hence unresilient. Arrangements alternative to it should have the quality of higher complexity, and the architecture of such complexity is a matter of the utmost consequence.

Third, some attention will be paid to the way in which the principal problems of politics—order and justice—present themselves in their context, and what requirements they impose upon the practice of politics in the global framework. The aim will be to offer for consideration models and constructions that might be helpful in appraising the world politics of the next generation. The principles themselves might then be seen as realizations of a conception of world interest, for this alone offers a secure basis for guiding and appraising conduct in the future.

Notes to Introduction, Part Three

1. Dubin, *Theory Building, cited*, pp. 9–25.
2. The *Yearbook* still carries, on its inside page, a quotation from Goethe: "Numbers may not govern the world, but they do tell us whether it is governed well or badly."

12

The
Vicious
Circle

THE DESCRIPTION AND ANALYSIS OF the nation-state system may now be supplemented by an explanatory sketch, an outline of the model underlying the present study. Such a model is required not only for purposes of explanation, but also as a vehicle of control and as a blueprint for the instituting of measures of change.

The nation-state system is one possible form of political constitution for mankind. Judged by the criteria of world interest, it has some positive features and also some negative ones. Both these aspects have been pointed out earlier, and at some length. It is a system that performs certain functions for world society; among these, the most important is the preservation of the substance and the spirit of autonomy and the maintenance of a degree of world order. Yet this political system cannot be seen only in purely functional terms: a good part of its performance is devoted less to fulfilling these functions than it is to pure self-maintenance. All systems maintain themselves and in time entrench themselves ever more firmly in the social matrix, without any explicit or necessary reference to social goals and purposes. The nation-state system is no exception to the rule of system inertia, so that explanations of its persistence must be couched in terms that are wider than merely functional ones, especially since an inertia that is as all-embracing as this is capable of misshaping the entire world society.

The principal explanatory model underlying this view of the nation-state system is one of circular causation. It implies a principle of cumulation and, in the form of the "vicious circle" has been introduced into social science literature in several of the works of Gunnar Myrdal.[1] As a dynamic equilibrium model of social change, intended to capture the wide range of interdependencies that characterizes social systems, it is also one of the basic conceptions underlying the social sciences.

Early Equilibrium Models

Early theory of International Relations has drawn, as has the rest of the social sciences, upon the notion and the theories of equilibrium. The most prominent of these, and possibly among the most influential in the history of science and learning, have been theories of the Balance of Power, underlying which are stable equilibrium notions; these specify that the direction of change for a given system is determined by the condition of balance. In a Balance of Power system, a disturbance will be followed by processes, events or policies aimed at restoring the equilibrium.

As an explicit statement of the conditions of the states system, such theory has been widely current since the seventeenth century and, in less explicit forms, even earlier. Its significance in shaping the global system has already been reviewed. In regard to its intellectual origins, it might have been linked closely with notions of symmetry in art, with the evolution of the balance measure in physics, with counterpoint in music and with double-entry bookkeeping in commerce, all of which also evolved during the late medieval period. Each of these was among the fundamental notions of these respective forms of endeavor; in physics in particular, it was among the basic notions of the natural sciences. In its turn, the stress on balance in political thought also had profound effects on the denial of monopoly in a variety of other social conditions. It is tempting to believe that science, the arts, and society in general could not have flourished as they did without the evolution of the political Balance of Power, first as between the Emperor and the Pope and later among the states of Europe and in the world. These may well have been the political preconditions for intellectual, scientific and economic growth.

Balance of Power theories continue to this day to be the staple fare of International Relations. Theories of the "arms race" or even theories of "nuclear deterrence" also derive from elementary balance or equilibrium concepts.[2] Richardson, for instance, writes differential equations for the "motions" of states members of his systems (European great powers, pre-World War I and pre-World War II). These states are related to each other by the quantity of armaments they hold and maintain. He then proceeds to find "solutions" for this system of equations; these might be either stable or unstable, depending on the form of the equations describing the relevant state behavior.

Balance of Power theories depict the world as divided among countries between whom a degree of equilibrium or equality has to be preserved. The real insight of such models is not to be underestimated. Up to a certain point, productive social systems do need such equipoise. But these models are nonetheless weak and deficient for being (1) unidimensional and (2) static.

Balance of Power theories are cast in the form of the nation-state paradigm. The units of analysis of these models are "states" pure and simple, and little else. In the cruder instances, the properties of these units are not even differentiated clearly enough; in some more developed versions, the one property of states that is singled out for special attention is their power. The effect upon other states of changes in the power (taking the form of armaments) of one state is then subjected to analysis, in terms that recall the Newtonian physics of bodies in motion. Admittedly, in some extreme conditions of stress and extreme violence, such unidimensionality may acquire significance in the global system; but this limiting condition need not be regarded as being theoretically the only relevant one. The working of the system depends on a wider set of interdependent circumstances.

The power balance, moreover, represents a static conception of world politics: it assumes an automatic tendency toward equilibrium or toward restoration of the status quo ante. It then seems to preclude changes away from a simple autonomy system toward one of more complex form— that is, toward new levels of political and social development. No doubt a good deal of stability is built into such systems, and the states system has in fact demonstrated a remarkable capacity for self-preservation. But there is also need for theoretical schemes that encompass the possibility of change as much as they do the fact of self-preservation.

In recent literature, the most important of the more elaborate models have been those of the conflict spiral and the war process.[3] They represent significant developments of theory, the first sophisticated attempts to fit data to a model of the war-propelling tendencies of the global system. But they are not models of the entire system of world politics, in that they do not explain system transformation. They are relatively simple explanatory models of war and violent conflict, which require causality to flow in one direction (as do other recent causal models of politics [4]) and do not allow for processes of feedback and circular causation.

Cumulation in Social Systems

Simple equilibrium models have been widely prevalent in the earlier stages of other social sciences, including economics and sociology. In economics in particular, the stable equilibrium form has been found wanting and recourse has been had in recent decades to more dynamic models.

The work of Gunnar Myrdal illustrates the fruitfulness of a model of complex causation, even in the absence of a highly sophisticated methodology for formalizing it. In *The American Dilemma* Myrdal took up the analysis of the Black-White relationship with the aid of what he called "a simplified . . . model of dynamic social causation." He saw that relationship as being determined by two sets of conditions: "a specific degree of 'race prejudice' on the side of the Whites, directed against the Negroes" and, on the other, a plane of living for the Negroes at a level considerably below that of the Whites. He took as given the existence of a relationship between these variables and saw it as being of such a kind that the Negroes' standard of living could be seen as being kept down by discrimination on the part of the Whites. Furthermore, the Whites' reason for discrimination was partly dependent upon the Negroes' standard of living. "The Negroes' poverty, ignorance, superstition . . . stimulate and feed the antipathy of the Whites for them."

To start with, it might be assumed that such a society is "in balance" —that is to say, that the two conditions check each other out, that there is sufficient prejudice on the part of the Whites to keep down the Negro standard of living to a level that will maintain the specific degree of prejudice and/or vice versa. "If now, in this hypothetically balanced state, for some reason or other, the Negro plane of living is lowered, this will, other things being equal, in its turn increase white prejudice. Such an increase in white prejudice has the effect of pressing down still further the Negro plane of living, which again will increase prejudice and so on, by way of mutual interaction between the two variables, *ad infinitum*. A cumulative process is set in motion which can have final effects quite out of proportion to the magnitude of the original push. The push might even be withdrawn after a time, and still a permanent change will remain or even the process of change will continue without a new balance in sight. If, instead, the initial change had been such a thing as a gift from a philanthropist to raise the Negro plane of living, a cumulative movement would have started in the other direction, having exactly the same causal mechanisms. The vicious circle works both ways." [5]

Myrdal's "Negro plane of living" is, however, a composite entity. It can be split into a number of components (such as wages, nutrition, housing, etc.) among which the cumulative principle is assumed to hold. "Any change in any one of these factors, independent of the way in which it is brought about, will, by the aggregate weight of the cumulative effect running back and forth between them all, start the whole system moving in one direction or the other . . . with a speed depending on the original push and the functions of causal interrelations within the system."

The subject for analysis then becomes not a stable system faithfully returning to its previous states, but rather "processes of systems actually rolling in one direction or the other, systems which are constantly subjected to all sorts of pushes from the outside." [6]

The "vicious circle" is an attractive model of macrosocietal analysis; it has been used by Myrdal, more recently, in an extensive investigation of problems of Asian underdevelopment. Importantly, it is multidimensional, for it can accommodate a series of variables and also variables of several different types. The variety of conditions it can take into account helps to ensure that the model will be flexible and able to accommodate continuous increments of complexity. It avoids the pitfalls of single-factor analysis, to which power theories and early balance-of-power models have been prone.

What is more, built into the "vicious circle" is a principle of cumulation—that is, a number of feedback loops. These are the mechanisms that can move the entire system to a new state upward or downward, depending on the pressures exerted on it. The cumulative process (a concept first used by Knut Wicksell for the analysis of monetary processes some two generations ago) is the product of an assumed interlocking of conditions—for example, when an increase in the plane of living is assumed to bring about a reduction in discrimination. The operation of this mechanism depends, of course, on the correctness with which these interdependencies were diagnosed in the first place.

Not all social systems are capable of such movement, either "down" the vicious circle or "up" the circle of virtue. Some such systems might be afflicted with inertia, which prevents the cumulation of forces and fails to stimulate secondary feedback processes that will be strong enough to sustain a primary change and to push it further. "True mutual causation is not enough to create this process; otherwise the ubiquity of mutual causation would be inconsistent with the widely observed stability of social systems. The relationship between the size of the coefficients of response and the spread of the response will determine whether mutual causation results in stable, neutral or unstable equilibrium." [7]

Should it be possible, however, to identify relationships that are not only mutual but strong, the "vicious circle" supplies a fine tool for the analysis of systems of world politics. Unlike structural-functional schemes, it does not lead directly into attempts at the rationalization of some existing social arrangements. Although the vicious circle ignores the wider social context, it does supply clues to the operation of the mechanisms that move it from within.

The Basic Model

World politics might be conceived as a system consisting of a number of conditions that are causally and circularly interrelated, so that a change in one will cause changes in all the others. The basic model consists of two sets of conditions: (1) nation-state dominance and (2) war. The relationship between these is represented in Figure 12:1. The Simple Model for the nation-state system can be seen as an elementary feedback loop, between a "level" (a state of the global system) and a "rate of change" (incidence of war).

The model assumes the existence of the nation-state system and also assumes what has been the conclusion of much of earlier analysis—namely, that the degree of dominance of that system in the world at large is a determinable and indeed measurable characteristic. There may be "more" or "less" of the nation-state system in the world—that is, the "level" of that system is a variable one. To be determined are the conditions that influence this system property, so that, by taking advantage of changes in these conditions, the status of the nation-state system in the world might be changed.

Nation-state dominance is assumed to be determined by the incidence of war and by the expectation of it, in the global system. The relationship is believed to be such that nation-state dominance is kept up by war and its expectation, but also that the incidence of war is kept up by nation-state dominance. This is a "vicious circle" of a most rudimentary kind.

As a starting assumption, such a global system might be "in balance," in such fashion that the two conditions check each other out. There is just enough war and violence in the system to maintain the level of nation-state dominance, and to the level that is maintained corresponds a degree of war tension and expectation. But if, in this hypothetically balanced state, the rate of war is increased, then this would tend, other things being equal, to increase the level of nation-state dominance, and change the character of the system. This would in turn have the effect of raising again the incidence of war and in turn still further enlarging the prominence of the nation-state system in the world picture, which will again add to the pressures for war—and so on, by a process of mutual interaction between the two variables, *ad infinitum* or, at least, up to some level of system transformation. A cumulative process can thus be set in motion, the ultimate effects of which could be out of proportion to the magnitude of the original disturbance. If, on the other hand, the original change had been in the opposite direction—for instance, toward reducing the rate of war processes (for instance, through arms control, or the erosion of public support for military activities), a cumulative movement

Figure 12:1
The Simple Model

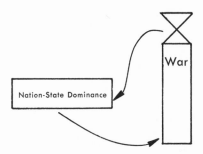

could start in the other direction, actuated by the same mechanism. Perhaps the vicious circle could be made to work both ways, even in world politics.

The relationship between war and the structure of world politics has been a persistent theme of earlier parts of this study. All the aspects of the evolution of world politics—globalization, the institutionalization of autonomy, the emergence of the strong state and its nationalization—were characterized by the pervasive influence of war and by the impact of demands for the organization of violence. Globalization took place through worldwide expansion of military power, and it built up the nation-state. Balance of Power wars have constituted the major process in European and world history, especially in the twentieth century. The nationalization of the state would have been inconceivable without the recurring and unsettling processes of war. In turn, war would not have reached that absolute degree of perfection that makes it possible to contemplate the end of humanity as its outcome, without recurrent reinforcement through the invention of organizations that have been ever more finely attuned to its requirements. The importance of war and of warmaking potential is most clearly seen in the role of the Great Powers in the system of world politics.

But, in a broader setting, war might be regarded as only one of the most striking manifestations of a set of dominant characteristics of modern civilization, with its orientation to achievement, hence also to performance, competition and its near-inevitable concomitant, violence—so much so that the question arises whether modern society and its prominent features, such as science, research and technology, industry, incessant building and instantaneous communication, are indeed compatible with any other system than the violence-prone nation-state system.

Importantly, however, the two conditions of war and nation-state dominance appear to be not only mutually related but also locked together in a cumulative process. The possibility of runaway arms races (which would constitute a strong positive feedback process) has long been recognized; equally interesting is the possibility of a descending spiral of armaments and war. The basic model postulates a mechanism of interdependence that has translated ascending arms spirals into changes in political structures; there is no reason to think that the process would not similarly hold in the opposite direction. The possibility of a negative feedback that would be strong enough to move the system out of its inevitable inertia lies in the same achievement orientation of contemporary society. The forces that processes of cumulation gather together in the nation-state system are truly explosive; but the science, technology and industry that are associated with the nation-state through war and planning could lend to the entire system a tremendous dynamism in the opposite direction as well. The possibility of large-scale political movement (which might conceivably present dangers also in the descending stage) inheres in the character of the modern world. It is in some ways a sign of instability; in other ways, however, it harbors the possibility of benign transformation—that is, the possibility of movement toward low or zero levels of nation-state dominance and of the incidence of war.

The simple model consists of two terms, each of which may be envisaged as a composite that might be split up into a number of component parts, and between which the cumulative principle holds once again. Thus, nation-state dominance as a descriptive condition of the nation-state system could be decomposed into such features as: Great Power dominance; power inequality or concentration; degree of nationalization; degree of organizational dominance, and the related properties of global and local networks. War might include, inter alia, such conditions as militarization and polarization rates; the incidence of global, national and local wars; general violence rates, and the expectations for a variety of types of violence. These are some of the relevant conditions reviewed in this study and others could be added.

A Vicious Circle

Figure 12:2 presents another possible model of the vicious circle. It is both a summary of what has been said so far about the global system

Figure 12:2
A Vicious Circle

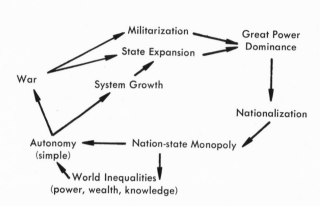

and also a research proposal for the future. The causal links indicated by the arrows have already been vindicated to some degree through previous arguments and their *prima facie* plausibility is now evident; but they do need to obtain additional analysis and substantiation. At the very least, the model conveys a picture of the interdependencies that characterize the system of world politics.

This particular vicious circle may be read both as a historical statement and as a statement of the conditions that now maintain the nation-state system. Read historically, the argument might commence with "autonomy." The conditions of autonomy that were experienced in Europe at the close of the Middle Ages were conducive both to system growth and to conflict. System growth at first took the form of globalization; then it also became population growth, expansion of commercial, financial and industrial activity, and finally economic and organizational growth. Conflict among the units of autonomy assumed the form of war; it was reinforced also by the tensions created by system growth. War became the great simplifier; it not only promoted the militarization of large sectors of activity and absorbed a large share of the proceeds of growth; it also led to a large expansion of state activities and to the rise of the state as the first modern organization. In other words, activities associated with war flourished, while others took second place. The premium placed upon military performance led to the emergence of the great military states and, within a century, to the assumption by those states of a large portion of global authority. The success of the great states was based upon a secure internal base, consolidated by nationalization; Great Powers that were unable to consolidate a national base disintegrated. The success of the Great Powers in the process of nationalization has been widely imitated; it has led to the worldwide dissemination of the model of the nation-state, irrespective of its local applicability.

The result has been the growth of a universal nation-state system, based on the monopoly of territorial authority by the nation-state and a corresponding discouragement of global and local activities. Global networks, as carriers of global cohesion, were weakened. Nation-state exclusiveness, moreover, consolidated the system of inequalities that had been brought about in the first place by system growth. The system affords nothing but extremely weak mechanisms of wealth redistribution; it contains no mechanisms whereby the strains created by it through war and system growth can be dissipated. National monopolies, in combination with world inequalities, tend to perpetuate the autonomy system and the problems it brings in its train; but because of the continued association with war and political activity, the resulting autonomy system is confirmed in a simple, rather than a complex form. A simple autonomy system does little more than reinforce the entire process.

The same process might be viewed not only as temporally sequential, but also as a system of simultaneous relationships. Autonomy stimulates competitiveness, which in turn finds expression in growth and violent conflict; the state affords protection from the uncertainties of competitiveness, and does so in particular through augmenting its military strength. Great Power authority is closely linked with nationality and with the privileges of nation-states; these in their turn reinforce inequalities and a system in which autonomy finds embodiment primarily in simple political forms.

This is, of course, no more than one possible statement of the web of relationships that has created a vicious circle in world politics. New links can be added to it, at any time additional analysis discloses the need for them. One element in the vicious circle of world politics might be, for instance, sex differentiation. Along the lines developed by Lionel Tiger,[8] it might be argued that the entrenchment of men in positions of political, military and generally social leadership is attributable in part to the complex of biological inheritance, which goes back two or three stages in man's evolution, to his pre-civilized beginnings (in terms of Figure 2:1). The dominant experience of early man was hunting; the nearest current equivalent to this might be war and other occasions for giving vent to competitiveness and aggressiveness. Given the fact that men occupy positions of political power and their need to demonstrate competitiveness, war affords them the opportunity to do so, and in turn the occurrence of war justifies the display of talents that are conventionally recognized as male, thus confirming male dominance. War consolidates sex differentiation, which might otherwise have abated sooner in the course of social evolution; in turn, it contributes to reinforcing the combative elements of the nation-state system.

But identifying the individual links of the vicious circle is at this stage less important than establishing the circular and cumulative character of such a process. For it is this circularity that affords such good clues about how the system maintains itself, while cumulation explains the movement in that system. Both enhance the possibility of tragedy that is inherent in world politics.

Patterns of Future-Orientation

In Knut Wicksell's scheme of monetary equilibrium—one of the influential analytical frameworks of modern economics, and a source of inspiration for Myrdal's work—the crucial element is the appearance of a disjunction between the monetary rate of interest prevailing in the market and the real or natural rate of interest. This disjunction sets in motion the process of cumulation through which the entire economic system may be moved; in other words, it offers clues as to how the system is able to move out of stationary equilibria.

The rate of interest is a device through which businessmen and economic planners relate the present to the future; it is the rate at which the calculations of future benefit will be discounted, if future-oriented activities are to be undertaken. It is also the rate that regulates relations between those who have the resources and those who need them, who want to act, and need support in order to do so, in larger undertakings. Inflation wreaks havoc with the rate of interest. Keynesian economics and contemporary economic planning are both built upon an understanding of these relations.

In broader purview, the rate of interest is only one facet of the universal problem of relating the present to the future. It is only one of the many devices that have been invented for mastering uncertainty, that inescapable aspect of the human condition. This particular rate formalizes the judgment that a market (the network of relevant financiers and planners) makes about conditions to come. Religious belief systems—those common to a circle of believers—have filled this need over major spans of human existence on earth, but political and social myths and utopias have become prominent in more recent centuries. The myths and utopias of a world system are its means of organizing its future, and its changes, the appearance of flaws in them and their inflation, the portents of stress and of impending change.

In Myrdal's analysis of White-Black relations in the United States, the "American dilemma" arises in the first place because the American creed, the dominant myth of personal equality and political democracy, finds itself at variance with the realities of inequality and discrimination. It is this disjunction that lends movement to the system, and might yet bring realities back into line with the dominant social myth, which Myrdal accepted as valid.

In world politics, too, disjunctions might make their appearance between utopias and realities. The ways in which mankind orients its future might be found to be inadequate, and the stars by which its trek is fixed false. The dominant myth of twentieth-century politics has been the nation-state, the virtues of nationalism and the thrills of nation-building. The rest of social life has at best been able to find its place within that myth, or else it has been left out of the mainstream. Does this myth correspond to social realities? Are its priorities congruent with real needs? Is there a need for new myths and fresh utopias, to give better formulations to the world interest and more reliable guides to the future?

Nation-state dominance has so far been used as a descriptive term, defining a particular distribution of resources and concerns within a world system; it is also a dominant myth, the accepted arrangement of future priorities for that system. Yet political leaders acting upon such priorities might find that the programs in which they invest fail to bring in the expected return; that, on account of movements in the realities of world society that they have failed to take into consideration, they are failing their constituents and cannot promote their real welfare. On some such grounds, it might be argued that today's dominant myth of the nation-state may have found itself in opposition to ordinary human desires and expectations. In that case, it may be the myth that needs changing, not the realities.

The myth of the nation-state could also be judged to be the last resort of traditional and in some ways archaic ways of thinking about world affairs—ways that are basically out of alignment with the requirements of modern world society whose creed of equality, democracy and pluralism has been making considerable inroads into all the institutions of the contemporary world. The disjunction occurs through the prejudices of extreme nationalism—that is, it takes place between the monopolistic claims of the nation-state, and the demands of everyday modernity, which correspond more closely to the realities of politics. To the extent that the modern creed is embodied in organizations other than the nation-state—the modern corporation, the university, the international organization—or is upheld through a variety of global networks in which these other organizations are embedded, it gains additional leverage whenever such organizations and networks move toward new levels of effectiveness.

The necessities of nationalism, the priority of national governmental claims, and the virtues of national sacrifice have been the hallmarks and the social cement of the modern world. Signs that the monopolistic loyalties of nationalism may no longer be commanding universal acceptance grew more numerous during the nineteen-sixties. The worldwide circulation of people, ideas and innovations has now begun to clash with the restrictive models of the nation-state. Awareness of interdependence has broken down its autarchic pretensions. The physical and social sciences are in need of broader horizons. The impact of developments toward a global layer has been particularly evident among the educated young. The life style that a large proportion of the population have assumed— with a distinctive dress and forms of recreation and art, with the whole adding up to something like a distinctive culture—could yet make a difference. There is strong evidence for substantial changes of outlook toward the future as the result of a college education. What is still lacking is evidence that such attitudes will prove to be long-lasting, as well as knowledge of the mechanisms that might translate such attitudinal dispositions into actual changes in world politics. In certain favorable circumstances, however, they could be influential in weakening the myth of the nation-state system.

Decumulation

The understanding and regulation of the "vicious circle" may prove to be the crucial problem of world politics. Since this amounts, in effect, to understanding the movement of the global system, it is a problem in system transformation. How can the system be propelled forward, beyond the vicious circle? How can it be "decumulated?"

Throughout the argument so far, war and organized international violence have occupied a role of great importance. Does this mean that the decumulation of the vicious circle depends on the solution of separate, smaller-scale conflicts before they reach the stage of war, through such means as the application of better rules, or the meting out of stern punishments? Does the world need more or better international law, or does it need improved arrangements for collective security to punish the aggressors? Analogically, the rate of traffic accidents could be controlled through either improved traffic legislation or stricter law enforcement on the road. Modern traffic management proceeds, however, on the assumption that, given the state of the road network and a certain traffic density, the rate of accidents is a predictable quantity. The way to cut the accident rate is to build a better road or else to reduce traffic density. Similarly, the way to cut down the rate of violent and organized conflict in the modern world is not so much to solve individual conflicts or police them better (because a conflictless world is in any event difficult to imagine, even though the forms of conflict are subject to change), as it is to create a structure that would be more suitable to contemporary traffic. Another drastic solution might be to cut down problem-density—for instance, through reducing growth rates.

The models here presented take a structural approach to world politics. The rate of war is one of the governing conditions of the vicious circle. But it is also the product of a number of interrelated conditions and structures, which both influence and are reciprocally influenced by the entire system. The regulation of the vicious circle must be governed not so much by the need to control war but rather by such wider system purposes as the maintenance of order and justice.

That the vicious circle can move the system up as well as down has been another theme of this argument. A movement of decumulation can be initiated by a favorable change in any one among the chain of conditions that compose it. Once set in motion and sustained by strong feedback beyond the point of inertia, such change could move the system toward fundamental alteration. This could be achieved both by accident, as the result of unanticipated consequences of action, as most such changes have indeed occurred in the past, or else by design, through conscious intervention. If such a decumulation were to be observed, or brought about, however, what could be put in its place? What are the guidelines for alternative world designs? These questions will be dealt with in the discussion to follow.

Notes to Chapter Twelve

1. Gunnar Myrdal, *An American Dilemma* (New York: Harper and Row, 1942), pp. 75–8, and Appendix Three, pp. 1065–70; see also his *Asian Drama* (New York: Atheneum, 1969), Appendix Two, pp. 1843–1878.

2. Lewis Richardson, *Arms and Insecurity* (Pittsburgh: Boxwood Press, 1960).

3. Dean Pruitt & Richard Snyder, eds., *Theory and Research on the Causes of War* (Englewood Cliffs, N.J.: Prentice-Hall, 1969), pp. 52–59; see also Robert North *et al.*, "Some empirical data on the conflict spiral," *Papers, Peace Research Society (International)*, Vol. I, 1964, 1–14.

4. Hayward Alker, "The long road to International Relations Theory" in Morton Kaplan, ed., *New Approaches to International Relations* (London: St. Martins Press, 1968), pp. 154–161.

5. Myrdal, *American Dilemma*, p. 1066.

6. *Ibid.*, p. 1067.

7. Myrdal, *Asian Drama*, p. 1875.

8. Tiger, *Men in Groups*, cited.

13
The
Architecture
of
Complexity

THE WEAKNESS OF THE NATION-STATE system lies in its absurd simplicity. The whole world is neatly divided up into a rather small number of near-identical and tightly organized compartments, for each of which, most often, one individual bears the responsibility; matters of common world interest are settled among even fewer of these same individuals. There is truly little mystery to the present political structure of mankind.

The world's organization could, of course, be even simpler: the entire world could be subject to one single ruler, or to one single overpowering organization; along a scale of complexity, a world state would be the simplest structure of all. While hardly a feasible solution for the world's politics, this type of arrangement does surface from time to time in the human imagination—for instance, in mystery or spy thrillers (as when James Bond sets out to deter evil designs for world domination), or in science fiction, with simplistic portrayals of political organization on this or other planets. Perhaps dreams do have to be kept simple.

But world order cannot be so simple because, in the scheme of life, simplicity equals vulnerability; complexity, by contrast, means adaptability, and thus survival fitness. Any life system whose ultimate interest is survival will deliberately promote complexity. The nation-state system, however simple it undoubtedly is, does bring at least a minimum degree of complexity to world organization. But a still higher degree of complexity than has been achieved so far is needed in the world today. World politics requires a form of ordering that will maximize the attaining of complexity.

The prime example of a healthily complex life-system is nature on earth itself. Its many intertwined ecosystems mutually support each other; changes in different elements often cancel each other out. A complex forest, which has a large variety of plants and animals, will persist year in and year out without interference. "Man, however," as Paul Ehrlich has pointed out, "is a simplifier of complex ecosystems." Among man's tools for reducing complexity are, for example, synthetic pesticides. When a complex system is treated with pesticide, some of the carnivorous species are exterminated and the pests become resistant. The removal of the carnivores simplifies the system. "One of the basic facts of population biology . . . is that the simpler an ecosystem is, the more unstable it is. . . . When man creates simple ecosystems, he automatically creates ecological problems for himself. For instance, he often plants strands of a single grass—wheat fields and corn fields are familiar examples. These lack the complexity necessary for stability and so are subject to almost instant ruination when not guarded constantly." [1]

Man is a great simplifier not only of ecosystems, but also of his own social and political systems. Areas of one-crop cultivation, or forests planted with one kind of tree, while tending to exhaust the soil and to suffer from the ravages of weather, pests and disease, are also frequently "productive," but in the narrowly specialized sense of economics. Single-crop cultivation systems frequently produce single-crop economies. Entire industries based on rubber and tin in Malay, on cocoa in Ghana or on rice in Thailand, freely supply the world market with important raw materials and produce profits for many participants; but they also expose the countries involved to disastrous price fluctuations and, at times of depression, they create regions of social devastation.

The political equivalents of single-crop economies are states that enforce a high degree of homogeneity or "purity," on the basis of a simple doctrine or of one-party rule, dictatorial or oligarchical. They, too, simplify political life beyond endurance. For a while, such systems appear productive of spectacular successes, as when military leaders are able to mobilize a whole population, or single-party dictatorships to focus national attention on some simple goal, such as steel production. But simple systems tend to run down: they lack the self-correcting ability to surmount repeated crises. Most often they bring disaster onto themselves: storms, diseases, corrupt predators.

The nation-state system is the most important "simple" political system, and the mechanism for its simplification has been war. A period of endemic wars converts populations into armies, and countries into armed camps; all purposes are subordinated to the supreme goals of surviving and winning. Not surprisingly, the periods of postwar readjustment are also those of profound malaise and strain. States, moreover, are organizations that are devoted to very specific purposes, especially in world affairs; the range of effectiveness of their "instruments of foreign policy" is narrowly and dangerously specialized.[2]

The basic reason why societies need complexity is the uncertainty of the future. Complexity is a form of insurance, a tribute man pays for his limited capacity to grasp the present and his even more tenuous hold upon the future. No current strides in science and technology can alter this aspect of the human condition. Only fools, or else men fatally afflicted by pride and conceit, could close their eyes to it.

In the story of evolution of life on earth, the advantage has consistently lain with adaptability. The dinosaurs grew to be truly huge, but they proved too large and too specialized in habits and behavior to be able to cope with changes in the environment, and they therefore succumbed to the mammals. Man, on the other hand, survived several ice-ages; he grew through adaptation and outdistanced the apes, not only because he developed his arms and hands as multi-purpose tools, but also because, with the help of an increasingly complex brain, he evolved language and the ability to establish lasting communications networks. His growth resulted from relative lack of specialization—that is, from his survival capacity. In the same way, the world's social system, man's greatest achievement on earth, needs a degree of flexibility and suppleness, and hence of complexity, in order to endure.

Complexity might be identified with what Johan Galtung calls "high entropy," which he believes to be a condition of "associative peace" (rather than peace through separation). He expects a system of high conflict-absorbing and conflict-resolving capacities to be one of considerable "messiness," lacking in clear, unique paths of interaction, and thus notable for high "disorder." "High entropy," together with high interdependence on a symmetric basis (that is, a strong world society), he sees as leading toward "increasingly complex systems." [3]

World politics is frequently, if unfeelingly, described as excessively complex—so complex as to defeat understanding and attempts by students in the field to put some conceptual order into it. Arguments have often been heard that it was this alleged complexity of its subject-matter that represented the major obstacle in the way of the development of International Relations theory. The fact is, however, that this is not so. The complexity bewailed by uninformed critics is no more than absence of understanding on their part and a lack of application to the subject; it gives evidence of a strongly ingrained tendency to forget the forest for the myriad trees. This is not to say that the subject of world politics does not demand intensive study. Increasingly interdependent large societies do need mounting investments in the human and social sciences and education in general; but there is nothing inherently and mysteriously enigmatic about the subject, such as is capable of defying the application of tested scholarly procedures and the ordinary search for knowledge.

Two forms of complexity might be distinguished at this point: network complexity and organizational complexity. Networks are lines and extend in space; their interesting dimension is spatial. Organizations, on the other hand, can be reduced conceptually to points in space, at the centers of decision-making, and their salient dimension would therefore be functional. Networks and organizations are the building-blocks of world society, and their mutually satisfactory interplay is a condition of world order. Organizational complexity will be looked at more closely in subsequent chapters, and in particular in Chapter Fifteen. For the present, attention will be confined to network complexity, which is achieved through the differentiation of a large social system into layers.

Layered Networks

The "layer cake" model of world society was first presented in Chapter Eleven (see in particular Figure 11:1, *Models of World Society*); but it was also implied in earlier discussions, notably in Chapters Two and Three, in the account of globalization, and in Chapter Seven, in the discussion of nation-state dominance.[4]

"Layer cake" is a term used by students of American government to depict the variety of levels encountered in its federal system. Morton Grodzins, who used it too, embellished it further by pointing out that the variety of interrelated programs undertaken by authoritative organs of all levels turned the layer cake into a marble-cake of government.[5]

The layer cake is a model of world society in two respects. For one, it is a device for organizing thought about and explaining the processes that take place in any world society. To this end, it is a taxonomic device, a method for classifying networks and the organizations that serve them and influence them. It has yet to be determined to what degree world interactions accord precisely with this model. On the other hand, the layer cake can also serve as a blueprint for ordering world processes so as to achieve an orderly arrangement of complexity.

This is one way of conveying the idea that world society, and politics too, can be organized in parallel network layers. It is a corrective to the hold that ethnocentric models (Figure 11:1 (a)) have on the popular imagination, and which is reinforced by conventional cartography, through its division of the world's land masses into a number of variously colored patches. It is a corrective, too, to the all-too-prevalent image of the pyramid as the arch-model of social organization. The pyramid has for millennia stood for hierarchy, the strong organization and the centralized state, bestowed upon civilization by the world's first fully mobilized political system. The modern organization chart still retains the shape of the pyramid; happily, however, the contemporary world may already be too complex to fall easily into that pattern.

The layer cake is therefore a scheme for identifying clusters of networks in accordance with their spatial structure. The characteristic features of networks being spatial, networks may be classified according to their spatial range. For historical agrarian systems, two main network layers have been distinguished: the Great Tradition, which is commonly regional in scope, and the Little Tradition of the villages, which is essentially local. For the contemporary world society, three basic network layers have been identified: global, national and local.

The assumption is that networks of similar spatial range tend to cluster into layers. The precise nature of this clustering is still an open question, however. It may mean no more than that networks operating over the same range use common communication facilities, share common languages and sources of information, develop complementary rules and conventions of behavior, and therefore generally come to face some similar problems. It does not necessarily mean that each network layer needs one government, but it may mean that some quantity of governance is required for each network layer. Thus people who live together in a city are enmeshed in a variety of networks, some of which are non-local. But to the extent that local networks develop a range of similar and common problems, they may be said to form a layer of local interaction which differs from the national and global layers. Each layer may therefore be expected to develop a range of specialized organizations serving it.

The stability and persistence of network layers, as of networks, may be accounted for more easily than the stability of organizations. Hierarchical structures have some difficulty in accommodating human interests to the overriding goal of the organization. Networks are systems of equal-status interaction; as such, they generate their own satisfactions solely by way of their functioning. One could apply here Homans' familiar interaction hypothesis, according to which mutual interaction in conditions of equality tends to generate feelings of liking and attachment.[6] This would make network and layer interaction less expensive to maintain, and generally a more efficient and flexible means of social coordination.

Each layer consists of networks and also of the organizations (or the portions of them) that are linked by these networks. All organizations exercise a large though varying degree of self-government, and networks too are, to a degree, self-regulating. But the whole still raises additional problems of politics, and each layer therefore requires arrangements for dealing with those that are relevant to it. The global layer might thus be seen to produce global politics, and the national and local layers, national and local politics. The total world system—its structure, its functioning and, in particular, the problems of the "coexistence of layers" —becomes the field of world politics.

The prototype of the present analysis is the federal political system. The centralizing tendencies of much of traditional political science have tended in the past to obliterate local politics, and to elevate to the front rank of attention problems of national politics. Students of federalism, on the other hand, have quite regularly acknowledged the viability and the independent quality of local politics, and the necessity of devising structures that would be capable of accommodating both within a comprehensive political system.

In terms of the layer cake model American history of the past two centuries has revolved around the gradual evolution, consolidation and expansion of the federal—that is, national—level of politics and society. For the United States did not come into the world as a full-fledged and powerful federal state; rather, it evolved into that form over a long period (see also Table 5:1). At first, in about 1750, there was no more than a network of personal and business relations, among a number of conspicuously elite families, in a few of the central states of what was later to become the Union.[7] Following the War of Independence and the signing of the Constitution, this network was institutionalized around Congress, the Presidency and the Supreme Court, and supplemented by the rudimentary common services of the army, the navy and the customs apparatus. Not until the Civil War was there a significant increase in the strength of the federal political layer: continental development—in particular by railroad—stimulated the growth of large organizations, and corporations began to serve a national market.

In contemporary United States, the national layer of society comprises significant portions of the population on a full-time basis: the Federal Government, and in particular its civil and military servants, both those that are liable to service in any part of the country, and the military, including the portion that is assigned overseas; the national corporations, whose executives in particular, along with other skilled workers, increasingly tend to circulate nationally (up to half a million people moved each year in the late nineteen-sixties); and the great universities, whose faculties and graduate schools are increasingly recruited from a national market. The communications and transport networks that hold all this together include radio and television, locally based but switched into a few large national organizations, as well as the airlines, which have displaced the railroad as a prime means of personal mobility. In some respects, this national layer was completed only in recent decades. In the nineteenth century, this country did not have (it still does not have) a national press (as England or France had); until the advent of the airplane, it has not had the personal mobility that people in the European states, which are smaller, enjoyed even during the nineteenth century.

The American example demonstrates that the growth of layers is uniquely a function of the quality of communications and transport. Primitive facilities do not permit the growth of multiple layers, they make only for links of the more tenuous and passing kind. The ability to sustain interactions over all but the shortest distances was in the past characteristic of all but a few of the most powerful organizations. All empires rested on such devices as relay-messengers, good roads and reliable shipping, and they were the wonders of their age. Independent communication networks, on the other hand, were few and far between: merchants plying regular trade routes, itinerant scholars, pilgrims. Cheap, reliable and independent means of long-distance communication bring into being clusters of activities that are no longer necessarily place-bound; as a result, the local community is eclipsed as the basis of social organization. Today a variety of organizations and networks sustain such transactions, and their intensity creates large clusters of relationships.

The growth of new layers disrupts the old established ones. The consolidation of national layers has everywhere affected and frequently led to the disorganization of local communities. Hence, such changes are by no means uniformly beneficial. The entire system must adapt to changes in any one of its layers. For instance, the effect of industrialization and urbanization, as part of national and world economic growth, has usually been the decline of small market towns, which had earlier served clusters of villages within a day's walking distance. In China, "progress" deprived these villages of their service centers, yet the lack of means has prevented the development of alternative networks. In the absence of measures for the equalization of opportunity, such progress has destroyed local communities, instead of helping them.[8] Yet in the United States, despite the increasingly prominent role of the federal layer of society, local life has not been obliterated, and its politics continues to function as a model for the functioning of complex systems.

By an extension of the federal analogy, the consolidation of world society may be seen as a growth of the global layer, in a fashion that would be comparable with the evolution of the federal network in the United States. World politics still remains at a primitive stage of that process, even though the rudiments of globalization have been in existence for centuries. Throughout this time, however, the emphasis has been on the intermediate level while the global layer has continued to suffer from neglect, as well as from fears and suspicions. Nevertheless, the expansion of the global layer was still able to proceed in a manner similar to the growth of federal politics on the American model: through the expansion of communications of a new type; the rise of new corporate enterprise, and new educational and social institutions, and, last but not least, through the evolution of new political functions, not necessarily of the centralized type. The emergence of world society, seen in Chapter Eleven as outgrowing the nation-state system, may also be regarded as a process of the necessary consolidation of the global layer.

Regional Networks

The character and arrangement of the layers that compose world society therefore consititute one determinant of the character of world politics. They define the framework within which world politics takes place. Two properties of this arrangement call for special attention: the number of layers, and their strength in relation to each other.

The number of layers into which a world system is differentiated is the single most important determinant of its complexity: in turn, this number is a close function of size. The larger a world system—in terms of such categories as population, spatial extent, social product or intensity of interaction—the more complexity it needs, and the greater the number of network layers it therefore produces. As the European system grew into a world system, it produced an additional, intermediate layer of interactions.

The basic layers of modern world society are thus three: local, with the city and the surrounding countryside as its basic unit; national, with the nation-state as its mainstay; and global. But this arrangement does not prevail uniformly on a world scale; large countries have important in-between layers, such as federal states or provinces, republics, or some regional constellations (such as Scotland in Great Britain). In some parts of the world, regional networks are gaining strength—for instance in Western Europe, in Africa and in Latin America. These world regional networks could constitute the next step in world complexity.

As world society grows in size during the next few decades, the number of layers into which it is articulated may be expected to increase, too. Population growth could be basic here: a world population in excess of ten billion will be within reach not long after the year 2000. Expansion of world regional layers is one possible response to this growth. That the possibility is a strong one is shown in the rising strength of regional intergovernmental contacts since World War II. A large proportion of international governmental organizations is now regional—about two-thirds of the total, according to Table 9:3. A similarly high proportion of contact and travel by government leaders also takes place within regional confines. Except for Europe, however, evidence for the existence of networks of a non-governmental kind in the several regions is insubstantial.

At the present time, the regional layer of world politics is still weak. Should it gain strength, the process could assume either of two forms: (1) a shift toward strong, state-like organizations at the regional level, the most likely model being the European Economic Community's assumption of an increasing range of functions, including those of finance and defense; or (2) a loser type of framework, within which each regional network is designed to fit its functions and possibly some broad cultural context, but without the whole being coordinated solely by a strong political organization.

Should pattern (1) prevail, a major shift of world organization could occur, away from nation-state dominance and toward regional-state dominance. The crucial questions would have to do with the control of military force. In the present-day system, the nation-state is the repository of that force; if, in Western Europe, the control of major forces were to shift to a European command, associated with a political authority, a new trend could be set in motion. The Arab states, some African states, and possibly some Latin American states might then pool their resources on a similar basis.

In the years during and immediately after World War II, students of International Relations recognized the shortcomings of the nation-state and forecast its replacement by wider, regional authorities. E. H. Carr saw this process as occurring in Europe in particular;[9] however slow the movement has proven to be, he was right. Quite a few states are too small in productivity and power, especially as compared with the United States and the Soviet Union, and their amalgamation into larger units could bring about all-round benefits. Should this process occur on a worldwide scale, large new regional states could arise and become the dominant actors of politics.

Some consolidation of the smaller nation-states is undoubtedly needed for the sake of world order; but it could take the form of new federal states (states at the national level), rather than regional superstates. Such amalgamations are, however, least necessary in Europe, although it is there that their probability is greatest. Aside from the question of the likelihood of such changes, the probable impact of a strong regional layer also needs to be evaluated. It is doubtful whether the drastic curtailment in the number of nation-states to, say, ten regional superstates would add much to world order or enhance justice. The problems of maintaining a viable global layer for such a system would be even greater.

A few strong states would be even less likely to permit diversity than does the contemporary system of a few very strong states and many weak states. A world that has been parceled out among a few regional states might have even greater tendencies toward self-sufficiency than is to be found at present, when the smaller and less affluent governments are in need of global services and often receive them from the world organization. If one of the large states broke down, the difficulties all around would be correspondingly large. Most generally, such a development would not seem to be conducive toward growth in complexity.

Barring a shift of dominance from the national to the world regional layer, feasible developments include a strengthening of that layer by means other than a drastic shift of military power, in some relationship to the world's major cultural areas. In the nineteen-sixties, the regional layer was weak, with the possible exception of the European Economic Community (whose financial strength was yet to be built up). Extra-European regional arrangements labored under the fundamental handicap of weakness: they were not, nor could they ever be, richer or stronger than the states that composed them and the populations that supported them. In the Third World, no amount of amalgamation can surmount this condition, and it might possibly even serve to aggravate it. In the absence of drastic shifts in world income and value distribution, no significant progress can be foreseen as deriving from the strengthening of regional cooperation alone. Rather, it should go hand in hand with strengthening the global layer as a means of income distribution and growth regulation. If Western Europe were to emerge as the only area to achieve significant regional consolidation, the sole result could be a strengthening of its own position as against the rest of the world, and an accentuation of the world's glaring inequalities, instead of their diminution.

Strength of the Global Layer

Layers of networks may be thought of as possessing the property or dimension of strength or width—most importantly in relation to the other layers. Thus, a convenient way of expressing the strength of such a layer would be as a fraction or percentage of the total of world society.[10] If world trade were to be regarded as an indicator of the strength of the global layer, it could be argued that that strength at present amounts to about 0.2, because such trade comprises close to twenty percent of the total of world economic activity (see also Table 11:1). Calculations of global centralization, however, suggest a much lower figure (see Table 7:5).

Different world societies might be envisaged, with network layers

Figure 13:1
Types of Layered Networks

A. Nation-state system   B. Balanced   C. Asymmetric

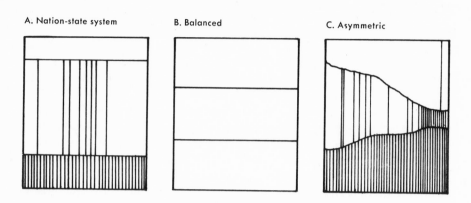

arranged in different ways and in different proportions. Figure 13:1 illustrates some important varieties. Type A represents a national arrangement of a nation-state system. It shows a weak global layer and a weak set of local layers, but also overwhelmingly strong national layers.

Type B model shows, by contrast, a world society with a balanced array of layers.[11] They are balanced because they are of equal strength, such that the weight of no one of them is sufficient to enable it to dominate the others. This could conceivably be the ideal type of arrangement for the world. The balancing of layers helps to assure autonomy. If layer autonomy is desirable, on the ground that each type of layer and each separate layer develops its own problems and purposes, to be solved within its own context and on its own terms, then a condition of equibalance would help to assure an absence of dominance. Grounds for believing this are largely intuitive at this stage, but they may not be for that reason irrelevant.

World systems, are, however, more complicated than the first two models would suggest. They are unevenly developed, so that the layers are actually unequally strong in various parts of the system. Type C model illustrates one particular kind of unevenness or asymmetry. It shows one part of the world as strong in the nation-state layer and weak in the global dimension, while the larger part of the world is strong in localism, weak in the national layers and strongly influenced by global forces. It may be that model C approximates the contemporary world more closely than does either A or B.

The implication of much of the argument so far has been that, overall, the global layer of contemporary world society is weak and needs strengthening. So much might also have been concluded from the analysis of nation-state dominance in Part Two, as well as from the study of diplomacy and international organizations. Some strengthening is indeed required, in both the political and the non-political parts of the global networks, up to the point of restoring a more balanced system; but some evening out of the asymmetrical features is also needed.

There is little conclusive evidence about twentieth-century trends in the relative strength of the global layer. International trade has been rising steadily, but at a rate that does not exceed the growth rate of the world product; its relation to world income does not therefore seem to have changed appreciably. In addition, the bulk of that trade takes place among the developed countries—which contributes greatly to existing asymmetries in world development. But there are grounds for believing that networks of various kinds—such as those based on science, education, migration and tourism, as well as on specialized elite structures of a global character—might have been expanding.

After analyzing some of these data, Karl Deutsch advanced the hypothesis of a "parochializing" trend—that is, a trend toward the weakening of global networks—and attributed it to the impact of industrialization. In his view, the process of fundamental democratization might effect different results at different stages. To begin with, mass politics, economic development, communications and mobility, all of which are centered in the national layer, grow faster than "acculturation to global processes." The collapse of the former imperial domains, too, would tend to produce the same effects. "As the result of all these processes, the propensities to international transactions might decline and prolonged periods of increased parochialism and nationalism might occur in many countries, just during the critical early decades of the nuclear age." But a second stage of development would ultimately permit the process of democratization to extend to the international level and to a higher level of global integration.[12]

Deutsch is, in effect, describing fluctuations in the strength of the global layer in accordance with a model of "temporary setback." The process that accounts for the setback is, according to him, "democratization"; but it could also be described as the nationalization of the state. Is the nationalization of the state, then, a temporary obstacle on the road toward the consolidation of global networks?

While the problem is an interesting one, the evidence is still far from being conclusive. The degree of globalization that existed earlier in the twentieth century is not known to any precise degree, so that trends cannot really be established. Such information as there is about world trade does not support any conclusion about a parochializing tendency.

There is no evidence showing a relative decline in the importance of commercial activities in the global network. Known trends documenting a rise in nation-state dominance (see Chapter Seven) could be accounted for by a relative decline in local activities, as much as by a fall in global participation, which was weak to begin with.

Much of the discussion of globalization (or "international integration") proceeds on the implicit assumption that "the more globalization, the better." This is not really so. Reliable knowledge about what constitutes a "desirable" degree of globalization is lacking. But the possibility of excessive globalization is not precluded by the present analysis; it is, rather, indicated by it.

A classical example of excessive identification with the global layer might be nineteenth-century Russia. The culture and even the language of the Tsarist Court and of the aristocracy was French and, in general, European: the ruling family was by marriage closely tied to the monarchical system; the aristocracy lived in French style and spent much of their time in Western Europe; it had little to do with the Russian peasants. The revolution that took place in 1917 destroyed this group; at the same time, it broke the links between Russia and the global system. Excessive participation at the global level may well have had the effect of weakening the national and local levels of society and ultimately of wreaking great havoc.

In general, the same type of process has occurred since 1945 in much of the Third World. The impact of globalization there was, in the long run, quite strong; it was reviewed earlier. In the overblown cities, as well as in many capitals, of Latin America, Africa and Asia, the symbols of the global system loom large over the landscape: the glass and concrete skyscrapers, the air-conditioned offices of the international airlines, the ever-present Hilton Hotels. A select few take part in the glamor of fashionable embassy parties and latest fashions; the many do not, and stand outside. In between there is a gap that is yet to be filled. The national layer may be strong governmentally; but many of the other networks—economic, cultural and educational—are lacking.

Maoist guerrilla warfare tactics, which seek support among the peasants who have been alienated from the governing political elite, attempt to exploit such possibly excessive absorption in the global layer. Guerrillas who seek to conquer the cities by first seizing the countryside believe that control over local communities will in time give them power in the nation's capital. This happened in China between 1933 and 1949, and it might or might not happen elsewhere again. But in Burma, a government that, over prolonged periods since the achievement of independence in 1947, has controlled not much else besides the capital city of Rangoon and some surrounding countryside, has nevertheless succeeded in preserving the national network, even while many local networks stayed under the control of a variety of insurgents. In Iraq, the Kurds have achieved a measure of local autonomy from national control, but only after prolonged guerrilla struggle. More often than not, the guerrillas are seeking national power. Under certain conditions, however, civil-war settlements could be devised by granting autonomy to some local layers of politics and society, even while leaving the national layer unchanged.

Nothing in this discussion is designed to suggest that one layer is superior to, better or more important than any other. A large society in particular must be a complex society: it needs all the layers it has. It is inconceivable that the world could form one undifferentiated society, just as it is unthinkable that it would break up into a congeries of unrelated and uncommunicative autonomies of merely parochial scope. Either situation is an extreme: all layers are important and further, in principle, of equal importance; all *a priori* claims to superiority on the part of any one layer, including the claims to superiority that are enshrined in the nation-state, seem unjustified.

World attention and the distribution of preferences does, nevertheless, shift from time to time, so that priorities are reallocated and values redistributed. Shifts in priorities and values sometimes bring about a reordering of relations between layers of world society. Nation-state dominance expresses the high valuation that is placed, on a worldwide scale, on the services of the nation-state and on some related elements of national networks. Such changes in evaluation would tend to reorder the priorities among layers.

The strength of layers thus in one sense reflects the prevailing conceptions of critical issues. For the nation-state, the critical issue is defense against outsiders and protection of the interests of nationals. If global problems, such as pollution, or world development, or some outer space challenge, were to assume a higher place in the rank ordering of world priorities, attention and resources could shift to the global layer and in effect restructure the system. On the other hand, the crisis of the cities might help to shift attention to the local layer. Presidential proposals for "revenue-sharing" among the federal and state and local authorities are among the ways of reallocating resources among levels of government.

The nation-state system keeps the global layer far under strength, by denying to it legitimacy or even visibility. A more balanced world system would shift its priorities, in order to compensate for this structural weakness. Nevertheless, unlimited expansion in the global layer would obviously be ill-conceived. Equally misplaced would be the idea of an inherent superiority or any claim to inherent predominance.

Students of world politics might wish to accept as self-evident the assertion that global problems are intrinsically superior to others. Some indeed are tremendously significant; in a fundamental way, the survival of mankind rests upon a continuing resolution of problems of world order. But does this justify an overblown expansion of global functions? Hardly so. Rather, ways must be devised to avoid a situation in which the needs of survival remain a source of perpetual blackmail against the organization of the world. It is indeed a sword of Damocles, suspended over a growing and still exuberant society. It needs to be recognized as part of the human condition, understood and kept in its place; but it must not become the embodiment of a death wish, casting increasingly long shadows over the entire world.

Cities in Network

The tendency to order human affairs into hierarchies is ever-present, and the layer cake might also lend itself to it. Could it not be, for example, the model of a world *class* system, with the upper classes dominating the global networks, the middle classes strong in the nation-states, and the lower classes confined to local affairs? Much writing on nationalism and national development has laid stress on the role of the middle classes, while the global layer has frequently been identified with upper-class pursuits. But there is really no necessity for this in optimum world organization: each layer requires its own self-sufficient social structure, rather than one that is dependent.

Students of geography have observed a tendency to hierarchy in the spatial arrangement of cities. According to the theory of "central places," first elaborated geometrically by Walter Christaller and then continued by a host of other theoretical and empirical studies, cities group themselves into hierarchies. Within such hierarchies, each larger city serves a predictable array of urban satellites and is, in turn, part of a more extensive network. On a world scale, and in the contemporary advanced economy, as many as nine or ten grades of cities have been identified —from world cities (such as New York or London), through world regional centers (such as Cairo or Singapore), national capitals, metropolitan and regional centers, small cities and towns, down to villages and hamlets. At each level, a city is part of a wider network of cities, and also provides the point at which two urban networks join together.[13]

In "central place" theory, the dominant relations are from the top down, along a hierarchy of functions arranged according to threshold size (the minimum market size required to support the organization)— from the highest-order function (with the greatest threshold; that is, with the largest market) to that of the lowest-order function with the smallest market). The highest-order centers cover the entire range of products, including the highest-order functions; "below them," a hierarchy develops that supplies an increasingly limited range of products.

The hierarchy of cities is generated by the assumption that any place that originates higher-order goods must also supply the entire range of lower-order products. It also assumes certain conditions of transport and communications. But if places (or organization-clusters) that supply higher-order functions do not supply all the other functions, and if transport and communications are without cost, then the need for a hierarchy disappears. So does the need for monstrous and unmanageable cities. There are indeed functions that require a world market; but these functions need not all cluster together, and they need not be met with at those places that also supply all national and local functions. The concept of layered networks provides a better rationale for remaking the map of human settlement.[14]

In any event, changes in income, scale and accessibility have already resulted in a progressive reduction in the span of the hierarchy, with the decline of the smaller hamlets, villages and cities coinciding with the universal trend toward urbanization. The great cities and urban agglomerations at the apex of the hierarchy of central places have become foci of attraction for the masses of the poor, who have been displaced from the land by industrial change and population growth. Their immense slums are fertile grounds for urban guerrilla warfare.

The diplomatic network of the nation-state system is, in one sense, a network linking the world's national capitals; it is thus one form of intercity network. But it is also to some degree isomorphic with the world's other global networks. For some important purposes, these might be seen as being centered on the world cities, those that serve as headquarters of international governmental and nongovernmental organizations: New York, Paris, Rome, Geneva; those that house the great corporations and the centers of world finance: New York, London, Brussels, Zurich, Beirut, Tokyo; and also, perhaps, those that accommodate universities and centers of intellectual and creative endeavor: Boston, San Francisco, Los Angeles, New York, London, Paris. Some of these are national capitals; some are not. The world itself has no capital city, nor does it need any cosmopolis, or single capital city. Although New York comes closest to being entitled to such a designation, because of its concentration of political (United Nations), economic (corporate and banking) and intellectual (university, publishing, foundations) activity, it is not self-sufficient and, in fact, labors under considerable strains. The global layer needs a broader base and a number of world cities.

There is a tendency to expect that the world cities must also represent the best there is in humanity: the best in men and women, wealth and power, the finest knowledge. But a system of balanced layers may not need a hierarchy of cities. There is no need to think that there must be cities that are best in every respect. A sane social system will not concentrate all that is good in it in one city or even in one network.

Layer Autonomy and Interdependence

If network layers represent self-organizing contexts of social organization, then the important principle arising out of this analysis is that of layer autonomy. Each layer of world society needs self-government in order to deal with the problems that are common to it; but layers are also interdependent and require some coordination. Once again, it is tempting to suggest that the function of global networks might be to coordinate (hence, in a sense, to rule over) the rest of the world system; but that is not really so. An artfully balanced world society would be so built as to require either no additional coordination or else would assign coordination as the task for all.

The justification for autonomy is the indispensability of each layer to the functioning of world society. None of the layers may lay claim to a monopoly of usefulness, or demand a monopoly of authority. Layers are not self-sufficient, however; this is evident, in particular, in the fact that layered networks operate not as exclusive, but rather as overlapping, closely meshed social systems.

The interweaving of layers results from the fact that to some degree individuals participate at the same time in all layers: they hold multiple network memberships. In fact, they can avoid doing so only at the cost of considerable effort. United Nations staff members are archetypical members of the global layer; but they are also nationals of member countries and, by living in New York, they cannot help being part of some local networks, with all the advantages and involvements that entails. A South-Vietnamese rice farmer, too, might principally be a member of his village community; but it is clear that he cannot avoid involvement in national affairs or, indirectly, even in global politics. Some individuals will, of course, specialize or do their principal work in only one particular layer; considered analytically, however, they all devote some attention to and participate in—or should participate in—all the other layers.[15] As a matter of daily life, participation in the global layer may for most people take the merely vicarious and indirect forms of newsreading and "tube"-watching; but if even very little time is spent on such activities, it does signify concern for, and participation in, what effectively constitutes world society.[16]

The precondition for broad participation in the global layer may be a similarly structured distribution of loyalties. An individual who participates in all three layers will also have his loyalty distributed among all three. A monopoly of loyalties in only one layer would thus appear to be unreal. Nationalistic extremism, viewed as the monopolization of loyalties, appears in such light to be on its way out.[17]

The necessity for layer autonomy becomes evident through an examination of the dangers of "layer fusion." [18] This is the process by which authorities, organizations and persons from one layer absorb the activities, authorities or organizations in a different layer. In simple terms, this constitutes interference. A common example might be intervention by national authorities in local affairs, or the usurpation of national authority by local and other parochial interests.

In world politics, two facets of this process assume prominence: intervention by some nation-states in the affairs of other nations; and the exercise of global authority by some nation-states. These are related issues, although they might be distinguished by using the term "horizontal fusion" for the first case, and "vertical fusion" for the second. In both instances, tensions and disruptions of order occur; among other things, both are hard to reconcile with the rules of the nation-state system.

Intervention by some governments in the affairs of others creates tremendous difficulties; but it is hard to avoid in a system in which inequalities of resources and opportunities are as great, and war is as frequent, as it is in the nation-state system. Intervention in the form of military deployment on foreign soil (for instance, Soviet troops in Hungary 1956; or United Arabic Republic forces in Yemen 1962–1967), military support for incumbent regimes threatened by civil war or rebellion, or by external military pressure (the Vietnam conflict; or Soviet aid to the U.A.R. before and after 1967), financial and economic assistance for "hard-up" governments (Arab states for U.A.R. and Jordan after 1967) —all these forms of intervention are bound up with war and war-critical situations. Wars of all kinds blur the distinctiveness of layers and networks, and override the universal preference for autonomy. Wars bring alliances and recognition of the interdependence of governments, as a result of which each becomes deeply concerned about the fate of others. In the absence of war, intervention could be expected to be less frequent and less unsettling.

More important still is "vertical layer fusion," which is represented in the assertion of global authority by nation-states and, in particular, by the Great Powers. Much already been said on this subject in Part Two. Suffice it to add at this point that, as a form of layer fusion, Great Power authority contributes greatly to the confusion of world politics. The autonomy of the national layer, which is a precondition of the nation-state system, strongly resists the exercise of global functions by other nations; but in the process it also develops a resistance to all other types of global function, and thus contributes to the weakening of the entire system.

The classical example of the dangers of "vertical fusion" is the fate of the Communist International, the world organization of the Communist Parties, which was set up in 1919. Conceived of as a world party, the Comintern was to be governed by an international executive body, controlled by a fully representative World Congress. Right from the start, the Russian party gained a strong influence in the executive; its influence was increased even further by the fact that Moscow was chosen as the headquarters of the new organization. The Comintern became one of the arenas in which the struggle between Trotsky and Stalin was carried out, and when Stalin won, he established complete control over it. Many Comintern employees, including foreign Communists, perished in the period of the Great Purges. When Soviet foreign policy objectives demanded it, the entire organization was summarily dissolved. In the meantime, its effectiveness as a world organization had been steadily declining.

All international organizations run the risk of being captured by one or a few of its member nations. When this condition obtains, their functioning is likely to be disrupted. The dysfunctions of vertical fusion bear out the importance of layer autonomy. More basically still, because the important global political functions continue to be controlled by national governments, fusion is chronic to the entire system. A progressive growth of layer autonomy at this level is a necessary condition of world development.

Demise of Geographical Units?

Johan Galtung has argued that, during the course of modernization and with the increase in communication capacity, the salience of geographical or spatially based units (such as cities, counties and also nation-states) will continue to decrease as a focus of unification, and at a rate higher than that of the decrease of organizations.[19] Galtung's arguments recall John Herz's long-awaited "demise of the territorial state."

The present chapter is based on the assumption that a modern world society must have both spatial and functional complexity. There is little reason to believe that communications advances will in the foreseeable future prevent the factors of location or distance from exercising an influence over the structure of politics. One set of men, organizations, and in particular, networks, occupy one space, while other men, organizations and networks occupy other spaces; this differential distribution in space gives rise to enduring problems. There is reason, of course, to hope that the nation-state monopoly of territorial authority will not continue forever, for it is that monopolization and the abuses to which it lends itself that create tensions, rather than the mere existence of national layers.

Notes to Chapter Thirteen

1. Paul Ehrlich, *The Population Bomb* (New York: Ballantine Books, 1968), pp. 49–51. Another form of ecological simplification is plant breeding, on which the Green Revolution of the nineteen-sixties was based.

2. See Chapter Seven above, Section on "Specificity of the Foreign Affairs Function."

3. Johan Galtung, "On the future of the international system," *Journal of Peace Research*, 1967, No. 4, p. 307.

4. See also Modelski, "World Parties and World Order," *cited*, p. 190.

5. *The American System: A New View of Government in the United States* (ed. Daniel Elazar) (Chicago: Rand McNally, 1966).

6. George C. Homans, *The Human Group* (New York: Harcourt Brace, 1950), p. 243.

7. Karl Deutsch, *Nationalism and Social Communication*, *cited*, pp. 32–36.

8. G. William Skinner, "Marketing and Social Structure in Rural China," Part II, *Journal of Asian Studies*, Vol. 24 (2), February 1965, pp. 195–228 ". . . the transformation of higher-level market towns into modern trading centers is achieved only at the cost of declining demand in neighboring markets . . . the process . . . involves a steady increase in the size of marketing areas as old markets are closed." (p. 215).

9. *Conditions of Peace* (London: Macmillan, 1942), Ch. 10; *Nationalism and After* (London: Macmillan, 1945).

10. Karl Deutsch discussed the same problem (within a nation-state framework) when he inquired into the "propensity to international transactions." He rated the "degree of the integration to the outside world" for a country as "high" if the percentage of "outside" transactions, as compared with total transactions, exceeded 50 percent, and as "low," if it ranged between six and nine percent. ("The Propensity to International Transactions," in Louis Kriesberg, ed., *Social Processes in International Relations: A Reader* (New York: Wiley, 1968), p. 249.

11. "Among equilibriums, equibalance describes a situation where the elements in balance have equal weight." J. A. Laponce, "An experimental method to measure the tendency to equibalance in a political system." *American Political Science Review*, Vol. 60 (4), December 1966, pp. 982–993.

12. Deutsch, *ibid.*, p. 254.

13. Brian J. L. Berry & Chauncy Harris, "Central Place," *International Encyclopedia of the Social Sciences*, Vol. II, pp. 365–370.

14. Lewis Richardson (*Statistics of Deadly Quarrels*, [Pittsburgh: Boxwood Press, 1960], pp. 154–156) notes the close similarity between the size distribution of wars and of towns. This might suggest that the hierarchical arrangement of cities is in some ways closely bound up with the structure of the international system.

15. The distribution of attention among the layers of politics has been studied with the help of survey research. A national probability sample of

the 1966 federal election showed the following percentages of respondents attributing first rank to the degree to which they followed public affairs: local, 30 per cent; state, 17 per cent; national, 32 per cent; international, 20 per cent. M. Kent Jennings and Harmon Zeigler, "The Salience of American State Politics," *American Political Science Review*, Vol. 64 (2), June 1970, p. 525.

16. A pilot project completed by Jon A. Christopherson ("Identity bonds in the global political process," paper presented to the Western meeting of the Peace Research Society (International), May 1970), showed that the distribution of identity bonds among various layers of the political process is indeed measurable. His research indicated important global identifications in the student sample he interviewed.

17. Another source of coordination among network layers are issue-areas (such as education, economic development, or population) which create "vertical" political systems. See James Rosenau, "Pre-theories and theories of foreign policy," in Barry Farrell, ed., *Approaches to Comparative and International Politics* (Evanston, Ill.: Northwestern University Press, 1966), esp. at pp. 71–88.

18. Modelski, "World Parties and World Order," *cited*, pp. 206–7.

19. Galtung, "On the Future of the International System," *cited*, p. 312; see also John Herz, "Rise and Demise of the Territorial State," *World Politics*, July 1957; and "The territorial state revisited," *Polity*, 1968, pp. 12–34.

14
Survival

I̶F THE OVERRIDING INTEREST OF MAN-
kind is survival, the condition most likely to assure it is, in the long run, complexity: only a complex social system can be expected to meet and to resolve the ever-changing problems of an unknown future. Without complexity, a system that specializes in coping with one kind of challenge only will be defenseless when confronted with other dangers.

If complexity is the basis of long-term survival, then the problem for the short run remains how to avoid global war. It is hardly a secret that the development and spread of thermonuclear armaments has put in question the ability of the human race to survive. Biological life, including human life, took several billion years to assume its present forms; contemporary weapons inventories could wipe it out in no time, and global war could be a precipitant of such an event. Prevention of a nuclear disaster may thus be viewed as the supreme concern of all humankind.

The avoidance of global war is imperative because of the likelihood of the mass use of nuclear weapons in such a war; it is less probable, although the possibility is not to be ruled out, that such weapons would be used in national or local conflicts. But the avoidance of global war is not the avoidance of global conflict; it is rather an effort to circumscribe and to institutionalize conflict, by dispersing it among the various layers of the body social, as well as among its various networks and organizational systems. For, if it is unchecked, war tends to spread, and no war more quickly than global war. It fuses the world system together, by involving it thoroughly in one single activity—that of waging war. War's tendency to spread induces a simplification of social problems: at times of global war, the issues deciding all others are those that have some bearing on victory. During times of peace, too, the expectation of war affects large segments of political action.

War is a great simplifier; it is, as a consequence, conducive to certain forms of productivity but is also the antithesis and enemy of complexity. War is therefore not only a direct and concrete threat to survival, but, through its tendency toward simplification, it may be undermining mankind's long-term capacity to adapt to changing conditions. It thus endangers survival in a doubly dangerous manner, which operates even in times of nominal peace.

The Simple Notion of War

Conventional thinking about International Relations is premised on the homogeneity of war. War is envisaged as a uniform phenomenon, which in its essentials has existed through the ages; however modern some of its forms may be, it is believed to have remained fundamentally unchanged to this day. What is more, the prospects for the future are viewed in terms of a simple war-peace dichotomy.

The unidimensionality of war appears most clearly in the conventional war-peace dichotomy. War and peace are portrayed as though they were two phases through which the international system has regularly passed. This makes peace no more than the simple absence of war, and offers no clues as to the conditions that constitute "normality"; indeed, it is war that assumes the stance of normality. The fact is that these are not true alternatives at all: at times, war can be waged in some areas without the entire global system being affected; at other times, it cannot.

The simple view of war contributes to the seductive and destructive simplicity of the institution. In a complex society, even war needs to be seen as complex, to be recognized as a multi-dimensional phenomenon. Above all, war must not be regarded as a natural phenomenon, occurring outside man's control and as the result of his "nature." It is a social institution—long involved in human affairs, but also subject to change, like all other human institutions.

War is not to be confused with conflict. It may be assumed that, in the history of the human race, some degree of conflict has been a permanent feature, and that it is likely to remain so. But war is only one of the many forms that human conflict can assume, depending on the social system within which it occurs. Should that one particular form outlive its usefulness, no theoretical reason exists why war should continue.

It could also be argued that a certain minimal amount of violence, of various kinds, should be expected to occur in all societies. In today's world, violence can take the form of individual and organized crime, domestic and traffic accidents, riots, violent strikes and civil war, violent speech, protests, demonstrations and bombings, and governmental terror and persecution. It is difficult to say to what extent violence is a "normal" part of the friction that is generated by every social system, and to what extent it is pathological. Under all conditions, however, violence must be kept under some degree of restraint and control, because it has a tendency to spread at an explosive rate, by infection or by demonstration effect.

The primary function of politics is to institutionalize conflict and to channel it in the least damaging directions, so as to contain violence and to organize it for social purposes. The international system so far has indeed institutionalized war, but it has failed repeatedly to keep violence from spreading into world war. War has become the predominant form of conflict and the preferred means of violence. Yet the dimensions that warlike conflicts have assumed in the twentieth century, and the tremendous efforts that have to be mobilized in order to wage them, have converted wars into a new type of game, which threatens the destruction of civilization. New rules and new institutions are needed to deal with global conflict and with the worldwide use of violence.

One process of limitation that could already be at work is a simple shift to less lethal means of conducting organized conflict. It is not so much that the *amount* of conflict would be reduced in that case, but rather that the means employed would shift toward less violent forms. The recent record of Europe has been rather good in this respect, despite the persistence of historical inclinations toward violence. In the nineteen-sixties, such far-reaching and large-scale national processes as, in the United States, the civil rights struggles of 1964-1967, the urban disturbances of 1965-1968 and the campus unrest of 1965-1970, and, in France, the general strike of 1968, occurred with only a minimum of bloodshed and did not rank as major events of organized violence. Perhaps a general civilizing tendency is at work, fostered by the diversification and pluralization of society.

Contemporary or future war may also be an entirely unique and novel phenomenon—part of the new social system from which it arises, and distinguishable from other, traditional types of warfare.[1] The analysis of complexity in world society that was carried out in the preceding chapter indeed suggests that war, which is part of that society, may also be subject to a similar complexity. In the past, war has of course been a simplifier, as well as a force for the fusing of layers. Yet, granted the possibility of layer autonomy, can it be that the several different layers of world society will develop different ways of conflict resolution? Can it be that the degree of violence that is permissible in one layer may not be allowed to occur in another (for instance, globally)?

The present chapter analyzes the phenomenon of war on the assumption that this complex process can in fact be broken down into three types: global wars, national wars and local wars. In each of these, the principal conflict is a network-deterioration event (a case of network malfunction), which would for that reason be confined to one layer of world society. There would always be the danger that it might spread to other layers; more often than not, however, it would be confined to the layer of its origin.

Avoidance of Global War

The major sources of violent threat to human survival are two: (1) global war, which must be avoided altogether, and (2) national and local conflicts, which must be limited and prevented from escalating into global wars. The classification of wars thus permits a differentiation of violent conflicts into those that are deadly and those that are not. Not all wars are equally dangerous nor do they all need to arouse equal or widespread concern; for the moment, the discussion will be confined to the problem of preventing global war.

Global wars are in a class all by themselves. They are conflicts that determine the constitution of the global political system. They are violent conflicts that are worldwide in extent, and occur above all in the global layer. But they have also been huge disturbances, absorbing immense resources and unlimited attention. In their character as Great Power wars, they have drawn on the bulk of the world's military forces. They have also played a decisive role in world politics and Table 14:1 presents a tentative list of these global phenomena. Yet, however terrible the losses they have inflicted and the violence they have engendered, global wars have not in the past posed a threat to human survival.

The loss of life caused by wars has always been considerable. There is some evidence that the proportion of military deaths in the total death picture has been rising. In France, for instance, it rose from 11 military deaths per 1000 deaths in the seventeenth century (which was hardly peaceful) to 63 in the 20th century, up to 1930; in Great Britain, during the same time, the figure rose from 15 to 48.[2] But the impact of war-induced casualties on population growth has so far been minimal. Even the terrible losses of World War II, comprising over three per cent of

TABLE 14:1   A List of Global Wars

Dates	War	Major powers participating	Outcome
1585–1604	War of the Armada	Spain, England, France	Spanish monopoly of the New World challenged; "prescription without possession availeth nothing"
1598–1669	Dutch War of Independence (ctd., also part of the Thirty Years' War	Netherlands, Spain, Portugal	Dutch seizure of Asian spice trade; weakening of Spanish power in Americas; Hapsburg Empire declines in Europe
1683–1715	Wars of Louis XIV	France, Austria, Spain, Netherlands, Portugal, England	Balance of Power reaffirmed in Europe; Louis XIV checked; England assumes paramount position in world trade
1756–1763	Seven Years' War	France, Britain, Austria, Prussia, Russia, Spain	France loses colonial empire in India and Americas; Prussia a major power
1775–1783	American Revolutionary War	Britain, France, Spain	United States of America independent
1792–1815	French Revolutionary and Napoleonic Wars	France, Austria, Prussia, Britain, Russia, Spain, Portugal, Sweden	Concert of Europe established; Slave trade abolished; England confirmed in overseas empire
1914–1918	First World War	Germany, Austria-Hungary, Russia, France, Britain, Italy, Japan, U.S.A.	League of Nations formed; German fleet destroyed; Austria-Hungary breaks up
1939–1945	Second World War	Germany, Britain, France, Italy, U.S.S.R., Japan, U.S.A.	United Nations founded; U.S.A. and U.S.S.R. emerge in super-power status

the world's people, if they are averaged out over six years are seen to have made hardly a dent in the annual growth rate of between one and two per cent. Yugoslavia and the Soviet Union suffered the heaviest losses, amounting to about 11 and 9 per cent of their populations respectively; but by 1970 the world as a whole had once again doubled its population.

Lewis Richardson has estimated the deaths from all causes, between 1820 and 1945, on a worldwide scale, to have been in the region of 3.8

billion.[3] On his data, deaths from what he described as "deadly quarrels" of magnitude $3 \pm \frac{1}{2}$ and above amounted to only about 47 million—that is, to 1.2 percent of the total. But out of the 47 million deaths that can be attributed to wars of this kind, the two world wars of the twentieth century alone, according to his figures, accounted for 36 million— that is, for close to four-fifths of the total of war-killed in more than a century.[4]

This confirms the fact that global wars are phenomena of a special kind, not to be lumped together indiscriminately with other types of wars and violent conflicts. Moreover, having listed wars of various magnitudes alongside estimates of the number of deadly quarrels of smaller size, such as murders—defined as quarrels of magnitude $0 \pm \frac{1}{2}$; that is, causing at least one death—Richardson also observed as "remarkable" the fact that "the heavy loss of life occurred at the two ends of the sequence of magnitudes—namely, the world wars and the murders. The small wars contributed much less to the total." [5] He drew no conclusions from this, but it could be argued that such data would show that the important problems of world order have been located at the global and local levels, and not in between, where most of the peace-keeping resources have been concentrated in the nation-state system.

Until recently, war has not posed any threat to the survival of the human race. In the future, however, it might, mainly because of nuclear weapons and the concurrent concentration of life and productivity in cities, which are ideal targets for mass destruction. Modern life makes entire populations dependent on city skills and city resources. Strategic doctrines of the nuclear powers therefore regard the threat of destruction of cities as the principal deterrent to nuclear war. Should that deterrent fail, the world cities would indeed be doomed and, with them, modern civilization.

One of the most acute problems of the twentieth century has been urbanization and, even more, the growth of very large cities. The expansion of city populations proceeds at a rate that is higher than the capital investment required to maintain an even standard of urban services, let alone to sustain an improvement. The growth is even more rapid in the Third World than it is in the developed areas; but everywhere the cities are being crowded as the outcome of high birth rates and by immigration from decaying rural areas. Between 1920 and 1960, the proportion of urbanized world population (people living in cities of over 20,000) rose from 14 to 28 percent, while those in cities of over a half a million people went up from 6 to 12 percent, now concentrated in 150 major metropolitan areas. The trend is still going on. This means that some 150 thermonuclear devices, representing only a minor part of the arsenals of the great powers (see Table 14:2), could now wipe out a substantial portion of the world's population and, what is more, with it the major nodes of global and most of the national layers of world society.

Precipitous urbanization has been the result of the deterioration of local communities in many parts of the world and their consequent inability to hold on to their populations. This undermines the health of the cities, bloats them up, turns them into breeding grounds of unrest, and weakens the entire world society. In itself, it is attributable to an excessive concentration of wealth and power in the national layer.

Urbanization renders world society particularly vulnerable to nuclear hazards. In intensity of destruction, the threat it presents has nothing like it to compare with in recent memory. It recalls only primitive and medieval horror stories of many cities being put to the sword and fire—for example, the career of Mongol conquerors, who wiped out entire cities for resisting them, laying waste large parts of Central Asia and the Near East, gravely weakening Moslem civilization of the late medieval period.

The plight of the cities in the nuclear age vividly illustrates the extreme vulnerability of the local layer of society to nation-state dominance. Why should wars that have been designed and contingency-planned at the national level entail the complete destruction of urban local life? Why should city communities be the hostages in a round of international nuclear blackmail? How is it that city-dwellers and urban leaders seem to accept this without question?

There is nothing that urban vulnerability brings out more clearly than it does the fact that, in global wars, as in most twentieth century wars, the cost of fighting is borne, even in the matter of fatalities, to a greater extent by civilians than by soldiers on active service. In both the world wars of the twentieth century, civilian losses exceeded military casualties by a factor of three or more. In these two wars, the total of soldiers killed was between 13 and 16 percent of those who were mobilized. This ratio may be compared with data for the late medieval period, which indicate that a participant in a battle may have had no more than a 50 per cent chance of coming out alive and unhurt.[6] The proportion has been declining steadily in modern wars, so that the paradoxical situation now obtains in which the life chances of a military man have been going up steadily, while those of civilians during periods of war have been going down. In a large war, the safest place to be (outside of the combat infantry, which is manned by conscripts) might now well be the military forces. Thus even ignoring the economic, social and moral burdens of a global war—the bombing, the hunger and the persecution—the question of personal survival is heavily weighted against civilians and the situation would deteriorate drastically in a nuclear exchange that involved cities.

The significance of past global wars has not lain in the absolute losses they have inflicted or in the property destruction they have brought in their train. The casualties suffered by the military forces have been the less important part of the whole picture; the armies and navies as a whole have emerged stronger from each successive confrontation. The meaning of these wars lies rather in their motivating and justifying a political system that is based upon force. The fear of war and the demand for protection from it, to be effective, needs to be instilled by example. Only a few need to suffer punishment in order that the many may be made to obey. Many political regimes use terror as a means of enforcing obedience, and the amount of force they have to exert need not be large —provided it is exerted at strategic points. In world politics, the nation-state system might well be based upon the same principle. The irony is that the prescription may not work in the future, because the losses inflicted by a global nuclear war may for the first time become catastrophic.

Deterrence

The terror now is real. In place of the possibility of a world war perhaps once every generation, and with adequate warning time, a global nuclear exchange can be visited upon the world at a moment's notice (as in the Cuban crisis of 1962, which built up and also subsided in a matter of days). Intercontinental strategic forces are part of the military forces of the two superpowers; each is ready, after a few minutes' warning, to launch a devastating nuclear bombardment against the adversary. The operational composition of these forces in the late nineteen-sixties is summarized in Table 14:2. The balance of power has reached a form that is quite perfect, yet still extremely crude and simple.

If it is remembered that one hundred strategic warheads would probably be sufficient to destroy either of the superpowers as an ongoing society, the plethora of armaments now being deployed on either side is obviously impressive. But the position depicted is unlikely to remain for long at that level; by 1975, the United States, through technological

TABLE 14:2 Intercontinental Strategic Nuclear Forces, October 1, 1968

	United States	U.S.S.R.
Intercontinental ballistic missiles (ICBM)	1,054	900
Submarine-launched ballistic missiles (SLBM)	656	45
Total missiles	1,710	945
Intercontinental bombers	646	150
Total force loadings: approximate number of warheads	4,200	1,200

Source: *SIPRI Yearbook 1968–9*, p. 33 (based on U.S. sources).

improvements, such as the installation of multiple independently-targeted re-entry vehicles (MIRV), may have as many as nine thousand vehicles deployed, and the Soviet Union, by new submarine construction and similar technical strides, perhaps five thousand. A technological arms race of this type has been in progress since 1945; while so far the system has not exploded in war, it has also been far from steady. Its instability recalls the earlier problems of Balance of Power systems: what one side sees as equity, to the other side looks like a design for dominance.

The basic distinction in nuclear deterrence theory is between two types of targets of a nuclear exchange: missiles (or launchers), and cities. A "first-strike capability" is the number of missiles that is sufficient to destroy all the missiles of the adversary. This also is called a "counter-force capability." A "second-strike capability" (or "countercity capability") is the number of launchers that would survive an enemy attack, yet still be large enough to inflict a punishing blow on his cities. Both sides in a deterrence situation strive, as a minimum objective, for a second-strike capability large enough for assured mutual destruction (which would be a situation of balance); but neither would reject the possibility of acquiring a first-strike capability and each suspects the other side of aiming precisely at that. Much of the momentum of the arms race has been due to this. In addition to the quantitative aspects of the missile deployment, important factors in this equation have been questions of missile accuracy and reliability, the hardening of silos, and the quality of command and communications systems. Since 1945, the United States has usually had a considerable quantitative and qualitative advantage over the Soviet Union, and hence a large element of first strike capability. Throughout the nineteen-sixties, however, the maintenance of peace has ultimately rested upon mutual countercity capacity.

Differentiation of Military Functions

Closely related to the problem of moving beyond the simple notion of war is the need for differentiation of military functions. The control of global war is bound up with the development of separate global military functions.

Some degree of differentiation and specialization of force obtains in all military systems. The evolution of the modern state has been marked by the segregation of police from military functions, the former being employed mainly for purposes of keeping local order and the latter for the establishment of national order and its protection, as well as, when needed, for the back-up of local police. This evolution is surprisingly recent: it dates from mid-nineteenth century, and has its source in the

growth of large cities and the distinctly modern problems of order they
have created. The London Metropolitan Police Force, which was established by Robert Peel in 1844, became the first of its kind, and was soon
imitated in other large urban areas. Most police forces now have their
own organizations—including budgets, recruitment, training and manpower policies, equipment, identity and political control; these are separate and distinct from those of the military forces at the national level,
which may also have its own police forces, sometimes taking the form
of secret police. Yet as aggregates of force they are not to be neglected.
The New York Police Department, with 30,000 officers, is larger than
quite a few national armies. Many such forces have not only light-
infantry armament, but also armored cars and good communications and
transport facilities. Some have helicopters (an air force); some even have
river and harbor patrol boats (navies). The problems that a mayor or
other local political leader faces in relation to a strong police department
are not unlike those that state authorities have faced in past centuries in
relation to military force: who will control the guardians?

At the global level, the differentiation had, until recently, been less
clear. Yet even here, naval forces—in particular, the Spanish and Portuguese and later the Dutch and British maritime power—filled specialized
functions that have come near to a conception of global military force.
The British navy, in particular, had a tradition of strong autonomy and
rigid discipline, and a fierce pride in being the senior service,—all of which
was combined with a global outlook. During the nineteenth century, for
instance, the British navy enforced the Vienna Congress prohibition of
the slave trade. It has often been said about British strength that it maintained world order through control of the seas.

In the system of 1945, the functions of British sea power have been
taken over by the intercontinental strategic forces of the superpowers. In
the organization of the armed forces, the strategic weapons forces now
constitute separate entities, with their own command and budgets, their
specific doctrine and sense of mission. They are elite services, attracting
the best, most trusted and most experienced military personnel. They do
not have their own recruitment and training academies, but they may
yet acquire them.

Contrary to the impression conveyed by the expense of the original
nuclear programs, the cost of maintaining and operating nuclear forces
is not, in world terms, excessive. Table 14:3 depicts the cost of the United
States strategic forces, as compared with the burden of Research and
Development, and of general-purpose forces. The strategic forces figure
for 1962—22.3 of the total defense budget; that is, some $11 billion—
reflects the early McNamara drive for additional missile sites. Those for
1965 and 1967—13.5 and 8.9 percent, respectively at about $6 billion

—show the stabilized cost of maintaining the program; by 1969 (at about $9 billion), the budget began to reflect the cost of MIRV and other technological refinements flowing from the large R&D program. It is evident that the total size of Research and Development had run at a level not much lower than that of the cost of the strategic forces; but R&D covers work for both global, and conventional or limited war forces. Over the years, and inclusive of a portion of R&D expenditures, the total cost of the strategic forces does not seem to have exceeded one-quarter of the total of the American defense budget.

Data in Table 14:3 make it possible to estimate the distribution of force among the several layers of world society. Table 14:4 gives this information and shows (to the extent that these estimates are credible) that, broadly speaking, the share of the global forces in the total of expenditures in the military fields is moderate, and the share of local police forces is modest, while national-level forces dominate the entire picture. In very rough terms, in that pre-Vietnam year, conventional and limited forces absorbed about two-thirds of the world military resources (two or three years later, that share was even larger); local police forces came next, with an estimated one-fifth; and global forces were third, with perhaps 15 percent of the total.

Such information as is at hand about the distribution of military forces at various levels of world society confirms what was already

TABLE 14:3 Share of Strategic Forces in the United States Defense Budget, 1962, 1965, 1967, 1969

	1962	1965	1967	1969
	($ million, current prices)			
Defense expenditures	52,381	51,827	75,451	81,460
	(per cent of obligational authority)			
Strategic forces	22.3	13.5	8.9	11.2
Research and development	8.6	9.3	6.5	5.8
General purpose forces	35.5	37.3	43.7	40.9

Source: *SIPRI Yearbook for 1968–9*, pp. 202–203.

TABLE 14:4 Distribution of Forces among Global, National and Local Functions, United States, World, 1965

($ billion)

	United States	World
Global (Strategic forces)	13	26 *
National (General purpose, conventional and non-conventional and limited war forces)	39	117
Local (Police, prison, etc. forces)	3	35 *

Source: Tables 7:8; 14:3; *United States Statistical Abstract for 1967*
* Estimate

apparent in earlier parts of this analysis: that the national layer of forces dominates the rest and absorbs an excessive share of the total resources. What is striking, in particular, is the underfinancing of local police functions. It may be the weakness of local forces in many areas (brought about by lack of autonomy in the direction of such forces, and their dependence on national governments) that is at the root of much of the current crisis of the nation-state.

Two types of forces do not easily fall into the classification just proposed: conventional national forces, disposing of global naval, and long-range air- and sea-lift capacity, and functional security organizations.

In addition to the strategic missile and bomber armories, the Great Powers also dispose of conventional forces; these provide them with the ability to operate at long distances from home bases, in particular on the world's oceans. Few national governments have such a capacity—probably only the United States, Britain, France (in Africa) and, increasingly, the Soviet Union. All others are restricted to operations that are carried on close to home bases, or else in a narrowly regional setting. These air-naval powers are the heirs to the global traditions of sea power, but they are no longer truly global forces; their actual significance lies in their ability to intervene in national and local conflicts. United States long-range lift capacity has also played an important part in mounting United Nations peacekeeping operations.

Analyses of the distribution of forces and of the increasing differentiation to be found in such distributions must also take into account the tendency for functional specialization. All large-scale organizations tend to develop their own order-maintaining organs, as well as functional security and police forces. Most corporations have their own guard and security detail (or perhaps just night watchmen); railways, airlines, port and harbor authorities have similar arrangements. Student unrest has recently spawned a rash of university forces. In some areas, political parties have paramilitary forces; households, too, sometimes have firearms and in that regard could also be viewed as force units. Nor should one ignore private firms and detective agencies, which provide security services, or the private arms trade. The total of non-governmental armament may, in certain areas, be quite large—especially at local levels—even though little is known about it. In the aggregate, nevertheless, these forces do not so far counterbalance the dominance of the national armies.

Controlling Global Power

The global strategic forces perform important functions for world politics: it is due to them that a worldwide balance of power prevails and autonomy is maintained. Their existence has positive consequences; yet, paradoxically, the use of the same forces could also wreak destruction. How can they remain in stable balance, without running away in some absurd arms-race spiral?

Like all power balances, the global deterrence system is simple and needs added complexity.

(1) The distribution of force among the various layers of world society is unbalanced. A harmonious system of world politics may call for greater effort at the local level and less at the national level. Between 1945 and 1970, the majority of incidents of major violence in the world have occurred in the national layer of politics. The disproportionate swelling of national military forces has much to do with this; but the relationship is far from simple, for it also points to some serious malfunction at that level, resulting in violence. The world could do with fewer brush-fire and revolutionary wars, as well as better police protection in public parks at night.

(2) The world effort in research and development—in military science, in particular, and in science in general—needs to be brought under control and slowed down. The dynamics of the scientific research complex constitute a volatile element in the global arms race. In a larger sense, the research that is spearheaded by military-oriented scientists (including nuclear energy work, and even the space program) continues to impose upon the whole of world society a system of values and a design of priorities that slants world development in the direction of large-scale industry, as producers of machines and other types of hardware, and toward the "hard sciences" in research and among the universities. This unbalances the world system, increases mechanization, and keeps technology in its position as the governing process of society. In turn, it reinforces the nation-state system, along with its propensity toward war organization, and thus feeds upon itself in a circular process. Moreover, technological pressure and high rates of weapon obsolescence (being analogous to annual model changes in the automobile industry) are ways of keeping down the number of competitors in the global arms race—hence also the roster of claimants to global authority. Research and development activities need to be subject to as much restraint as any other important social process, so that technological logic may not wind up imposing its own pattern upon global processes.

(3) Finally, global power has to be made responsible to a global constituency. Since the end of World War II, the power to destroy the world has been held at first by one, and then by two, superpowers. On the whole, this power has not been utilized irresponsibly. But terrible dangers lurk in the background, and experience warns that ultimately

such power over global destinies will have to be brought into a relationship of responsibility toward all those whom it directly affects.

This is a necessary and inevitable development—and not only because of the general principles of political responsibility, according to which those whose interests are affected by decisions must be consulted about them. It is only in that way that a healthy political system can function; otherwise, trouble ensues. But the exercise of supreme power, almost absolute power, is dangerous to its holders; in Lord Acton's dictum, it corrupts absolutely. For the exercise of power, being more than merely a source of pride and dignity, threatens even the most powerful. It is not too hard to imagine a set of circumstances in which a major nuclear exchange could wipe out the substance of life in the two superpowers, yet leave the rest of the world relatively unharmed. This would hardly be a fitting end to a period of world authority.

It is therefore in the general interest, and not only in the interests of those who now lack world authority, that the burdens and the responsibilities of superpower status (and of Great Power authority in general) be defused, dispersed, and diffused more widely in the global system. If power is not shared, and its rewards are instead monopolized, then new claimants to world authority are bound to rise sooner or later. This would do little more than repeat the cycle that brought on earlier world conflicts—for instance, at the beginning of this century, when the German Empire, through its naval and overseas policy, directly and even ostentatiously challenged Britain's status on the seas.

Concretely, this could take place as a continuation of the process by which, by 1970, thermonuclear weapons became available to five national governments, representing between them close to 40 per cent of the world's population. In addition, a number of other states had facilities that were well enough developed to permit the construction of a smaller arsenal of nuclear weapons at short notice (India, Canada, Israel, Sweden, Switzerland, etc.). The cost of a global strategic program is, of course, considerable—probably between five and ten billion dollars annually. In 1970, no states other than the superpowers had defense budgets that were large enough to accommodate such expense; but if long-term prospects are taken into account, other considerations intervene: (1) A United (Western) Europe could afford such a program without excessive difficulty (the combined defense budgets of France, West Germany, Italy and the United Kingdom at that time were already approaching the 20-billion level).[7] (2) A continued rise in world production combined with technological innovation might make these armaments relatively cheaper, and thus their diffusion could become even simpler than it was in 1970.

Since 1968, the spread of such weaponry has been regulated by the Nuclear Non-Proliferation Treaty. This has established a new set of ascribed international statuses—those of "nuclear-weapon" and "non-nuclear-weapon" states—and prohibited "non-nuclear-weapon states" from manufacturing or otherwise acquiring nuclear weapons, although not from pursuing research in this field. The "nuclear-weapon states" (defined by the Treaty as those that had already "manufactured and exploded a nuclear weapon or other nuclear explosive device prior to January 1967") are forbidden from transferring operational nuclear weapons to any country;[8] but the Treaty does not rule out transfers of technology between nuclear-weapon states, or joint planning for the use of these weapons. The nuclear powers also undertook to continue further the disarmament negotiations "in good faith" (and in 1969 began talks on strategic arms limitation) but refused to commit themselves in any detail. The net effect of this agreement should be to slow down the process of proliferation; but it is still too early to be confident about this.

Would the world be better off if every national government were in control of nuclear weapons of at least some kind—even if only, for example, tactical weapons designed to counter local incursions? Or should this privilege be extended to *all* large organizations, many of which, including corporations, could easily afford them? Or might these weapons ultimately become so universal that, for instance, through theft from government arsenals, black market sales by bribed officials, or illicit production by private entrepreneurs based on fuel from nuclear power plants, they could become widely distributed, even among private persons? Would *this* be conducive to order, and help to stabilize a situation in which *no one* would be threatened with attack, out of the fear of universal destruction?

If in this particular regard "lessons" are to be "learnt from history," the conclusion would have to be that nuclear weapons would inevitably be diffused. This does not necessarily mean that all states and other interested organizations would have to possess global strategic weapons systems; rather, the situation could come to approximate what has been observed to prevail in respect to other weapons. Thus, by no means all of the world's maritime states have aircraft carriers: less than a dozen did as of 1970. Only three had more than one attack carrier (United States, Britain and France); others had smaller capital ships, such as cruisers or missile destroyers, and still others had hardly any navy at all. Not all of the world's airforces acquired their advanced aircraft at the same time; yet such weapons systems do tend to spread at a predictable rate. In the Third World, the number of "supersonic-fighter states" rose from four in 1958 (Israel, Taiwan, India, Turkey) to 30 in 1968 (the three airforces acquiring such craft in that year were those of Jordan, Kuwait and Peru).

In the same time span the ranks of "long-range-surface-to-air-missile-states" in the Third World swelled from one (Chinese P.R.) to eighteen.[9] Why not expect nuclear weapons to spread in a similar way, even if over a longer time period?

Indeed, a strong probability exists that they will. The structure of the nation-state system favors such a process of diffusion, in a hierarchical fashion. The pressures are strong, both in the general sense of the difficulty of compelling abstention from what "comes naturally" (as armaments do to states), and in the marginal case of the $N+1$ state: the next most likely government to test or take advantage of such weapons would most likely have a good case for doing so—conceivably, India or Japan under Chinese pressure, or perhaps Israel, in the face of great odds.

Prohibitions on nuclear proliferation run counter to the expectations of the nation-state system, in favor of independence and for self-choice of weapons of self-defense. They can work only if it is demonstrated that the value of such armaments is low—both specifically, for defense purposes, and as a source of political authority and general advantage in world affairs. The success of anti-proliferation measures therefore depends in part on the continued limitation of national conflicts and the minimizing of external intervention in such conflicts, as well as on the reduction and the wider sharing of Great Power authority, which derives from superior armament.

Some fruitless experiments in nuclear sharing have already been undertaken. Between 1958 and 1964, much was heard in NATO of a project to man and equip an allied nuclear fleet (the "MLF" proposal), to be owned and operated jointly by the participating nuclear and non-nuclear powers. The project came to nothing, as the result of technical difficulties, all-round lukewarmness in allied military and political circles, and vehement Soviet opposition to German participation in it.

Beginning in 1966, NATO devised a new process, whereby the members of the alliance were brought into consultation on the planning for the possible use of nuclear weapons, even though most of these weapons would remain subject to United States control.[10] The Nuclear Planning Group, a committee composed of eight NATO Defense Ministers, kept these matters under continuous review; its work included, for example, the formulation of political guidelines for the use of tactical nuclear weapons. No information is at hand as to whether parallel developments have been at work among the members of the Warsaw Pact.

The processes of sharing (which basically are those of power equalization) could be extended in three ways. First, the number of participants in the process of consultation could be gradually enlarged, so as to go beyond NATO and the Warsaw Pact alliances to include, for instance, Japan or India. A special United Nations Security Council resolution of June 1968 promised assistance by three nuclear-weapon states (United States, United Kingdom and the Soviet Union) to any non-nuclear weapon state that became the "victim of an act of aggression in which nuclear weapons are used." Second, arrangements could be made for international contributions to the financing of global strategic forces; this would amount, in effect, to "buying shares" in the global strategic forces. The sharing of some military expenses in Europe has been a long-standing NATO practice. Third, the distinctiveness of the strategic forces could be enhanced by giving them more of a "world status," as well as some links with United Nations and other global purposes. In this way, the habit of viewing these forces as subject to special restraint and governed by considerations of world interest might be institutionalized.

Disappearance of the world's nuclear, missile and other arsenals is rather difficult to imagine: their existence gives the states the measure of autonomy that guarantees their vitality. But the dangers that they create must also be guarded against, through the development of effective institutions for their *non-use*; in that process, changes might well be wrought in the nation-state system. Great Power authority would not be eliminated outright, but it might be reduced to more modest proportions than it now enjoys.

Limiting National Conflicts

Next to avoiding global nuclear war, the most important task is to prevent the spread of national wars and, in particular, their escalation into global wars. Such escalation (or layer fusion) would represent a malfunctioning of the global system; it would not occur normally, but it could occur under conditions of stress or misjudgment.

First of all, a distinction might be drawn between "national war" or "national conflict" and the conventional idea of war. The conventional or simple concept represents war as an interstate conflict, an armed clash between two or more nation-states; it takes this to be the characteristic and prevailing, as well as the problematic form of international disturbance. Elaborate procedures have been devised for dealing with this type of armed interstate collision; most of the provisions of the United Nations Charter for dispute settlement and for dealing with threats to peace assume this to be the type of conflict involved.

The present analysis, on the other hand, employs the concept of national war as a conflict that occurs primarily within the national layer of society, with or without external participation, and thus distinguishes it from both global and local conflicts. The classical interstate (non-

Survival *305*

global) conflict may take the form of national war, if it is seen as a disturbance of the national networks of politics; as a general rule, however, the national layer generates its own malfunctions, its own large and violent conflicts. More often than not, such conflicts can be contained within the geographical framework of that network. Evidence on violent conflicts in the period 1945-1970 lends considerable support to this view.

Table 14:5 *Armed Conflict 1945-1970*, lists all the instances of organized violence in which the casualties attributable to an event amounted

TABLE 14:5   Armed Conflicts, 1945–1970

Dates	Conflict	Magnitude	Source
	NATIONAL		
1945	Syria-Lebanon	3	B
1946–1949	Greek Civil War	5	A
1946	Bolivia	3	A
1946–1949	Chinese Civil War	6	B
1947–1948	Kashmir	3	A
1947	Paraguay	3	A
1948–1949	Israel I	4	A
1948–1952	Philippines (Huks)	3	A
1948–1964	Colombia	6	A
1950–1953	Korean War	6	A
1952	Bolivia	3	A
1954–1958	China (Quemoy)	3	A
1956	Sinai and Suez	3	A
1956–1959	Cuba (Castro)	3	A
1956	Hungary	4	A
1957–1961	Indonesia	4	A
1958	Lebanon Civil War	3	A
1959–1962	Laos	4	A
1960–1963	Congo	5	A
1961–1962	Nepal Civil War	3	B
1961	Cuba (Bay of Pigs)	3	A
1961–	Vietnam	6	B
1962–1967	Yemen Civil War	5	B
1962	Burundi	3	A
1962	India-China Border	4	A
1962	Guatemala	4	B
1963–1964	Cyprus	3	A
1964–1967	Malaysian Confrontation	3	A
1964–	Laos	5	B
1964	Zanzibar	3	B
1965	Dominican Republic	4	A
1965	India-Pakistan War	4	A
1965–1966	Indonesia	5	A
1967–	Philippines	3	B
1967	Israel (Six Days)	4	A
1969	El Salvador-Honduras	3	B
1969	China-USSR Border	3	B
1969–1970	Suez fighting	4	B
1970	Cambodia	4	B
1970	Jordan	4	B

TABLE 14:5   Armed Conflicts, 1945–1970 (continued)

Dates	Conflict	Magnitude	Source
	SUB-NATIONAL AND LOCAL		
1945	Algeria	4	B
1945–1949	Indonesia	4	B
1945–1954	Indochina	5	B
1947	Taiwan	4	B
1947–1948	Indian communal	6	A
1947	Hyderabad	3	A
1947	Madagascar	3	A
1947–1952	Malayan Emergency	3	A
1948–	Burma	4	B
1952	Tunis	3	A
1952–1954	Kenya (Mau Mau)	4	A
1954–1962	Algeria	5	A
1954–1964	Nagas	3	A
1956–1961	Cameroons	3	A
1956–1959	Cyprus	3	A
1959	Ruanda-Urundi	5	A
1959	Tibet	4	A
1961–1970	Kurds	4	B
1962–	Angola	4	A
1963–1967	Aden	3	B
1963	Sudan	4	B
1965–	Mozambique	3	B
1965–	Eritrea	3	B
1967–	Chad	3	B
1967–1970	Biafra	5	B

Sources for magnitude: A   *SIPRI Yearbook for 1968–9*, pp. 366–373
                          B   Estimate

Lists all armed conflicts of magnitude 3 and above begun after January 1, 1945; status as of December 31, 1970. All estimates of magnitude are rounded.

to $10^{3\pm0.5}$ or more; $10^{3\pm0.5}$ indicates a conflict of magnitude 3, meaning 1,000 fatal casualties within a range of from 317 to 3162. All listed conflicts fall within the magnitudes of either 3, 4, 5, 6, 7 or 8. It is assumed that the salient feature of a conflict is the quantity of fatal violence that goes with it and that that quantity supplies an indication of the magnitude of the conflict.[11] But this is only a rough absolute measure of the intensity of violence; to give it more precision, one would also have to index its relation to the size of the population and the time covered.

One consequence of classifying conflicts by the number of casualties they have entailed is the exclusion of important violent clashes that have caused lesser degrees of fatalities. The list thus omits, for instance, the Cuban confrontation of 1962, or the Warsaw Pact occupation of Czechoslovakia in 1968, because the number of deaths in each instance was quite low. Another warlike event left out is the Indian seizure of Goa in 1961.

Second, this is a list of events of organized violence—that is of political or other violence, involving at least one, if not more, organizations in a conflict situation. This criterion would exclude spontaneous riots and such other forms of violence as crime and traffic collisions, but it would include all those events that are conventionally recognized as wars, provided they reach a minimum level of violence. Governmental violence—for instance, mass purges and executions, as in the anti-landlord campaign in China 1951-1953, or government-incited and -tolerated riots, are marginal cases; they have been largely omitted. Natural disasters, such as floods or earthquakes, are of course, omitted, whatever the amount of governmental negligence that may be involved.

A listing of organized violence for 1945-1970 shows few cases that can be clearly labeled "wars," as the term is known in nation-state theory. Those closest to the classical conception of interstate conflict have been the wars in the Middle East; the Indo-Pakistani war of 1965, and the El Salvador-Honduras war of 1969. The six amount to some 15 per cent of the total in the column of "national conflicts," and to less than ten per cent of the total of world conflict events in that period. Nor is their magnitude outstanding. Of the fourteen largest conflicts—that is those, of magnitude 5 and 6—only two belong clearly to the class of interstate conflicts—namely, two of the Middle Eastern wars. Two others are ambiguous cases, Korea and Vietnam; both are on the borderline between civil war and interstate war, which has been part of the difficulty in dealing with them. All others are either civil wars or cases of national disturbance.

Some contrasts may be observed between the system of 1945, and the Versailles system of 1919-1970, for which data are also shown in Table 14:6. During the earlier period, interstate wars were also a minority

TABLE 14:6   Distribution of Armed Conflicts, 1945–1970, 1919–1945

Type of Conflict		1945–1970	1919–1945
Global		—	1
National		21	13
magnitude	6	4	3
	5	5	5
	4	12	5
Local		14	9
magnitude	6	1	—
	5	4	3
	4	9	6

Sources: for 1945–1970: Table 14:5; for 1919–1945: Richardson, *Statistics of Deadly Quarrels, cited*, Chapter II.

of all conflicts that could be labeled "national," but their relative strength was somewhat higher (five out of 13, or some one-third) and they "looked" more convincingly like interstate wars: the Japanese attack on Manchuria in 1931; the Chaco War of 1930-1935; the Ethiopian war of 1935-1936; or the Russo-Finnish War of 1939-1940.

It is as though the salience of classical interstate war was fading in world politics. Since 1945, the "use or threat of force" has been illegal under the Charter for members of the United Nations. Hence, the legal paraphernalia of classical war have not been observed: there have been no war declarations or peace treaties, and only a few cases of truce negotiations. Armed clashes of short duration—such as the Indo–Chinese and Russo-Chinese border clashes of 1962 and 1969 respectively—are now more often the case, and these are assuredly easier to contain. For none of these strictly interstate wars had much potentiality for fusing the global layer, and thus for endangering world order. The only exception to that rule might be the Middle Eastern conflict since 1967, which could even now involve the superpowers. But the chances of this happening are equally strong with regard to all the other larger or even smaller national conflicts—for instance, those in Laos, Yemen, Cyprus or Biafra.

For this reason, a conceptual scheme that abandons the simple concept of war promises greater insight. Table 14:5 distinguishes violent conflicts according to whether they have occurred in the global, the national or the local layers of politics. Since 1945, the world has known no global war and none appears in this listing (World War II is included as a war of the Versailles system, in Table 14:6). Such conflicts as the Algerian war of 1954-1962, or the Biafran secession of 1967-1970, were important disturbances that, at the time of their occurrence, affected only one portion of their respective state networks: the first, the Algerian, brought about separation and the establishment of a new nation-state; but the second, the Biafran, failed in this respect. All local conflicts have a potential for leading to separateness; between 1945 and 1970, as many as one-half of the conflicts labeled "local" sooner or later brought into being a new nation-state. Finally, incidents such as the Greek civil war or the Indo-Pakistani war have been classified as primarily nation-level conflicts. At issue in these is the constitution of the national authority, or the delimitation of national boundaries and the consolidation of a new state. The Middle East wars may be regarded as wars fought over the determination of Israel as a nation-state and its place in the world; so were the Korean, Vietnamese and Jordanian wars, which were fought over how the basic constitutions for these nations should be established.

A fourth category of wars—regional—might yet prove to be necessary. The wars in the Middle East might alternatively be regarded as concerning the political structure of a regional network of relations. But it is not yet clear that regional networks exist that are strong enough to support wars, nor is it clear that they should be encouraged to grow in that way.

The labeling of conflicts as occurring "in the national layer" does not rule out the possibility of extra-national involvement. About one-half the conflicts listed in Table 14:5 had substantial outside participation—in part by Great Power military forces, in part by United Nations' and other international peacekeeping operations. In virtually every single case, the outside world participated, at least to some degree—for instance, through arms supplies to incumbents or insurgents, through moral support or encouragement for one or both sides, or through affording an ultimate safe exit and exile.

Irrespective of their status as national or local conflicts, more than one-third of these have also been the object of United Nations and other international involvement. This has ranged all the way from the dispatch of forces, in a case in which the United Nations Secretary-General was acting in effect as the principal (Congo), to such milder forms of intervention as attempts to put the question on a United Nations agenda for discussion (Algeria, Tibet). A few cases included the participation of regional organizations—for instance, the Arab League in Yemen and Jordan; the Organization of African States in Biafra, and the Organization of American States in the Dominican Republic.

The classification of armed conflict as national or local, therefore, has little predictive value as to the extent of intervention by an international organization; in both categories, the proportion of such participation has been about the same—that is, it has taken place in about one-third of the cases. The United Nations, in particular, is of course debarred by its Charter from intervening in the "domestic affairs" of its members. International intervention is warranted by the acknowledged danger that conflict escalation and spillover may create a generalized "threat to peace"; the more violent the conflict, the greater such possible danger. But such intervention has also usually done little more than bring into being a new nation-state, or consolidate a new or a weak one; it has not been designed for preserving any specific condition in "domestic affairs" or strengthening local autonomy. Perhaps the provisions of the Charter should be more strictly observed in the future, and the role of the international organization confined to conflict limitation and isolation, rather than its serving for intervention on behalf of national authorities.

Conflicts recorded in Table 14:5 should be labeled "organized" as a reminder that all serious violence in world politics is organizational—that is, it represents a conflict in which at least one organization is a party. In each and every case of violence listed, a nation-state has been one of the participants; in at least one-half the cases, Great Powers were involved to some degree. The role of international organizations has already been noted. Sometimes component parts of nation-state organizations have also played their separate part: political parties have at times been organizing agents of civil war—for instance, the nationalist parties of Algeria or Angola, or the Communist parties of China, Malaya or the Philippines. At other times, the military as such has seized the center of the stage, as in Indonesia in 1965-1966. Guerrilla organizations —for example, the Palestine guerrillas in Jordan 1970—represent yet another type of actor in this arena, as do the organized units of other ethnic, minority and community organizations—for instance, in Cyprus or Kurdistan. Churches have not played any prominent role in recent events of organized violence, except in the theocracy of Tibet, in Cyprus, and in Vietnam, where a number of sects have had military branches and the Buddhists have been active. Corporations, too, have had only a small part of this fighting—except for some cases of behind-the-scenes influence in such instances as the Congo. The university, finally, has not been party to any conflict; but in cases such as Hungary, student activities have contributed significantly to the momentum of the conflict spiral.

Violence and the Nation-State

The nation-state (and those intent on capturing it—such as political parties, guerrillas or the military) is therefore the principal agent of violence of the intermediate kind—that is, the kind that lies between global wars on the one hand and, on the other hand, violence of a sort for which the activity of the police is a satisfactory remedy. Conflicts over national authority and the definition of the state are the principal sources of such middle-level disturbances. Two interpretations of the incidence of this violence could be argued: (1) national violence is a phase in the consolidation of the nation-state, and therefore is transitory in character; (2) national violence is an indicator of strains that the nation-state exerts upon world society, and that are thus endemic to the system.

Nearly all the violent events appearing in Table 14:5 occurred outside Europe. In the quarter-century since the holocaust of World War II, Europe has been free of major violent disturbances, the exceptions being Greece (1945-1949) and Hungary (1956). This is to be compared with a total of fourteen incidents recorded between 1919 and 1945. It could mean that Europe did indeed settle its major constitutional problems in the two world wars and is now free to enjoy peace. But the world wars also affected and in part devastated large areas of the Far East and of Southeast Asia, and these still were among the world's most disturbed regions. It could also mean that the nation-state system is reaching a state of repose in Europe, and that the rest of the world has yet to pass through the "shaking down" phase before it can attain peace. But this, too, could be deceptive: even in peaceful Western Europe, the constitution of national society remains under revision: tensions could easily flare up in Ulster, in Belgium, in Spain, among the Basques, in France on regional issues, and so forth. Well-governed states, such as Canada, are not immune to difficulties, and a record of domestic tranquility is never a conclusive guarantee of future peace (even though it may help). Even established countries, such as the United States, have not been able to avoid urban violence and unrest.

The consolidation thesis appears to be convincing in part because some of the violent events—in particular, the successful independence wars, which have been listed under "local" conflicts, such as those in Indonesia, Algeria, etc.—seem to have been once-for-all affairs, whose outcome was conclusively settled upon the attainment of sovereignty. But that is not the whole story. Indonesia has continued to generate violence, and there is no clear evidence that, taken by itself, national independence is a guarantee of peace. Conversely, such peace could be no more than the silence imposed by oppression.

The universalization of the nation-state during the twentieth century imposed new strains on world society. The homogeneity that European and North American societies had painfully attained by that time (and which they may not sustain for long) had no equivalent outside that small area—for example, in places where communications were poorer and distances much greater, and where the tradition of dominant national governments was not as well-established as, and even less appropriate than it was in Europe. Moreover, even in European societies, strains have again begun to manifest themselves, even though they have been less given to major violence than in other types of confrontation—for example, student unrest, strikes, terrorism and urban riots.

While the world of Versailles was still in part imperial, the system of 1945 is clearly nation-state dominant. If the incidence of violent conflict is compared for the two systems (see also Table 14:6), two significant points emerge. The total number of observed conflicts was almost identical (62 for 1919-1945 and 65 for 1945-1970); and the quality of the conflict was more characteristically national than local in both periods. In the system of nation-state dominance, the major conflicts all were also national; furthermore, the total magnitude of the conflicts had somewhat risen. World War II apart, in magnitude 6 the Versailles world saw three conflicts, and the system of 1945, five; in magnitude 5, Versailles had eight events, and the post-1945 world, nine. The evidence tends to show that in the past 25 years the global system had not grown any more peaceful than it had been during the preceding quarter of a century.

The prevalence of purely national wars, which have not escalated in the contemporary system, suggests that some principle of self-limitation may already be at work. It may be a form of the principle of layer autonomy, strong enough to forestall tendencies to layer fusion. Despite the frequency of their occurrence, only a few national conflicts and those for only short periods have deteriorated into interstate wars, and none has brought on a global war.

Processes of Limitation

The fact that global war has been avoided since 1945 may be a matter for congratulations; but it does not dispose of all the problems involved. It may show only that a certain incidence of national wars can be tolerable for world society as a whole. Yet the effort to limit such wars to the network directly involved remains the major principle of conflict limitation. The incentives for escalation (and for breaking down limitation) are both internal and external: the parties to national wars need and expect external help, and outsiders may find some advantage for themselves in supplying it.[12] Only a small proportion of national and local wars have had little or no external intervention—perhaps one-quarter of them. The Great Powers, with their worldwide interests and large military capacity, exhibit the greatest propensity to intervene, and thus to create the risks of layer fusion. The greatest degree of self-limitation is therefore incumbent upon them; the same considerations also apply, however, to international organizations.

The national wars that have been the subject of this analysis were not just discrete events but also parts of larger, possibly global patterns. Even though the Great Powers did not themselves collide in global combat, they did clash indirectly in conflicts they were involved in, sometimes through third parties. Some of the conflicts in Table 14:5 might therefore be linked together in Great Power patterns, such as the following:

Communist internal wars, in which a national Communist party was a principal to the conflict: Greece, 1945-1949; Philippines, 1948-1952; China, 1946-1949; Korea, 1950-1953; Indochina, 1945-1954.

The Dulles phase of American foreign policy: Indonesia, 1957-1961; Laos, 1959-1962.

The Khrushchev doctrine of support for "national-democratic" regimes in the Third World: the Suez War of 1956; the Six Day War of 1967; Vietnam, 1961-   ; Yemen, 1962-1967; Nigeria, 1966-1970; Cuba, 1961.

The Maoist challenge to the 1945 order: Indonesia, 1965-1966; India–Pakistan, 1965; Laos 1964-   ; Cambodia, 1970; Congo, 1965; Zanzibar, 1964.

A direct Great Power involvement is not necessarily arguable in each of these cases; yet the patterns are too striking to be ignored, and Great Power activities on a worldwide scale bear much of the responsibility for the extent and intensity of national violence, if not for its precise cause and timing. The abatement of this violence must await an attenuation of Great Power rivalries and a reduced salience of Great Power status.

Notes to Chapter Fourteen

1. Wright, *A Study of War*, cited, pp. 639–640, also Chapter IV, distinguishes among Balance of Power Wars, civil wars and imperial wars and, elsewhere among animal, primitive, historic and modern wars.

2. *Ibid.*, p. 665.

3. Richardson, *Statistics of Deadly Quarrels*, cited, p. 153.

4. Note that Richardson's estimate of war casualties are lower than Wright's in *A Study of War* (cited, pp. 1542-3), 40 million total casualties in World War I, and 60 million for World War II, the latter figures including civilians killed by war-borne epidemics.

5. Richardson, *Statistics*, p. 153.

6. Wright, *A Study of War*, cited, p. 242; in World War II, United States battle casualties were less than two per cent of the total of those who had been mobilized for active duty.

7. A division of opinion exists as to whether the Nuclear Non-Proliferation Treaty precludes a European federation (with French and possibly British membership) from possessing such weapons. The Soviet interpretation would define a European federation as a "non-nuclear weapon state," while the West views it as a "nuclear-weapon state" to succeed French and British rights in this matter.

8. Despite the general "clubbiness" of postwar alliances, such as NATO or the Warsaw Pact, intergovernmental cooperation on nuclear weapon questions has in fact been quite limited. The only important instance of it is the American-British cooperation, which was based on war-time experience; but that was abruptly terminated in 1945, and taken up again only in 1958. A Soviet–Chinese nuclear weapons accord was reached in 1957; it lasted only until 1959. France has had only marginal assistance from the United States; but, prior to 1967, it gave some help to Israel. There are no known instances of actual transfers of nuclear weapons, but cooperation for "the peaceful atom" is quite another story. Much of that cooperation has contributed greatly to the dissemination of nuclear power technology in all parts of the world.

9. *SIPRI Yearbook for 1968-9*, pp. 48, 47.

10. W. F. Ekelen, "Development of NATO's Nuclear Consultation," *NATO Letter*, July 1970, pp. 2–6.

11. See Richardson, *Statistics of Deadly Quarrels*, cited, pp. 4–12.

12. See George Modelski, "The International Relations of Internal War," in J. Rosenau ed., *International Aspects of Civil Strife* (Princeton, N.J.: Princeton University Press, 1964), p. 18 ff.

15
Order

MERE SURVIVAL IS, OF COURSE, NOT enough. In terms of world politics, it is true, survival means the avoidance of nuclear catastrophe, through preventing global war and limiting other conflicts to manageable proportions. These might be called the negative aspects of order. But order is more than mere conflict-management. It is the product of a social system that is characterized not just by control, but also by comfort, allied to a feeling of esthetic rightness. An "orderly" system in this sense would have all the variety of its vital elements articulated in freedom, yet so artfully poised that the result would be *positive* harmony, a *harmony in diversity*.

In relation to world society, the elements for diversity are innumerable. This is a hopeful feature and not at all a cause for despair. The world's variety of peoples, organizations, networks, races, communities, climates and environments is a source of strength, inasmuch as it is the raw material of flexibility and hence fulfills one important precondition of survival. But diversity could deteriorate into chaos; the structure of world politics requires the articulation of the elements of diversity into a meaningful whole.

In Chapter Thirteen, the system of network layers was seen as one of the ingredients bringing order in complexity into global society; further, autonomy of layers and avoidance of dominance relations were viewed as the fundamental elements of such a harmonious arrangement.

The second and complementary approach toward encouraging complexity—hence, greater autonomy—is through functional differentiation. World society knows no total institutions; a variety of organizations and networks is necessary to take care of all social needs.

The typical organizations of modern world society are the government, at all levels, the corporation, the university, and the household. Each of these supplies certain vital services to the individual throughout his life. The government offers the services of order, redress of grievances and a variety of associated enterprises; the corporation, along with other economic organizations and arrangements offers consumption and other goods, as well as employment, for a large portion of the population. The university (a periodic return to which for brainpower-recharging is becoming a feature of contemporary life) is the apex of the school system: it offers both education and socialization at a higher level. The household is the organizational unit of family life, providing intimacy, happiness and a secure refuge from the vicissitudes of daily living. Each of these fulfills distinctive functions in ongoing society, and each is essential to its orderly existence.

The basic organizations of world society might be distinguished according to the network layers toward which each is predominantly oriented. There is local and national government, and international organization; local stores and enterprises, national business organizations, and world corporations; community colleges, four-year colleges and universities of global stature. Even households although they participate in all layers, may be predominantly oriented to one (thus, European ruling families operated chiefly in the global layer of their time). In turn, each of the network layers already discussed exhibits a degree of functional complexity.

In recent memory, the most important claimant to the status of total institution has been the state and, in particular, the nation-state. In a variety of contexts, the state has not only assumed dominance; in some circumstances, it has also absorbed vital portions of other functional areas into its own organization. In Communist countries, the state (through the Party) organizes the economy, and the various departments of state serve as functional divisions of society. In many other countries, the universities are state-controlled and state-financed. For some purposes, nationalism has even taken on some of the characteristics of a religion, and the nation-state the features of an organization of believers. Thus, in contemporary society, the main trend of functional differentiation has to be the assumption of special and autonomous identities by forms of functional organization other than the state.

Functional differentiation has another, less familiar aspect. It proceeds along lines whereby a balance is attained between the physical and the moral bases of social organization. For the purposes of this analysis, the economic and political aspects of society may roughly be identified with the instrumental concerns for the production of certain tangible social assets—that is, of goods of various types: material goods, for more or less immediate consumption and gratification, and those political goods that result from the exertion of power. More often than not, these are the products of organizations. But society also needs nutrients for its moral resources, and attention to the quality of its normative and personal order. At the local level, this is the work of the sphere of family, church and school; their main functions, in this regard, consist of giving meaning to life, establishing orientations toward the past and the future, and aiding in the process of the shaping, clarification, restoration and reconditioning of values. As often as not, networks are decisive in this area. In the global layer, too, a balance must be struck between physical and moral concerns.

Specifications for World Order

The structural conditions of world order may be summarized along three lines: (1) spatial: the maintenance of a number of autonomous layers; (2) non-political: the maintenance of viable and autonomous non-political organizations, to complement the political structure at all levels of world society; (3) moral: the cultivation of moral resources in all aspects of world organization, especially through network development.

Implementation of such principles will lay the foundations for the preservation of public order on a world scale. It might be expected that successful differentiation of a variety of organizations would produce, even on a world scale, not only complexity and a balancing effect, but also units of social organization that are small enough to meet the requirements for personal participation and for the possibilities of personal identification. Complexity and diversity favor participation and also facilitate conditions of voluntariness, insofar as the variety of organizations provides avenues of affiliation and opportunities for partial, rather than total commitment.

But how does this entire structure cohere? Why does it not fall apart? The principles of cohesion are two: the need for balancing (that is for complex balancing), and the need for some moral consensus. Both are conditions that would be met by the flowering of many networks, as well as the flourishing of organizations. Both are also essentially principles of harmony: the coexistence of a multiplicity of elements, in conditions of creative tension. Thus the specification of a "normal" world order (against which existing world order must be judged, and against which the costs of disorder might also be evaluated) proceeds also along aesthetic lines: world order must be beautiful in order to be viable. An unharmonious world is ugly, and therefore liable to descend into disorder.

This argument must be taken up further to show that world order not only needs to be beautiful; the beauty it possesses (or lacks) will stand in some determinate relationship to the aesthetic criteria of the members of world society. What that relationship may prove to be is difficult to say; but the consensus of society has customarily contained some agreement on what constitutes a harmonious world order, and the notion of world harmony will also have a moral component. The structural principles of world order thus show an affinity to principles of artistic and architectural construction. An early example in the history of social and political thought is Aristotle's concept of the mean as the characteristic of virtue: "Goodness . . . is a mean condition in the sense that it aims at and hits the mean." "Virtue (is) a disposition of the soul in which, when it has to choose among actions and feelings, it observes the mean relative to us." [1] For Aristotle, the mean also became the principile for the construction of the ideal political system, the best constitution: "If we were right when in our *Ethics* we stated that Virtue is a Mean and that the happy life is life free and unhindered and according to virtue, then the best life must be the middle way . . . and the same principle must be applicable to the goodness of cities and states. For the constitution of a city is really the way it lives." [2]

Aristotle's principles recall the rules of classical Greek art, in which the "golden mean" and the canons of symmetry occupied such an important part. They support the view that order is an aesthetic principle, and that world order must therefore rest upon tested and widely recognized criteria of beauty.[3] For that reason, artists, poets, writers and critics —all those who shape, clarify and elaborate the prevalent conceptions of beauty—need to be recognized (for they have not been so recognized well enough) as essential and active participants in the making of that order.

Nevertheless, the specifications indicated above never give only one solution to the problem of order. World society is capable of sustaining a range of solutions, however circumscribed that range might be. While harmony might be postulated as a general principle, the particular harmony and the balance implied in it is a shifting one. This will be so because world society, and the global layer in particular, may be exposed to a variety of problems, and at different times these problems may hold different positions of priority.

In its problem-solving capacity, the nation-state system is a "one-problem" system. It is a system that is designed specifically for the exhaustive and optimal handling of the problem of war. The war-peace cycle is the essence of the system: the simple concept of peace is as much a necessary part of it as is the simple concept of war (there are as many kinds of peace as there are of war). The system has functioned on this basis for several centuries, and as one result has acquired a permanent structural slant toward large-scale war.

Growth in spatial, functional and moral complexity, particularly at the global level, makes possible the processing of problems other than war-peace issues. It is this that holds out the prospect of a real possibility for the attainment of fundamental change in the character of world politics.

The conventional mechanisms that are available for dealing with world problems have until recently been slanted in one direction. Great Power authority, along with the network of bilateral and multilateral diplomacy supporting it, have been devices for dealing with war-peace problems. Hand in hand with this institutional constraint have gone prevailing doctrines stressing the incompetence of global structures. Issues outside the war-peace complex have occasionally occupied diplomatic agendas—questions, for instance, of the slave trade, the status of minorities, the regulation of trade or the control of epidemics—but, they have never assumed the status of major and autonomous issue areas.

Since 1945, evidence has begun to accumulate of an accelerating trend toward the generation of new issues within the world context. This is the process that was previously referred to as the strengthening of the global layer. As awareness, interdependence, and the commonality of values increase, so does the necessity for the regulation of these processes. For instance, enhanced global awareness has made it universal knowledge that world wealth is distributed in a most unequal fashion and that the inequality of that distribution is actually rising. This promotes feelings of injustice and movements of dissatisfaction—hence also pressure for measures to cope with what has become a global problem. A panoply of programs and institutions has developed in the decades following World War II to deal with that problem: the World Bank, the United Nations Development Program, the Colombo Plan, a variety of national aid and Peace-Corps-type programs, the United Nations Development Decades and the rest. A substantial proportion of the work of universal and regional international organizations has been channeled into efforts to cope with inequality.

In a similar manner, a number of other global problems has arisen. Demand has made itself felt for other public goods—that is, for goods that are produced by global public authorities. Those frequently cited include world population growth, the food problem, environmental pollution and the control of the seabed—all of these being aspects of the overriding problem of the survival of man on earth. They all raise issues of order and of justice, and it is for that reason that they involve world politics. The leaders and the institutions of world politics must provide the mechanisms with which both to meet such demands and to attack these problems, without necessarily becoming involved in the myriad technical questions surrounding them. In the process, however, world politics itself would change.

The nature of any system of world politics is determined in part by the type of problems it handles. A complex system can handle a variety of problems, reallocating attention and resources in accordance with shifting demands, because no single problem (or layer, or function) is allowed to grow unchecked and unchallenged toward irreversible ascendancy over others. There is movement, but it is bounded.

Once again, an analogy to artistic creation may not be out of order. The "golden mean" of classical art forms is not a fixed proportion, nor is it a single solution, equally applicable to every enterprise. Rather it is a formula, allowing for movement within limits and for tension between counterpoised proportions; it creates asymmetries and seeming imbalances, which it then embraces in an essential condition of harmony. The golden mean has also been observed in organic life forms—for instance, in the structure of a leaf or of a seashell; it is a framework of meaningful growth. Unchecked, growth that dislocates established proportions and upsets balances constitutes a threat to order. All growth must be contained within a harmonious framework of spatial, functional and moral institutions.

Pluralistic World Politics

The specifications for world order detailed in the preceding section may conveniently be summarized under the label of "pluralism." They are, in fact, a restatement or a reinterpretation of pluralist doctrines of the late nineteenth and early twentieth century, within the context of contemporary world politics. Because pluralism is also the unarticulated (taken-for-granted) essence of Western political liberalism, however, it represents a position that needs to be examined, with some care for its relevance to global politics.

The practice of pluralism in the European setting goes back to the medieval world and to the vigorous and flourishing variety of its political and social structures. The major "achievement" of the modern state system has been to eradicate this variety in the name of fighting feudalism, and to simplify the complexity in the interests of military and industrial efficiency. The thinkers of the Enlightenment—such as Voltaire and Diderot —in the name of progress decried the Middle Ages, about which they knew little. Yet even then, in the seventeenth and eighteenth centuries, the practice of pluralism received a good fillip through the transplantation to America of English, Dutch and Swiss political habits that had never been so fully streamlined as in the great military monarchies of Europe. These then gave birth to that powerful experiment in applied pluralism: the American constitution.

The theory of pluralism was formulated first by English political thinkers who were concerned over the dangers to individual freedom that were being posed by the emergence of the sovereign nation-states, and who were also becoming increasingly aware of trends toward the concentration of industrial power in the hands of newly consolidating business organizations. Alarmed by developments in Bismarckian Germany, whose hegemonic strivings and military bearing even then set bounds to human freedom, they sought to devise means for protecting the individual against unified and monolithic power—in particular, the power that hides behind the fictions of state sovereignty. The remedy for monopolistic power they saw in the fragmentation of power; hence their advocacy of voluntary and intermediary associations, those that alone (in their eyes) would make possible the cultivation of wholesome communities and thus avert the trend toward the mass society of undifferentiated individuals.

The foremost English pluralists were Frederick Maitland (who brought out the relevance of Otto von Gierke's researches on the Middle Ages), John Neville Figgis, Harold Laski (especially in his earlier work) and G. D. H. Cole. Léon Duguit's work developed the conception of the state as a servant of the community. In American political thought, Arthur Bentley and David Truman, with their model of the group basis of politics, have been influential in shaping generations of political science research.

In its early state, pluralist thought also spawned works that shed light on world affairs and that stand apart from the mainstream tendencies of International Relations. Among these might be mentioned Leonard Woolf's *International Government*,[4] which foreshadowed the rise of specialized international agencies and helped to shape the structure of the League of Nations, and the works of H. G. Wells (both his novels and his political writings), which gave expression to a vision of a new world, freed from the threat of war and organized by a variety of new associations, including corporations.[5] More recently, David Mitrany has formulated ideas that have proven to be significant in giving shape to the post-World War II reconstruction period; his war-time pamphlet *A Working Peace System*[6] is still of considerable interest.

These latter writers on international affairs, and especially Mitrany, came to be known as functionalists. Not directly related to the structural-functional school of modern sociology, they are part of the same climate of thought that produced political pluralism (and also, incidentally, Bronislaw Malinowski's anthropology of functionalism).

The Great Depression and World War II sapped some of the vitality of pluralist thought, even though serious criticism of American pluralism did not come until the nineteen-sixties. Early pluralists may be criticized on two points: (1) for their failure to take account of the world outside their own nation-state; and (2) for not making certain that a system of group life or group pressures (which can descend to pure pressure group politics) is also a *just* system. Yet the original debt of the functionalists to pluralism ought not to be forgotten, because the connection is indeed central. The same conditions that moved the early pluralists are now evident on a world scale, because the state occupies a more prominent role than ever. It has also become clear what was wrong with the earlier pluralists: their inability to conceive of the political process, without the helping hand of the state to inject a sense of purpose and a sense of the common weal.

Pluralism, as originally conceived, is untenable without a global conception of politics and without the activation of a variety of influences within a framework of world politics. The problems of pluralism cannot be resolved within the confines of a single state, and especially not by a Great Power. In each individual nation-state, international pressures put enormous powers into the hands of the particular government and thus undermine pluralism from within and from without, even in successful and well-entrenched federal systems. If pluralism were to be projected on a global scale, significant changes could be expected to occur in world politics, and in the structure of Great Power authority.

Such changes are possible. The questions identified earlier by pluralists are now more pertinent than ever. Even if pluralism does need to be supplemented by conceptions of world interest and of world justice, it points to significant problems. The questions posed still stand; they serve as a reminder that issues of national politics cannot be resolved within single states, but instead need a conscious awareness of global interdependence.

The Corporation and World Order

The remainder of this chapter will spell out in more detail two aspects of the specifications for world order: first, the role of corporations (and business enterprises) will be reviewed in relation to world politics, in the light of the requirement that political power be balanced by non-political power; and second, the role of universities will be examined in the light of the belief that the increase of physical power must be counterbalanced by the growth of the society's moral resources.

The "commercial interest" has been prominent in a number of world systems—especially in those that have fostered the growth of autonomy.

Among the most important of these have been the Greek states, the city states of the Italian Renaissance, and the worldwide operations of Dutch and British trading enterprise. Reference has already been made to the role of the great trading companies in the era of globalization. But the rise of the modern corporation has been more recent; it has followed that of the modern nation-state. Corporations rose to national significance in the United States during the second half of the nineteenth century; by the beginning of the twentieth century, the exploits of such international entrepreneurs as Cecil Rhodes in South Africa had already drawn attention to the role of companies in world politics. Interest was focused on their role in the Third World—the extractive (gold, oil and copper) and plantation (rubber) industries being characteristically involved in such scrutiny. But none of the commentators on the subject of "economic imperialism" at that time regarded the companies as anything but close allies of their governments. Their role could be that of prime mover, or that of tool of the politicians; but it was never conceived of as being actually or even potentially independent. Commercial enterprise either planted the flag or followed it; the one thing it never did was to go afield without it.

The system of 1945 witnessed the rise of a new type of world organization: the global corporation. Table 15:1 gives instances of this new type of organization; it must be regarded as purely tentative, however, and useful mainly for illustrative purposes. The global corporation is so far insufficiently studied, and not yet well-known enough to political scientists, to produce accurate empirical observations.

A global corporation is a business organization that: (1) operates in the world market—that is, in the global layer of the world economy (a distinction is implied here between world, national and local markets); (2) is significantly independent of national governments, and (3) is significantly responsive to a conception of world interest. This definition makes it possible to deploy knowledge about the organization of the world economy within a theory of world politics, the decisive factors being participation in a global network, and two elements of political significance: autonomy (based on power), and responsiveness to wider purposes.

Table 15:1 has been put together in the light of that definition. The primary criterion for inclusion has been the number of subsidiaries and affiliates that are being maintained on a worldwide scale; in other words, a corporation has been judged to be global if it has maintained a sufficient wide sales and operations network. In one respect, such a network is also an aspect of the company's market power, of its ability to control the world market. In 1967, sixteen organizations had more than 41 foreign subsidiaries; this has given universal dimension to their operations. But

TABLE 15:1 Some Global Corporations, 1967 *

Name	H.Q.	Number of affiliates	Employees (000)	Sales (US$ m)	Per cent of sales outside H.Q. country	Net income (US$ m)
International Business Machines	New York	80	222	5,345	30	652
Singer Sewing Machine	New York	62	105	1,138	50	50
Pan-American World Airways	New York	59	36	950		66
National Cash Register	Dayton, Ohio	56	84	955	44	35
Socony Mobil Oil	New York	54	80	5,772	45	385
British-American Tobacco	London	54	95	1,321		155
British Petroleum	London	50	68	2,974	90	243
Imperial Chemical Industries	London	46	187	2,962		206
Pfizer	New York	46	33	638	48	58
Standard Oil of N.J.	New York	44	150	13,266	68	1,232
Unilever	London–Rotterdam	43	312	5,560		206
Royal Dutch–Shell	The Hague–London	43	171	8,376		935
The East Asiatic Co.	Copenhagen	42		1,000		
Paramount Pictures, subsidiary of Gulf Western	New York	42	46	644		46
Bank of America	San Francisco	42	32	21,268		130
Colgate–Palmolive	New York	41	25	1,025	55	34
Texaco	New York	37	80	5,121		754
Ford Motor	Dearborn, Mich.	28	394	10,516	36	84
Chase Manhattan Bank	New York	27	19	17,771		105
Chrysler	Detroit, Mich.	25	216	6,213	21	200
General Motors	Detroit, Mich.	22	728	20,026	14	1,627
General Electric	New York	15	375	7,741		361

* Defined as business enterprises with subsidiaries and affiliate companies in more than 41 countries; also industrial corporations with sales exceeding $5 billion and banks with assets exceeding $17.5 billion in 1967.

Sources: *Yearbook of International Organizations 1968–9*, pp. 1203–1214, *Fortune* issues for June 15 and September 15, 1968.

these were no more than the tip of the iceberg: in the same year, as many as 595 corporations (45 per cent of them American-based) were listed as having such affiliations in ten or more countries. On preliminary estimates, at least 7,000 companies had affiliates in at least one country outside their own base of operations.[7] Thus the total universe of global corporations is potentially quite large.

The secondary criterion has been sales volume: this, too, is an indication of market power. The list includes all those industrial corporations whose sales exceeded $5 billion in 1967 (a total of ten), along with two banks with exceptionally large assets. The corporations with large sales also have extensive networks of subsidiaries (none has fewer than 15); large sales volume generally coincides with global market coverage. Thus, in general, the global corporations also tend to be the world's largest business organizations; it seems that global extension is one route to business power.

A tertiary criterion of worldwide market impact should have been but was not applied in this short list: it would include those moderate-size organizations that have few or no external branches or subsidiaries, yet are crucial to the world market. Among those are manufacturers who supply advanced technical equipment for world airlines or for the various space programs.

The products of world corporations are among the most characteristic goods of modern society: computers and business machines; automobiles and other engineering products; oil and gas to make them run; films; world-brand consumer goods (such as Colgate–Palmolive or Singer); banking, air and shipping services. Most of the company names are household words, on a nearly worldwide scale. Some of these are commodities with a clear world market: world airlines, some banks, films of universal appeal. In oil, for instance, a world distribution network has been deliberately constructed, and a world market created, as a means of controlling the terms of exploitation. In the case of computers, a high rate of technological progress, or a high cost of initial investment, serves to preserve a dominant share of the market for the leading companies. There are also cases in which companies have secured an early lead for such commodities as soap, toothpaste or frozen foods, in markets that could just as easily have been preserved as national markets. Not that in every case global status is necessarily justified; in each case, however, it is true that a broad clientele is being served.

More important questions have to do with autonomy: if corporations are to play a balancing role in world society, are they in fact independent, can they become *more* independent, in relation to their home governments? Such independence has undoubtedly been less than the concept of a global corporation would require. The ownership and management of most business organizations is restricted to the nationality of the headquarters' state: the mere fact of having many affiliates does not make companies truly geocentric, inasmuch as home governments are anxious not to lose control over their major revenue sources. Furthermore, corporations are not randomly distributed among the world's nations: about one-half of the large multinationals are American-based companies. In the eyes of non-American observers in the host countries, they are not global organizations, carrying whatever halo might be associated with that status, but merely American business firms. Many such companies pursue profit maximization as their chief objective and care for little else; they rely on the home government to "bail them out," should an emergency arise. Finally, governments are good customers for many of the products of industry and commerce, especially those designed for the military sector. It is of some interest, however, that none of the companies with a large global network is oriented in the main to military production.

There are other circumstances, however, to take into consideration. The first is the undoubted power of the global corporation. By any yardstick, companies such as I.B.M. or Ford or Royal Dutch–Shell constitute substantial aggregations of world resources: their liquid cash and investment funds compare favorably with those of most governments.[8] Their large and potentially diverse staffs, often brain-drained from many countries, give them a pool of loyal, well-trained and well-paid manpower. Their research establishments and planning facilities, as well as communications apparatuses, match any to be found in the most progressive governments. The larger global corporations can meet all but the most powerful states on equal terms.

Another important factor is the flexibility that is afforded by worldwide operations in a loosely structured system; a single national government could not control any but a fraction of these activities. Its displeasure can in the long run always be circumvented—for instance, by a change in plant location, or a shift of operations across its borders. Even expropriation in most cases holds no terror; aside from the fact that it is frequently costly to the nationalizing government, it can most often be taken in stride by the particular firm that is involved. Even the oil companies—most frequently subject to confiscation, as in such *causes célèbres* as Mexico, Iran or Peru—are hard put to demonstrate any adverse long-term effects resulting from such moves.

For a truly global corporation, worldwide operations are in themselves a source of autonomy. This is attributable in part to the fact that, in the global layer, the political factor is a weak one: autonomy would be more restricted, if global political organizations acquired more substance. But, except for the case of global war, the autonomy of the corporation is now substantial and it is still growing. Inasmuch as this contributes to the diversification of world society, it could be rated as a positive factor.

But the question might also be asked: are this power and this autonomy being used in accordance with world interest? Is the substantial freedom from national control being employed responsibly and for wider purposes? Here, the responsiveness of the corporation to the values of a world community must be rated less highly. Few corporations have so far escaped the circumscribed conditions of the national environment. To begin with, notice must be taken of the hierarchical, even authoritarian, features of many corporations. By comparison with states and with local and international governments, most corporations do not maintain more than a fiction of responsiveness, either to their own members or to their clientele. The staff and labor forces are viewed as interchangeable machine-parts, rather than as communities of people who work and live together. Customers are seen as gullible audiences, to be manipulated by lavish advertising circuses, if need be, rather than to be heeded. The power of the corporations is yet to be tempered by a feeling of responsibility for the welfare of the world—the *whole* world, whose wondrous ways have made it possible for such power to accumulate.

Internally weak, the great corporations have also failed to develop an institutional structure that would bind them to the fabric of world society. They lack that feeling of responsibility to the world at large that, in some countries, national corporations have toward the nation. These external responsibilities have been left unarticulated, and no leadership for world problems has emerged from the ranks of world corporations. Their links to the United Nations are weak, while their financial contributions to the political structure on which their own global operations so substantially rest are shortsightedly non-existent. Propelled onto the world scene largely by their own momentum, the great corporations have not associated themselves with any wider purpose, such as world development. Their record in this area, as in respect to other world problems, has been poor. Arguably, their activities may have aggravated, rather than lessened, the existing imbalances between the richer and the poorer nations. Their failure to develop a sense of mission and of purpose leaves the door open for the nation-state to step in, to circumscribe their activities and at times even to take over their functions.

Finally, the corporations (and observers of corporations) tend to confuse global functions with bigness; they have therefore pursued bigness at the expense of service. A global corporation is, by definition one that serves a world market; but the entire world need not be a world market for all commodities. The ultimate in such gigantomania would be one world corporation, as the counterpart of one world state. Just as world politics requires a variety of levels, so the world economy too calls for a variety of markets. The corporation that pursues market dominance is seeking monopoly power through mergers and absorptions; it is pursuing a course that is equivalent to conquest in the more purely political realm. The pursuit of market power, without considerations of service, invites retaliation through politics. In small national markets, the only organization that is sizable enough to take on the superior power of the great corporation may well be the nation-state.[9]

The global corporations could be a source of strength for world society; but their mission and their tasks in relation to world interests are yet to be set out more persuasively, and their role as corporate world citizens is yet to be defined precisely.

The Role of Universities

A world order needs more than corporations and the "profane" promise of a material cornucopia that they hold out. In its institutional base, world order also needs a "sacred" component—one that lifts mankind out of its daily concerns, and enables it to face with some equanimity the uncertainties of the future. In earlier times, religion and its organizational arm, the church, was expected to meet this task; an important feature of the world since 1945 has been the degree to which education, and especially the universities, has entered this field and thereby contributed to altering the entire system.

The rise of the universities has been truly phenomenal. In the United States universities and colleges had, in 1930, about one million students; by 1978, that number could well go up to ten million. Universities have become the focal points for large self-sustaining academic and research communities, which enjoy considerable autonomy. An increasingly large proportion of the population is well-educated: among the young adults, high school diplomas are now held by the great majority (75 per cent), while the proportion of those with some college education went up from 13 per cent in 1940 to 31 per cent in 1970. Elsewhere in the world, the rise in student numbers has been equally if not more striking. The world population of university and college students rose 185 per cent between 1950 and 1965, to over 18 million; the ranks of teachers increased by 135 per cent, to 1,325,000; and the system of higher educational institutions expanded by 110 per cent by 1964, to exceed 12,000 units.[10]

This expansion of the student population was accompanied by the evolution of the large graduate university, as a separate and distinct type of academic institution. Supported by generous government research grants, the large university has become a spearhead of technological development and scientific invention. It has also tended to become more interdependent with other universities—that is to say, global in its operations.

The result might be described as the incipient growth of global universities within the world system of higher education. Table 15:2 supplies some illustrations of this: it includes those universities that award the highest number of doctorates and that also meet a number of additional criteria bearing on quality and worldwide service: a large graduate student body with a considerable foreign student component (indicating a complex and potentially global clientele); a large full-time faculty, a large library (two good indicators of research capacity), and substantial revenue (part of which goes into financing research).

The global university is, above all, an institution of quarternary— that is, graduate—education. Its chief "products" are doctorates, as well as learning, research (including post-doctoral research), and professional training. In undergraduate education, most countries are now largely self-sufficient; but postgraduate training is more specialized and more expensive, and absolutely necessary: for every ten undergraduate students, an adequate system of higher education needs one faculty member who has been trained up to doctoral standards. The worldwide expansion of the student population has brought in its train a worldwide demand for graduate education. Because of the degree of specialization, and on account of the expense involved, the number of large and well-endowed graduate schools is truly small, and they are all concentrated in the United States and Europe. These schools nevertheless serve the world, by instructing large bodies of foreign students. Centers of graduate and post-doctoral training together make up a global layer of education.

A large graduate university absorbs prodigious resources. It maintains a large library; extensive research laboratories or teaching hospitals; a full-time faculty of several thousand, of high professional repute, and a variety of ancillary facilities. A revenue of one hundred million dollars is not unusual, a sum that compares favorably with the ordinary budget of the United Nations Organization and with those of many independent states. But the species of global university is not exhausted by the examples given in Table 15:2. The most prominent and best endowed universities are found in the North American–European region, but other parts of the world also have centers that, in favorable conditions, might grow to global stature. Cairo University and the American University in Beirut serve as magnets for the Middle East; Al-Azhar, the world's oldest university, still functions in Cairo. India's universities are huge but underfinanced; as a rule, they lag behind in quality graduate work. Japan's are larger and better endowed, but are not as yet attracting many foreign students. Some Latin American centers are large, but understaffed (Buenos

TABLE 15:2 Some Global Universities, 1967

Founding Date		Doctorates awarded	Faculty	Students	Graduate students	Foreign students	Library (m vols)	Revenue ($ m)
1868	U.C. Berkeley	722	1,018	26,963	10,101	2,703	3.3	175 (est)
1848	Wisconsin (Madison)	627	1,966	31,120	8,222	1,480	1.9	100
1100	Paris		5,848	117,911		9,371	3.9	
1867	Illinois (Urbana)	568	1,930	29,120	7,418*	1,430*	3.7	175*
1754	Columbia	557	1,866	17,377	9,272	2,565	3.8	134
1836	London	536	3,000	28,108	8,557	4,694		103
1638	Harvard	524	2,151	14,986	9,059	1,266	7.6	151
1851	Minnesota	501	2,111	43,997	7,120	1,337	2.5	100
1885	Stanford	498	1,037	12,423	6,520	1,016	2.8	129
1821	Michigan	475	2,343	36,063	13,149	1,546	3.7	202
1755	Moscow		2,469	31,729		2,091	5	
1303	Rome		4,955	42,304		1,256		
1919	U.C. Los Angeles	396	1,116	26,898	9,411	2,300	2.5	175 (est)
1861	M.I.T.	386	912	7,567	3,718	935	1	200
1865	Cornell	367	2,936	14,123	4,041	1,107	3	119
1200	Oxford	324	1,220	10,262	2,513	1,244	3.5	
1365	Vienna		1,045	18,276		2,905	1.8	
1209	Cambridge	293	1,000	10,103	1,921	1,000	3.5	
1894	Chicago	293	1,534	8,399	5,614	617	2.6	211
1701	Yale	277	1,252	8,654	4,360	867	5.2	90
1861	Washington	266	1,834	26,431	5,308	1,174	1.6	125
1754	Pennsylvania	263	1,636	19,297	8,900	1,114	2	118
1919	Hamburg		1,177	19,076		1,374		

Each university meets the following criteria for selection: more than 250 earned doctorates awarded 1966–7; over 2,500 graduate students (except Cambridge); more than 1,000 full-time teaching faculty (except M.I.T.); over 1,000 foreign students (except M.I.T., Chicago, Yale); library of over 1.5 million volumes (except M.I.T.).
* All campuses.
Sources: *American Universities and Colleges 1968*; *Commonwealth Universities Yearbook 1968*; *International Handbook of Universities 1968*.

Aires has 65,000 students, but only 600 full-time faculty; Mexican National, 79,000 students and 515 full-time faculty). Graduate universities need not be large, however: they can be small in faculty and in numbers of graduate students, and nonetheless maintain excellence in training and research and a global impact. Rockefeller University in New York is one example of a small but high-quality operation.

The distinguishing characteristics of a global university are therefore the following:

(1) *Substantial autonomy*. As in the case of corporations, this is in part a function of their power—that is, of the resources they absorb and the facilities they deploy. That is the reason why large graduate universities are important and their continued viability crucial: they are large aggregations of brain-power, the wise exercise of which will go a long way toward preserving academic freedom, that traditional rallying point for university autonomy. Neither the small specialized graduate university, the large teaching institution inundated by students, nor the advanced and well-financed research institute can by itself exert an influence comparable to that of the large graduate university—especially as far as the moral climate of society is concerned.

(2) *Operation in the global layer*. This is the result of the shift of emphasis to graduate and post-doctoral work which, because it is taking place at the frontiers of knowledge, involves awareness of similar activities elsewhere in the world of learning. It must, therefore, at least with regard to the chosen field of specialization, be global. Membership in the "invisible colleges" of learning is an indispensable part of such work. This is the world inhabited by Nobel Prize winners and others like them.

(3) *Responsiveness to world interest*. Universities have always been marked by a certain detachment from society and a measure of seclusion; these have been aspects of that autonomy that is essential to their functioning. But they cannot detach themselves altogether and, when they function in the global layer, they cannot isolate themselves from the influences that shape world affairs. Members of the great graduate universities have proven themselves to be specially responsive to universal political issues: civil rights, Vietnam, the environment. What has been dubbed "the Berkeley invention" has been the fusion of these issues with campus protest during the nineteen-sixties. In one sense, the campus of the global university has thus become the focal point of the operation of global interdependence. The precise manner in which responsiveness to the world interest is implemented by the great universities may take a variety of forms; but its substance will be grounded in the concerns of younger, better educated generations.

The great graduate university makes a positive contribution to world order. This cannot and will not forever take the form of campus unrest.

Their first contribution is to the diversification and enrichment of world society and to the raising of the quality of life. The worldwide university community is now substantial enough to be itself a significant component of the world social system. Its second contribution lies in the direction of educating a large and rising proportion of the world's younger generation, especially those who are destined for positions of leadership. It not only educates them but also facilitates links among them; in that respect, it is instrumental in the development of global networks. Its universal quality can bridge other sources of global division, including religious and ideological traditions. Third, members of universities help to identify world problems—for instance, dangers to the environment—and to create a climate of opinion in which the attacking of world problems becomes a matter of urgent public policy. Finally, the global university constitutes an element in the building up of the moral order of world society, which has so far been dominated excessively by the motives and the mechanics of power. Admittedly, the university contributed, through its earlier investments in scientific research, to the present dangers to mankind's survival; it may be that, without the universities making as significant a contribution to our moral resources, our prospects are indeed slim.

Doubts arise on two grounds. The protean strength and the vitality of the great universities during the past few decades has been a peculiarly American phenomenon. Just as, with regard to world corporations, 15 out of the 22 most prominent enterprises were American-based, so 14 out of the 22 global universities are also American. Perhaps the impetus will prove to be contagious and such splendid creativity an example to be emulated even more widely. On the other hand, their difficulties may serve to discourage others and to divert them into less ambitious forms of organizing learning—forms that will make fewer demands on the moral character of their contribution. As a worldwide institution, universities have yet to demonstrate a positively constructive capacity, on the strength of their own political and moral constituency and their recognized place in world society.

Second, much of the recent flourishing of the universities has been based on their service to the state and to industry. In the conventional justification of university services, a large place has been held by research, science and technology. These do not have to be minimized on the grounds that scholarly activity remains the heart of the university; yet overemphasis on the profane and utilitarian functions of science and technology and the consequent diminution of the role of the arts and the humanities, which cultivate the qualities of beauty, harmony and goodness, tends to slight the university's moral functions and to weaken its impact on the general education (directly, as well as indirectly, through the training of teachers) of all members of society, and thus on the social and moral climate of their times.

The principal route to augmenting the moral resources of world society might well be by way of raising the quality of the education that is available to its members. A better educated society is also a better society: its members are each better able to cope with the future and, since they are all educated to a high standard, they also see themselves as better able to join in common enterprises. Education is a powerful mechanism for equalizing political resources, and thus for creating conditions that are conducive to the effectiveness of moral considerations and the realization of justice. By facilitating network formation, education also leads to cohesion and cooperation, and hence to order. H. G. Wells saw man as engaged in a race between education and catastrophe; the future of the university will have a crucial bearing on the outcome of that race.

Order Is Not Enough

Corporations and universities are two of the dimensions along which world society—and not the global layer alone—may be moving toward greater complexity, and hence toward a greater potential for survival and order. In respect to the moral sphere, there is no need to give undue prominence to universities, however dramatic their recent growth. The moral resources of society extend beyond university and education to include religious forms and manifestations, the province of law, the sphere of art, and matters of public taste and public judgment. They make themselves felt strongly through all societal networks. While each of these spheres also has direct links with education, they all form autonomous and self-restructuring fields of activity.

Much emphasis has been placed so far on organizations as sources of order, and little emphasis on individuals. Yet individuals are in some sense the ultimate sources of complexity. While many people work through organizations and others in networks, some represent areas of individual autonomy that are significant within a global context. Two classes of individuals might be adduced as examples: men and women of great personal wealth, and individuals of outstanding intellectual or moral distinction. Of the latter, Nobel Prize winners might be taken as outstanding representatives. How can these people contribute to the establishment or the maintenance of world order?

In the preceding generation, portions of three large personal fortunes—those of the Carnegie, Rockefeller and Ford families—were set aside for public purposes, and they thereby made an impact on world

affairs. To give but two examples, the early study of International Relations, especially in the United States, owed much to Carnegie and Rockefeller support; after 1945, international studies, in American and other
universities, benefited greatly by injections from the great resources of
the Ford Foundation. In a different way, the Green Revolution of the
nineteen-sixties owes much to early sponsorship of the International Rice
Research Institute by the Ford and Rockefeller Foundations.

Wealthy persons add to the textural richness of some dimensions
of society. In 1968, in the United States alone, as many as sixty-six individuals were identified as possessing a personal fortune in excess of
$150 million, and two of these were classed as billionaires, Howard
Hughes and Paul Getty.[11] These are large resources, even on a world
scale; yet in recent years, they have not been used with any evident
concern for world order. This most recent generation of the very rich
seems less notable than its predecessors, in terms of the degree of its
concern for the world; it evinces instead a sense of detachment and self-
centeredness that is best embodied in contemptuous references to the
"international jet set."

Nor have those individuals who have been outstanding in intellectual attainment—as, for example, Nobel Prize winners—been notable for
world leadership, either. The dominance of the sciences among the Nobel
Prizes has tended to add impetus to the scientific and technological race,
instead of helping to moderate it. The Prize has become a coveted attainment in the race for discovery, and a spur to competition. Only in the
Peace Prizes has moral eminence been recognized to any great degree.
Cases of individual impact on world politics have thus been rare. The
Pugwash Conferences on Science and World Affairs (sponsored by Cyrus
Eaton) could be adduced in evidence, while the clearest single instance
might well be that of Bertrand Russell, twice a Nobel Prize Winner—
another representative of the milieu in which pluralist thought originated
—who, at times of international tension (for instance in 1962), conducted
correspondence and maintained contact on equal terms with heads of
the Great Powers.

Potential contributors to complexity are almost as numerous as
individuals and the infinite number of combinations they might be involved in. In the present emphasis on organizations, these various combinations have been recognized as constructive elements of world order.
The view that large-scale organization is bad, that it is inherently inimical
to human purpose and automatically brings alienation to all who come
within its purview, cannot be supported.

Large-scale organization undoubtedly brings problems. These may
become particularly acute in relation to global organizations having to
operate effectively over long distances; they are particularly liable to

gigantomania. But hopefully such growth can conceivably be channeled and limited, through concepts and devices such as layering, differentiation and decentralization. Provided they did not exceed a size of the sort that dwarfs not only human perception but even human imagination, the large organizations might be accommodative to individual purposes.

In addition to size, all organizations tend toward rigidity and oligarchy; sometimes they descend into tyranny. The tyranny practiced by private associations that are unresponsive to the public interest and bent on maximizing narrow sectoral demands can be as real as is oppression by public authorities, even if it is less often recognized. The cozy community that is governed with an iron hand by the resident oligarch; the private business that is ruled autocratically by the boss-owner; industrial associations piously administering a public trust, but for a private purpose—all these are cases in which territorial autonomy or functional differentiation do not in and of themselves assure orderly progress or enhance justice.

There are no shortcuts to order: organizations need to be enmeshed in networks; when these latter function as they should, they can soften and moderate the crushing force of the organizations' power. Universities are the basic producers of the raw material out of which networks are constructed; that is their significant contribution to order, rather than their organizational power, which, like all other forms of power, is also liable to deterioration. The networks, with their suppleness, resilience, and textural richness, are also elements of complexity, perhaps essential elements.

In addition to organizations and networks, there is another, passive element of order—and that is withdrawal. This may take the form of a temporary retreat, recreation, meditation, or a period of study, but it may also take the socially less predictable and occasionally more damaging forms of apathy, along with the withholding of support, which results in social and organizational anomie and the withering of the networks. In world systems, there might thus be phases of isolationism and intense self-preoccupation. The universities serve in some of their aspects as harbors of safe withdrawal, "ivory towers" on a world scale, so to speak.

In summary, one could say that the complexity whose elements have been suggested in this chapter does go some way toward bringing about a sounder structure of world politics. Yet inasmuch as order is not the only concern of politics, complexity and pluralism are not enough; they need to be enriched, continuously reinvigorated by a basic concern for justice.

Notes to Chapter Fifteen

1. *The Ethics of Aristotle*, J. A. K. Thompson ed. (Baltimore: Penguin, 1955), Book II, Ch. 6, p. 66.

2. *The Politics of Aristotle*, T. A. Sinclair tr. (Baltimore: Penguin, 1962), Book IV, Ch. 11, p. 171.

3. Leo Spitzer (*Classical and Christian Ideas of World Harmony* [Baltimore: Johns Hopkins, 1963], p. 138) laments the decline of the Greek concept of world harmony which occurred in the seventeenth and eighteenth centuries.

4. Leonard Woolf, *International Government* (London, 1916).

5. See in particular *The World of William Clissold* (New York: Doran, 1926); also *Imperialism and the Open Conspiracy* (London, 1929).

6. Re-issued in Part I of D. Mitrany, *A Working Peace System* (Chicago: Quadrangle Books, 1966).

7. *Yearbook of International Organizations 1968-1969*, p. 1195.

8. Compare Table 15:1 with Table 7:9, *Classes of Military Power, 1967*.

9. See, for example, Stephen Hymer and Robert Rowthorn, "Multinational Corporation and International Monopoly: The Non-American Challenge," in Charles Kindleberger ed., *The International Corporation* (Cambridge, Mass.: M.I.T. Press), 1970, esp. p. 87 ff.

10. *UNESCO Statistical Yearbook 1965, 1967*; all figures exclude China, North Korea and North Vietnam.

11. Arthur M. Louis, "America's Centimillionaires," *Fortune*, May 1968, pp. 152–7.

16
Justice

IN THE COMMON UNDERSTANDING, THE question of justice is alien to international politics. Indeed, the irrelevance of justice is seen by some to be the distinguishing characteristic of this universe of behavior.[1] Whereas justice appears to be attainable, and therefore worth striving for, in the comparative security of domestic society, to seek it in the jungle-like conditions outside the nation-state appears extremely hazardous, if not quixotical. Justice being the good of others, the narrow vision of the nation-state system rules out the extension of its authority to those "others" who may be found beyond any set of national frontiers.

War Knows No Justice

An early authoritative statement of such views can be found in Aristotle's *Nicomachean Ethics*:

Political justice is manifested between persons who share a common way of life, which has as its object a state of affairs in which they will have all that they need for an independent existence as free and equal members of the society. Between persons who do not enjoy such freedom and equality, there can be no political justice but only a simulacrum of it.[2]

Yet the passage is not unambiguous: although it asserts the possibility of justice in the *polis*, and implies the impossibility of it in external relations, the point is not elaborated. A little further on, Aristotle acknowledges the existence of natural justice, which "has the same validity everywhere." [3] The basic point was spelled out more clearly by Thomas Hobbes; his has remained to this day the classical statement of the problem.

Crucial to Hobbes' entire argument is his position that men naturally tend toward a state of war "of every man, against every man," which is not just a matter of actual fighting but also "the known disposition thereto." It is only when men live under "a common power to keep them all in awe"—that is, when they have formed a state—that they attain the condition of peace. In interstate relations, however, the condition of war continues to prevail:

In all times, Kings and Persons of Soveraigne authority, because of their Independency, are in continuall jealousies, and the state and posture of Gladiators; having their weapons pointing, and their eyes fixed on one another, that is their Forts, Garrisons and Guns upon the Frontiers of their King-domes; and continuall Spyes upon their neighbours; which is a posture of War . . .

To this warre of every man against every man, this also is consequent; that nothing can be Unjust. The notions of Right and Wrong, Justice and Injustice, have there no place. When there is no common Power, there is no Law; where no Law, no Injustice. Force, and Fraud, are in warre the two Cardinall vertues.[4]

While it has by no means gone unchallenged, Hobbes's position has nevertheless remained representative of the mainstream of International Relations. The gradual evolution of International Law has indeed en-tangled states in a growing web of written and unwritten obligations, the breach of which would commonly be regarded as unlawful and unjust; the "natural law" tradition has for centuries suggested the idea, found in Aristotle's alternative formulation, of justice with equal validity every-where. Yet International Law has not organized more than the fringes of world politics, and has done not much more than apply a thin veneer of respectability to all kinds of behavior, some of it outrageous. The main structures of world politics—the nation-state system and its sequelae—have commonly been held to be outside the considerations of justice. For this reason they acquired, for some, certain inherently sinister, apocalyptic qualities, insofar as they seemed to place, as indeed they did, unusual and unscalable obstacles in the path of that progress that was commonly thought to be realizable in domestic affairs.

Hobbes may have been the world's first "organization man," in that he explicitly stated that the solution to man's problems lies in the creation of an "artificial man"—that is, the organization. He expected the organi-zation to rescue man from the deterioration that is endemic in the human condition and thanks to which life would become "solitary, poore, nasty, brutish and short." But his vision was circumscribed by the jurisdictional boundaries of the organization he was designing, and he ignored the problems he was creating for world order, in part by virtue of the Leviathan's inability to deal with world injustice.

The Hobbesian view of the irrelevance of justice in interstate relations has some superficial validity. General or global war damages the fabric of world society, and the universal expectation of war can have the same effect. These processes also strengthen the nation-state system, and thereby diminish the chances for solutions that will be favorable to justice. To an important extent, the question of justice on a world scale is bound up with the structure of world politics.

But just as the nation-state system is not the only possible—or "natural"—state of the world, so conditions can be specified in which considerations of justice could assume greater than the marginal positions they now occupy. In the first place, insofar as the degree of "disposition to war" (and also nation-state dominance) varies in the world system, the disposition to attend to injustices can also vary. A period of widespread peace would in this respect show characteristics different from those to be seen, for example, in the middle or the closing stages of a global war.

Second, the strength of the global layer is also a relevant variable. "Independence," which in the Hobbesian scheme causes war, is not a necessary condition for war. Depending on a variety of other factors, including the strength and resilience of those networks in which organizations are enmeshed, independence (or autonomy) is compatible with the absence of violence, and hence does not preclude justice. Nor does autonomy (and there are degrees of autonomy) preclude change and progress.

Third, world order may in fact be quite unattainable in the absence of justice. The possibilities for the redress of grievances are the surest guarantees of order, while the combination of injustice with the absence of remedies for it undermines order and reinforces the vicious circle of the nation-state system. In world politics, injustice functions as a "self-fulfilling prophecy"; but the injection of processes of justice could slow it down and, in favorable conditions, could even help to reverse it.

Finally, the Hobbesian argument holds true in conditions of ignorance, based on lack of adequate information, about the world, world order and the worldwide consequences of political action. If an act or a political arrangement is to be regarded as unjust, there must be an element of voluntariness attached to it. In Aristotle's terms, the actors must act: (1) in full knowledge of the consequences, (2) in a situation where they have the power to decide either way, and (3) outside the influence of *force majeure*. In world politics, insofar as political action tends to be regarded as being beyond the power of the participants to control and therefore as assuming an irresistible momentum, it could also be categorized as outside the purview of justice. But to the extent that society moves toward higher levels of awareness and global communication, as well as toward improved understanding of the consequences of decisions, the burden of responsibility that lies upon all actors of world politics increases immensely. In that sense, the contemporary information explosion and the ability to organize large flows of high-grade intelligence, also have significant moral consequences: they take away from policy-makers the excuses of yesteryear and make them more responsible to the concepts of justice. Progress in the study of world politics might itself be a contributory factor toward augmenting the place of justice in world affairs.

Justice in world politics is the concern for the good of all of world society; it is the ethics of world politics, and as such is informed by the ethical notions that are appropriate to this context. At this point, no advantage is to be gained from laying down standards of world justice; rather, as in the case of world order, note will be taken of the fact that, while justice may be difficult to define, injustice is quickly felt and deeply resented. Justice is a quality that informs the conduct of world politics, and among the possible outcomes of any action is the creation or the perpetuation of injustice. The system as a whole may be less or more unjust.

In the pages that follow, the distinction will be made between distributive (or substantive) and procedural justice. In part, it will be argued that world politics needs to face up to the fact of world inequalities; what distributive justice deals with is the concern that the distribution of resources and rewards should proceed on the basis of recognized criteria of merit and fairness. In part, it will also be argued that world politics requires adequate procedures for the airing and the accommodation of grievances, and that such procedures must satisfy the conditions of both responsiveness and responsibility. In both respects, justice is a counterweight to power; it offers criteria and mechanisms that give substance to the long-run wisdom of social coexistence.

World Inequalities

Today's world is plagued by great inequalities. Several of these have already been remarked upon—among them, the concentration of trade and the lopsided distribution of military power and of wealth. Not only are these inequalities distressingly deep, they are cumulative—and they are still growing. They put to question the viability of world society.

Yet at the same time the perception is gaining currency that these inequalities are essentially unjust. There is no doubt that explanations can be advanced with regard to each kind of inequality, and the processes that brought it to its present level can be subjected to causal analysis.

Some degree of inequality is also undoubtedly justified, on the grounds that justice demands not mechanical equalization but a fair allocation, related in a determinate manner to relevant merit and to past achievement. But sentiments of injustice must not be allowed to deteriorate into feelings of uncontrollable envy or the desire for revenge—the customary ingredients of tragic situations. World inequalities extend beyond mundane rationalizations and activate "the sentiment, inchoate yet profound, that no matter how unequal men may be in their abilities, in some deeper sense all men are equal, merely by virtue of being men." [5]

The idea that equality is in some sense a norm from which inequality represents a deviation has a strong hold on man's imagination. Wollheim and Berlin have pointed out that (1) men are all members of one species, of a simple class of objects (i.e. human beings) and (2) all members of a class should be treated uniformly, unless there is good and sufficient reason not to do so.[6]

In other words, inequality is perceived as unjust because of the postulated unity of mankind. Just as inequalities are among the principal forces maintaining the nation-state system, so the idea of equality might be a motive force for world society. Alexis de Tocqueville called it "the great democratic revolution" and he studied its early manifestations in his *Democracy in America* (1835). He saw it taking hold among all the "Christian nations" with the force of a process of nature: "it appears to me beyond a doubt that, sooner or later, we shall arrive, like the Americans, at an almost complete equality of conditions." [7] But he also pleaded for its control and regulation, for finding means of "rendering it profitable to mankind."

Why is it that de Tocqueville's projection has not, so far, been realized? In the past century and a half, conditions have changed toward a greater, yet far from complete, equality in Europe; in America, the level of equality may even have declined. In the world at large, however, inequality has been decidedly on the rise.

The basic datum with regard to present-day world inequality is the diparity in the distribution of the world product, summarized in Table 16:1. This shows, in the first place, the gap between the income levels of the developed (and, in part, rich) countries, and the developing, and poor, countries. The developed areas, with just over one quarter of the world's population (28 percent), absorbed (in the years 1965-1967) over four-fifths, or 83 percent, of the gross world product. This is one of the basic facts of contemporary politics, and one of the striking forms it assumes is the gap between the levels of living in Western and other populations—especially in such matters as nutrition, health, and general vitality.

Even more striking are the trends indicated by absolute magnitudes.

TABLE 16:1   Distribution of World Product, 1965, 1967

(billions of constant US 1967 dollars)

	1965		1967	
World	2,259		2,481	
Developed	1,870	(82.8 p.c.)	2,054	(82.9 p.c.)
Developing	389	(17.2 p.c.)	427	(17.1 p.c.)

(per capita)

	1965	1967
World	684	772
Developed	1,983	2,151
Developing	165	172

Source: *World Military Expenditures 1969*, p. 10.

Between 1965 and 1967, per capita income in the developed areas rose by $168, but in the developing areas the increase amounted to only $7. Thus, in a period of two years, the income increment obtained by ordinary economic growth in developed areas was as large as the *entire* per capita income for the developing countries. The absolute disparity in income levels rose from $1,818 in 1965 to $1,979 in 1967; in other words, the gap has been growing and not narrowing down at all, at least as shown by this information.

This would suggest that the "developing" countries have not been developing at all, but retrogressing. No analysis of their growth rates can obscure the fact that their relative share of the world product has been declining. According to Table 16:1, that share declined in the space of two years from 17.2 to 17.1 percent, all the while their share of world military expenditures was rising from eleven to twelve percent.

TABLE 16:2   Trends in World Income Inequalities

(Gini index)

1860	.465	1958	.545
1880	.470	1959	.551
1900	.508	1960	.548
1913	.503	1961	.554
1929	.506	1962	.555
1952–54	.531	1963	.560
1960	.612	1964	.562
		1965	.568
		1966	.568
		1967	.567

1860–1960: index calculated by Douglas Grandquis, from L. J. Zimmerman, *Arme en Rijke Landen* (1964), pp. 134–135, Table 6.5: Distribution of World Income (1953 prices, for 10 out of 12 world regions).

1958–1967: index calculated by Douglas Grandquis from standard United Nations sources covering 190 reporting units; current prices.

What is more, the trend of retrogression is no mere accident of the two years depicted in Table 16:1. Longer-range data, also on hand, give additional support to the suspicion that recent tendencies have been little more than a continuation of entrenched secular trends. Table 16:2 summarizes the relevant information, in the form of a Gini index of inequality, derived from two different sets of statistical data. (The higher the index figure, up to the level of one, the greater the inequality in the distribution of the relevant value.)

The global trends are unequivocal in their decisiveness. Over a period of more than one hundred years, a clear worldwide trend of steadily rising income inequality may be observed. In 1860 world income was distributed fairly unequally, with a Gini index level of .465 which might be compared with the average level for the United States in 1959 of .439. Present-day levels of world income inequality are, by contrast, the highest on record, the nearest comparison to the high .567 for the world in 1967 being the .510 recorded for the state of Mississippi in 1959.[8] It might be said, without much exaggeration, that in some respects the world is like Mississippi—only more so.

The explanation for the continual rise of income inequality is not at all obvious. In a most general sense, the growing gap could seem to be the consequence of growth. Rapid growth benefits the community, yet the benefits are distributed selectively. Those areas that spearheaded growth reap major benefits; those that have been left behind by progress may have to carry its major burdens. At times of depression or lack of growth, the weakest find it more difficult to protect themselves. Thus growth has benefited Europe, North America and lately Japan, yet has weakened societies throughout the rest of the world. A stationary (or non-growth) economy would pose the same problem, but in an even sharper form. But students of the nation-state system cannot help noticing that the steady increase in the wealth gap has also coincided with the rise of the nation-state and its universalization. The greater the nation-state dominance, the greater, it seems, the nation-state inequalities. This is no more than an association, and the causal influences might well be running in both directions; the nation-state system itself might be the product of rapid growth. Whatever the precise connection, however, the mere association is too striking to be ignored.

One last dimension of inequality is cumulation. The data here adduced bear only on income and therefore indirectly on income-generating wealth. But, as far as can be discerned, the top quarter of the world's population, commanding over four-fifths of its wealth, also has preferred access to most of its organizational resources (the global corporations, in Table 15:1), and to most of its knowledge-generating and value-shaping institutions (the global universities, Table 15:2). Most international organizations are located in the metropolises of the developed areas (Table 9:4), along with most of the headquarters of the non-governmental organizations. Finally, the affluent states also dispose of the bulk of military power (Table 7:8), proportionately to an even higher degree than wealth. In other words, the world's values are not distributed in a random fashion over the surface of the globe, but rather cumulate in a determinate section, a minority of its population.

The causality of accumulation is an open question. Robert Dahl links it to the agricultural character of the relevant society, by contrast with modern society, in which he expects value distributions to be non-cumulative. He writes: ". . . in an agricultural society, if the distribution of landed property is highly unequal, the distribution of all political resources and skills tends to be highly unequal . . . this is why a popular ·government is unlikely to exist in an agricultural society unless landed property is divided with a considerable degree of equality." [9]

Whether contemporary world society can be characterized as industrial, or whether it is still basically agricultural, in terms of Dahl's definition, is a moot point. Is it still a society in which the value of land owned determines not only wealth and income, but also education, political and military power and social status? World population has long outdistanced the level known to have existed for any previous agricultural world society; on the grounds that a larger society needs a more complex organization, the present-day world is functionally industrial and could not work without its industrial framework. But, as far as world-wide trends are concerned, close to one-half of world manpower is still in agriculture (as against a small percentage in the United States), while urbanization still covers less than one-half the population. Most importantly, perhaps, in the nation-state system a man's (or woman's) status is still basically derived from his (or her) ownership, however indirect that may be, of land—namely, the stake in the national territory, and the rights and privileges deriving from it on the basis of citizenship. In the world at large, citizenship, or nationality, is still the dominant status, and immigration and other such restrictions, which are enforced at the national boundaries, consolidate this territorial distribution. World society therefore remains, in Dahl's sense, an agricultural society, even though the meaning of that term is somewhat stretched beyond the intentions of its author.

The cumulation previously diagnosed might therefore be attributed to the lingering "agricultural" features of world organizations. But it is also self-evident that large parts of the world have passed beyond this stage, and that the more advanced areas are moving rapidly ahead in a number of directions away from agrarian simplicities. An agricultural society prefers self-contained communities and, since its contacts are intermittent, requires few comprehensive systems of communications. Modernity has destroyed the coziness of small communities, so that knowledge about world distributions is now widely dispersed. Hence, in a variety of ways, the tensions that exist are set up by friction between the surviving agricultural features of world organization and the requirements of the modern world.

Approaches to World Welfare

Students of world politics are keenly aware that inequalities of income and wealth are closely linked to power inequalities. Military power distributions, and the Great Power system, are particularly relevant. The chain of causality is probably circular, a part of the circle of the nation-state system. In a fundamental sense, the reduction of income inequalities must therefore be related to processes of diminishing nation-state dominance. The principles of complexity as a condition of order are also the conditions for wider power distribution.

The two issues must be kept analytically separate, even though the income gap—or the poverty and the degradation of large masses of the world's people—cannot remain a matter of indifference to world politics, even in the face of power inequalities. A modern society cannot conceivably be shaped in the image of a caste system, with the so-called underdeveloped majority of the world assigned permanently to a lowly life. The traditional Hindu model of a static society, composed of rigidly demarcated, non-communicating castes whose membership is determined by birth, offers little attraction or even application in the modern world. Yet this was also a system that was originally based on a racial division; basically non-centralized, it was held together at the top level, above all by a priestly caste of Brahmins.

Nor will any lasting improvement in world welfare be found by way of increase in intergovernmental assistance funds—a "remedy" that has grown remarkably popular and has been assiduously applied in the years since 1945. Whatever the multifarious effects of the various foreign aid programs, funds and resources that have been given by nation-states to other nation-states have brought about no perceptible reduction in global inequality. This is not to deny that some programs of that sort did have a notable success: the European Recovery Program, and early postwar assistance to Japan proved to be hugely effective. But as a form of world organization, intergovernmental aid benefits first and above all governments and states: the donor government, because it is usually attuned to specific foreign policy objectives; and recipient governments, because such a government will arrange its projects in accordance with its own priorities, among the foremost of which will undoubtedly be the desire to fortify its own rule or its hold on power, by rewarding its supporters, and frequently even a wish for personal enrichment. But the bulk of aid funds is not even of this kind but rather military: weapons and supplies, whose sole purpose is to strengthen the nation-state and its armed forces. Because of this tendency, intergovernmental aid of the past few decades has contributed greatly to nation-state dominance, and possibly also in that very way to the steady trend toward *increasing* inequality.

Measures and designs for reducing inequality in the past have emphasized speeding up the growth rate of the "underdeveloped" areas, so that they might contribute their share to meeting the pressures for ever-faster world growth. In the future, the approach might be directed toward slowing down the growth that unrelentingly accentuates and aggravates inequalities in the present world system. This negative approach would place the onus for dealing with problems of development where it belongs —that is on the developed areas and their resource-rich organizations. The excesses that have characterized recent developments in the major industrial centers; the worship of growth, which approaches the status of a religion among vice-presidents in charge of sales, state economic planners or even wide sections, for instance of the Japanese populations —all these may have to be replaced by concern for a broader range of objectives. The motor of this growth has been organizational competition and technological pressure, fueled by research and development funds and by an overemphasis on science and technology. The balance of growth may be restored by establishing the goals of moral awareness, through the development of social and humanistic values at a level at least equal to the present tendencies toward technological gadgeteering and pyramid-building.

Positively, the institutions of the global layer can be strengthened by giving them greater financial capacity and, thereby, the ability to effect income transfers. A large part of the activities of the United Nations family, budgetwise, is already concerned with assisting the developing states. Above all, the global layer needs sound financing, as well as sources of revenue that are independent of member government subscriptions and contributions. The constituency of national governments should not be expected to finance global purposes as well. Rather, organizations that are profitably active in the global layer—the world corporations and other members of world markets—should regard it as one part of their policies of enlightened self-interest to contribute to the growth of a community of purpose, within which their own activities could proceed more smoothly. Oil companies that now buy protection through royalties to absurd potentates could operate more securely as agents of a global system. Revenue from the seabed is another obvious source of finance for global purposes.

In line with such measures, there is a call for a world welfare function that will ultimately guarantee a world minimum standard of living. The United Nations Children's Fund is already fulfilling this function in relation to young children. Its enlargement, in the form of income maintenance for the whole world, is not beyond the bounds of reason. The assurance of a minimum standard of subsistence would absorb much of the competitiveness that is now driving the world system. More concretely, only income transfers of global proportions can prevent the proliferation of global centers of urban infection on the scale and model of Calcutta.

Advocates of revolutionary class warfare, or of self-reliance and isolationism, inspired by China's Cultural Revolution, have little to contribute to this debate. The injustice of world inequalities is now clearly established. But if those who are concerned about them do little else than engage in warfare or terrorism, they are not likely to change things in the direction of greater world equality. Most of all, they will add to the strength of the nation-state system and thereby delay necessary changes in world priorities. The nation-state already serves to contain and to stabilize areas of potential disorder within its own boundaries; national violence must be contained, for otherwise it could endanger world survival. Revolutionary governments are unlikely to do much to modify the nation-state system, which has little capacity for intergovernmental solidarity on behalf of income redistribution. It is more likely that the sources of the impetus for change lie in every other part of the world system.

World distress over wealth inequalities, however, by a process of displacement (that is, displacement of aggression from primary to secondary objects), may take the form of national and regional wars and create generalized disorder. The decade-long persistence of such conflicts as the Indo–Pakistani or Arab–Israeli wars, is indeed difficult to account for in other ways. In any case, their effect is not to soften inequalities but rather to accentuate them. In the nation-state system, all problems tend to assume the form of international conflict; they are rarely solved in that way; in the process, however, they reinforce the system.

Power Equalization

A precondition for greater equality of income and wealth, as it is of all justice, is power equalization. This is a topic that has rarely been touched upon by students of economic or even political development, yet it is one that cannot be ignored by students of world politics.

The historical states system has been an important mechanism of power equalization, principally through the working of the Balance of Power. During the course of modern history, a degree of equality has been institutionalized among the sovereign princes of Europe and later among the Great Powers. In the nineteenth century, the idea of the equality of states made further inroads. The concept burgeoned in the early functional international organizations, and grew strong roots with the increasing practice of international conferences. Upon the foundation of the universal international organizations, the League of Nations and the United Nations, it came to be accepted as a normal condition of international intercourse, with Great Power privileges as an exception qualifying that rule. The nation-state system has confirmed the basic rule of equality; in part, therefore, it has provided a mechanism whereby some power equalization has already been injected into the world system.

To that degree, its influence has been beneficial. The position of political organizations in the national layer has been regularized and put on an equal footing—in a status of equality and symmetry, so to speak—much in the same way in which states that are members of a federal system enjoy status equalization. A modern world system could not function without this streamlining of the intermediate political layer; it could not otherwise cope with problems of wealth distribution.

But the degree of equalization in the states system has been only limited. (1) Power equalization was confined primarily to the North Atlantic-European region and, within that area, resources and rewards were in any event distributed more equally. But in the process, an imbalance was created between these privileged nations and the rest of the world. (2) Formal status of independence and political equality is not enough to compensate for striking inequalities in the population and resource base of existing nation-states. The variety of political units claiming equal political status in 1970 (some 130 units, ranging all the way from the United States or China to Fiji and the Maldive Islands), was excessive. It strains both common sense and political analysis to regard them as all equal. For reasons of political effectiveness and sound constitutional engineering, and for as long as states remain as salient in world politics as they are in the nation-state system, the range of diversity may have to be reduced. A number of independent states could arrange mergers into international organizations, if only for purposes of external representation, while others might possibly benefit from subdivision. A number of alternative schemata can be envisaged, the result of which should be a reduction of political inequality.[10] (3) Power equality is an attribute only of states; it does not extend to other organizations. This makes the states system a simple system, and accounts for some of is instability. Such a simple system will tend to accumulate other forms of power, including wealth, with concentrations of political and military power.

In most general terms therefore, the principle of decumulation and the principle of complexity, both of which have been previously detailed as directions for possible change, are also principles of power equalization. Instead of devoting their time to studying the present fine gradations of international power and prestige, students of politics would do well to pay more attention to working out possible processes of equalization. If the world is viewed as one single society, which shares its finite resources among all its members, then with regard to the basic needs of food, clothing, and shelter all humans are entitled to equal fulfillment. They will not obtain such fulfillment, however, until and unless their political resources are correspondingly equalized.

Procedural Justice Through Representativeness

A world political system must not only *be* just; it must also be *seen to be* just: its processes and procedures must be such as to maximize the probability that justice will prevail. Procedural injustice occurs when established political processes and mechanisms are capable of being disrupted, negated or invalidated through the exercise of power. An earlier chapter discussed weaknesses of that sort in the nation-state system. Suffice it to say here that Great Power authority, along with its characteristic military and coercive power presents a large number of obstacles to the attainment of procedures that will be just to all concerned.

In relation to world politics, attention will at this point be focused on one important feature of procedural justice: the representativeness of world elites. A just world political system should also be representative; its institutions will be representative if their leadership represents all the legitimate interests of the society, and if changes in the content of those interests are promptly and adequately reflected in the relevant leadership. The nation-state system is not, to say the least, conspicuously representative: in fact, it is primarily the inequality of nation-states that detracts from their possible usefulness as constituencies of representation at the global level. Furthermore, the world system as a whole is governed in a manner that recalls models already known from earlier, agricultural and other pre-modern societies: dominant castes, aristocracies, and ruling classes.[11] To a system that is still "agricultural" in its distribution of income and wealth, corresponds a largely agrarian ruling elite, the current prevalence of which raises some questions about the possibility of obtaining free government in world society.

The fundamental fact about the world elite—that is, about the occupiers of strategic positions in the global layer of world politics—is that it is not adequately representative, in that it is recruited from a narrow segment, in the main from the North Atlantic portion, of the world population.[12] This condition may be observed in a wide range of the world's organizations and elite networks.

Conventional diplomacy reserves the positions of influence to the Great Powers and, among the latter, it is the North Atlantic world that has long been dominant. The United Nations family proceeds on a somewhat broader basis: the General Assembly, which is the most representative of its organs, is indeed capable of reflecting a range of other interests (in recent years, for example, a strong anti-colonial coalition); but the authority of the General Assembly is strictly circumscribed, and its moral influence limited by the vagaries of its make-up. In all the other United Nations organs, the Great Powers wield large influence, while in the Secretariat, positions of major importance have, since its inception, never departed from being held by men who are part of that same tradition.

The world of the great corporations is inhabited by men from the United States, Japan, Britain, Germany and France; this holds true as well of the worlds of finance, transport and communications. In the world of learning, the vast majority of Nobel Prizes regularly go to scholars from the same area, which is also the domain of the great universities. This means that scientific and technological progress, along with the organization of growth, and therefore of the governing world process, belong to this same area.

Of particular interest is the distribution of Nobel Peace Prizes—awards made to individuals and organizations that have rendered distinguished service in the cause of world peace. Here too, in the years between 1901, when the first award was made, and 1967, out of fifty-two personal awards, only two went outside the North Atlantic area—in 1936, to an Argentine statesman, and in 1960 to Chief Luthuli, a South African. Of the remaining fifty, nationals of the three Western Great Powers accounted for 28 (including fourteen Americans), while the Scandinavians, the Swiss and the Low Countries between them received fifteen more. It would seem as though the search for peace-makers had been limited only to one small corner of the globe; is it that the world's most dangerous conflicts were also born here? or does it signify that the rest of the world simply does not care about peace? The paucity of non-Western representation is striking, yet also puzzling.

Another useful, and more comprehensive sample of the world elite is Donald Robinson's list of the one hundred most important people in the world.[13] Admittedly a somewhat impressionistic compilation, it nevertheless does bring together people of merit and achievement from all over the world, and from all fields of social enterprise, including politics, business, science, religion and letters, as of about 1969. In Robinson's survey, the major sources of the world's most important people are the developed countries, led by the United States (27 out of 100) Britain (11) and the Soviet Union (11). The developing countries supply 22 representatives (out of 100)—that is, less than one-quarter of representation for three-quarters of the world's population. The fact is that this is a marked improvement over an earlier edition of the same work: a doubling of representation from the developing countries, in the space of seventeen years!

The world system therefore now discriminates more moderately, perhaps, against non-Western recruits to world elite positions; but it does discriminate. Those who have succeeded in attaining this status show two important characteristics: fifteen of the twenty-two belong to religions or ideologies that are Western in origin, although universal in aspiration (Christianity, Communism); nineteen of the twenty-two had attended universities and colleges (including three military colleges), and seven of those nineteen had been students at a university that can be described as global.[14] The religions and ideologies, and the universities, have acted as avenues of recruitment into the world elite and sources of elite mobility; of them all, the university, and in particular the global university, might become the most important.

The world elite is disproportionately European—in fact, North-west European and North American. Occupancy of elite positions corresponds closely to the known distributions of such values as power, wealth and knowledge; the two conditions obviously bear a close relationship to each other. But the skewed character of elite distributions is probably even greater than the inequality of value distributions. The unrepresentativeness of the world elites is therefore closely associated with lack of equality in world value distributions; but is this a necessary connection? Are only the wealthy, the powerful and the knowledgeable entitled to be represented in world politics? Is achievement a sufficient criterion of representation, if achievement itself is the result primarily of the unequal possession of resources and opportunities for action—and further, the product of a value system that defines what is worth achieving in terms of what has been achieved?

Indeed, why *should* world elites be representative? Might it not be that all that is needed is the proper attention to global problems and global interests? Might it not be enough for world elites to be austere and unselfish guardians of the world interest, without one's having to

raise troublesome and "political" questions of proportionality and representativeness? Might these guardians not do better if they were not
distracted by such "petty" concerns? Do attorneys who represent such
clients as, say businessmen or criminals, themselves have to be businessmen or criminals, in order to be good surrogates for their clients?

Traditionally, such have been the arguments put up on behalf of
imperial rule and imperial civil services.[15] Some merit might attach to
them. Stable and self-confident social systems do not require strict, literal,
numerical representativeness; indeed, in relation to world politics, it is
not clear what the constituency is by which representativeness is to be
judged. If it were the global layer of politics alone, then the quality of
representation might adequately reflect current involvement in those networks of activity. It is only if the representativeness of that very layer
is questioned that the more difficult questions arise. Yet it is nevertheless
the received experience of generations of students of politics that the
proper representation of interests does seem to entail some degree of
representativeness, that a certain degree of correspondence is indeed
required between elites and their societies. World elites, which in a
broad sense and through their participation in global networks express
global purposes, need also to be brought into a closer relationship with
the entire world community.

The Global City?

The elementary fact of globalized politics for the past few hundred years
has been Western dominance—specifically, North-west European, and
lately North American dominance—and that elementary fact would seem
to be among the basic determinants of world politics. The conditions of
inequality and unrepresentativeness that underlie the injustices of the
global system are but reflections of this fact.

Since the inception of the age of globalization, this dominance has
been supplying a hierarchy for global society, as well as those elements
of coherence and gradually increasing interdependence that have transformed it. The core of this society has been the London-Paris axis—
extended in the twentieth century across the Atlantic, to New York and
Washington. This region has been at one and the same time the source
of immense creativity, both cultural and physical, as well as the generator
of tremendous tensions. Theodore von Laue recently pictured the West
as a "conelike volcano which spouts forth . . . an endless variety of cultural outpourings which spread . . . down slope into the lower regions
along its base." Yet this Great Outpouring has also visited fire and destruction upon the "lower regions": the Western metropolis has "burdened

the unprepared societies under its sway with unbearable and dehuman-
izing challenges," and made them subject to the sweeping absolutism
of a universalized Western culture. Stresses of Western societies have
been transformed into global contests that have everywhere wreaked
destruction.[16]

Western dominance has elements of caste and aristocracy about it;
it has given rise to a privileged stratum, rendered well-nigh impermeable
by the restrictiveness of the nation-state, and carrying with it some notably
racist overtones. This dominance also contains quite visible elements of
class rule, in that it goes hand in hand with the ownership of a major
portion of the world's resources, both landed and industrial. Put all these
together, and it adds up to a social system that is in disjunction with the
major value premises of modern society. For, in the end, modern society
cannot be kept alive solely in a few islands of order, security and freedom, in certain select and privileged areas, while progressive "slumifica-
tion" [17] is tolerated in the rest of the world. For even slums have a
tendency to insinuate themselves into what may have been regarded as
the most secret recesses of privilege.

Western predominance could yet be replaced through some major
upheaval—a race war?—by a dominance that was based on some other
cultural-ethnic-racial-political coalition. In the age of nuclear weapons,
the merits of such upheavals, let alone of such a shift of power, do not
appear overwhelmingly promising for world society.

The whole could yet crystallize into a modern-day caste system—
especially if the world were to be shaken by great civil and international disturbances. Whatever the present probabilities of such retro-
gressive tendencies, however, the outlook is not altogether dark. The
privileged sections of the contemporary global system have never been
entirely closed, or exclusive on ascriptive grounds—not even during the
short phase of the heyday of Western imperialism, c. 1870-1900. They
have always been impressed by evidence of achievement, if only of the
achievements of power. Japan was a member in good standing for nearly
a century, and her recent economic growth has given her a position
equivalent to North America's and Western Europe's in the industrial
field. In a broader sense, the worldwide consolidation of the nation-state
system during the twentieth century has brought into world councils a
wide range of new interests and untried orientations.

There is some scattered evidence that, in recent decades, world elites
have grown more widely representative. Symbolically charged appointments, such as those to the office of United Nations Secretary-General,
and to positions of leadership in other international organizations; the
recruitment policies of some world corporations; and, above all, the role
of the educational system and the universities in opening up paths of

advancement—all these raise hopes that, with time, the makeup of the world elite will assume a character that is more in keeping with the requirements of world interest. Hopefully too, these changes in elite personnel would not merely be the result of processes of co-optation, but would instead promote (and, in turn, be reinforced by) measures for the control of world growth and world wealth, the management of world welfare, and a general loosening up of world society.

In sum, the prognosis need not be entirely hopeless. There is promise in the conception of a complex, pluralistic world that can move toward a more just society. It is a promise that was inherent in the American society of the nineteenth century, as that was witnessed by Alexis de Tocqueville. The promise is not a prediction. But it might yet come to pass.

Modernization of World Politics

The future of world politics cannot be envisaged adequately in terms of possible choices among a range of discrete alternatives. It is never a matter of selecting one from a list of suitable scenarios. Short of a world catastrophe that threw everything into disarray, it is hard to imagine statesmen, or the world public, actually finding themselves face to face with a decision between say, a nation-state system, a regional bloc system or a world government. The global system is indeed changing from day to day, and from year to year; and on this road it is being steadily and continuously guided by the myriad choices made by states and organizations, and in fact by all men and women. If there is to be any degree of consistency and purpose to this path, the choices have to be related to ideas that are at once less grandiose than those mentioned, more practical, and yet also more pervasive and more fundamental. Both for predictive purposes and in practical decisions, the best rule still is that tomorrow's system will be largely (but not entirely) like today's; the range of freedom is not great. Yet a steady accretion of meaningful changes, informed by a long-term purpose, can make a great difference.

Part Three, now concluded, has been propelled by the thought that the nation-state system, the contemporary constitution of the world, is in fact capable of just such steady change, improvement and adjustment. The impact of this thinking was intended to be architectural, in a special sense: presenting design blueprints not for one ideal structure but for a world habitat that will be capable of an infinite number of additions, accretions and modifications, subject only to the overriding determination to reconcile order with justice. These are not blueprints, to be carried out by one world authority, but rather guides to universal conduct—principles in terms of which day-to-day decisions may be ranked by all members of world society. For, in the ultimate analysis, world order rests not on the actions of any one such organ or agency, but on the responsibilities that are knowingly assumed by all of them.

Some principles of modern world politics have been enlarged upon in some detail so far, chiefly through elaborating the imperatives of order and justice. These may be summarized as follows:

(1) decumulation of the vicious circle of the nation-state system;
(2) construction of the framework of complexity for world networks;
(3) insulation of global from national and local military problems;
(4) harmonization of a variety of elements in world society;
(5) reduction of world inequalities; and
(6) representativeness of world networks and organizations.

In themselves, the principles are not really novel: they are the principles of sound politics, derived from centuries of political experience within the more limited context of particular political systems. The question is: are they, or can they become, relevant to the politics of a global system?

The answer is: Yes, they can, because their time has come. From their application, no immediate solution of world problems can be expected to emerge. Yet, taken together, they tend toward the gradual evolution of a more orderly and less unjust, and perhaps even more catastrophe-proof world society. This emergent type of world structure could be described as a system of multiple autonomy; being open-ended, it allows for a multiplicity of possible successful outcomes in complexity. On the other hand, since the nation-state system, with its continued institutionalization of war, might well be among the most backward features of world society, this could be a recipe for the long-overdue modernization of world politics—a design for finally putting world politics on a truly modern basis.

Notes to Chapter Sixteen

1. Morgenthau, *Politics among Nations, cited,* p. 470–3.
2. *Aristotle's Ethics, cited,* Book V, Ch. 6, p. 156.
3. *Ibid.,* Ch. 7, p. 157.
4. Hobbes, *Leviathan,* A. D. Lindsay ed. (London: Dent, 1914), Ch. XIII: "Of the Naturall Condition of Mankind, as concerning their Felicity and Misery," esp. pp. 65–66.
5. Irving Kristol, "Equality as an ideal," *International Encyclopedia of the Social Sciences,* Vol. 5, p. 108.
6. *Ibid.,* quoting Richard Wollheim and Isaiah Berlin.
7. Author's Introduction to *Democracy in America.* De Tocqueville pressed his themes strongly—for example, in relation to poetry in democratic

nations (that is, those favoring conditions of equality); he expected it to attempt an expression of "the destinies of mankind": "all that belongs to the existence of the human race taken as a whole, to its vicissitudes and its future, becomes an abundant mine of poetry" (Book I, Ch. 17).

8. Data from Thomas Dye, "Income Inequality and American State Politics," *American Political Science Review*, Vol. 60(1), March 1969, pp. 157–162.

9. Dahl, *Political Analysis, cited*, p. 85.

10. The Gini index of the inequality of states (measured by population) could be reduced from the present excessive level of about 0.7 to a more manageable 0.4 or 0.3, the latter being the measure of the United States federal system in the nineteen-sixties.

11. Suzanne Keller, *Beyond the Ruling Class* (New York: Random, 1963), pp. 30–32.

12. For purposes of this section, world elite structures are analyzed in terms of their representativeness; they can also be viewed as showing inequalities of wealth and income distributions, because elite positions carry with them special rewards.

13. Donald Robinson, *The 100 Most Important People in the World To-day* (New York: Putnam's, 1970); the reliability of Robinson's selection is affirmed by a random sampling of the *International Who's Who 1969-70*, which yields approximately similar distributions of nationalities and fields.

14. For the world elite as a whole (the entire sample of 100), the same proportion had attended colleges and universities (84 per cent), although fewer had military training.

15. Analogous arguments have been made about British rule in India.

16. Theodore von Laue, *The Global City* (Philadelphia: Lippincott, 1969), pp. 68, 75, 233.

17. Phrase used by H. G. Wells in *The World of William Clissold, cited*, pp. 619–620.

17

Conclusion

WORLD POLITICS HAS BEEN DE-
scribed in this study as a system that processes, for the world at large,
certain problems that impinge upon issues of order and justice. The
world regularly throws up for processing a variety of problems (that is,
threats to values)—not all of which require or deserve attention at the
global level. Those that do need and do receive attention at the global
level become the substance of world politics.

World politics is also more than this. It cannot be divorced from
questions of a broader, architectonic kind—questions about the make-up
of society on earth. The way in which all the elements of world society
—its organizations, its networks, and the individuals that constitute both—
interrelate and interact harmoniously is also the substance of world politics.
In other words, world politics has to do with both global level politics
and the structure of the entire world society, insofar as it gives rise to
problems of order and justice.

The Possibility of World Order

The world political system cannot assume an infinite number of forms;
for every century or every generation, only a very few true alternatives
are open. In recent periods, these alternatives have been of two kinds:
(1) those that have been opened up by global wars, and (2) those arising
from gradual and cumulative changes in various properties, or combinations of properties, of the global system.

In past centuries, the first type of political system change—unsettling, indeed profoundly revolutionary in its effects—has been predominant, overshadowing the second, more evolutionary kind of system transformation. In earlier chapters, the impact of global wars and the utility of a system demarcation, based on these wars as watersheds, has been demonstrated. The contemporary world lives in the system of 1945, and that system could conceivably, and not altogether improbably, terminate in a global and nuclear combat. Just as conceivably and more desirably, the system of 1945 might remain undisturbed by a major holocaust, while still undergoing major changes.

A world system that has been caught in a regular war-peace cycle tends to maximize the value of order. The awesomeness of global war— the worst catastrophe ever conceived by man or as yet devised by nature—so overwhelms human consciousness that all other concerns subordinate themselves to it. In a climate of impending disaster, injustice goes unnoticed, and justice becomes an irrelevant luxury.

It is just conceivable that mankind could extricate itself from the global war cycle. In such conditions, its politics could still assume a variety of forms—each a distinct combination of the values of order, justice and autonomy. The import of the argument so far has been to demonstrate the feasibility, though not necessarily the inevitability or even the probability, of a movement toward types of world political systems that combine order with justice. Such movement is feasible in conditions of decumulation of the nation-state system; it is not necessarily probable, chiefly because of the indeterminacy of such developments and the possibility that the vicious circle may continue to function relentlessly.

Through a conjunction of conscious effort with the unintended consequences of large processes and small-scale activities, great and necessary changes may be brought about. The development of the social sciences and of the study of world politics will steadily enlarge the area that is amenable to self-conscious influence. Through more reliable evidence and better understanding, through creative theory, world politics could become the object of more effective control, not by a few but by a worldwide audience concerned about survival. Given sufficient knowledge, the nation-state system need no longer be regarded as a "fact of nature." Development might be guided toward forms of world political structure whose precise shapes cannot now be forecast but whose general outlines might nevertheless be capable of specification.

To move the world, what is needed is powerful ideas of wide appeal. The aesthetically pleasing but possibly sterile appeal of "order" must be combined with the emotional force of ideas of world justice. Both must in turn be undergirded by a sound knowledge of world conditions and by a sturdy theory of world politics. The social sciences, and political science in particular, are called upon to supply the real foundations of a true world order with justice.

World Politics as Basic Politics

If an understanding of world politics is among the necessary foundations of world order, so too it is the fundamental portion of the study of political science. For too long now, political science has been the science of the state, the handmaiden of the nation-state system. It has made great strides and attracted a great audience, so that it is now part of the great world of learning; but in its basic orientation it has not moved much beyond Aristotle and his preoccupation with the small-scale *polis*. Paradoxically, Aristotle's greatest pupil was Alexander the Great, founder of the first universal empire, but one would not know that from reading the *Politics*. The old world of city-states was fast crumbling all around him, yet Aristotle provided no guidance to meet the problems of organizing a new world.

Contemporary political science faces another replay of the Aristotelian paradox—except that this one has been magnified a thousand times in its import. The learning of the world is still literally built up on the classic heritage (medieval universities in general expounded little else but Aristotle's accumulated wisdom), and the bulk of political knowledge is still cast in term of the nation-state (a *polis* enlarged, but still basically a *polis*). The world political structures are not really collapsing, and the possibility of a world conqueror on Alexander's model seems remote. Yet real-world processes are moving toward a global ambit and rapidly altering habitual modes of thought. While the nation-state system has been imposing increasing stresses upon the social fabric of the world, political science has been doing little to ameliorate the strain.

The recognition is now due that the study of world politics is the foundation of contemporary political science, just as world politics, understood as the world's fundamental constitution, is today the world's basic political problem.

The great processes that have shaped world society for the past few centuries have been globalization, power equalization and the creative momentum of the great political organizations. All these have been large-scale social and political events, truly comprehensible only as global processes. They may have had their origin in one corner of the globe, but they also cascaded over the rest of it, in what von Laue has called the "Great Outpouring"; in any event, whatever their origin, their action now is worldwide, and the political system they created is global. Even though it has molded life everywhere in a peculiarly strong fashion, that fact alone does not necessarily make it an ideal system. It was brought into existence in part through accident and lack of design, and it now needs reviewing by techniques of social-scientific observation, based on a new perspective. The world's political structure is *one*, and it can only be understood as such.

In this fundamental regard, the parameters of all politics are global: earth politics, like all human activities on earth, operates within the constraints of the finite nature of the earth's resources. This sets an upper limit to all human endeavor, and places politics as only one among the many claimants on the Gross World Product.

But the finite datum of earth resources is not the only datum of politics. World Politics also has at its disposal the flexibility and adaptability of the human response, its capacity for vision, its moral creativity and its potentiality for infinite empathy. Man is capable of a multiplicity of loyalties and enthusiasms, a plethora of objectives and an indefinite expansion of knowledge. Traditional international politics has pandered to the meaner instincts in man, and for that reason could not build into its structures this human capacity for expansive strength. Once this can be done, perhaps politics itself will change its character, and such classical problems as authority and obedience or freedom will take on a new and different cast.

In that sense, the future might be viewed as the construction and management of an earth habitat out of finite resources and infinite sympathy. In this edifice, the study of world politics will inevitably gain a central place in political science. No longer can American politics, for instance, be studied separately from international politics. In the nineteen-sixties, a large part—at least one-third (perhaps as much as one-half)—of the latter was actually American politics, as when presidential elections in the United States set the tone for years of world political debate, and when political and economic disturbances in the country sent tremors throughout the body social and politic of the world.

The foundation of the study of politics thus lies in acquiring an understanding of the actual political conditions on earth today. Politics must be introduced and framed into perspective on a global basis: in essence, basic political science is earth politics, and within it can be accommodated all the politics arising from global, national and local problems.

World politics since 1945 has not been unrelated to the emerging problems of world organization. The dilemmas of survival in a nuclear world have rightly occupied considerable attention. If pluralistic complexity is the basic recipe for world order, then the model of the ideal American society is much nearer to it than is the Soviet Communist exemplar, which is held firmly in the grip of the world's perfect embodiment of the all-powerful state. If greater justice is to be attained on a world scale, however, another set of models will have to come into play: the Western world will have to come to terms with the non-Western majority of mankind. Here the pale palliatives of the era of "foreign aid" will obviously not suffice, and transformations in world structure could be in order.

The intellectual point of departure for this discourse was the study of International Relations; but its ultimate point of arrival has been the general study of politics and world politics, as the embodiment of that study in an understanding of the structure of world political arrangements. The nation-state system confuses that understanding, and its political science has been found wanting. World politics replaces it with a concern for the whole of earth society and a sense of that interdependence that binds this society together and substantiates the workings of infinite empathy.

The Need for Vision

In 1939, E. H. Carr published *The Twenty Years Crisis 1919-1939*, subtitled "An Introduction to the Study of International Relations." This proved to be one of the seminal works of this field and clarified the issues for a number of intellectual debates. Carr depicted the study of International Relations, and of all politics, as perpetually alternating between two extreme poles, those of Realism and Utopia. Realism represented the factors of power and understanding, while Utopia supplied the elements of value, perspective and vision. Carr's own book marked the beginning of a reversal, and strongly pushed the entire field in the direction of Realism—a tendency that has strongly persisted in all of contemporary politics, but especially in International Relations.

Carr himself recognized, however, that politics must contain elements both of Realism and Utopia, if it is to produce generally acceptable outcomes. He also clearly recognized the weaknesses of unadulterated Realism, as when he wrote:

The impossibility of being a consistent and thoroughgoing realist is one of the most certain and most curious lessons of political science. Consistent realism excludes four things which appear to be essential ingredients of all effective political thinking: a finite goal, an emotional appeal, a right of moral judgment, and a ground for action. Any sound political thought must be based on elements of both utopia and reality.[1]

In spite of such injunctions, however, the actual impact of the writings of Carr, and of others that followed him, has been to reconsolidate within International Relations the already strong tendency toward a narrow, suspicious and even cynical view of world realities. While such a view might be justified in extreme situations, or at times of great crisis, it does not serve well as the daily diet of large portions of mankind. The state-system has traditionally encouraged such an outlook, and the weak shoots of utopianism that started to sprout during the early interwar years were soon overwhelmed by the clamor and the blasts of World War II battles. The years of the cold war have not been hospitable to utopias, nor has the Vietnam war made things any easier in this regard. The pendulum of politics is always in motion, but it may be that the extreme points of realism have now been passed. In political science, signs abound that, in all its areas, the mines of national and realistic "fact" are nearing exhaustion, and that *new* visions and *new* bearings are needed to direct the miners toward new and richer lodes.

In world politics today, the nation-state system is the institution that defines political reality. But is it the be-all and end-all of politics? Hardly so. This institution too needs to confront the test of the ideals of order and justice and, if it fails that test, it needs to be adjusted. In the long run, it is in the interplay of institutions and ideals that the major interest of politics lies.

Too much of both past and contemporary study of politics has proceeded from a myopic conception of political reality. Modern social science has given realism the tools for becoming more perceptive; but realism must also be informed by a vision of a better world. It needs a good strong dose of utopia, as well as a steady diet of optimism and faith, so that the world can truly be made a better place.

Note to Chapter Seventeen

1. Carr, *Twenty Years Crisis, cited*, pp. 89, 94.

Index

Acheson, Dean, 166, 206
Alger, Chadwick, 17, 188, 205
Alker, Hayward, 75, 226, 266
Allison, Graham, 89
Angell, Norman, 234
Ardrey, Robert, 108
Aristotle, 317, 335, 336, 354, 358
Aron, Raymond, 4, 17, 185, 205
Austria, 91, 117, 150, 164; involvement in war, 82; as Great Power, 144
Autonomy: as type of world order, 30–31; and historical systems, 31–32; and globalization, 53–54; legitimacy of, 63–66; benefits of, 66–68; maintenance of, 70–73; simple and complex, 73–74; as property of organizations, 79; and corporations, 324–326; and universities, 330

Bacon, Francis, 64
Balance of Power: wars of, 58–62; mentioned in Treaty of Utrecht, 61, 63; legitimized, 63–66; as constitution of the global system, 64; costs, 69–73; and equilibrium theory, 254–255; as mechanism of equalization, 347
Barnard, Chester, 75, 89, 108, 178, 179, 181, 205

Belgrade Conference of Non-Aligned States (1961), 148, 214
Benoit, Emil, 245
Bentham, Jeremy, 223
Bentley, Arthur, 320
Berlin, Isaiah, 340, 354
Berry, Brian J. L., 286
Bismarck, Otto von, 5, 61
Bolingbroke, Viscount, 64
Borgstrom, Georg, 57
Boulding, Kenneth, 139
Brams, Steven, 188, 205
Brandi, Karl, 75
Brezhnev Doctrine, 158
Butterfield, Herbert, 75

Cairo Conference of Non-Aligned States (1964), 214
Carnegie Endowment for International Peace, 3, 333
Carr, E. H., 4, 89, 226, 275, 360, 361
Cassinelli, C. W., 108
Centralization, 126–129; lack in primitive societies, 27–28; and classification of world orders, 29–31; in Ch'in China, 37; and globalization, 53; in political history, 126–127; at global level, 127; non-centralization, 127–129; as response to war, 165; in U.N. family, 199